Perform or Else:

FROM DISCIPLINE TO PERFORMANCE

JON MCKENZIE

First published 2001
by Routledge
2 Park Square, Milton Park, Abingdon, Oxon OX14 4RN

Simultaneously published in the USA and Canada
by Routledge
270 Madison Ave, New York NY 10016

Transferred to Digital Printing 2008

Routledge is an imprint of the Taylor & Francis Group, an informa business

Typeset in Baker sans by Matt Broughton
Printed and bound in Great Britain by TJI Digital, Padstow, Cornwall

British Library Cataloguing in Publication Data
A catalogue record for this book is available from the British Library
Library of Congress Cataloging in Publication Data
McKenzie, Jon, 1960-
Perform or else: from discipline to performance / Jon McKenzie.
p. cm.
Includes bibliographical references and index.
1. Performance—Psychological aspects. 1. Title.

BF481 .M395 2001
302—dc21
00-046014

ISBN 10: 0-415-24769-1 (pbk)
ISBN 10: 0-415-24768-3 (hbk)

ISBN 13: 978-0-415-24769-6 (pbk)
ISBN 13: 978-0-415-24768-9 (hbk)

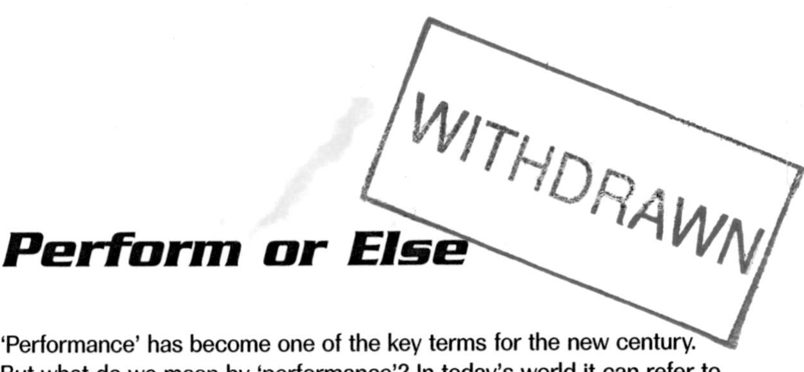

Perform or Else

'Performance' has become one of the key terms for the new century. But what do we mean by 'performance'? In today's world it can refer to experimental art, productivity in the workplace, and the functionality of technological systems. Do these disparate performances bear any historical relation to each other?

In *Perform or Else*, Jon McKenzie uncovers an uncanny relationship between cultural, organizational, and technological performance. In this theoretical tour de force, McKenzie demonstrates that all three paradigms can operate together to create powerful and contradictory pressures to 'perform—or else'.

His startling readings of the Challenger mission will ignite new lines of research, while his explosive conclusion—that performance will be to the twentieth and twenty-first centuries what discipline was to the eighteenth and nineteenth—is an exhilarating realization of how culture, business, and science have become hyperlinked through globalization. McKenzie then goes on to outline a vision of resistant strategies for the future.

This is an urgent and important intervention into contemporary critical thinking. It will profoundly shape our understanding of twenty-first-century structures of power and knowledge.

Jon McKenzie is Assistant Professor of interface design and multimedia at The University of the Arts (Philadelphia). He also consults in the new media industry.

LONDON AND NEW YORK

"It seems to me not unlikely that with the publication of this book McKenzie will become, like Deleuze, Foucault and Butler, a point of orientation for future work on modes of Western Thought."
Marvin Carlson, author of *Performance: A Critical Introduction*

"This tour de force introduces 'perfumance' as a new practice giving access to a secret network connecting "performance" in all its uses across the divisions of knowledge. The liminal hinge of this network is 'the Challenger Lecture Machine,' to whose seven Challengers may be added this eighth wonder of the performance world."
Gregory L. Ulmer, Professor of English, University of Florida

"Wholly original. Extremely valuable. A truly remarkable book."
Philip Auslander, author of *Liveness*

for ij, vw, & sloo

CONTENTS

Illustrations

ACKNOWLEDGMENTS

Buried deep within the writing of this text there lies a paradox of sorts, one that came to my attention years ago. I had just discovered the performance art of Laurie Anderson and happened to read Jean-François Lyotard on the postmodern condition of performativity. What struck me then still resonates today: "performance" can be read as both experimentation and normativity. This paradox, if it is one, forms the kernel of *Perform or Else*.

The performance I began studying years ago is not the same performance I study today. Nor is the writer the same writer. Foucault once said that the books he wrote constituted an experience for him, noting that an "experience is something you come out of changed." *Perform or Else* constitutes such an experience-book for me. I have attempted to theorize performance in a general framework and in doing so my world has been transformed.

The theory proposed here is framed as a rehearsal, for the performance it addresses is not yet in full production. Even as currently installed, however, this performance exceeds the scope of my inquiry, and I have tried to indicate areas where additional study and reflection are needed. I suspect other areas may be found. Whether these tasks fall to me or another, I trust they will be taken up at some point.

My research's early development was guided by Peggy Phelan, Richard Schechner, Barbara Kirshenblatt-Gimblett, and Michael Taussig, the first three of whom read an early version of this text, as did Joseph Roach and José Munoz. Their comments and critical insights have been invaluable. More recently, readings by Janelle Reinelt and Herbert Blau have been most helpful as I refined the manuscript into the present text.

Diana Taylor, Peggy Phelan, Una Chaudhuri, and Arthur Bartow provided me the opportunity to develop some of this research into studio and seminar courses at New York University's Tisch School of the Arts. I would also like to thank the many students who participated in these courses and the folks I've worked with through NYU's Innovation Center: Vincent Doogan, Jeffrey Lane, Joseph Hargitai, Jodi Arlyn Goldberg, and Sana Odeh.

Paul Clark, Gwyneth Campling, and Miranda Lowe of the British Natural History Museum contributed to my research of HMS *Challenger* specimens and Dennis Jenkins to my research of *Amerika Bomber* documents.

I'd like to give the warmest of thanks to Talia Rodgers, my editor at Routledge, for her enthusiasm, support, and insight into this project; kind thanks also to Kate Chenevix Trench, Matt Broughton, Rosie Waters, Alison Kelly, and Heather Vickers at Routledge for their hard work in turning this project into a book.

Special thanks to Peggy Phelan and Richard Schechner for all their support, criticism, and generosity.

The sites of one's writing brush up against the places where one lives and loves. In New York, I have been fortunate to draw upon a wealth of friends and colleagues. I am especially grateful to the following people for their generous support and friendship-Jeffrey Schulz, Karin Campbell, Melissa Goldstein, Laura Trippi, Ken Weaver, Fabio Roberti, Erika Yeomans, Jane Yeomans, Deborah Velick, Cathy Lynn Gasser, Andruid Kearne, Melissa Lang, Amanda Claybaugh, and Martin Puchner.

I've also been enriched by the support and work of Ilana Abramovitch, Gabrielle Barnett, Amanda Barrett, John Bell, Lori Brau, Jessica Chalmers, Jan Cohen-Cruz, Angelika Festa, Jackie Hayes, Christian Herold, Elke Lampe, Jill Lane, Dell Lemmon, Gary Maciag, Richard McKewen, Frédéric Maurin, Jessica Payne, Jim Peck, Rebecca Schneider, Mady Schutzman, Robert Sember, Joseph Simmons, Mark Sussman, Nicole Ridgeway, Judy Rosenthal, Mariellen Sanford, Leslie Satin, Louis Scheeder, Teresa Senft, Marta Ulvaeus, Amy Underhill, Scott Westerfeld, and Martin Worman. Special thanks to Toni Sant and Cindy Rosenthal.

In Philadelphia, I've received support and encouragment at The University of the Arts from Virginia Red, Laura Zarrow, Chris Garvin, Jeff Ryder, Barry Dornfeld and my students in the Multimedia Department. Special thanks also to Dan Rose and Matt Rumain. Extra special thanks to my extraordinary friends Craig Saper, Lynn Tomlinson, and their young son Sam.

In Gainesville, the proto-elements of this project owe much of their formulation to my studies and conversations with Gregory Ulmer, John P. Leavey, Jr., Robert Ray, Robert D'Amico, and the late Robert Long.

Dispersed at distant sites and providing long-range support and friendship have been Mady Schutzman, Rebecca Schneider, Kathleen McHugh, Michael Jarrett, Doug Whittle, Randy Rutsky, Steve Kurtz, Ricardo Dominguez, Mark Turner, and Steve Bottoms.

My family has been incredibly patient in supporting my research and teaching interests over the years. These interests have been nourished by the love and care of my parents, Ina Jo and Victor McKenzie, my brother and sister, Wade McKenzie and Betty Wallen, my cousins, Marshall and Robert Wigglesworth, and my aunt and uncle, Virginia and Julian Clark. Additional long-term nourishment has been given by my dear friends Samuel Hill, Sally Hadley Dickinson, and Caroline McGriff.

Finally, the trajectory of my life and work has been dazzled beyond brilliance by Caroline Levine, who is the wisest companion I could ever dream of having alongside me while wandering about the world, yes-"and then what?"

JM
Philadelphia
December 2000

Nephrops challengeri,
88.22
Types.
Betw. Australia
& N. Zealand.

SO—IN THIS MY LAST GOOD NIGHT TO YOU AS YOUR PRESIDENT—I THANK YOU FOR THE MANY OPPORTUNITIES YOU HAVE GIVEN ME FOR PUBLIC SERVICE IN WAR AND PEACE. I TRUST THAT IN THAT SERVICE YOU FIND SOME THINGS WORTHY; AS FOR THE REST OF IT, I KNOW YOU WILL FIND WAYS TO IMPROVE PERFORMANCE IN THE FUTURE.

Dwight D. Eisenhower

Farewell Radio and Television Address to the American People

HE WAS, AFTER ALL, BY NOW WELL ABLE TO PLAY ON THIS DEPARTMENTAL MACHINERY, THIS DELICATE INSTRUMENT ALWAYS TUNED FOR SOME COMPROMISE OR OTHER. THE ART OF IT LAY ESSENTIALLY IN DOING NOTHING, LEAVING THE MACHINERY TO WORK BY ITSELF AND FORCING IT TO WORK BY THE MERE FACT OF ONESELF BEING THERE, IRREMOVABLE IN ONE'S PONDEROUS MORTALITY.

Franz Kafka

A passage deleted by the author from *The Castle*

THERE IS NO OFF SWITCH TO THE TECHNOLOGICAL.

Avital Ronell

The Telephone Book

INTRODUCTION

OF ALL THOSE PERSONS WHO HAVE PROPOSED THE IDEA OF ROCKETING THEMSELVES INTO SPACE, THE FIRST MAN WHO SERIOUSLY TRIED TO DO SOMETHING ABOUT IT WAS PERHAPS THE BRAVEST. THE FIRST, ACCORDING TO CHINESE HISTORY, WAS A [FOURTEENTH-CENTURY] SCHOLAR AND SCIENTIST NAMED WAN HU. HE HIT UPON THE IDEA OF PROPELLING HIMSELF WITH THE CRUDE ROCKETS KNOWN TO THE CHINESE AT THAT TIME. SO, AFTER LASHING SEVERAL DOZEN OF THESE "JATO" UNITS TO HIS SEDAN CHAIR, HE PROCEEDED TO HAVE ALL THE ROCKETS FIRED SIMULTANEOUSLY. WE DO NOT YET KNOW JUST HOW SUCCESSFUL WAN HU WAS, FOR IN THE BLAST THAT FOLLOWED HE DISAPPEARED, AND NOTHING HAS BEEN HEARD FROM HIM SINCE.

Major Nels A. Parson, Jr., 1956

CHAPTER 0. CHALLENGES

10, 9, 8 . . .

Perform or Else initiates a challenge, one that links the performances of artists and activists with those of workers and executives, as well as computers and missile systems. From congressional attacks on performance artists to the performance specs of household appliances, from the iterative training of high performance managers to the performativity of everyday speech, performance so permeates US society that it evokes that mysterious circle of mist which Nietzsche said envelops any living thing and without which life becomes "withered, hard, and barren." "Every people," the philosopher wrote, "even every man, who wants to become ripe needs such an enveloping madness, such a protective and veiling cloud."[1]

If performance is our mist, our mad atmosphere, it's also capable of becoming stratified, of leaving an historical sediment of effects that we can read in both words and actions. Herbert Marcuse, professor to Angela Davis and other student radicals of the 1960s, argued as early as 1955 that postindustrial societies were ruled by what he called "the performance principle," a historical reality principle founded on economic alienation and repressive desublimation.[2] Yet around the same time, researchers in the humanities and social sciences were beginning to use a theatrical concept of performance to understand social rituals and everyday interactions, and this performance concept would later be applied to political demonstrations and experimental art happenings. Today, as we navigate the crack of millennia, work, play, sex, and even resistance—it's all performance to us.

Because performance assembles such a vast network of discourses and practices, because it brings together such diverse forces, anyone trying to map its passages must navigate a long and twisting flight path. The challenge initiated here: *to rehearse a general theory of performance.*

The possibility that a general theory is called for—and perhaps long overdue—may be gauged by posing *Perform or Else* as a response, as a reply in dialogue with other performative challenges, the first of which I cite not from a scholarly text, but from a popular business magazine. The 3 January 1994 issue of *Forbes* magazine published its "Annual Report on American Industry" under the dramatic cover reproduced here:

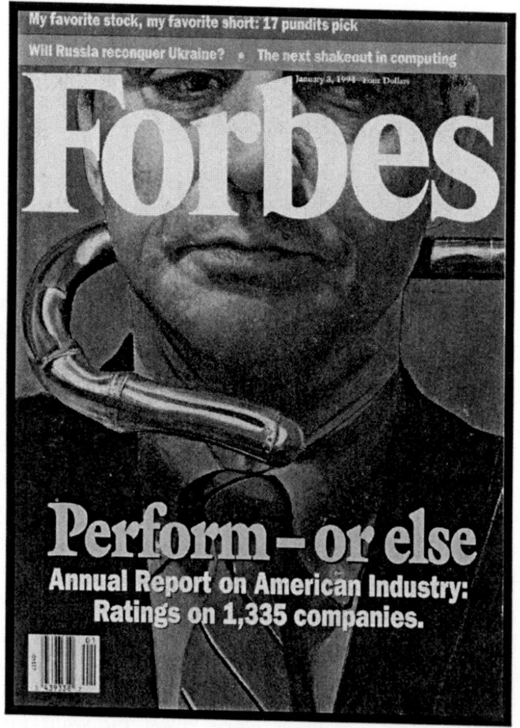

Let us begin here a patient, if partial, reading of this scene, taking apart its elements—its script, its cast, its props—while also tuning and retooling them with the care of a motorcycle mechanic.

The *Forbes* challenge: suspended under the name of this well-established magazine is the headline "Perform—or else," printed in a loud caution of yellow. These words and the white *Forbes* name in turn frame a detail of the image behind them, focusing our eyes on a stilled gesture: a cane hook wrapped menacingly around the neck of a white-skinned, gray-haired businessman. His eyes peer out between the magazine's title and top banner, staring wearily off in different directions: one straight ahead and slightly down as if to face the music, the other down and off to his left, perhaps sizing up a burly escort, perhaps seizing a line of escape. Below this bifurcating gaze, his almost forgotten nose is pinched between the letters "r" and "b," while lower still, a stiff upper lip and strong jawline prepare to take things on the chin. The cane itself embodies the challenge, brandishing a high-gloss polished gleam; more subtly still, its hook casts a shadow across the executive's red-striped tie. This shadowy adornment gathers the pathos of our tableau, for it ties together the cane's gesture and the words "Perform—or else," knotting them in a fashion that's got this performer by the throat.

ORGANIZATIONAL PERFORMANCE

What performance is challenged forth by this *Forbes* cover? And what is its "—or else"? To commence one reading: From the executive figure and the title "Annual Report on American Industry: Ratings on 1,335 Companies," to the publication itself and its namesake founder, the cover directs us to the performance of companies, of business management, of economic power. It directs us to the high performance of US corporate executives—and to their occupational risks. Inside, an introductory article by Dana Wechsler Linden and Nancy Rotenier reprints the cover image and runs this callout which encapsulates the gist of their text: "For too long boards sat passively while chief executive officers blamed below-par performance on all manner of things: recessions, foreign exchange fluctuations, strikes. Chief executives would fire vice presidents in the way that Stalin would shoot commissars, but the boss tended to be sacrosanct. No more."[3] This performance is evaluated in terms of profits, stock prices, and organizational efficiency, and the risks to poor performers are occupational and reach high up the US corporate ladder. Linden and Rotenier's article features a chart showing how 1993 was "The year heads rolled," namely, those of GM's Robert Stempel, IBM's John Akers, Apple's John Sculley and nine other corporate heads axed by their boards of directors.

The *Forbes* challenge can thus be paraphrased as "Perform—or else: you're fired!" The challenge is that posed by organizational performance. And though it seems directed to a rather small but powerful group—the top brass of 1,335 companies—this challenge affects not only all levels of corporate structure, but also workers in a wide variety of organizations, from businesses to non-profit organizations, from government agencies to educational institutions. As part of their administrative practice, thousands upon thousands of organizations administer "performance reviews," formal evaluations of the work performed by their employees. These reviews, conducted by immediate supervisors, human resources staff, and/or the employees themselves, occur at regular intervals, in most cases annually, but also semi-annually or quarterly. The reviews themselves traditionally take both oral and written form, though increasingly digital technologies also provide numeric calculations of workplace activity. Depending upon the work, performance reviews evaluate such things as productivity, tardiness, motivation, innovation, and the ability to establish and fulfill goals which support the organization's own goals. High performance ratings may produce rewards: salary increases, special bonuses, official recognition, perhaps a promotion. With low ratings comes the "—or else," which may be that of getting fired or "outsourced" (and often later rehired without benefits), though other options include receiving little or no pay increase or bonus, being retrained or transferred to another job, or being presented with such difficult working conditions that one "chooses" to leave the organization. This broader "perform—or else" challenge of organizational performance thus affects not only the group of (primarily) white males who make up the top management of US organizations. Its call addresses all members of a workforce whose ranks, from shop floors to cubicles to office suites, are increasingly composed of women and minorities.

At a more abstract level, the challenge of "perform—or else" also enacts a self-described paradigm shift in the theory and practice of organizational management. The literature of this new management paradigm, which I will read as "Performance Management," describes the displacement in the following terms. Scientific management or "Taylorism" has been the dominant organizational paradigm in the US since early in this century, when it was articulated by Frederick Taylor. Aptly equipped for a manufacturing-based, nationally oriented, and highly industrialized economy, scientific management calls for organizing work upon rational, scientific principles designed to make work more productive from both managerial and labor perspectives. According to contemporary organizational theory, however, the decades-long application of Taylorism produced highly centralized bureaucracies whose rigid, top-down management styles were—and still are—perceived by workers and managers alike as controlling, conformist, and monolithic. Performance Management, in contrast, attunes itself to economic processes that are increasingly service-based, globally oriented, and electronically wired. Since the end of the Second World War, theorists from Herbert Simon to Edwards Deming to Peter Drucker have argued for decentralized structures and flexible management styles, styles that, rather than controlling workers, empower them with information and training so they may contribute to decision-making processes. The principles regularly cited in management are not uniformity, conformity, and rationality, but diversity, innovation, and intuition.

Performance Management doesn't sell itself as scientific management: instead, it articulates an *ars poetica* of organizational practice. In the business realm, this artistic approach can be seen in the 1994 text, *Corporate Renaissance: The Art of Reengineering*, in which authors Kelvin F. Cross, John J. Feather, and Richard L. Lynch detail the mechanics of the paradigm shift using terms and figures from Renaissance painting. John Kao's *Jamming: The Art and Discipline of Business Creativity* (1996) theorizes the displacement with discursive riffs taken from improvisational jazz music. And in *Cultural Diversity in Organizations* (1993), Taylor Cox argues that diversity in the workplace contributes to creativity and problem-solving. Yet along with its ennobling discourse, high performance management has also generated practices so distressingly familiar to US workers that they are lampooned daily in Scott Adams' nationally syndicated Dilbert comics. These practices include reengineering, restructuring, TQM programs, downsizing, outsourcing, part-timing, flex-timing, hoteling, and multi-tasking.

While Dilbert has made millions laugh by tapping into the anxiety and cynicism produced by these and other microeconomic practices, we can only begin to imagine the sick jokes which may arise as these practices are connected to broader, macroeconomic developments, such as the rapid flow of capital worldwide, the corresponding decline of organized labor movements, the opening of global consumer and labor markets, and the integration of computer and communication technologies throughout all strata of society, both in the US and abroad. Thus, the *Forbes* challenge and its hold upon throats around the world: Perform—or else: be fired, redeployed, institutionally marginalized.

CULTURAL PERFORMANCE

If the *Forbes* challenge of "perform—or else" were readable solely in the manner just outlined, mounting a response to it here would pose a daunting enough task. Yet by citing another challenge our path becomes even more twisted. Close at hand, the *Forbes* cover can generate another reading of performance, one that takes the threatening cane as a citation from a different performance site, that of the vaudeville stage. Here, performers who brought forth boos and missiles from the crowd were sometimes yanked from the planks by wily stage managers yielding long wooden hooks. At first blush, this seems to enact the same "perform—or else" challenge associated with organizational performance, and in fact the *Forbes* cover design plays precisely upon this coincidence of theatrical and managerial performance. That's its hook, as it were, the same one that gives "show business" its resonance, and here the play between stage and business crafts produces a stunning headshot and a punning headline. By following this hook off the cover and back into the wings of the vaudeville stage and pausing there to learn a few things from the brothers Marx—namely, to strategically mix up the literal and the figurative, the real and the fictive, the serious and the joke—one can gather another sense of performance, one that directs us to a different challenge of "perform—or else."

In contrast to the organizational sense of performance, the activities that once animated the vaudeville stage—music and dance, comedy and melodrama, daring feats of skill—all these can today be read as cultural performances, as the living, embodied expression of cultural traditions and transformations. Today, the most common uses of this performance concept still come in the contexts of theater, film, and television, where acting performances are routinely discussed, reviewed, marketed, and consumed. However, cultural performance extends far beyond those genres often considered "mere" entertainment. Over the past five decades, the presentational forms associated with theatrical performance have been transformed into analytical tools, generalized across disciplinary fields, and reinstalled in diverse locations. Anthropologists and folklorists have studied the rituals of both indigenous and diasporic groups as performance, sociologists and communication researchers have analyzed the performance of social interactions and nonverbal communication, while cultural theorists have researched the everyday workings of race, gender, and sexual politics in terms of performance. Here, Richard Schechner's concept of "restored behavior"—as the living reactualization of socially symbolic systems—has been one of the most widely cited concepts of cultural performance.

The concept of performance as the embodied enactment of cultural forces has not only informed many disciplines of study, it has also given rise to its own paradigm of knowledge, called in the United States and other English-speaking countries "Performance Studies."

The intellectual history of this paradigm has been sketched several times, most notably by John J. MacAloon in his introduction to the 1984 anthology *Rite, Drama, Festival, Spectacle: Rehearsals Toward a Theory of Cultural Performance*; and by Carol Simpson Stern and Bruce Henderson in the introduction to their 1993 *Performance: Texts and Contexts*. The first book-length attempt to examine the development of the concept of cultural performance was Marvin Carlson's *Performance: A Critical Introduction* (1996). In this long-awaited intellectual history, Carlson culminates his text by stressing that the "growing interest in the cultural dynamics embedded in the performance and theatrical representation itself was primarily stimulated by a materialist concern for exposing the power and oppression in society."[4] Indeed, within Performance Studies, performance has taken on a particular political significance; with increasing consistency, performance has become defined as a "liminal" process, a reflexive transgression of social structures. Marginal, on the edge, in the interstices of institutions and at their limits, liminal performances are capable of temporarily staging and subverting their normative functions. Through the study of such genres as demonstrations, political theater, drag, public memorials, performance art, and everyday gestures of social resistance, performance scholars have sought to document and theorize the political practices enacted in performances around the globe. At the same time, scholars in the Departments of Performance Studies at New York University and Northwestern have used liminal performance as a generative model for theorizing their own institutional practices of research and teaching.

This cultural understanding of performance is by no means limited to scholars, however. In the early 1990s, performance formed a front line in the highly publicized "culture wars" waged in the US by politicians and journalists, lawyers and judges, artists and grassroot activists from both the right and the left.[5] In early 1990, when Senators Alfonse D'Amato, Jesse Helms, and other conservative politicians renewed their calls for defunding the National Endowment for the Arts, they targeted their rhetorical wrath at sexually explicit performance art. Responding to political pressure, NEA chairperson John Frohnmayer vetoed Theater Program grants that had been approved for four performance artists, Karen Finley, John Fleck, Holly Hughes, and Tim Miller, who would later become known as the NEA 4. Though the courts later forced the Endowment to honor their original grants to these artists, the Endowment—and, arguably, performance art and the art world in general—have been under siege ever since.

This cultural sense of performance allows us to cite another challenge. From the perspective of the NEA 4 and those for whom performance means liminality, subversion, and resistance, this challenge reads: Perform—or else: be socially normalized.

TECHNOLOGICAL PERFORMANCE

In the reading proposed so far, *Perform or Else* responds to two challenges, one that calls us to perform organizationally, to help improve the efficiency of companies and other institutions; the other calls us to perform culturally, to foreground and resist dominant norms of social control. A general theory of performance must somehow account for these two types of performance staged by *Forbes*, must respond to their two contrasting challenges.

One might easily construct a table and attempt to draw up the challenge of *Perform or Else* by extending the fronts of the culture war and declaring them also to mark the border between organizational and cultural performance. A long series of oppositions could then be generated between Performance Management and Performance Studies, starting with their two challenges and then continuing with Establishment/margin, standardization/deviation, and structure/play. Such a table could in turn direct many other readings of performance, and perhaps even a general theory or two. The challenge of *Perform or Else*, however, involves a slightly different response, one that sets up tables so they may twist and turn on their own shaky legs. At this particular table, one can already hear Performance Management theorists objecting that they've been recast as neo-Taylorites, that they're as interested in creativity as Performance Studies scholars, though within a different context. For their part, theorists in Performance Studies might point out that sociologists such as Erving Goffman have conducted performance research in corporate and institutional environments. But the more significant twist underlying this table lies in this observation: these two performance paradigms know very little of one another's research, even though their practitioners encounter, and often enact, one another's concept of performance on a daily basis, even as their fields have grown ripe alongside one another.

Where might this twist take us? Rather than stage an oppositional front between the organizational and the cultural, rather than set up shop with just these two senses of performance, let us take another direction. Let's continue reading the cover of *Forbes*, for another performance unfolds on this magazine cover, a third performance whose script remains plainly on view for us. And though the script is inscribed and even translated on this and nearly every other product we buy, it remains almost totally illegible to us. What is this third performance, what is its script, and who—or rather what—is its performer? We see the script down in the left corner, stuck there like a sinister lapel button marking this performer for executive execution. Yet it rides not the plane of his lapel, but that of the cover itself: printed black on white, the script is a bar code, a cryptic cipher composed of vertical lines and spaces. The bar code contains the magazine's Universal Pricing Code, which is also written in Arabic numerals. Who reads bar code? Nobody, really—few, if any, human bodies read it directly; but many, many machines read it, specifically, laser scanning technologies. Bar codes, when scanned by systems attached to databases and interactive terminals, facilitate the on-site processing of such data as price, inventory, ordering, and other product information.

Bar code is a script of technological performance, a performance embodied in such items as high performance sports cars, stereos, and missile systems. When we talk about how a car performs, or when we ask about the performance specifications of a computer, we are citing a sense of performance used by engineers, technicians, and computer scientists. Concepts of technological performance help guide the design, testing, and manufacture of thousands upon thousands of industrial- and consumer-grade commodities. The performance specs of materials and products are often regulated by federal and/or state governments and monitored by their agencies, as well as by industry associations, insurance companies, and consumer groups. Performance specifications also play an important function in consumer information literature, such as owner's manuals. Beyond these relatively specialized discourses, technological performance is perhaps most familiar to consumers through the use of "performance" to market brands and products.

What performs? Air fresheners, roofing insulation, bicycles, carpets and rugs, powerboats, wallcoverings, drain panels, cleansing towels, car-stereo equipment, bakeware, aquarium filters, tires, fabric, window film, woodworking knives, automotive timing chains, foil containers, audio antennae, deep-fat fryers, embossing tools, mop handles, music synthesizers, casement windows, and eyeliners—to name just a selection of those products marketed in the US with some form of the word "performance" actually appearing in their names. One industrial giant, Phillips Petroleum, even markets itself as "The Performance Company."

The most profound enactments of technological performance, however, are those cast and produced within the computer, electronics, and telecommunication industries. To cite the range of performing computers and their users: on one end, the Macintosh Performa, a popular line of computers marketed by Apple in the 1990s; toward another end, the Maui High Performance Computing Center, a facility maintained by the University of New Mexico and the United States Air Force that offers state-of-the-art parallel processing for highly select research projects. The Performa is but a single line of computers, the Maui facility but one of dozens of high performance computing centers in the US. The extent of technological performance within the computer industry must be mapped both in terms of its own specific operation there and in light of the computer's function as a virtual metatechnology, a technology used to design, manufacture, and evaluate other technologies. Technologies no longer go back to the drawing board; instead, they go back to the desktop with its CAD or computer assisted design programs. The computer not only performs, it helps produce performances of other products and materials and thereby greatly extends the domain of technological performance, a domain whose reach into our own lives can be grasped in the ubiquity of bar codes.

Despite its massive extension, however, technological performance does not yet have a significant body of critically reflexive research corresponding to Performance Studies and High Performance. That is, although performance functions as a working concept in a number of technical sciences and an array of manufacturing industries, although its application in the computer sciences is so vast that it has been institutionalized in High Performance Computing Centers, and although product information and marketing campaigns have placed this highly technical performance in our garages, kitchens, and living rooms, despite all this, technological performance has largely escaped the critical attention of historians and philosophers of science. Although technologies perform, very few researchers have asked, "What is this performance?" and "How does it function in different scientific and technical fields?"

In an attempt to respond to such questions, I shall call this rigorous yet amorphic paradigm of research, "Techno-Performance." Despite the absence of critical literature, I shall also make this hypothesis: like Performance Studies and Performance Management, the paradigm of Techno-Performance has emerged in the US since the Second World War. To specify this hypothesis more: the formative stages of Techno-Performance were engineered within the American Cold War apparatus, that vast "military-industrial complex" which President Eisenhower warned the nation about in 1960 and which Senator William Fulbright also called the "military-industrial-academic complex."[6] Concepts of technological performance developed by this "MIA complex" have been, shall we say, instrumental to the deployment of successive generations of military systems, and despite the thaw of the Cold War, the criteria of "high performance" and "very high performance" still attain their most rigorous formulation in such fields as aeronautics and computer science.

If the MIA complex guided the first stages of Techno-Performance, its effects are not limited to arms races and the space race, and even in its more modest performances this paradigm stages its own challenges. Posed to a given product or material by its developer, its challenge might read: Perform—or else: you're obsolete, liable to be defunded, junkpiled, or dumped on foreign markets. And we can also imagine a computer displaying this message to a befuddled user: Perform—or else: you're outmoded, undereducated, in other words, you're a dummy!

THE PERFORMATIVITY OF KNOWLEDGE

In articulating the challenge of *Perform or Else*, I have introduced three performances, organizational, cultural, and technological, each of which poses different kinds of challenges. These performances, paired with their respective research paradigms, form one level of the general theory under construction here. With three, rather than two, performance paradigms on our unstable table, we can perhaps avoid building a reading machine out of binary oppositions while unfolding performance in other ways as well.

The fields of organizational, cultural, and technological performance, when taken together, form an immense performance site, one that potentially encompasses the spheres of human labor and leisure activities and the behaviors of all industrially and electronically produced technologies. As extensive as these combined fields might be, the paradigms of Performance Management, Performance Studies, and Techno-Performance do not exhaust the performance research now operating in the United States. In linguistics and philosophy, the concept of "performative" has been employed to theorize utterances that constitute rather than represent social actions. In the health sciences, performance has emerged as a field studying the effects of pharmacological and physical therapies on activities such as work, sports, and everyday life. And in the realm of finance, individual stocks and bonds, mutual funds and pension investments, and even entire markets are daily, if not hourly, analyzed in terms of their short- and long-term performance. These and other paradigms deserve study in their own right, and we shall at times draw upon their research, especially that of philosophy. However, detailed readings fall outside our current mission. The general theory rehearsed here is partial, and part of this partiality involves focusing initially on the three paradigms of performance research introduced above and leaving others for later research.

Three paradigms may indeed be challenge enough, but immediately the question arises: what is the relation among these different paradigms, and how have they emerged in the US since the Second World War? I should stress that I am not arguing that the application of performance concepts to objects as diverse as cultural activities, organizational practices, and technologies originated during the past five decades. The *Oxford English Dictionary* cites related uses of "performance" dating back over several centuries. No, the term "performance" has not been coined in the past half-century. Rather, it has been radically reinscribed, reinstalled, and redeployed in uncanny and powerful ways. What has occurred has been the articulation and rapid extension of performance concepts into formalized systems of discourses and practices, into sociotechnical systems that have themselves become institutionalized first within the United States and then subsequently worldwide. To get some sense of this rapid extension: between 1861 and 1944, only some 127 dissertations were written pertaining to the subject of "performance." Since then, there have been over 100,000.[7] There has been, in short, an explosion of performance research in the past half-century, one whose expansion includes and exceeds the immense object terrains produced by researchers of organizational, cultural, and technological performance.

Here one could raise the following objection: however impressive this explosion of performance research might be, it is merely indicative of a much more massive expansion in research and teaching over the past half-century. Performance research must be understood as part of an unprecedented growth in new methodologies and specializations, a sudden expansion in disciplines and degrees, in the number of colleges, universities, and graduate institutions in the US and abroad, and in the number of students and faculty involved in primary, secondary, and higher education. Further, this expansion must be situated within the context of a complex and worldwide set of geopolitical, economic, technological, and cultural changes, changes that have come to be called "globalization."

And yet what if this explosion in knowledge was itself "performative"? What if the diversification and proliferation of researchers, projects, and fields over the past fifty years signal not only a quantitative leap in research initiatives, but also a qualitative mutation in what we call knowledge, the becoming-performative of knowledge itself? With this question, we begin to sense a level of performance quite different from that of the paradigms.

The possibility of such an "event" of knowledge can be cited in what has become a classic text of cultural theory, Jean-François Lyotard's *The Postmodern Condition: A Report on Knowledge*. Here Lyotard argues that the status of knowledge has radically changed in postindustrial societies and that this change has been underway since at least the end of the 1950s. Modern knowledge fully emerged in industrial societies of the nineteenth and early twentieth centuries and legitimated itself upon what Lyotard calls "grand narratives," epic stories of history such as "the dialectics of Spirit, the hermeneutics of meaning, the emancipation of the rational or working subject, or the creation of wealth."[8] Depending upon their defenders' political commitments, even highly specialized knowledges were socially legitimated by arguments that their truths served the progress of humanity, the revolution of the working class, and/or the liberation of historically oppressed groups. Postmodern knowledge, by contrast, legitimates itself by "optimizing the system's performance—efficiency."[9] Its emergence marks the decline of grand narratives within academic and public discourse and the growing hegemony of computer technologies. Significantly, Lyotard names this postmodern legitimation "performativity."

In a certain sense, performativity is the postmodern condition: it demands that all knowledge be evaluated in terms of operational efficiency, that what counts as knowledge must be translatable by and accountable in the "1"s and "0"s of digital matrices. But performativity extends beyond knowledge; it has come to govern the entire realm of social bonds. Because performativity is the mode through which knowledge and social bonds are legitimated in contemporary societies, we must investigate how it conditions—and is conditioned by—the paradigms of Performance Management, Performance Studies, and Techno-Performance. For now, I will only note that Lyotard associates performativity with a certain challenge, "a certain level of terror, whether soft or hard: be operational (that is, commensurable) or disappear."[10] In other words, performativity involves its own challenge to perform—or else.

THE PERFORMATIVITY OF POWER

We are assembling the components of a general theory of performance, the rehearsal of which forms the challenge of *Perform or Else*. At one level, our mission consists in analyzing the connections between the challenges posed by Performance Management, Performance Studies, and Techno-Performance. Studying how their performances embed themselves within one another, we must also situate their workings at a second level, one characterized by the rise of performative knowledge, and also by the recent installation of performative power circuits.

Modern legitimation operates by opposing knowledge and power, with the latter conceived primarily in negative terms. The asserted objectivity, rationality, and universality of knowledge—not only of its formal truths, but also of its methods of research and teaching, as well as its institutes and universities—purportedly allow it to demystify and master subjective, irrational, and particular forces of power. Performative, postmodern legitimation, however, challenges this opposition and realigns the relation of power and knowledge. It takes as its slogan: knowledge is power, with knowledge increasingly understood to mean information and power conceived in terms of productive potential. But this realignment of knowledge and power, while troubling to some social critics, also allows us to entertain another reading, one that exposes the specific ways in which knowledge always entails questions of power. Lyotard puts the equation this way: "knowledge and power are simply two sides of the same question: who decides what knowledge is, and who knows what needs to be decided?"[11]

Although *The Postmodern Condition* has been in translation for well over a decade and is frequently cited by cultural theorists, it is significant that Lyotard's concept of performativity remains strangely uncited, even by those theorizing postmodern cultural performance. We begin to sense that, in contrast to the theories of transgressive performance long articulated by Performance Studies scholars, other theories have emerged which directly concern the normative power of performance. Indeed, Lyotard's performativity stands as but one critical site where performance is analyzed as a regime of normative force.

Another such site can be found in the field of gender studies, where Judith Butler's work has focused on the ways in which discursive practices underlie the social construction of women, gays, and lesbians. To this end and other ends, she has articulated a theory of performativity which draws upon J.L. Austin's concept of performative speech acts, as well as Jacques Derrida's deconstructive reading of Austin. In "Critically Queer," Butler writes, "Performative acts are forms of authoritative speech: most performatives, for instance, are statements which, in the uttering, also perform a certain action and exercise a binding power. . . . The power of discourse to produce what it names is linked with the question of performativity. The performative is thus one domain in which power acts as discourse."[12] Over the past few years, Butler's work on the citationality of performatives has had a very influential effect within Performance Studies, yet the normative valences of her performativity concept were initially passed over—in favor of her incisive analyses of drag performance's subversive potential—and have only of late become fully appreciated by scholars.

One other theory of normative performance must be cited here, or rather, re-cited. It is that of the performance principle, which forms the guiding thread of Herbert Marcuse's *Eros and Civilization*. Marcuse wrote in English and did so in the United States, the country to which he fled from Nazi Germany in the 1930s. Through a critical conjunction of Marx's theory of labor and Freud's theory of drives, he set out to define the historical reality principle, the regime of repressive forces, which he saw as guiding postwar, postindustrial civilization. From this place, in this language, Marcuse called it "the performance principle," for "under its rule society is stratified according to the competitive economic performances of its members. . . . Men do not live their own lives but perform pre-established functions. While they work, they do not fulfill their own needs and faculties but work in alienation."[13] Crucial to Marcuse's theory, however, is that individuals not only tolerate performative alienation; through a process of repressive desublimation they can even take pleasure in it. Further, the effects of the performance principle extend throughout society.

Marcuse's theory of the performance principle was published in 1955. That he made this call so long ago is telling, for it indicates that the power of performance was already operational in the US early on in the Cold War, which is also the time when Techno-Performance, Performance Management, and Performance Studies were initializing their reading machines. But Marcuse's call has been on hold for some time; today, the performance principle remains largely unread and uncited, even by cultural theorists trained during the 1960s, when his texts and teachings at the University of California at San Diego became a lightning rod for both student activists and conservative politicians such as then Governor Ronald Reagan. This putting on hold of Marcuse's call, when connected to the strange (non)citation of Lyotard's and Butler's own calls and then to calls held up on the communication lines of the MIA complex—this cumulative holding pattern suggests something other than lax reading practices on the part of individual scholars. It suggests that the (non)citation of different performance concepts across and even within paradigms may itself be generated by the power of performance.

If the power call has been left up in the air, circling or orbiting about us, this is not due to incompetent scholarship here on the ground; on the contrary, it arises from the very competencies which form and inform our fields of research, from the hows and whys and whens and wheres of pointing to and saying that "this—*this* is performance." If different researchers have known little about one another's performance concepts, if they have remained largely out of the loop with respect to different performances, it is because their reading machines have been programmed by codes and protocols barring them from performing at one another's evaluative sites. The question then becomes: who—or what—decides what performance is, and who—or what—performs that which is decided? And more challenging still: how to characterize the power/knowledge formation that underlies the different challenges to "perform—or else?"

DISCIPLINE AND PERFORM

Let us circle back toward our point of departure, navigating our way through the mist in hopes of touching down and taking off again, but not before digging in a little. Picking up *Forbes*, the issue whose cover let us in on Performance Management, Performance Studies, and Techno-Performance, let's now uncover a reading of onto-historic proportions, a reading of power and knowledge. The statement "Perform—or else" and the image of the threatening gesture are gathered together most tightly in the performer's neck tie. Statement and graphic elements form a circuit of power, the binding of word and image by normative forces. Word and image are bound together, but they are not static, for each is a production, an active formation of knowledge, the one an audible discourse, the other a visible practice. Here we see and hear a demonstrating and a commanding, and such normative circuits operate in the showings and tellings of school children, as well as the big pictures and moral callings of the more highly trained and educated. The entire cover calls out to us: "Look, hear, what counts is this—perform—or else—⊃ "

In the small text *This Is Not a Pipe*, Michel Foucault writes of René Magritte's famous drawing by the same name, a drawing of a pipe, under which is drawn the words *"Ceci n'est pas une pipe."* Of this last element, Foucault writes, "They are words drawing words; at the surface of the image, they form the reflection of a sentence saying that this is not a pipe. The image of a text. But conversely, the represented pipe is drawn by the same hand and with the same pen as the letters of the text; it extends the writing more than it illustrates it or fills its void."[14] Foucault's interest in Magritte's works lies in the artist's calligraphic experiments into the relation of word and image, of discourse and practice, or rather, into their relation of nonrelation, their forced cohabitation which makes up our world. If we cite this interest here, it is because Foucault's own writings on statements and visibilities have been operating in the background of our text, guiding from afar our reading of the *Forbes* cover. In *Discipline and Punish*, Foucault argues that the power regime of eighteenth- and nineteenth-century Western Europe was modeled on a particular arrangement of statements and visibilities, specifically, "the legal register of justice and the extra-legal register of discipline."[15] Discipline proper is an onto-historical formation of power, an *episteme* based upon the juxtaposition of two forms of knowledge: the discursive statements of penal law and the concrete mechanisms of surveillance embodied in Bentham's panoptic prison. To read the extent of disciplinary power and knowledge in the eighteenth and nineteenth centuries, Foucault documented its normalizing effects within discourses and practices far beyond the prison, such as those of hospitals, factories, and schools. Moreover, he concluded from his research that an understanding of discipline was essential to studying the effects of power and knowledge in contemporary society.

A central argument of *Perform or Else* is that performance must be understood as an emergent stratum of power and knowledge. More specifically, the performance theories of Butler, Lyotard, and Marcuse, as well as readings of Foucault, Deleuze and Guattari, and many others, lead me to make this speculative forecast: *performance will be to the twentieth and twenty-first centuries what discipline was to the eighteenth and nineteenth, that is, an onto-historical formation of power and knowledge.* This formation is ontological in that it entails a displacement of being that challenges our notion of history; it is nonetheless historical in that this displacement is materially inscribed. Though it obviously draws upon and recombines other knowledge forms and power forces, this "performance stratum" coalesced in the United States in the wake of the Second World War, and its effects have been going global for some time, expanding especially fast with the thaw of the Cold War.

Let me outline the contours of the performance stratum in a few bold strokes, strokes whose details we shall read more closely later on. Like discipline, performance produces a new subject of knowledge, though one quite different from that produced under the regime of panoptic surveillance. Hyphenated identities, transgendered bodies, digital avatars, the Human Genome Project—these suggest that the performative subject is constructed as fragmented rather than unified, decentered rather than centered, virtual as well as actual. Similarly, performative objects are unstable rather than fixed, simulated rather than real. They do not occupy a single, "proper" place in knowledge; there is no such thing as the thing-in-itself. Instead, objects are produced and maintained through a variety of sociotechnical systems, overcoded by many discourses, and situated in numerous sites of practice. While disciplinary institutions and mechanisms forged Western Europe's industrial revolution and its system of colonial empires, those of performance are programming the circuits of our post-industrial, postcolonial world. More profoundly than the alphabet, printed book, and factory, such technologies as digital media and the Internet allow discourses and practices from different geographical and historical situations to be networked and patched together, their traditions to be electronically archived and played back, their forms and processes to become raw materials for other productions. Similarly, research and teaching machines once ruled strictly and linearly by the book are being retooled by a multimedia, hypertextual metatechnology, that of the computer.

The geopolitical, economic, and technological transformations associated with the performance stratum give us insight into the formation of its fractal subjects. The desire produced by performative power and knowledge is not modeled on repression. Performative desire is not molded by distinct disciplinary mechanisms. It is not a repressive desire; it is instead "excessive," intermittently modulated and pushed across the thresholds of various limits by overlapping and sometimes competing systems. Further, diversity is not simply integrated, for integration is itself becoming diversified. Similarly, deviation is not simply normalized, for norms operate and transform themselves through their own transgression and deviation. We can understand this development better when we realize that the mechanisms of performative power are nomadic and flexible more than sedentary and rigid, that its spaces are networked and digital more than enclosed and physical, that its temporalities are polyrhythmic and non-linear and not simply sequential and linear. On the performance stratum, one shuttles quickly between different evaluative grids, switching back and forth between divergent challenges to perform—or else. "Perform—or else": this is the order-word of the emerging performance stratum.

PERFORMANCES, PERFORMATIVES AND THE LECTURE MACHINE

The general theory of performance is multilayered. Already it comprises the levels of performance paradigms and performance stratum. In addition, if one wanted a forceful indicator that performance is indeed a contemporary formation of power and knowledge, it might lie in this observation: the stratum's knowledge forms of statements and practices can readily be understood as, respectively, *performatives* and *performances.* Discursive performatives and embodied performances are the building blocks of the performance stratum and, thus, they form a third level of the general theory.

The performances are multiplying and dividing, and their relationship may be growing a little unclear. The diagram below sketches the general theory's preliminary rehearsal site.

1. Performance Stratum
2. Performance Paradigms
3. Performance-Performative Blocks

Starting with the most abstract level, performance is a stratum of power/knowledge that emerges in the United States after the Second World

War. Its emergence can be traced, in part, through at least three research paradigms which rest atop it: Performance Management (organizational performance), Performance Studies (cultural performance), and Techno-Performance (technological performance). At the most concrete level, the power of performance can be analyzed in terms of blocks of discursive performatives and embodied performances, audio and visual knowledge forms bound together by normative forces and unbound by mutational ones. These blocks make up the paradigms, yet their composition resonates with that of the stratum itself.

Here I must address another possible objection, namely, that the attempt to outline a general theory of performance is itself outmoded, even anachronistic, and to mount this project in today's critical scene is either misguided or naïve on my part, for general theories are too abstract, too detached, and too overarching to capture the workings of concrete performances. Yes—perhaps general theories are a bit anachronistic and their generalizations may sometimes risk obliterating the specificity of particular performances. However, something along the lines of a generalized performance is, shall we say, hardwired to our future. For now, it is enough to recognize that it has been at work for some time. Performance theory cannot do without movements of generalization, nor, for that matter, can any theory, whether it be of radical difference, differential equations, or the management of differences in the workplace. To theorize is to create and critique concepts, concepts that bind together—and inevitably disseminate—diverse materialities. To study different activities, to gather up diverse events, behaviors, and processes, to analyze them all as "performance" using a variety of methods and tools, such theorization presupposes the possibility of generalization.

The task of theory is not to dismiss generalization, but to situate its movement within a matrix of sociotechnical and onto-historical forces, while also allowing it to deviate itself into idiosyncratic passages of experience, something that can only be done with immanent partiality and detachment; that is, it can only take place by taking part while simultaneously taking apart one's own part in the unfolding machinations of generalization. Thus, while the challenge lies in rehearsing a general theory of performance, it also relies on performing this theory, in staging its generalizations, its genres, and its genesis in relation to one's current site and situation. To this and other endless ends, I will launch the general theory via an immanent performance, one that I call the lecture machine.

Like the term "performance," "lecture machine" is polyvalent within the passages of our text. It will come to frame and embody a series of case studies introduced later in the book, performances that all involve lectures and scenes of instruction. The term "lecture machine" gathers divergent senses, and I will touch upon a few of the most important here.

First, at a relatively simple level, "lecture machine" designates a lectern, the piece of furniture commonly found standing or, in truncated form, sitting atop a table in lecture halls and classrooms. As lectern, the lecture machine supports a body and a script, and perhaps such props as a pen, a glass of water, a microphone, a small reading lamp, or the remote control of a projection device. Through its installation within various institutions, the lectern has become an emblem of knowledge and power, a symbol standing upright between lecturer and audience, separating the one presumed to know and thus empowered to speak the truth from those presumed not to know and thus empowered to seek the truth.

We move now to a second, broader sense of lecture machine, one indicated by Derrida, who once lectured that the entire academic institution forms a *"une puissante machine de lecture,"* a powerful reading or lecture machine. "Lecture machine" thus also designates the university itself, with its books, its desks for reading and writing, its libraries and catalogues, its logocentric protocols of research and teaching. Beyond the obvious synecdochal relation, the lecture has been the dominant performance of modern pedagogics. One might think here of specific lectures that have impacted one's own life, a disciplinary field, or an entire period of intellectual history. I'm thinking of a high-school chemistry lecture, Woolf's lecture on "Oxbridge" which formed the basis of *A Room of One's Own*, and Kojève's influential lectures on Hegel, but other readers would certainly cite other lectures—and there are lots to cite. From room to room, institution to institution, nation to nation, in short, from one locality to all corners of the university's universe, lectures are not only a popular and powerful pedagogical performance, they stand as a crucial educational norm.

There is an even broader sense of lecture machine that I will make use of here. In addition to lectern and university, I will also use "lecture machine" to refer to any system that processes discourses and practices, any assemblage that binds together words and acts or, alternatively, that works to disintegrate their bonds and erode their forms and functions. Pulpits, podiums, indeed any desktop—actual or screenal—operates as a lecture machine, as do the institutions in which they are installed. Schools of thought, research paradigms, and disciplines can likewise be understood as reading machines, as sociotechnical systems that join together and break apart specific practices and discourses. Performance Studies, Performance Management, Techno-Performance—these are all highly specialized, finely tuned machines that connect up specific infrastructures and seek to discover, invent, analyze, measure, interpret, evaluate, and produce certain acts and certain words as performance.

Finally, we can understand the lecture machine in terms of the performance stratum itself, and here its most profound reading occurs. With the emergence of this formation, there has been a radical transformation of our reading machines, an epochal shift in the citational network of discourses and practices: the global emergence of technological media—television, tape recorders, satellites, copy machines, faxes, beepers, and most profoundly, interconnecting and overwriting them all, information technologies such as digital computers and electronic networks. The emergence of this hypermediating media affects all cultures, all organizations, all technologies, for the digitalization of discourses and practices enables them to be recorded, edited, and played back in new and uncanny ways. Highly localized ensembles of words and gestures can now be broken apart, recombined, and hyperlinked to different ensembles in ways unlike anything in the past, at speeds incredible from all perspectives except those of the future.

Perform or Else constitutes a lecture machine itself, one that engages and disengages diverse readers and scanners. Its mission, in part, lies in reading the ways discourses and practices have been joined together to become different kinds of "performance." Because the project is both interdisciplinary and multiparadigmatic, the different performances it theorizes may not be familiar to many readers, and thus we will, to put it mildly, do a bit of reading. The task is to generate some sense of "performance" as it has been invented by different researchers over the past half-century, to trace the ways it has become caught up in different processes of generalization. We shall come to attempt this by studying the performance of Challenger lecture machine.

FLIGHT PLAN

The text unfolds in three stages.

Part I focuses on the performance paradigms, providing genealogical readings of their respective concepts. My approach to each one is guided in part by the terrains of their practices and discourses, in part by the path of my training and interests. Each of the three chapters of Part I takes a different perspective, while also seeking to get perspectives on these perspectives. I thus seek to distill a sense of "performance" through different sets of eyes and ears, while also examining their inter- and extra-paradigmatic connections.

In Chapter 1, I analyze cultural performance and its challenge of social efficacy. I first trace how the concept of cultural performance arose in the 1960s and 1970s from the convergence of two trends: social scientists using theater as a model to study ritual, everyday life, and other events; and artists and theorists challenging traditional notions of Western theater and other art-making practices. In the wake of this convergence emerged a research paradigm we now call "Performance Studies." I argue that, in the face of civil rights and Vietnam War protests, theater initially served as its formal model of cultural performance and liminal rites of passage as its functional model. Together, theater and ritual gave form and process to the challenge of efficacy. Privilege was given to embodied practices, presence, and live bodies. I go on to argue that in the late 1970s and 1980s, the study of cultural performance was rocked by a "theory explosion," the impact of Continental philosophy on the paradigm's reading machines. In the context of new struggles—revolving around gender, racial, sexual, ethnic, and class differences—new modes of social efficacy emerged, modeled on performance art and critical theory. Liminality becomes rearticulated in terms of discursive statements, representation, and mediated bodies. I close Chapter 1 by introducing the concept of the "liminal-norm," asking whether the very focus on liminal cultural performances has not forestalled an awareness of how performance functions in other areas of contemporary life.

Chapter 2 focuses on organizational performance and its challenge of efficiency, of maximizing outputs and minimizing inputs. To study some of the most important aspects of organizational performance, I track the concept through several different approaches to management. I start with human relations and its emphasis on developing rather than controlling the performance of workers, on encouraging diversity rather than mandating conformity. This approach, which first came to prominence in the 1940s, found renewed relevance in the 1960s and 1970s with the passage of Affirmative Action laws. Another school of management also sought to counter the machine model of Scientific Management, and did so by drawing on the field of cybernetics or systems theory. Here the focus on individual performance is replaced by attention to the overall performance of a sociotechnical system. The model of feedback emerged from this system's approach to management. I then turn to a school called information-processing and decision-making, which forcefully shifts attention toward managerial performance and the growing impact of information technologies. From this perspective, organizational performance can be defined in terms of managers' abilities to process information and make decentralized decisions. Organizational development is yet another school of performance, one that stresses the need for constant learning and reinvention throughout an organization. Empowering employees, diversifying corporate cultures, and engineering innovation—according to proponents of organizational development, these are key to producing "high" or "peak" performance in the workplace. Because it synthesizes different approaches to organizational performance, I argue that organizational development best exemplifies the paradigm of Performance Management. I conclude Chapter 2 by probing the relation of Performance Studies and Performance Management, beginning with the respective challenges of performative efficacy and efficiency. I argue that as different as these two challenges may be, they should not be seen as opposed to one another, showing that each has already produced effects upon the other.

Concentrating on technological performance and the challenge of effectiveness, Chapter 3 sketches the formation of the Techno-Performance paradigm. I argue that it crystallizes in the military-industrial-academic complex that emerged in the US after the Second World War. At the cutting edge of this complex was research devoted to high-performance weaponry, especially that of rocket science. Given the importance of this research to both the military and the nation, I contend that the guided missile has served as a metamodel of technological performance. In the wake of the Soviet Union's launch of *Sputnik*, the discourse and practice of Techno-Performance spread throughout American science, industry, and education. Because there has been relatively little reflection upon the concept of technological performance, I devote a substantial portion of Chapter 3 to examining the specific ways in which engineers, computer scientists, and other applied scientists employ the term "performance." I demonstrate that performance is central to the design, testing, and evaluation of virtually all types of consumer products and technological systems. Especially crucial has been the emergence of the digital computer. The development of computer-assisted design programs, computer simulation models, and global information networks such as the Internet have helped to extend and consolidate the research of Techno-Performance. Because of its role in designing, testing, and evaluating other technologies and, in addition, marketing, selling, and distributing them, I argue that the computer has come to function as a metatechnology, one that has joined the guided missile as a metamodel of technological performance.

Part II explores the emerging performance stratum. In the course of three chapters, it resituates the paradigms within the worldwide circuits of performative power and knowledge. Part II starts with an encased study of how cultural, organizational, and technological performances become entangled in a specific yet extremely complex event, the NASA *Challenger* disaster. Part II ends by surveying global performance.

Chapter 4 recounts the case of the *Challenger* shuttle accident, a disastrous mission on which Teacher-in-Space Christa McAuliffe was to have given two astronautic lectures. Reading Diane Vaughan's sociological study of the disaster, I examine the ways in which cultural, organizational, and technological performances can become embedded in one another. Vaughan explicitly focuses on the "performance pressures" created by cultural, organizational, and technological imperatives, and thus I read her in-depth study as a textbook for conducting multiparadigmatic performance research. At the same time, I examine how challenging operates within the performance of her own text. I come to suggest that performance and challenging are intimately connected and that by exploring this performance-challenge, we can situate the three paradigms' movements of generalization within an even more general movement.

Chapter 5 opens up our theory rehearsal in this direction. I begin by citing a second lecture, a 1955 talk by Martin Heidegger that served as the basis for his essay "The Question Concerning Technology." Reading this essay, I track how Heidegger questions technology in terms of its mode of truth, which he calls "challenging-forth." While Heidegger traces this mode of truth back to the Cartesian *cogito*, I situate it in relation to contemporary readings of performance. Examining Lyotard's "performativity," Marcuse's "performance principle," and Butler's "punitive performatives," I contend that performance is a mode of power, one that underwrites the reading machines of Performance Studies, Performance Management, and Techno-Performance and, beyond them, challenges forth the world to perform—or else.

This global performance-challenge takes center stage in Chapter 6. Engaging yet another *Challenger* lecture, I introduce Deleuze and Guattari's notion of stratum or onto-historical formation. Performance, I argue, is the stratum of power/knowledge that emerged in the US in the late twentieth century. Discursive performatives and embodied performances are the knowledge-forms of this power. I survey the performance stratum in terms of the subjects and objects it produces, the geopolitics and economics of its history, the media of its educational and citational networks, and the modulations of performative desire and power. Chapter 6 thus produces a geology of global performance.

While Part II addresses the formation of the performance stratum, Part III explores processes of destratification, particularly as they apply to strategies of resistance in an age of global performance. For if this age entails a new and emergent arrangement of power-forces, this arrangement necessarily includes mutant as well as normative potentialities and these deserve our utmost attention.

In Part III, I engage destratification as a resistant force that erodes and breaks up the forms and processes of performative power/knowledge. While performativity stratifies the world with performatives and performances, destratification operates through an atmosphere of forces and intensities, an atmosphere that I call "perfumance." Perfumance is the nonstratified element, the outside of the performance stratum. Perfumative resistance, I argue, destabilizes this formation through pockets of iterability, self-referential holes in which this outside is turned inside. Such pockets are located not only at the limits of social formations but also at their very core.

The reader is here forewarned: beginning in Chapter 7, the reading of performance-challenge repeatedly tests the uncertain limits of theory and practice, generality and specificity, proper and common, gravity and levity. For some, this experiment may border on the excessive; for others, it may read as an instance of performative writing; for others still, it may fundamentally bore. Chapters 8, 9, and 10 engage strategies of perfumative resistance on three distinct levels. At the level of performatives and performances, it consists of catachrestic uses of language and catastrophic restorations of behavior. At the level of sociotechnical systems, it gives rise to multiparadigmatic, polytonal research experiments. At the level of onto-historical formations, perfumative resistance channels "minor" histories and "minor" anachronisms.

To repeat: the challenge of *Perform or Else* is to rehearse a general theory of performance. The machine that stages this theory here and now takes it apart there and then: it sometimes says one thing and does another, shows this and tells that, all the while emitting a faint sense of its inner workings, an outside that puts everything at risk. Derrida's remarks on Phillipe Soller's *Numbers* suggest the direction our reading takes: "The text is remarkable in that the reader (here in exemplary fashion) can never choose his own place in it, nor can the spectator. There is at any rate no tenable place for him opposite the text, outside the text, no spot where he might get away with not writing what, in the reading, would seem to him to be *given; past;* no spot, in other words, where he would stand before an already *written* text. Because his job is to put things on stage, he is on stage himself, he puts himself on stage. The tale is thereby addressed to the reader's body, which is put by things on stage, itself."[16] This, then, is the flight plan of *Perform or Else*.

PART I: PERFORMANCE PARADIGMS

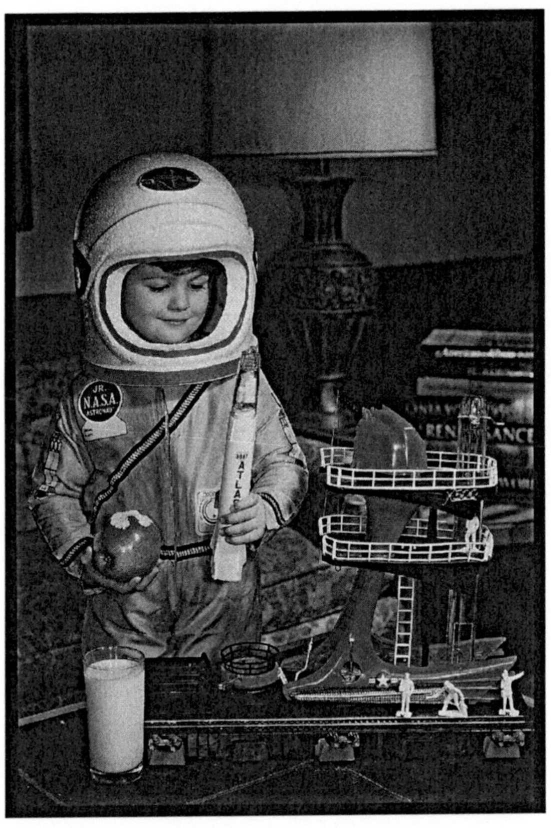

I BELIEVE THAT THIS NATION SHOULD COMMIT ITSELF TO ACHIEVING THE GOAL, BEFORE THIS DECADE IS OUT, OF LANDING A MAN ON THE MOON AND RETURNING HIM SAFELY TO THE EARTH.... [I]N A VERY REAL SENSE, IT WILL NOT BE ONE MAN GOING TO THE MOON—IF WE MAKE THIS JUDGMENT AFFIRMATIVELY, IT WILL BE AN ENTIRE NATION.

John F. Kennedy, 25 May 1961

CHAPTER 1. THE EFFICACY OF CULTURAL PERFORMANCE

THE CHALLENGE OF EFFICACY

To construct a general theory of performance, we first examine different models or paradigms which help to compose it. These performance paradigms are themselves composed of movements of generalization, by which diverse activities are gathered together and conceptualized *as* performance. This chapter focuses on the Performance Studies paradigm and its field of cultural performance, and I analyze both in terms of the challenge of social efficacy. To theorize this challenge, we will look at its interdisciplinary origins, its practical and theoretical models, and the development of the paradigm over the past five decades.

The field of cultural performance that has emerged over the last half century includes a wide variety of activities situated around the world. These include traditional and experimental theater; rituals and ceremonies; popular entertainments, such as parades and festivals; popular, classical, and experimental dance; avant-garde performance art; oral interpretations of literature, such as public speeches and readings; traditions of folklore and storytelling; aesthetic practices found in everyday life, such as play and social interactions; political demonstrations and social movements. This list is open to additions, subtractions, and debate, but from it one can see that cultural performance is cultural in the widest sense of the term, stretching from "high" to "low" culture, though its most ardent proponents stress its *counter*cultural aspects.

Given the great diversity of activities, how can we call them all "performance?" Identifying different practices and discourses as "performance" first requires gathering them together and conceptualizing them as a field of study, a field of objects, a field of performance. It simultaneously requires a gathering of subjects, a community of practitioners and researchers constituting itself around and indeed *through* performance. Today, there are students, teachers, and practitioners of performance, as well as programs, departments, and professional organizations devoted to its study. The field of cultural performance and the paradigm of Performance Studies thus co-create and co-legitimate one another. To identify different activities as performance; to study and teach such performances in terms of individuals, peoples, genres, movements, and periods; to apply diverse methods across institutional disciplines; to establish performance departments and programs; to organize panels and conferences and, of late, an international professional association—to do all this under the name of "Performance Studies" presupposes a movement of generalization capable of gathering all these differences under the concept of "performance." It presupposes that such questions as "What is performance?" and "What is Performance Studies?" if not definitively answered, have nonetheless been proposed, contested, and recast innumerable times and in numerable sites.

The history of cultural performance and Performance Studies is precisely the history of such questioning. To follow the movement of generalization that has produced the field and paradigm of cultural performance, I shall engage a number of texts that not only define performance, but also outline intellectual histories of the paradigm.

What, then, is the performance of Performance Studies? From the perspective of the general theory under construction here, this performance can best be distinguished from other performance concepts by its *challenge of efficacy*. That is, at the heart of its movement of generalization, Performances Studies scholars have constructed cultural performance as an engagement of social norms, as an ensemble of activities with the potential to uphold societal arrangements or, alternatively, to change people and societies. While performance's efficacy to reaffirm existing structures and console or heal peoples has consistently been recognized, it is its transgressive or resistant potential that has come to dominate the study of cultural performance. It has long been its cutting edge. From the happenings, rock concerts, and political demonstrations of the 1960s to the drag shows, raves, and Culture Wars of the 1990s, cultural performance has been theorized as a catalyst to personal and social transformation. Richard Schechner provides guidance here concerning the efficacy of cultural performance. Writing in 1976, he addressed the notion that theater and other performing arts functioned as simple entertainment or, at best, as a reflection of changes occurring elsewhere, arguing instead that entertainment and efficacy are two strands of a braid that cross one another throughout history.

"At each period in each culture one or the other is dominant—one is ascending while the other is descending. Naturally, these changes are part of changes in the overall social structure; yet performance is not a passive mirror of these social changes but a part of the complicated feedback process that brings about change. At all times a dialectical tension exists between efficacious and entertainment tendencies."[1] From this perspective, the emergence of cultural performance entails the reascendance of efficacy over entertainment.

The importance of efficacy to the conceptualization of performance can be seen in key definitions provided by various cultural theorists. John J. MacAloon provides one such definition in his 1984 anthology *Rite, Drama, Festival, Spectacle: Rehearsals Toward a Theory of Cultural Performance*.[2] In rehearsing this theory, MacAloon introduces his collection by citing the definition of cultural performance provided by the symposium organizers, Barbara Babcock, Barbara Myerhoff, and Victor Turner. Cultural performances are "'occasions in which as a culture or society we reflect upon and define ourselves, dramatize our collective myths and history, present ourselves with alternatives, and eventually change in some ways while remaining the same in others.'"[3] This citation of a citation identifies three functions which scholars have regularly attributed to cultural performance: 1) social and self-reflection through the dramatization or embodiment of symbolic forms, 2) the presentation of alternative arrangements, and 3) the possibility of conservation and/or transformation. Given the imperative of social efficacy, theorists have largely concentrated on performance's transformational potential.

Another definition can found in *Performance: Texts and Contexts*, a 1993 book by Carol Simpson Stern and Bruce Henderson. Stern and Henderson's *Performance* is a textbook, a work intended to assist the teaching of performance studies. As such, it also attests to the institutionalization of performance study, to its courses, curricula, syllabuses, canons, evaluations, examinations, and theses. Significantly, Stern herself served many years as chair of the Department of Performance Studies at Northwestern University. The authors write that the "term *performance* incorporates a whole field of human activity. . . . In all cases a *performance act, interactional* in nature and involving *symbolic forms* and *live bodies*, provides a way to constitute meaning and affirm individual and cultural values."[4] Like MacAloon, Stern and Henderson define performance by citing its social functions, those of constituting meaning and affirming values. They also cite two forms, those of human symbols and human bodies. These functions and forms have been routinely employed by researchers, although as we will shortly see, the precise functions and forms have changed over the past half century.

The definitions provided by MacAloon and Stern and Henderson demonstrate how cultural performance has been conceptualized as social efficacy. Performance gives us an occasion to "change in some ways while remaining the same in others;" it "provides a way to constitute meaning and affirm individual and cultural values." To theorize the ways in which performance produces this efficacy, scholars have also drawn upon specific genres of performance and deployed them as models to think about the transformative potential of cultural performance in general. Such models have thus been crucial to the paradigm's movement of generalization, to the theorization of its field, and to the articulation of its challenge of efficacy.

Challenging, in fact, may be one of the most insistent gestures of Performance Studies, and thus my framing of *Perform or Else* as a challenge has been rehearsed many times. Across different sites, the tonality of challenging carries a force of efficacy. In the general introduction to their anthology *Critical Theory and Performance* (1992), Janelle Reinelt and Joseph Roach attribute "an inherently political character to the performance analysis that has emerged from critical theory; it revises, *challenges*, rewrites, interrogates, and sometimes condemns received meanings."[5] For his part, Marvin Carlson, in his *Performance: A Critical Introduction* (1996), writes that "almost any contemporary performance project" involves many cultural, social, and intellectual concerns, including "the varying *challenges* of gender, race, and ethnicity, to name only some of the most visible."[6] In a closely related though slightly different manner, Peggy Phelan opens her *Unmarked: The Politics of Performance* (1993) with another challenge. "*Unmarked* examines the implicit assumptions about the connections between representational visibility and political power which have been a dominant force in cultural theory in the last ten years. Among the *challenges* this poses is how to retain the power of the unmarked by surveying it within a theoretical frame."[7]

Given the role which challenging plays in Performance Studies, one might say that *performance challenges*, it provokes, contests, stakes a claim. And there is some uncanny feedback here: not only does performance challenge, challenges perform. J.L. Austin includes "challenge" in his list of performative speech acts, words that "do something." Specifically, Austin lists "challenge" as a word with illocutionary force.[8] Challenges do something: they incite, demand, assert, accuse, and oppose. And as performance scholars have sharpened our challenges over the past several decades, perhaps we have witnessed the launch of something like "the Performance Studies challenge," akin to the one which Lawrence Grossberg, Cary Nelson, and Paula Treicher cite in the introduction to their 1992 anthology *Cultural Studies*:

> Through the last two decades, when theory has sometimes seemed a decontextualized scene of philosophical speculation, cultural studies has regularly theorized in response to particular social, historical, and

> material conditions. Its theories have attempted to connect to real social and political problems. Now that "theory" is more broadly returning to material concerns and interrogating the social effects of its own discourses, it finds its enterprises clarified and facilitated by the cultural studies challenge.[9]

Performance Studies, like cultural studies, has challenged theory to get real, while also challenging itself with theoretical questions concerning the status of that "real" ("real bodies," "real materiality," "real life"). Over the past half century, this paradigm has emitted many challenges and counter challenges in its study of cultural performance. In theorizing performative efficacy, Performance Studies has mimed its object of study; our scholars have launched their own challenges to the institutional norms of research and teaching. Developing specific models to theorize cultural performance generally, we have also deployed them as paradigms of the paradigm itself. To understand this process, let us now turn to the initiation of Performance Studies.

THE PASSAGE TO PARADIGM

To compose a field as diverse as that of cultural performance—and to compose itself as a paradigm—Performance Studies has drawn upon many different, even disparate, disciplines. These disciplines range from "a" to "z": anthropology, art history, cultural studies (especially gender, ethnicity, class, and, of late, queer and postcolonial theory), dance history, ethnography, folklore, history, linguistics, literary criticism, media studies, philosophy, political science, psychology, sociology, speech and nonverbal communications, theater studies, and zoology.

Because the fields upon which it draws are so diverse, the intellectual history of Performance Studies is quite complex, though there is general agreement that its formation began in the 1950s. MacAloon, for instance, cites "certain initially independent intellectual developments in the 1950s that have served as a foundation for the now rapidly expanding and coalescing interests in the study of cultural forms."[10] He goes on to discuss the importance of four concepts: Victor Turner's "social drama," Milton Singer's "cultural performance," Kenneth Burke's "dramatistic pentad" and Erving Goffman's "social psychology of everyday life." These theorists are significant, for Stern and Henderson also discuss four authors important for their contributions to defining *performance* and *performers*. Despite their different disciplinary orientation, Stern and Henderson cite three of the same four theorists as MacAloon, namely, Turner, Burke, and Goffman. Instead of Singer, they stress the importance of Richard Schechner and his concept of "restored behavior." The overlapping casts of performance theorists indicate that, despite the different perspectives and debates in the field, these differences circulate in a shared citational network of discourses and practices.

While MacAloon, writing in 1984, argues that "the study of cultural performance is in, as yet, a 'preparadigmatic' stage,"[11] Schechner outlines a more detailed intellectual history of a full-fledged research paradigm just five years later. In "PAJ Distorts the Broad Spectrum," he writes:

> The performance studies paradigm came to the fore in the mid-'50s. Gregory Bateson's "A Theory of Play and Fantasy" was published in 1955, the same year as J.L. Austin's Harvard lectures on the 'performative' *(How to Do Things with Words)*. Erving Goffman's *The Presentation of Self in Everyday Life* was published in 1959; Albert B. Lord's *The Singer of Tales* in 1960; and Roger Callois' *Man, Play, and Games* in 1961. My "Approaches to Theory/Criticism" was published in 1966; Dell Hymes' "Model of the Interaction of Language and Social Setting" in 1967. Victor Turner's *The Ritual Process* came out in 1969, his *Drama, Fields and Metaphors* in 1974. Milton Singer's *When a Great Tradition Modernizes* appeared in 1972. *Folklore: Performance and Communication* (editors, Dan Ben-Amos and Kenneth Goldstein) was published in 1974 as was Barbara Myerhoff's *The Peyote Hunt. Secular Ritual* (edited by Myerhoff and Sally Moore) appeared in 1977, the same year as Richard Bauman's *Verbal Art as Performance.*[12]

This paragraph reads as a dramaturgy of the paradigm, an expansive reading of its citational network. Though both Schechner and MacAloon date the field's origins back to the 1950s, Schechner incorporates MacAloon's "'preparadigmatic' stage" into the paradigm. And with the exception of Burke, he cites all of the authors cited by MacAloon, Stern, and Henderson—and then some.

The intellectual histories cited thus far are quite brief, limited as they are to but a few paragraphs or pages. Recently, however, a book-length survey of the field has been published, Marvin Carlson's *Performance: A Critical Introduction.* The depth of this survey is unparalleled, as is its breadth: not only does Carlson reference over 300 theorists from a wide range of fields, he provides discussion of almost all of them. Needless to say, he cites all the authors we have cited above and, beyond this, all of the authors they cite (and, one suspects, all of the authors that *they* cite). In short, Carlson's *Performance* delivers the most extensive reading yet of the paradigm's formation and development, the most detailed mapping of its citational network. He states that the concept of performance is "heavily indebted to terminology and theoretical strategies developed during the 1960s and 1970s,"[13] yet also discusses uses of the term dating back to the 1950s and earlier.

Carlson's intellectual history of performance focuses on the concept's development in the fields of anthropology and ethnography, psychology and sociology, and linguistics. I am interested here not only in the theorists and disciplines that contributed to the early formation of Performance Studies, but also in the ways that scholars have since theorized this formation itself. We find in Carlson's introduction a telling description of the paradigm's movement of generalization.

> With performance as a kind of critical wedge, the metaphor of theatricality has moved out of the arts into almost every aspect of modern attempts to understand our condition and activities, into almost every branch of the human sciences—sociology, anthropology, ethnography, psychology, linguistics.[14]

Moving out of theater, out of a field taken by many to be its proper home, performance becomes the cutting edge of a critical wedge. Slicing into the human or social sciences, performance here brings with it the metaphor, the figure of theatricality and, at the same time, inscribes its own movement of generalization. This reading cuts its way through Carlson's *Performance*, for in his conclusion he describes performance as a "metaphor or analytical tool,"[15] suggesting that performance first enters the sciences as an unfamiliar metaphor and, after extended use, becomes a critical tool of analysis. But he also stresses a feedback effect: "as performativity and theatricality have been developed in these fields, both as metaphors and analytical tools, theorists and practitioners of performance art have in turn become aware of these developments and found in them new sources of stimulation, inspiration, and insight for their own creative work and the theoretical work of understanding it."[16] Theater thus provides the human sciences with metaphors and tropes which are developed into conceptual tools for analyzing other activities, and these tools may then pass back to humanities scholars and become applied anew. From theater to metaphor to analytical concept and back to theater and other performances: such is the general movement of Performance Studies according to Carlson.

Although the disciplinary matrix of Performance Studies contains many fields of study, the passageways between theater and anthropology are the ones most often cited as generative of the paradigm. During the 1960s and 1970s, the feedback between theater studies and ethnography generated powerful and influential models of cultural performance. Theater provided anthropologists and ethnographers with a model for studying how people and societies embody symbolic structures in living behavior. Social actors, role playing, the scripting and rehearsing of interactions, the importance of gesture, costume, setting, and dramatization in maintaining and transforming social relations—all of these concepts were explicitly developed from the study of theater and applied to the analysis of ceremonies, festivals, and rituals. Over these same two decades, however, concepts developed by ethnographic studies of performance were used by theater and humanities scholars to theorize the social dimensions of theater and other emerging genres of performance. The work of Victor Turner was especially influential here, in particular his concepts of social drama and liminal rites of passage. In his essay, "Liminality and the Performative Genres," Turner writes that liminality "is a complex phase or condition. It is often the scene and time for the emergence of a society's deepest values in the form of sacred dramas and objects. . . . But it may also be the venue and occasion for the most radical skepticism."[17]

Liminal rites were first theorized by Arnold van Gennep at the beginning of the last century.[18] Through Turner's critical dialogue with Schechner in books such as *From Ritual to Theatre* and *Between Theatre and Anthropology*, liminal rites of passage provided performance scholars with another important model, one used to theorize the ways in which theater and other arts can help to transform individuals and society at large. Peggy Phelan poses the "fecund collaboration" between Turner and Schechner in this way: "In bringing theater and anthropology together, both men saw the extraordinarily deep questions these perspectives on cultural expression raised. If the diversity of human culture showed persistent theatricality, could performance be a universal expression of human signification? If performance communities continually remade themselves into mini-cultural ensembles, how did their rules and responses reflect larger cultural imperatives?"[19]

Between theater and anthropology emerges the paradigm of Performance Studies. Theater provided anthropologists and ethnographers with a *formal* model for "seeing" performance, for recognizing its forms in society, for conceptualizing the ways in which social meanings and values become embodied in behaviors and events. In turn, liminal rites of passage gave theater scholars a *functional* model for theorizing the transformational potential of theater and other performative genres. Like theater, liminality would become a pervasive model of cultural performance itself: separated from society both temporally and spatially, liminal activities allow participants to reflect, take apart, and reassemble symbols and behaviors and, possibly, to transform themselves and society. And even more than theater, liminality would become key to theorizing Performance Studies itself.

Drawing upon the reflexivity found in rites of passage, cultural performance scholars have also theorized our own activities in terms of liminality, arguing that we operate in the interstices of academia as well as the margins of social structures and seek to reflect upon and transform both the academy and society at large. Performance scholars have been interested, in other words, in the efficacy of our own performance, and we have used liminal rites of passage as a metamodel of the very formation of Performance Studies. MacAloon, for example, theorizes its early development as a breakthrough, a passage:

> Dell Hymes has coined the phrase "breakthrough into performance"

to describe the passage of human agents into a distinctive "mode of existence and realization." "Breakthrough into performance" equally well configures certain initially independent intellectual developments in the 1950s that have served as a foundation for the now rapidly expanding and coalescing interests in the study of cultural forms.[20]

What is Performance Studies? Casting Hymes' "breakthrough" within the orbit of MacAloon's analogical reading, we get this response: it is a dramatic rite and ritualized drama of passage, a rehearsed movement that carries theory-builders into a distinctive mode of existence and realization. Theory becomes performance (and performance becomes theorized) as an assemblage of liminal processes: reflection and definition, alternative embodiment, transgressive transformation. Liminal rites of passage thus have played several functions in Performance Studies. First, as theorized by Turner, they have been an important *object of study*. Second, through the work of Schechner, Turner, and many others, the concept of liminality has been applied to different cultural activities, thereby contributing to the generalization of the concept of performative efficacy. Liminal rites have therefore functioned as an *exemplar* of the entire field of objects, guiding not only the descriptive analysis but also the theoretical and practical construction of other performances. Over the course of several decades, performance scholars have downplayed the potential for rites of passage to conserve social structures and emphasized their transgressive possibilities instead. And finally, as MacAloon demonstrates, liminal rites have been used to theorize the very emergence of Performance Studies. They have become an *emblem* of the paradigm itself. Turner himself wrote that the university functioned as a "liminoid" site in industrialized societies. Performance scholars have not only extended this transformational potential to other cultural activities, we have theorized our own activities as liminally efficacious.

As object, exemplar, and emblem, liminality has served as a paradigm of the paradigm. Even more than theater, rites of passage have provided Performance Studies a metamodel for its own initiation as a discipline, its passage to paradigm. This passage can be understood in relation to a series of conceptual shifts, shifts defined in different terms by different disciplines, but now cited as formative of the concept and study of cultural performance.[21] With respect to theater, the movement from entertainment to efficacy came via a shift in emphasis from the playscript to the actor's body; in dance, attention moved from formal choreography to movements of everyday life; and in both dance and experimental theater, there was a shift away from theatrical to environmental spaces. In the visual arts, artists and critics turned from the art object to the art-making process itself. In anthropology, ethnographers shifted their attention from mythic structures to their embodiment in rituals. Similarly, in folklore studies, attention moved from the text of a tale to the context of its telling. In linguistics and communication, researchers turned their focus from *langue* to *parole*, from studying grammatical structures to analyzing the pragmatics of utterances. And in political science and social activism, there was an attempt to move US culture away from serving "the Establishment" and toward the creation of an authentic form of social relations between genders, races, and classes.

In general, between 1955 and 1975 and across a wide range of cultural practice and research, there was an attempt to pass from product to process, from mediated expression to direct contact, from representation to presentation, from discourse to body, from absence to presence. Performance Studies' passage to paradigm was initially driven by this general movement. But by the early 1980s it had become evident that something had happened, something had altered this movement subtly yet radically. The repercussions of this event would reroute the passage to paradigm, engender other models of performative efficacy, and bring the paradigm itself into crisis.

THE THEORY EXPLOSION

A paradigm is coming to pass: a gathering of subjects staking out a field composed of a gathering of objects. Performance emerges here as the efficacy of certain activities, activities capable of challenging of social norms and symbolic structures. To conceptualize this efficacy, scholars study diverse cultural practices, generalizing, differentiating, and theorizing them *as* performance. This movement of generalization depends upon a process of selection, one that not only delimits the field of cultural performance, but also selects paradigms of the paradigm, specific models of the general model. In its first two decades, the formation of the Performance Studies paradigm was guided by two dominant models, theater and ritual. These were not the only ones by any means, but between them, in their limen, the challenge of efficacy took on a particular form—the theatrical body, the physical presence of actor and audience—and a particular function—the transformation of society through liminal transgression. Through this form and function, Performance Studies fashioned its field and itself.

Reflecting back on the efficacy attributed to the body in the 1960s, Herbert Blau writes that there was "a liberating energy in the libidinal thinking which—seeking a 'body without organs' or instituted power—subverted the repressive text and disrupted, along with the universities, the institutions of literature and theater, which were exposed in their collusion with other instruments and agencies of power."[22] The immediacy of what Blau calls "Love's Body" offered both the means and the ends, the passage and the destination of those working to connect the arts with social struggles over civil rights, the Vietnam War, and women's liberation. At its most polemical, cultural performance opposed the physicality and passion of body to the rationalized alienation of modern society. From the Living Theater to

Woodstock, from Birmingham to the streets of Chicago, bodies performed and transgressed the power of the Establishment, the System, the Machine. Performance Studies emerged as witness and participant of this performance, and its memory still haunts us. Commenting on the convergence of history and theory, Sue-Ellen Case remarks, "I have become aware that something like a narrative keeps haunting my discussion of this convergence. It's as if something happened in the 1960s and is marching through time."[23]

Something has happened along this march, however; the passage to paradigm has been redirected. Beginning in the mid-1970s, there has been a profound shift in the ways in which performance scholars articulate the challenge of efficacy. Its form and its function have been altered, its models mutated, its field blown wide open as new sites of cultural performance and research emerged. Schechner marked this transformation in 1989: "Since the mid-'70s there has been an immense body of performance studies work. It is not possible to name even a fraction of the scholars—some well known, some just emerging—currently working the field." But perhaps Reinelt and Roach put it best in 1992 when they wrote: "There has been a theory explosion. . . ."[24]

Documents and analysis of this explosion can be found in Reinelt and Roach's anthology, *Performance and Critical Theory*. The categories into which the editors structure their anthology indicate some of the new approaches that have emerged in the last two decades: "Cultural Studies," "Semiotics and Deconstruction," "After Marx," "Feminism(s)," "Theater History and Historiography," "Hermeneutics and Phenomenology," and "Psychoanalysis." Discussing the consequences of the theory explosion, Reinelt and Roach write that "the new theory has provided a methodology and an impetus to specify the meaning of an old cliché: a text is different on the stage than it is on the page. Theory has done so principally by radically questioning the idea of what a text is. . . . Perhaps most important, performance can be articulated in terms of politics: representation, ideology, hegemony, resistance. In a way, theory gives theatre back again to the body politic."[25] The theory explosion—in particular, the translation, publication, and reading of Continental philosophy by artists, activists, and academic researchers—further expanded the concept of performative efficacy while also subjecting it to a rigorous philosophical examination, one whose methodological focus on textuality has had the effect of returning theater to the body politic or, to put things differently, to an embodied *and* discursive politics. For the fallout from the theory blast has entailed a radically renewed interest in many of the sites left behind in Performance Studies' initial passage to paradigm, especially the topics of discourse and text.

The concept of cultural performance developed in the 1950s and 1960s had emphasized the presence of the theatrical body. The theory explosion of the 1970s and 1980s challenged the efficacy of this body through a radical questioning of presence itself. Among the most important texts in this regard are Jacques Derrida's readings of Artaud in "The Theatre of Cruelty and the Closure of Representation" and of Lévi-Strauss in "Structure/Sign/Play in the Discourse of the Human Sciences." Between theater and anthropology, these deconstructive readings argue that presence and absence are inscribed within a system of conceptual hierarchies, an evaluative network that also includes such oppositions as truth/falsity, science/art, speech/writing, reality/representation, and body/language. In *Of Grammatology* (1974), Derrida defines this system and its history as "logocentrism," the dominance of the spoken or written word which he characterizes as "nothing but the most original and powerful ethnocentricism, in the process of imposing itself upon the world."[26] The critique of presence, and the reevaluation of values it entails, have become a signature event of French poststructuralism, itself a signpost bearing—rightly or wrongly—the names of Bataille, Baudrillard, Barthes, Bourdieu, Cixous, Clement, de Certeau, Deleuze, Derrida, Foucault, Girard, Guattari, Irigaray, Kristeva, Lacan, Levinas, Lyotard, and Serres.

In the wake of the theory explosion, amidst the decline of 1960s and 1970s activism and the startling rise of 1980s Reaganism, critical theory gradually took on the efficacy that artists, activists, and scholars had long attributed to the body. Blau records this shift in his essay, "(Re)cycling the Sixties," arguing that "when the radical activism of the sixties abated or went underground it surfaced in *theory* as a new erotics of discourse. . . . The lifestyle desires and polymorphous perversity which were celebrated at Woodstock and seemed to be savaged at Altamont also went under, retreating across the Atlantic, and entered the high intellectual traditions of continental thought, given the *ideology* they were charged with *not* having in the sixties, and are being recycled, biodegradably, as an assault on the phallogocentric structure of bourgeois power, with its invisible ideology."[27] This theory was not restricted to French structuralism and poststructuralism, for the works of the Frankfurt School and the Centre for Contemporary Cultural Studies at Birmingham also contributed to the explosion of new approaches. At stake in this recycling was not the simple introduction of theoretical discourse—for such discourse had obviously been employed by earlier performance theorists—but the heightened element of philosophical critique. Reinelt and Roach comment that "the 'new' theory has returned the humanities to philosophy: performance history and criticism, along with other humanities disciplines such as English, modern languages, and history, have returned to a fundamental examination of the underlying assumptions and their understanding of objects of inquiry in general."[28] In short, to the critique of dominant social norms, the new theory added a critique of performance research.

Blau's "recyling of the sixties" and Reinelt and Roach's "theory explosion" help us mark an important shift here, one I will call "from *theater* to *theory*." Over the course of the past two and a half decades, the impact of critical theory has helped transform the "what" and the "how" of performative efficacy while also contributing to its movement of generalization. This shift from theater to theory, however, itself marks an even more profound passage, *for there has been a passage in the passage itself.* The efficacy, the transformative potential of cultural performance has itself been transformed.

This transformation can be situated by looking at the models of performative efficacy, the paradigms of the Performance Studies paradigm. Theater, which had served performance scholars as the most productive formal model for analyzing cultural performance, has gradually ceded this role to theory itself. If theater helped performance scholars "see" performance as embodied practices, critical theory challenged this vision and, indeed, the very field of its theoretical visibility, its form as presence. In posing the challenge of how to frame the unmarked within theory, Phelan writes that "Visibility is a trap. . . .; it summons surveillance and the law; it provokes voyeurism, fetishism, the colonialist/imperial appetite for possession."[29] Because practitioners and researchers alike had originally located the efficacy of performance in the presence of performing bodies, the poststructuralist critique of presence contributed to a whole new series of conceptual shifts within the study of cultural performance.

Among the most evident developments: the influence of Winnicott and Piaget's psychologies has been eclipsed by Lacanian psychoanalysis which, with its stress on the structural relation of desire and language, displaces the presence of the subject into the insistent deferral of signifying chains. Similarly, the importance of Goffman's work and, for that matter, of sociology in general, has steadily declined as the notion of the social has been fragmented and dispersed among multiple and competing voices. Even anthropology, so essential to the formation of the paradigm, no longer plays the same role it once did, owing in large part to the critiques of its own cultural constructedness and to the increasing importance of an array of approaches associated with cultural studies, including ethnic studies, theories of gender and sexuality, and postcolonial studies. Obviously, each of these developments has involved different challenges posed at different times and places, but all have also been informed by the poststructuralist critique of presence.

Over the past decade, one of the most significant challenges to performative presence has come through deconstructive readings of Austin's speech act theory. Through the work of Judith Butler and others, Austin's analysis of performative utterances has provided scholars a rigorous means of studying how performance embodies symbolic systems, and more radically, how such systems help to construct and constitute the body as such.

The body has in no way disappeared from Performance Studies. Indeed, bodies have multiplied and diversified as more and more people have taken up cultural performance as a means to challenge social norms.

A second and more profound transformation of performative presence has been the hypermediation of social production via computer and information networks. In terms of cultural performance, this has entailed the incorporation of media technologies into live performances and vice versa. Media have long been commonplace in performance spaces, but now these spaces are themselves being mapped by and into digital media. With programs such as LifeForms, choreographers can generate individual movement sequences and compose entire dance pieces on computers and then "download" them in the studio into dancing bodies. Conversely, movement sensors can track a performer's gestures so that the movements can be digitally stored and processed to create computer animations. Connecting themselves to and between older media such as film, audio, video, synthesizers, etc., computer systems can break up and recombine elements, "distributing" or rather redistributing performative presence. Words and acts break down, embodied performances can be recast in relation to discursive performatives, as both performances and performatives are immersed in networks of citationality.

If the shift from theater to theory can be understood as occurring along a series of fronts, it has also been accompanied by a transformation in the functional model of cultural performance. As we have seen, ritual processes provided early performance scholars with an important model of efficacy, one which they generalized across the entire field of cultural performance. In the social and political context of the 1960s and 1970s, this model helped to articulate strategies of embodied transgression, strategies deployed in performances ranging from Grotowski to Spiderwoman. In the 1980s and 1990s, however, the role of ritual as a general model of efficacy has declined, or rather, ritual has itself become the raw material for another modelization process, one centered around performance art. Especially in its most recognizable form—a body and some stories—performance art has emerged as an incredibly critical and fertile site for researchers theorizing the mediated play of embodied practices and discursive statements. Through the work of Laurie Anderson, Karen Finley, and Guillermo Gómez-Peña (to name but a few of the innumerable individuals and groups who have turned to performance art to engage cultural representation), the tactics of appropriation, parody, and cross-cultural detournement have become central to the articulation of efficacious performance. Other genres, most notably drag, voguing, and rap, have also contributed to this theorization, but over the past two decades performance art has been the most productive site of practical and theoretical experimentation. Carlson, in fact, devotes two thirds of his survey to the history and theory of performance art. And for many in the experimental arts, performance *is* performance art.

This transformation of performative efficacy has been discussed many times, often in reference to the differences between modern and postmodern performance art. In *Presence and Resistance*, Philip Auslander describes postmodern performance as involving a shift from transgression to resistance, which can be understood here as two different strategies of performative efficacy. Transgressive efficacy posits itself as a presence outside an alienating power, taking its position in opposition to dominant social structures and forms. By contrast, resistant efficacy arises from within, necessarily inscribed within the very forces of power whose arrangement of presence and absence it seeks to challenge. The difference between these strategies corresponds also to a difference in the ways power is conceived: while transgressive efficacy seeks to overthrow the totalitarianism of the Establishment, resistant efficacy seeks to subvert the hegemonies of ethnophallogocentricism. Auslander argues that postmodern performance does not attempt to oppose social norms and institutions but instead infiltrates them through subtle critiques and/or parodies of representational media. The title of one chapter succinctly articulates this change: in "From the Politics of Ecstasy to the Ecstasy of Communication" he writes that "the social subject can no longer take up a position in a social drama but is always already absorbed into society as electronic communication."[30]

The shift from transgressive to resistant efficacies reflects the growing reluctance of artists, activists, and theorists to ground performative efficacy in either an ideal or a material presence. Debates over these models of efficacy have been intensified by the increasingly divergent cultural differences at work in performance theory and practice. In "Performance and Contemporary Theory," Part III of his *Performance*, Carlson devotes his final chapters to two strategies of political performance art, one based in the identity politics of the 1960s and early 1970s, and the other in the postmodern critique of presence. The differences between these two strategies generated a subtle yet profound change in performative tactics.

> Instead of providing resistant political "messages" or representations, as did the political performances of the 1960s, postmodern performance provides resistance precisely not by offering "messages," positive or negative, that fit comfortably into popular representations of political thought, but by challenging the processes of representation itself, even though it must carry out this project by means of representation.[31]

Again, these changes can be situated in relation to the retooling of critical values that has occurred since the theory explosion. One efficacy has challenged another. The critique of presence has challenged the very core of identity politics, the position of the subject, the authentic presence from which oppositional transgression can take place. Given the political stakes, it comes as no surprise that the emergence of postmodern performance has generated the most heated debates within Performance Studies over the past two decades. This is not to say that identity politics have been eclipsed; as Carlson points out, there has been a productive tension "between the desire to provide a grounding for effective political action by affirming a specific identity and subject position, and the desire to undermine the essentialist assumptions of cultural constructions."[32] Yet the very space between these desires attests to their difference, their alterity.

There has been a passage in the passage itself. The theory explosion marks a threshold between thresholds, a limit-experience where one liminality challenges another, where paradigms of efficacy are reflected upon, taken apart, reassembled, and transformed. The feedback between ritual and theater, so productive for an earlier generation of performers and scholars, has itself been appropriated, parodied, and recycled in the reverb of theory and performance art. While the initial paradigmatic passage from discourse to body was often posed as a rejection or exclusion of the first term and a corresponding valorization of the presence found in the second, the later passage has tended to include both terms while displacing them within a more general terrain of inquiry. The post-explosion passage thus is by no means a simple reversal or return: it has altered the very site of performance. Displaced but not replaced, the efficacy of embodied transgression has been reworked as the efficacy of discursive resistance, and, in passing, performative presence gives way to performative iterability.

PAS DE PARADIGM

The transformation of efficacy from transgression to resistance, the shifts in models from theater to theory and from ritual to performance art, all of these changes must be understood in relation to another important process that was well underway in Performance Studies by the late 1970s. I refer here to its institutionalization as a discipline and profession. The passage to paradigm, in short, has led from the streets and barricades to the classroom and conference hall. In 1980, the Graduate Drama Program at New York University was renamed the Department of Performance Studies. Soon after, Northwestern University transformed its Oral Interpretation program into a second Performance Studies department. Other programs of study have since emerged at Arizona State, Southern Illinois, North Carolina-Charlotte, and, overseas, in Great Britain and Australia.

What to make of the fact that the formal institutionalization of Performance Studies has occurred over the same period as its transformation from transgressive to resistant strategies of efficacy? One might argue that theories of "resistance from within" are ultimately self-serving, because those of us who articulate them are merely legitimating our own activities within the academy. The valorization of performance theory could be also interpreted in a similar manner: of course theory has displaced theater as a guiding model of Performance Studies; theory is what scholars produce, not theater, etc. Such arguments cannot be dismissed altogether. But the impact of theory and the emergence of resistant efficacy have not been limited to scholars; artists and activists have also responded to Continental theory and put resistant strategies into practice. One could thus counter that performance scholars have merely followed the lead of those they study and that, to facilitate the research and teaching of performance, the paradigm had to institutionalize itself. Such arguments also cannot be rejected out of hand.

Rather than choose between these two readings, we might instead draw them together and understand the paradigm's reevaluation of efficacy and its own institutionalization as two mutually reinforcing developments. That is, performance scholars have responded simultaneously to changes in the performances they study and in their own performances *of* study. Again, both of these developments must be situated within a broader sociopolitical context. Let us recall Blau's memory of the 1960s' libidinal thinking which "subverted the repressive text and disrupted, along with the universities, the institutions of literature and theater." Performance scholars' suspicion of institutions and discursively based methods and their theorization of embodied transgression were responses to normative forces at work both outside and inside the halls of the academy. More specifically, they were directly connected to the civil rights movement, to anti-war demonstrations, and to the emergent feminist movement, all of which positioned themselves, both conceptually and physically, in opposition to established social institutions.

In terms of the university, scholars studying cultural performance struggled to define its distinctiveness as an object of research and teaching. Reinelt and Roach argue that

> the history of the discipline of theater studies [a term I'm actively reading here as Performance Studies] is one of fighting for autonomy from English and speech departments, insisting on a kind of separation from other areas of study. It was necessary, politically necessary, to claim this distinctiveness, even at the expense of becoming somewhat insular and hermetic—a result that unfortunately became true for many departments of theater.[33]

However, the development of "resistance-from-within" strategies and the expansion of research to include both embodied practices and discursive statements have contributed to a rethinking of this separatist approach. Institutionally, if pre-explosion disciplinary tactics vis-à-vis English, speech, and traditional theater departments had been to break away and seal up, postexplosion tactics have sought to relink and forge alliances. Reinelt and

Roach write that "[n]ow it is even more necessary to recognize and insist on the interdependency of a related series of disciplines and also on the role of performance in the production of culture in the widest sense."[34] As in the 1960s and early 1970s, this institutional impetus merges with larger social forces. In the 1980s and 1990s, the embracing of discourse and theory and the practices of resistant efficacy have cut across artistic, activist, and academic communities, communities working under a different set of normative forces, such as those revolving around abortion rights, the treatment of AIDS, apartheid, federal funding of the arts, gay and lesbian rights, and multiculturalism. This wider sociopolitical context allows us to understand how changes in strategies of efficacy and disciplinary formation supplement each other: from this perspective, the strengthening of institutional alliances is itself a tactic of resistant efficacy.

Two models of efficacy, an explosive transformation in between: one can read here traits of what Kuhn would call a paradigm shift within Performance Studies. The immense body of new research, the theory explosion, the recycling of Love's Body, these striking figures trace the rerouting and detouring of Performance Studies' passage to paradigm. Yet this reading of Performance Studies is haunted by another paradigm shift. As we read in Stern and Henderson's 1992 textbook, the field of oral interpretation has contributed to the formation of Performance Studies and its conceptualization of performance. Though Stern and Henderson cite most of the early theorists mentioned by MacAloon, another pair of theorists offer a different perspective on the relation between oral interpretation and Performance Studies and, in doing so, they trace an alternative paradigm shift.

In a 1987 essay entitled "A Paradigm for Performance Studies," Ronald J. Pelias and James VanOosting depict Performance Studies not as the emergence of a revolutionary new paradigm, but rather as a paradigm shift occurring within an established discipline. Posing this shift as a starting hypothesis, they set out to measure "the explanatory power of the paradigmatic presumption."[35]

> Performance studies asserts a theoretical orientation framed squarely within the discipline of human communication and enriched by such fields as anthropology, theatre, folklore, and popular culture. From within speech communication, performance studies derives from the interpretation of literature and focuses on the performative and aesthetic nature of human discourse. It is based in art, carries epistemological claims, posits methodological procedures, and calls for new pedagogical approaches.[36]

Pelias and VanOosting conclude that it is "too early to say" whether there has been a paradigm shift. We can see, however, that their hypothesis frames it as a paradigm shift *to* Performance Studies, whereas the reading I have been developing suggests there has been a paradigm shift *within*

Performance Studies. Their history repeats and yet differs from the "theater meets anthropology" passage I have tracked here; it rehearses another path to performance.

Having placed Performance Studies squarely within speech communication, Pelias and VanOosting conclude their text by gathering up different genres with this round figure: "the paradigmatic relationship between oral interpretation and performance studies might display the performance of literature as the central circle in a concentric figure widening outward to include social dramas, rituals, storytelling, jokes, organizational metaphors, everyday conversations, indeed any communication act meeting the criteria of aesthetic discourse."[37] I am tempted to say that this figure, evocative of a large target, marks the site where oral interpretation met anthropology, a site located somewhere in Illinois (Pelias and VanOosting's 1987 article lists them as "assistant professors of performance studies in the Speech Communications department" at Southern Illinois University; Northwestern University is located in Evanston, north of Chicago). The contrasts between what we might call the Midwestern and Eastern passages are many, but the most significant involves the different emphasis each gives to discursive and embodied practices. For researchers with presumptions informed primarily by the oral interpretation of literature, discursive practices have long taken analytical precedence; their paradigm shift to Performance Studies heightened the importance of embodied practices while simultaneously introducing new bodies to analyze and new methods with which to do so. By contrast, for researchers holding presumptions informed by theater studies, the emergence of Performance Studies emphasized embodied rather than discursive practices. This difference can be read in the contrast between Schechner, who often excludes literary texts from the field of performance, and Pelias and VanOosting, who, when gathering together the genres of performance, do not mention performance art, arguably the genre that has most tested the body's limits. But as East meets Midwest, theater-based scholars have shifted more of their attention to discourse while the literature-based scholars have turned toward embodiment.[38]

The convergence of these two passages to paradigm has been formalized over the course of the 1990s. In 1990 graduate students at NYU organized PSI (which originally stood for "Performance Studies International"), a major conference and festival co-hosted by the NYU and Northwestern departments. Beginning in 1995, the two departments have co-hosted a series of conferences, two in New York (one of which was also co-hosted by the City University of New York) and one each in Evanston and Atlanta (co-hosted by Georgia Institute of Technology). Out of the 1997 conference in Atlanta came the formation of the first professional organization of the field, which somewhat coincidentally took the name of the 1990 conference, Performance Studies international or PSi. Subsequent conferences have been held at the University of Wales and Arizona State University.

Despite such regular conferences and organizational development, the institutionalization of Performance Studies is a history of contestations and reconciliation. Performance scholars have for decades asserted the social efficacy of our own research and teaching activities, not only calling for but also participating in challenges to the norms of scholarship and pedagogy. From this perspective, the very notion of a Performance Studies paradigm is paradoxical, if not misguided. Schechner writes that "any call for or work toward a 'unified field' is, in [his] view, a misunderstanding of the very fluidity and playfulness fundamental to performance studies."[39] Joseph Roach has suggested that Performance Studies constitutes not a discipline, but rather an "interdiscipline" or "postdiscipline."[40] For Performance Studies scholars, myself included, these arguments are familiar and important, as they form part of our image as a field of radical research. Yet someone researching the field from the outside might disagree. Citing our genres of performance and canons of literature, our methods and disciplines, our courses and curricula, our programs and departments, our professional organizations and intellectual histories, and even our contests and fluidity, this other researcher from the outside might comment: if it walks like a paradigm. . .

The twisting and detouring of Performance Studies' passage to paradigm, the debates over whether it is or is not a discipline, these result from a tension between two desires: the desire to create cultural performance as a field of study, one with institutional and professional legitimacy, and the desire to avoid recreating the norms of the academy, norms that are themselves tied to extra-institutional forces. As we have seen, in inventing performance as an object of cultural analysis and ourselves as subjects of knowledge, performance scholars have taken two different strategies regarding institutionalization: break with traditional fields of theater, speech, and English and, alternatively, seek alliances with these same fields as well as others. But to maintain the challenge of efficacy which we have attributed both to our objects and ourselves, we have also invented a paradigm that challenges the Establishment, the Ivory Tower, the university lecture machine, and all the paradigms that shift about in them. This tension has been and continues to be at once productive, reproductive and counterproductive—if not destructive and deconstructive. There is no one paradigm of Performance Studies, but instead an explosion of paradigms, a gathering and dispersion of models and modellers, a complex and sometimes contradictory process of analysis, modelization, and blasting of paradigms. *Pas de paradigm*. Step (and stop) of paradigm. There is no paradigm, no passage; there are only more paradigms, more passages.

THE LIMINAL-NORM

Let us again assemble two paradigms of efficacy, two models of cultural performance legible from our readings. In the first, efficacy grounds itself in embodied transgressions, in practices honed by theater, ritual, and other trainings of the body. Performance here is between theater and ritual: its limen is the theatricalization of ritual and the ritualization of theater. Face-to-face encounters, site-specific events, the co-presencing of individual and social bodies—these instantiate the transformative power of performance in the first decades of Performance Studies, prior even to its appellation. The second model of efficacy, that of resistance, takes off from the discourses of critical theory and the experiments of performance art: its cutting edge is the theory of practice and the practice of theory. Mediated encounters, parodic appropriations, bodies constructed by and through discourse: increasingly (though not exclusively) these have come to make up the efficacy of performance in the last two decades. Passing between the two models, the challenge of efficacy turns itself outside in: from transgressing a totalitarian power from an outside site to resisting a hegemonic power from within that very power arrangement.

Theater and ritual have in no way been left behind in this passage from transgressive to resistant efficacy. They remain two of the most important objects of study, and while their role as models has diminished, it has not been eliminated. Today, the field of cultural performance and the paradigm of Performance Studies cannot be *thought* without citing theater and ritual. They remain, as it were, specific and historical touchstones for any general theory of cultural performance. Theater continues to offer an important formal reference for conceptualizing cultural performance; in addition, theater departments and organizations such as the Association for Theatre in Higher Education and the American Society for Theatre Research provide important bases for its teaching and research. Similarly, the discipline of anthropology continues to provide performance scholars with important methodological approaches, especially those related to ethnographic fieldwork.

Furthermore, between theory and performance art, liminality remains one of the most frequently cited attributes of performative efficacy. Carlson, for instance, closes his 1996 survey with a section entitled "Conclusion: What is Performance?", which ends with the following definition, one that touches upon both liminality and theatricality.

> [Performance] is a specific event with its liminoid nature foregrounded, almost invariably clearly separated from the rest of life, presented by performers and attended by audiences both of whom regard the experience as made up of material to be interpreted, to be reflected upon, to be engaged in—emotionally, mentally, and perhaps

> even physically. This particular sense of occasion and focus as well as the overarching social envelope combine with the physicality of theatrical performance to make it one of the most powerful and efficacious procedures that human society has developed for the endlessly fascinating process of cultural and personal self-reflexion and experimentation.[41]

Scholars also continue to stress the liminality or "in betweenness" of the paradigm itself. In a 1998 essay, "What Is Performance Studies Anyway?", Schechner writes: "Performance studies is 'inter'—in between. It is intergeneric, interdisciplinary, intercultural—and therefore inherently unstable. Performance studies resists or rejects definition. As a discipline, PS cannot be mapped effectively because it transgresses boundaries, it goes where it is not expected to be. It is inherently 'in between' and therefore cannot be pinned down or located exactly."[42] Liminality, then, remains key to articulating the efficacy of both cultural performance and Performance Studies, whether that efficacy be conceived as transgressive or resistant.

Cutting-edge practices, fringe groups and marginalized peoples, border crossings, transgressions of boundaries and limits—these can and have been theorized in terms of liminality. What is performance? What is Performance Studies? "Liminality" is perhaps the most concise and accurate response to both of these questions. Paradoxically, the persistent use of this concept within the field *has made liminality into something of a norm*. That is, we have come to define the efficacy of performance and of our own research, if not exclusively, then very inclusively, in terms of liminality—that is, a mode of activity whose spatial, temporal, and symbolic "in betweenness" allows for social norms to be suspended, challenged, played with, and perhaps even transformed. The concept has not simply been applied to performances; it has also helped us to *construct* objects of inquiry by guiding the selection of activities to be studied, their formal analysis, and their political evaluation. And as we have seen, the liminal rite of passage also functions as a striking emblem of the paradigm itself, both of its initiation and of its subsequent development.

To underscore the normative dimension of liminality, I have come to call it the *liminal-norm*. More generally, the liminal-norm operates in any situation where the valorization of liminal transgression or resistance itself becomes normative—at which point theorization of such a norm may become subversive. I made up the term "liminal-norm" not long after reading another citation of rites of passage, this one by Michel Foucault. In an interview entitled "Rituals of Exclusion," Foucault discusses how capitalist norms are inscribed pedagogically:

> There is the first function of the university: to put students out of circulation. Its second function, however, is one of integration. Once a student has spent six or seven years of his life within this artificial

> society, he becomes "absorbable": society can consume him. Insidiously, he will have received the values of this society. He will have been given socially desirable models of behavior, so that this ritual of exclusion will finally take on the value of inclusion and recuperation or reabsorption. **In this sense, the university is no doubt little different from those systems in so-called primitive societies in which the young men are kept outside the village during their adolescence, undergoing rituals of initiation which separate them and sever all contact between them and real, active society. At the end of the specified time, they can be entirely recuperated or reabsorbed.**[43]

In other words, the very same rituals which performance scholars have long cited in theorizing the efficacy of performance, Foucault cites to explain the university's normative function within contemporary society.[44]

Turner himself recognized the conservative function that liminal rites of passage ultimately play in agrarian, pre-industrial societies, where they almost always reinforce existing social structures. Turning to cultural performances found in industrial societies, he came to distinguish the liminal from the liminoid, the latter referring to cultural activities found in "advanced" societies marked by the sharp separation of labor and leisure.[45] However, there is little doubt that Turner's interest and passion lay in the anti-structural elements he theorized in both liminal and liminoid activities, and it was these elements which he stressed in his critical dialogue with Schechner and other performance scholars (elements Foucault does not mention in the text cited above, although elsewhere he does emphasize the importance of "limit-experiences" to his own theoretical work).[46]

The liminal-norm is important here for several interrelated reasons. *First*, it demonstrates how forces of normativity can become mutational, and vice versa. In his ethnographic research, Turner recognized that the liminal practices of Ndembu society could lead to either schism or reinforcement of existing social structures, with reinforcement being the most common outcome. However, as liminality was generalized across the emerging field of cultural performance—that is, as it was re-cited, decontextualized, and recontextualized—the relatively rare instances of schism and radical transformation quickly came to the fore as performance scholars sought to theorize the efficacy of cultural performance during the social unrest found in North America and Western Europe during the 1960s and early 1970s. Liminality almost exclusively became a space and time of transgression and subversion; thus, a concept and practice primarily associated with normative forces had become the embodiment of mutational forces. However, the very success of this generalization process inevitably produced the normalizing effects already noted: the concept of liminality has helped to guide the selection and construction of objects as well as their analysis and evaluation, and in addition, it has shaped Performance Studies' image of itself, the self-representation of the paradigm in relation to both the academy and society at large. Again, re-citation, decontextualization, and recontextualization, only here liminal efficacy has become a liminal-norm.

Second, the liminal-norm also suggests that any given conceptual model, even one constructed and deployed to theorize transgression or resistance, is necessarily limited in terms of both its formal and its functional aspects. This does not imply that one must—or even can—avoid modelization or generalization altogether. As indicated earlier, the formation of theoretical concepts presupposes movements of generalization, as does the emergence of a research paradigm such as Performance Studies. The challenge, then, is not to abandon conceptual modelization, but rather to inscribe this movement within one's specific situation, to fold generalization back on itself in order to avoid reducing performance to any one model, be it theater or ritual or performance art or such theoretical models as formalism, psychoanalysis, feminism, deconstruction, queer theory, or postcolonial theory. These models have all been extremely productive to the study of cultural performance, yet all have their own perspectives, their own limits. The task is thus also to multiply the models at one's disposal while at the same time opening up these models to their "own" alterity. To cite another yet model: Félix Guattari describes schizoanalysis as a process of "metamodelisation," one that, "rather than moving in the direction of reductionist modelisations which simplify the complex, will work toward its complexification, its processual enrichment, toward the consistency of its virtual lines of bifurcation and differentiation, in short towards its ontological heterogeneity."[47] I have attempted here to analyze the workings of not one but several models crucial to the emergence and development of Performance Studies. In doing so, I have focused special attention on liminal rites of passage because they are a particularly rich and productive model of the paradigm's movement of generalization. This modelization process I have nicknamed the "passage to paradigm." In other words, liminal rites provide us with *a* (and not *the*) metamodel of the paradigm, one that I have tried to crack open by citing its normative and mutational dimensions, as well as other models and movements.

Third, as a metamodel, the liminal-norm can help us resituate the borders and limits of Performance Studies itself. This resituation or displacement of borders is crucial to the challenge guiding our entire project, the rehearsal of a general theory of performance. This project entails challenging Performance Studies, that is, challenging ourselves. By focusing on liminal activities, on transgressive and resistant practices, or, more generally, upon socially efficacious performances, we have overlooked the importance of *other* performances, performances whose formalization and study also took off in the United States and which have since gone global. These other performances are not metaphorical displacements of theatrical or cultural activities, though they certainly and mistakenly can be reduced to them. Nor would we describe these other performances as primarily transgressive or resistant, far from it. As we shall see, their function is for the most part highly normative, so normative in fact that one might justifiably align them with the Establishment, the System, the Machine—in short, with the very institutions and forces against which cultural performance has directed much of its efficacious efforts over the past half century. But recognizing one's own involvement with these normative performances is, paradoxically, essential to making such efforts more diverse, more concrete, more efficacious. It is also essential to our general theory.

The development of such a theory is highly problematic. Carlson writes that if we "consider performance as an essentially contested concept, this will help us to understand the futility of seeking some overarching semantic field to cover such seemingly disparate usages as the performance of an actor, of a schoolchild, of an automobile."[48] I agree. But at stake in such usages is not simply different meanings of the term "performance," but also entirely different sets of discourses and practices, different infrastructures and histories, different paradigms of performance. More profoundly, what's at stake in our general theory is not an overarching semantic field of performance, but rather an underworldly stratum of performative power and knowledge, a pragmatic formation upon which all this contesting of performance unfolds. The question "What is performance?" perhaps remains inescapable, especially when surveying a paradigm or defining a field, but to map different terrains of this stratum—which is less a metaphysical foundation than an onto-historical sedimentation of forces—a more urgent question becomes "*which* performance?"

Philosophically speaking, to pose the question "What is?" presupposes a unified form while promising a single, correct answer, while the question "Which one?" assumes a multiplicity of forces that must be *actively* interpreted and evaluated.[49] This will be my assumption. Rehearsing a general theory of performance, we must not only use different concepts, nor only contest and critique them; we must also *create* concepts, *initiate* models, *launch* movements of generalization. Performance Studies scholars have obviously created multiple and diverse concepts and continue to do so. However, this multiplicity and diversity is itself largely determined by our paradigmatic perspective, which I have called here the challenge of efficacy. Direct, or rather internal, analysis of this perspective can only proceed so far, for we cannot easily get a perspective on our perspective, on the critical and affective investments in a field we have constructed and to some extent been constructed through. To open an angle on what amounts to our paradigmatic presuppositions and prejudices, we must turn elsewhere, for "prejudices are found by contrast, not by analysis."[50] Our rehearsal of a general theory must thus seek out other sites, other premises, other performances.

CHAPTER 2. THE EFFICIENCY OF ORGANIZATIONAL PERFORMANCE

THE CHALLENGE OF EFFICIENCY

For corporations, nonprofit organizations, government agencies, and other US institutions, performance reviews have long meant something other than theater criticism. Throughout the twentieth century they played an important role in the management of human labor, in measuring work activity, developing skills, and making decisions regarding the hiring, firing, and promotion of workers. Performance reviews are an important tool in the field of organizational performance, a field of research and practice that includes the manual labor of factory workers, the office and information skills of pink- and white-collar employees, and the decision-making processes of top managers. Like cultural performance, the field of organizational performance is a highly contested one. Similarly, it must be understood as a construction: its performances are not simply "out there" in the world, but have been generated by a paradigm of research, which we shall call "Performance Management."

The emergence of Performance Management can be traced back to just after the Second World War and situated in the United States. Through a process of generalization, however, its concept of performance steadily altered and expanded during the last half of the twentieth century, as did its field of application. Organizational performance is now in the process of going global, in part through the worldwide influence of US business schools, in part through the American style of management found in multinational corporations, in part through the role which the US plays in such organizations as the United Nations, the World Bank, and the International Monetary Fund.

Performance Management, like Performance Studies, is not a unified research paradigm, but rather a gathering of diverse conceptual models, discourses, and practices. Its passage to paradigm occurs through such schools as human relations, systems theory, information processing and decision making, organizational development, and more recently, the peak performance cult composed of theorists and practitioners of excellence, high performance, and maximum performance. These models all define performance in a slightly different manner, and thus they enable different ways of generating and evaluating specific performances. Yet gathering together this multiplicity of models, a specific challenge guides Performance Management: the challenge of "working better and costing less," of maximizing outputs and minimizing inputs, the challenge of *efficiency*.

To theorize this performative challenge, we shall read from this paradigm's citational network. The origins of organizational performance as a field of inquiry actually date back to the first decades of the twentieth century, when Frederick Winslow Taylor and other efficiency experts began to systematically analyze the performance of individual workers. But according to its proponents, Performance Management is precisely not Taylorism. From the early 1950s onward, the concept of performance has been radically redefined and recast, becoming increasingly applied to larger and larger organizational entities. By the 1980s, entire institutions were regularly being evaluated in terms of their performance. Further, they were, and still are, being *designed* for "high performance."

The generalization of performance over the past half century will be the main concern of this chapter. We can get an initial understanding of organizational performance and its challenge of efficiency by beginning at the level of individual workers, where performance reviews take place under many names, including *performance assessment*, *performance appraisal*, and *merit rating*. In 1954 Joseph Tifflin and Ernest J. McCormick defined merit rating as "a systematic evaluation of an employee by his supervisor or by some other qualified person who is familiar with the employee's performance on the job. Merit ratings are usually made by means of a standardized form that is adapted to the needs of the particular industry. Usually the ratings are made at periodic intervals. A merit rating thus becomes a permanent part of an employee's record with a given company, and, at least in theory, is a part of the record that may be used by management in subsequent promotion, transfer, or layoff."[1] Although efficiency or workplace productivity is the primary criterion, individual performance may also be evaluated by such criteria as absenteeism, dependability, problem-solving ability, project management, and work ethic, as well as professional and community service.

Performance reviews underwent a profound change in the 1960s, as their function expanded beyond the primarily evaluative purpose of past performance. In their 1984 *Performance Appraisal*, Evelyn Eichel and Henry E. Bender write:

> In the 1960s, the purpose of performance appraisal broadened to include development of the individual, organizational planning, and improving the quality of work life. Management now used performance appraisal to try to increase employee's productivity, effectiveness, efficiency, and satisfaction. Performance appraisal provided a basis for development of employee job skill, career planning, and motivation through effective coaching and information exchange between appraiser and appraisee.[2]

The changes Eichel and Bender describe here entail not only asking "How much is this individual's performance contributing to the organization?" but also "How much is the organization contributing to this individual's performance?" Organizational theorists often describe this change in the performance review process as moving the managerial emphasis from controlling workers to empowering them, from giving orders to creating participatory interactions.

This shift from controlling to developing an individual's performance reflects a larger movement of generalization, a generative process that has gathered together an ever widening range of practices and discourses under the term "performance." Besides this expanded approach to an employee's actions and "quality of work life," performance research and development has also been extended beyond individual workers. As deployed by managers, organizational theorists, and policy makers, the referential universe of performance has steadily been enlarged and transformed, and the term's usages now include the activities of small workgroups, departments, and divisions within an organization, as well as the overall organization, groups of organizations, and even entire industries and economies.

One of the most ambitious recent projects in this regard is the National Performance Review (NPR), a federal program begun in 1993 by the Clinton administration. The purpose of the NPR has been to evaluate and make recommendations concerning the performative efficiency of government agencies. In his Report of the National Performance Review entitled *From Red Tape to Results: Creating a Government that Works Better and Costs Less*, Vice President Al Gore writes that the "National Performance Review is about change—historic change—in the way the government works. The Clinton administration believes it is time for a new customer service contract with the American people, a new guarantee of effective, efficient, and responsive government."[3] This initial report, based on a six-month study, covered twenty-seven federal agencies and fourteen government systems (such as budgeting, personnel, and procurement practices). The report made some 384 recommendations on ways to make government work better and cost less, recommendations that, in general terms, included simplifying rules and processes, improving interagency coordination, stimulating innovation at all organizational levels, and reforming procurement procedures.[4] Early in the first Clinton administration, to popularize the efforts of the NPR, Al Gore went on *Late Night with David Letterman,* where the Vice President picked up a hammer, donned protective goggles, and smashed a costly, "over-regulated" ashtray in order to demonstrate the extent of government waste and inefficiency.

Waste, inefficiency, high costs and poor quality: organizational performance is an ongoing matter of the state. The National Performance Review has continued beyond its initial study and report and is still in operation as of this writing. It received its founding legislative support when Congress passed the Government Performance and Results Act of 1993, whose purpose included initiating "program performance reform with a series of pilot projects in setting program goals, measuring program performance against those goals, and reporting publicly on their progress."[5] This Act and the NPR were not, however, the first attempts to improve government performance, but rather the latest in a long series of national performance reviews. More than four decades earlier, for instance, the 81st Congress passed the Performance Rating Act of 1950. Section 3 defines the Act's executive directive: "For the purpose of recognizing the merits of officers and employees, and their contributions to efficiency and economy in the Federal service, each department shall establish and use one or more performance-rating plans for evaluating the work performance of such officers and employees." The Performance Rating Act of 1950 was itself enacted to supersede the Uniform Efficiency Act of 1935, which had also focused on individual performance.

Far from generating uniform efficiency or efficient uniformity, organizational performance has a long history of debates, disputes, and challenges regarding its own inefficiency and waste. This history marks the Acts of 1935, 1950, and 1993. The 1935 Act's five-level rating system purportedly led to misuse and ineffectiveness. The 1950 Act passed to correct it created a more striking uniformity: a 1954 congressional report based on departmental surveys compared the two Acts and found that the 1950 Act's three rating levels ("outstanding," "satisfactory," "unsatisfactory") served as one meaningless level, with up to 99% of individuals being ranked as "satisfactory." We observe here something repeatedly commented upon in the literature of organizational performance: performance reviews are themselves objects of intense debates and appraisal, and they are consistently deemed "unsatisfactory." Vice President Gore's National Performance Review, with its focus on agencies rather than individuals and its goals of innovation and "reinvention" rather than command and control, has itself been appraised and, well within the norm, has come under fire both for its promises and its programs.[6] Not surprisingly, the Clinton administration counters that its NPR has contributed to eliminating the national deficit and restoring confidence in the federal government.

The challenge of efficiency extends from measuring and evaluating performance to creating and developing it. Organizational performance is produced at the level of individuals, teams, departments, organizations, and industries, and it takes place across a wide variety of sectors, including business, nonprofit, educational, and government organizations. Because it stretches across different institutions, performative efficiency has come to be a social imperative in the United States, making it something of a national challenge. In early 1994 PBS broadcast *Challenge to America*, a four-part program that addressed the challenge of being a "high performance" competitor in the emerging global economy. Hosted by Hedrick Smith, *Challenge to America* compared aspects of the US economy and educational systems with those of Japan and Germany, two nations cast as challengers from whom Americans could learn something and thus better address this nation's "crisis" in education and productivity. President Bill Clinton, interviewed by Smith in a supplemental fifth part, echoed the call of *Challenge to America*: the US must link its domestic educational and economic policies to international high-tech, high-wage economies, in short, to the efficiencies of the world economy. The challenge of efficiency thus has global implications.

FROM SCIENTIFIC TO PERFORMANCE MANAGEMENT

The contemporary field of organizational performance, like that of cultural performance, is a discursive and practical construct, one whose sites of construction have been overseen by a paradigm of performance research, a gathering of subjects who collect different activities together under the concept "performance" and who participate in this movement of generalization by developing certain models drawn from other fields. In their preface to the 1962 anthology *Performance Appraisal*, editors Thomas L. Whisler and Shirley F. Harper write that the performance appraisal literature "covers a number of fields—industrial psychology, personnel administration, social psychology, and sociology—with contributions coming also from military psychology, industrial engineering, accounting, and public administration."[7] Though performance appraisal is an important aspect of organizational performance, it is only one model contributing to it. Performance Management utilizes many other models, including those of systems theory, computer science, behavioral science, and even the performing arts.

Here I must clarify my use of the term "performance management." Richard

S. Williams, in a 1998 text titled *Performance Management*, writes that, though the "idea of performance management is nothing new. . . . the term performance management itself may be seen as yet another philosophy or system, and as such it came to particular prominence in the late 1980s/ early 1990s."[8] The term is sometimes used to describe recent attempts to integrate the performance of individuals and the organization itself. Theorists also use "performance management" to designate organizational strategies that focus primarily on *ends, results*, or *targets*. Such strategies can be found in Joseph H. Boyett and Henry P. Conn's *Maximum Performance Management* (1988). The sudden prominence of such performance theories in the 1990s even led to warnings of a "peak performance cult" among managers and organizational theorists.[9] In our general theory, the term "Performance Management" is being employed in a very specific though far more general sense. Working with a variety of models of organizational performance, I am defining "Performance Management" as a paradigm of organizational theory and practice that has come to dominate the management of US organizations since the Second World War and which, through this nation's economic and political hegemony, is becoming installed in organizations worldwide.[10]

While annual performance reviews of workers provide one of the most familar examples of Performance Management in action, there are many other highly publicized strategies associated with it, strategies that have become so well-known as to be ridiculed almost daily in the comic strip *Dilbert*. These practices include *restructuring*, wherein an organization's divisions or departments may be combined, divided, or eliminated, requiring dramatic changes in management structure. Another is *reengineering*, which focuses less on an organization's structure and more on its operational procedures. *Reinvention* may include both structural and procedural changes, but it seeks an even more comprehensive transformation, one that focuses on an organization's fundamental mission and its day-to-day working culture. *Total quality management* or TQM emphasizes the importance of providing excellent service to customers and/or clients. *Pay for performance* programs tie pay incentives to specific achievement targets. *Outsourcing* refers to the practice of contracting out certain internal activities (which may range from production or assembly of parts to back-office functions such as payroll or mail service). *Downsizing* and *rightsizing* are euphemisms for laying off workers or whole departments, often as part of a restructuring or reengineering program. Despite the differences in these practices, they all have the same aim: to improve an organization's performance and fine-tune it to create *excellence, total satisfaction, high performance*.

As suggested above, these contemporary practices can be read as the outgrowth of early twentieth-century attempts to improve the organizational performance of individual workers. In *The Principles of Scientific*

Management (1911), Taylor referred to his approach as "task management" and used the term "performance" to describe the execution of specific workplace tasks. "These tasks are carefully planned, so that both good and careful work are called for in their performance. . . ."[11] If contemporary organizational theorists use "performance" in a much wider sense than did Taylor, this is because researchers from a variety of schools cite the Second World War as a turning point in organizational theory and practice; more specifically, they argue that a paradigm shift has since occurred, one that challenges and moves away from Scientific Management. There have been many different articulations of this shift, each made by champions of rival models of performance. Performance Management is the name I use to theorize the related emergence of these different paradigmatic articulations. Because they all differentiate themselves from Scientific Management, I will briefly discuss Taylor's paradigm of organizational performance before turning to a detailed investigation of Performance Management.

It is difficult to overestimate the influence which Frederick Winslow Taylor had upon the twentieth century. Peter Drucker, a key organizational theorist of the postwar era, has described Taylorism as "the most powerful as well as the most lasting contribution America has made to Western thought since the Federalist Papers."[12] Prior to the First World War, Henry Ford used Taylor's principles of Scientific Management to create the assembly lines and factories that mass-produced his automobiles and revolutionized industrial manufacturing in the United States. In the 1920s the Soviet Union utilized Tayloristic principles as part of its massive, crash program to industrialize its fledgling modern economy. Taylor's task-oriented approach even influenced the biomechanical techniques developed by theater director Vsevolod Meyerhold, who, as Joseph Roach writes, "sought to humanize Taylorism by introducing an aesthetic element into the performance of efficient movement."[13] Today, the principles of Scientific Management can still be found in everything from the preparation of fast-food hamburgers to the manufacture of personal computers, and thus Taylor is still regularly cited as the "father of modern management."

What are the principles of Scientific Management? According to Taylor, there are four principles: "First. The development of a true science. Second. The scientific selection of the workman. Third. His scientific education and development. Fourth. Intimate friendly cooperation between management and the men."[14] Taylor's mission was nothing less than to reconceptualize work itself by redefining and expanding the role of management in an unprecedented fashion, one that involved "the substitution of a science for the individual judgment of the workman."[15] Managers were to become the scientist-kings of the workplace, transforming the long-established ways that workers entered into particular jobs, as well as the traditional rules of thumb they used to perform those jobs. Taylor advocated "the scientific selection and development of the workman, after each man has been studied, taught, and trained, and one may say experimented with, instead of allowing the workmen to select themselves and develop in a haphazard way."[16] Where previously there had been little or no direct management beyond a foreman, now workers and managers would work together according to scientific principles, sharing "almost equally in the daily performance of each task, the management doing that part of the work for which they are best fitted, and the workmen the balance."[17]

In polemical terms, Taylor set forth Scientific Management as the solution to the increasing tensions between labor and top management, tensions that he argued arose from the inadequacies of the established approach to organizing work, in which "the attitude of the management is that of 'putting the work up to the workmen.' "[18] According to Taylor, the old "Initiative and Incentive" approach relied far too much upon the workers, be they work gangs or individuals, who had neither the time, the inclination, nor the intelligence to maximize output and, in fact, often operated by *"systematic soldiering"* or loafing.[19] Taylor thus championed Scientific Management as a rival to the established model of management. Whereas the old approach operated by self-selection, rules of thumb, and encouraged a variety of methods, Scientific Management demanded scientific selection, rational formulae, and the determination of "the one best method."[20] Informal knowledge and knowhow that had been handed down verbally from worker to worker must give way to formal knowledge and methods involving meticulous time and motion studies, recordkeeping, and planning. Old tasks must be broken apart into their component motions, each motion studied and made more efficient, and then the motions reassembled into new and more efficient tasks. Thus, "to work according to scientific laws, the management must take over and perform much of the work which is now left to the men."[21]

Taylor framed his project in nationalistic terms. *The Principles of Scientific Management* begins with a citation from President Theodore Roosevelt: "The conservation of our national resources is only preliminary to the larger question of national efficiency."[22] Taylor considered Roosevelt's statement to be prophetic, arguing that as yet "there has been no public agitation for 'greater national efficiency,' no meetings have been called to consider how this is to be brought about."[23] Scientific Management was, for Taylor, "the one best method" for improving national efficiency. Though he stressed that this "one best method" was unique to each situation and could be determined only by thorough and patient experimentation, this method must rest upon his scientific principles. And once it was found, Taylor believed it must then be *enforced*. "It is only through the *enforced* standardization of methods, *enforced* adoption of the best implements and working conditions, and *enforced* cooperation that this faster work can be assured. And the duty of enforcing the adoption of standards and of enforcing this cooperation rests with the *management* alone."[24] The oxymoron "enforced cooperation" provides a clue to the limits of Taylor's "friendly" approach to educating and developing of workers, as well as to Performance Management's point of departure.

Though it met with resistance by workers and labor organizations, Scientific Management was widely perceived as a successful and influential business strategy in the first part of the twentieth century. During his lifetime, Taylor's *Principles of Scientific Management* helped launch an "efficiency craze" in the United States and later contributed to the rise of social engineering, a movement that culminated in the election of the first engineer to the White House, Herbert Hoover.[25] However, with the economic collapse of the Great Depression and the immense administrative requirements of implementing New Deal policies and, later, of fighting a world war on two fronts, managers in US business and government organizations had neither the time nor the resources to determine "the one best method" and then enforce it. Taylorism was not abandoned, but its limitations and drawbacks began to emerge. With the recovery of the US economy and the Allied victories in Europe and the Pacific, managers and organizational theorists began to articulate other models of performance, models that often defined themselves in sharp contrast to Taylorism. From the perspective of the late 1990s, these new models mark the initiation of Performance Management.

Performance Management develops out of Scientific Management by challenging many of its basic tenets and seeking to redress its drawbacks. First and foremost, Performance Management attempts to displace the rational control of workers by empowering them to improve efficiency using their own intuition, creativity, and diversity. Second, Performance Management seeks to counter the monolithic, "machine" model of bureaucracy described by Max Weber and instituted by Taylor, Ford, and others, offering instead a more "organic," systems-oriented model, one that resituates performance within larger organizational and socioeconomic environments. Third, while Scientific Management was developed and deployed in an industrializing economy, Performance Management has become the organizational paradigm for an information economy hardwired to computer and communications technologies, wherein information processing and decision-making no longer take place only from the top down, but are diffused throughout an organization. Fourth, at its most progressive, Performance Management challenges the challenge of efficiency itself, or at least its exclusivity, by introducing a diversity of values and organizational cultures.

Performance Management, therefore, is not the replacement of Scientific Management, but its displacement and overcoding. Taylor's principles can still be found in manufacturing industries, which increasingly have been established or relocated outside of the United States and

Western Europe, in developing countries where wages are lower and labor laws either weak or nonexistent. However, the executive management of such local industrial operations has gone electronic, gone global, gone high performance. To track more closely the passage from Scientific to Performance Management, let us now look in detail at some of its models, each of which traces its own passage to paradigm.

HUMAN RELATIONS, DIVERSITY, AND THE BOMB

Taylorism sought to establish a science of organizational performance, a rational methodology for selecting and training workers. While Taylor also stressed the importance of cooperation between management and employee, the very introduction of managers into each and every task, their sharing "almost equally in the daily performance of each task" previously executed by workers alone, meant that such cooperation would only come grudgingly and would thus itself need to be enforced. Further, as Taylor recognized, the practices he introduced into the workplace—the use of time and motion studies, slide-rules, recordkeeping, and day-to-day planning—only reinforced the division between worker and manager, a division he stressed time and again: "the workman who is best suited to actually doing the work is incapable of fully understanding this science, without the guidance and help of those who are working with him or over him, either through lack of education or through insufficient mental capacity."[26] A worker could suggest ways to improve performance, but it must first be subjected to "careful analysis" and "if necessary a series of experiments to determine accurately the relative merit of the new suggestion and the old standard."[27] In other words, any innovation in practice must itself have a "rational" managerial basis, that is, it must be translated into and evaluated by scientific discourse. Needless to say, such a requirement does not encourage innovations based on either creative intuition or common sense.

Even more restricting to workers is the day-to-day work environment which results from lengthy application of Scientific Management. Organizations ruled by "the one best method" strive to insure that all performances are standardized. Anyone who has ever worked on an assembly line, even if only for a short time, knows that variety there is not the spice of life, but grounds for reprimand or dismissal. Stress, repetitive motions, and boredom—these are what one experiences when performing on the line.[28] The standardization of organizational performance is not conducive to creating cooperation between workers and management, especially when management's role is to set and enforce performance standards. Because of such rationalization and standardization, postwar organizational theorists frequently characterize Scientific Management as a "machine" model, one that treats the employee "as though he were a product under inspection on the assembly line."[29] Nor is it surprising that the development of new social and technological forces would lead to an alternative model for managing workers.

To track the emergence of Performance Management, I will take as a guide a 1981 text, *Performance Appraisal on the Line*, by David L. DeVries, Ann M. Morrison, Sandra L. Shullman, and Michael L. Gerlach. This text provides an intellectual history of performance appraisal (PA) dating back to 1900, one that also charts the influence of different schools of organizational theory. The authors write: "Scientific management was followed by the human relations school, but the latter's impact on PA was not felt for nearly 20 years until the proliferation of participative PA systems in the 1960s. These systems incorporated at least some of the elements of the human relations approach—in particular, the emphasis on collaboration between the manager and employee."[30]

Human relations first came to prominence in the 1940s, in the wake of the Hawthorne Experiments, George Elton Mayo's research into the boredom, apathy, and absenteeism often exhibited by industrial workers. The result of Mayo's research was to direct attention to the social factors which help determine an individual worker's output. In *The Social Problems of an Industrial Civilization* (1945), Mayo stressed that successful management techniques relate to working groups rather than individuals, groups with "appropriate customs, duties, routines, even rituals."[31] Using teamwork, effective communications, and even appeals to patriotism, managers could exploit the underlying social dynamics to dramatically improve organizational performance. Over the past half century, this "human relations" approach has radically transformed the relation between managers and workers, for it helped initiate the move from controlling to developing workers' performance.

While Mayo stressed the social dimensions of the workplace, another human relations theorist, Douglas McGregor, sought to unleash the creative potential latent in all employees, a potential that had been stifled by Scientific Management. Interestingly, McGregor drew upon a powerful and timely analogy to physical science. In a 1957 essay, he characterized the changes in management strategies with this explosive image.

> A quarter century ago basic conceptions of the nature of matter and energy had changed profoundly from what they had been since Newton's time. The physical scientists were persuaded that under proper conditions new and hitherto unimagined sources of energy could be make available to mankind.
>
> We know what has happened since then. First came the bomb. Then, during the past decade, have come many other attempts to exploit these scientific discoveries—some successful, some not.
>
> [. . .]

> To a lesser degree, and in a much more tentative fashion, we are in a position in the social sciences today like that of the physical sciences with respect to atomic energy in the thirties. . . . We are becoming quite certain that, under proper conditions, unimagined resources of creative human energy could become available within the organizational setting.[32]

Tapping into and developing these creative energies became a major concern of the human relations model of organizational performance. For McGregor, this requires leaving behind the old, mechanical world and absolute time-space of Scientific Management and entering into a new relativistic cosmos of management, one that releases the explosive force of human creativity.

To distinguish further between the old and new management models, McGregor discusses them in terms of "Theory X" and "Theory Y." Both theories assume that management's role lies in organizing productive elements (capital, materials, equipment, and personnel) in an efficient and economical manner. However, Theories X and Y differ in their assumptions about workers and, consequently, in their approach to managing and evaluating their performance. In Theory X, management's organization of employees "is a process of directing their efforts, motivating them, controlling their actions, modifying their behavior to fit the needs of the organization?" Without this active intervention by management, people would be passive—even resistant—to organizational needs. They must therefore be persuaded, rewarded, punished, controlled—their activities must be directed."[33] While Theory X assumes workers to be passive or resistant, McGregor contends that they have only become so due to their experience in poorly run organizations. Theory Y, by contrast, assumes that employees have the motivation and potential to direct their own performance toward desired goals. "The essential task of management is to arrange organizational conditions and methods of operations so that people can achieve their own goals *best* by directing *their own* efforts toward organizational objectives."[34] McGregor states that management must also "involve the individual in setting 'targets' or objectives for *himself* and in a *self*-evaluation of performance annually or semi-annually."[35]

We see in these two models of organizational performance one of the most fundamental differences between Scientific and Performance Management. For Taylor, worker performance is something that must be experimented upon, modified, and tightly controlled under the close supervision of scientific managers. Efficient performance results from minimizing or removing individual initiatives and differences, "tayloring" them to fit "the one best method." Management's rigid enforcement of such standardization is hardly conducive to the stimulation and release of creative energies. By contrast, Performance Management draws upon the human relations model of management and emphasizes the intuitive as well as the rational, the creative as well as the scientific. Some contemporary theorists go so far as to give primacy to creativity, calling this the "age of creativity." John Kao, a management consultant and long-time professor at Harvard Business School, contends that this "is the age of creativity because management is transforming its role from controller to emancipator—of creativity. This is the new managerial mindset."[36] Creativity, innovation, invention, reinvention—these have become buzzwords of Performance Management. But they are buzzwords with a sting, for creativity and innovation are no longer perceived as luxuries or activities that occur only in research and development divisions. "Corporations today must live in a permanent state of mobilized awareness—of themselves, their performance, their customers, and their competitors."[37] In the face of unprecedented changes in the workforce, in commodity and capital markets, and in the area of information technologies, some managers see creativity as an organizational necessity.

Another closely related difference? between Scientific and Performance Management concerns the organizational *cultures* produced by each paradigm. Perhaps the very discussion of such cultures has become possible only with the emergence of Performance Management, for it articulates a widespread desire to "humanize" organizations. Besides characterizing Taylorism as the "machine" model, postwar organizational theorists have also argued that Scientific Management's stress on standardization inevitably creates a monocultural environment, one defined by a uniform set of values and "ways of being and doing." This monotonal, monotonous, monoculturalism has long been emblematized by the "Company Man," a figure who entered popular culture in the 1950s through such films and books as *The Man in the Gray Flannel Suit* and *The Organization Man,*[38] not to mention the existential reading of Kafka that became fashionable after the war. These works all recognized and struggled against institutional conformity. The Company Man was also, not coincidentally, precisely a man, white, preferably Protestant, and of Anglo-Saxon descent. The US workforce, of course, never fully embodied the Company Man, but management acted as if it should and, further, it succeeded in creating glass ceilings and other structural barriers to ensure that top executives matched this emblem as closely as possible.[39]

Performance Management, by contrast, has come to emphasize a culturally diverse work environment. Initially, the impetus behind this development stressed equality rather than diversity and was largely reactive rather than proactive, in that serious and sustained action only arose as a response to the 1964 Equal Employment Opportunity Act. Under Title VII of this Act, the function and norms of performance appraisal were adjusted; no longer determined solely by professional and technical standards, performance appraisal suddenly became a regulative and judicial tool. Enforced by the Equal Employment Opportunity Commission (EEOC), the 1964 Act protects individuals from discrimination based upon certain group membership.

Barry R. Nathan and Wayne F. Cascio write that a "primary concern of the EEOC . . . is whether an assessment or selection procedure results in adverse impact against members of a protected race, sex, or ethnic group. In general, the EEOC will consider a performance assessment procedure that has no adverse impact as complying with Title VII. However, if adverse impact is found in the use of performance assessment, it will have to be justified."[40] Performance reviews have thus been used by claimants in both individual and class-action suits against discriminatory practices. At the same time, they have also been central to organizations' attempts to explain and justify decisions relating to promotion, remuneration, and termination procedures.

In recent years, organizations have come to stress diversity rather than equality in the workplace. Facing a culturally diverse workforce, on the one hand, and, on the other, seeking to create niche markets at home and new markets abroad, managers have begun to take a more proactive approach to cultural diversity. Rather than simply tolerating diversity, many organizations create work environments that promote it. R. Roosevelt Thomas, Jr. describes this as a shift from affirmative action to *affirming diversity*, from controlling differences to managing them.

> Affirmative action gets the new fuel into the tank, the new people through the front door. Something else will have to get them into the driver's seat. That something else consists of enabling people, in this case minorities and women, to perform to their potential. This is what we now call managing diversity. Not appreciating or leveraging diversity, not even necessarily understanding it. Just managing diversity in such a way to get from a heterogeneous work force the same productivity, commitment, quality, and profit that we got from the old homogeneous work force.[41]

This stress on getting the full potential from a workforce harkens back to McGregor's Theory Y, yet the additional element of diversity has led to the development of multicultural models for improving performance. Reporting on a diversity program at Digital Equipment Corporation, Barbara A. Walker and William C. Hanson write: "The philosophy is anchored in the conviction that the broader the spectrum of differences in the workplace, the richer the synergy among the employees and the more excellent the organization's performance."[42]

While fears of EEOC actions are still present, managers are increasingly promoting the positive dimensions of cultural diversity, including not only gender and ethnicity, but also sexuality, age, and physical ability.[43] Among the benefits often cited by theorists are improved organizational reputation *vis-à-vis* potential employees, greater worker morale, increased problem-solving capabilities, and greater competitive advantages in the global economy. In addition, Walker and Hanson argue that a multicultural workforce leads to greater creativity and innovation: "When people value differences, and can truly value divergent, and perhaps opposing perspectives, they are creatively forced to come up with some different ideas that allow them to have both. . . . Valuing both leads to other alternatives and other values."[44] These authors even argue that diversity has displaced efficiency as the primary goal of organizational performance.

The human relations model that first emerged in the 1940s initiated several developments that now help to define Performance Management's approach to managing individual workers. Rather than seeking to control them, this paradigm's stated goal is to empower employees by unleashing their full human potential. It has sought to do this not by emphasizing scientific methods, but by developing workers' creativity and intuition. And in place of a monocultural environment built upon "the one best method," Performance Management advocates the creation of a multicultural workplace that affirms a diversity of values, traditions, and life experiences. As we have seen, these changes are all dramatic shifts away from the principles of Scientific Management; nonetheless, like Taylorism, they still focus primarily on individual performance. Other models employed by Performance Management have, however, extended the concept of performance far beyond the practices of individual workers, and it is to this extension that we now turn.

AWAY WITH THE MACHINE: ALL SYSTEMS GO

A second model that has contributed to the formation of Performance Management is systems theory, which became influential in organizational theory during the 1950s and continues to be important to the paradigm. This approach reconceptualizes organizational performance by generalizing it to include the overall operation of the organization, which it defines as an open system constantly adjusting to internal and external circumstances. In management systems theory, not only do employees perform, so too does the entire organization in which they work.

Like the proponents of human relations, those of systems theory characterize their approach in contradistinction to Scientific Management, though the paradigm shift they describe focuses on a different set of concerns. David P. Hanna, in his 1988 *Designing Organizations for High Performance*, argues that until the Second World War, organizations operated under "Machine Theory," whose "premises stem from the assumption that an organization is like a machine: a collection of parts that need to be standardized and centrally controlled. The leading spokesmen for this theory were an American, Frederick W. Taylor (the father of Scientific Management) and a German, Max Weber (creator of the Bureaucratic Model)."[45] Management systems theory instead sets forth the model of a living system open to changes from the outside. In contrast to the rigid, static "Machine" organization, systems theorists defined organizations as flexible, dynamic "organisms." "The basic premise of Open Systems Theory is that organizations have common characteristics with all other living systems; from microscopic organisms, to plants, to animals, to humans. Understanding these characteristics allows us to work *with* the natural tendencies of an organization rather than struggling against them needlessly."[46] Hanna cites the contributions that human relations theorists made to rectify the faults of Machine Theory, but credits Austrian biologist Ludwig von Bertalanffy's general systems theory as crucial to the development of more comprehensive management strategies. Thus some Performance Management theorists not only argue for a more humanistic approach to management, but also for a naturalistic one.

Systems theory, however, draws upon other disciplines besides biology, and these have also been influential in recasting organizational performance. Another of its constitutive fields, electrical engineering, provides Performance Management with one of its most important models for evaluating performative efficiency: the calculation of inputs and outputs through *feedback*. In classical systems theory, feedback is defined as a process by which part of a system's output is reentered or "fed back" into the system as an input, thus allowing inputs and outputs to be compared. The reentering of outputs as inputs gives feedback a circular or looped structure, and electrical engineers use such "feedback loops" in the design of thermostats, engine governors, guidance mechanisms, and innumerable other technologies. In Performance Management, feedback is used to measure, analyze, and adjust an entire system's performance in relation to its component systems and to its environment.

The pervasive use of feedback models in organizational discourse and diagrams reflects the widespread application of systems theory to analyze, produce, and manage performance throughout an organization, from the level of individual workers and teams, to departments and divisions, and on up to the organization itself. Feedback is so pervasive, in fact, that we can read it as a metamodel of this organizational paradigm. In *Performance in American Bureaucracy* (1976), Robert C. Fried suggests that we "think of the administrative organizations as systems that take inputs of resources and demands from society and convert them into socially desired outputs or activities. . . . The performance approach . . . stresses the 'payoff' phases of the administrative process (outputs, impacts, and feedback)."[47] While Fried emphasizes the "payoff" phase here, it is important to understand the processual aspect of systems theory: over time, outputs become new inputs in the ongoing performance of the organizational system. The "payoff" phases are actually those times when managers use feedback to measure and evaluate that performance.

Feedback can also be used to make changes in organizational goals, changes brought about by internal or environmental factors. Hanna explains: "Knowing whether or not the system is on target is a function of feedback. This term refers to information inputs that measure the acceptability of both outputs and the purpose and goals. The terms *negative* and *positive* feedback, from the field of cybernetics, distinguish between two important types of feedback. Negative feedback measures whether or not the output is on course with purpose and goals. It is also known as *deviation-correcting* feedback. Positive feedback measures whether or not the purpose and goals are aligned with environmental needs. It is sometimes called *deviation-amplifying* feedback."[48] Both negative and positive feedback can occur internally and externally to create "positive" effects: negative feedback (whose most familiar model is the thermostat) can adjust performance to maintain a desired norm, while positive feedback can provide a means to adjust that norm itself, potentially leading to the creation of a "virtuous circle" of ever increasing efficiency. Yet both negative and positive feedback can also have "negative" effects: the dynamics of positive feedback can lead to "runaway" deviation (the familiar model here is the vicious circle), while the stasis of negative feedback can lead to organizational inflexibility and obsolescence; in both instances, the guidance system breaks down and the performance becomes inefficient at best, catastrophic at worst.

Though systems theorists often disparage the "machine model" of Scientific Management and advocate a more naturalistic approach, their reliance on feedback means that systems theory and Performance Management cannot be simply posed as a nonmachinic alternative. This becomes particularly evident in a branch of organizational systems theory called "sociotechnical systems" or STS. In *Performance by Design* (1993), James C. Taylor and David F. Felten write that "all organizations are sociotechnical systems. Every organization contains a technical subsystem to produce the core output and a social subsystem to coordinate activities among people to assure the flexibility and long-term survival of the enterprise."[49] Taylor and Felten also conceptualize a paradigm shift from "machine thinking" to "systems thinking" and diagram their differences in relation to the organization, management, unions, and employees.

"Discovery": The Paradigm Shift from Machine Thinking to Systems Thinking

The Changing Organization

From:	**To:**
Purposive	Purposeful
Focus on tasks	Focus on product
Quantity	Quality
Closed	Open
Tall—many levels	Flat—few levels
Short term	Focused balance

The Changing Role of Management

From:	To:
Risk-taking avoided	Innovation encouraged
Directive	Participative
Control of people	Enabling control of product
Inform if need to know	Inform if want to know
Commitment to boss	Commitment to purpose
Competitive	Collaborative

The Changing Role of Unions

From:	To:
Protecting	Empowering
Opposition	Active involvement
Resistance	Innovation
Reactive	Proactive
Separation	Partnership
What's in it for us	What's best for the whole
Adversarial	Collaborative

The Changing Role of Employees

From:	To:
Dependent	Empowered
Passive	Assertive
Childlike	Mature
Cynical	Optimistic
Competitive	Cooperative
Distrustful	Trusting
Ignorant	Informed
Unskilled	Skilled
Assumed lazy	Motivated

The most significant aspect of the STS approach is that it broadens the concept of performance to include the operations of technological systems. As we will see in the next chapter, sociological researchers of technology have also turned to this concept of sociotechnical systems precisely because it focuses on the interface of social and technological performances.

Systems theory thus makes a number of important contributions to the development of Performance Management. By theorizing organizations as systems, it generalizes performance beyond simply referring to the work performed by individuals within an organization. Systems theory offers a radically different model of organizational performance than does Scientific Management. According to systems theorists, high performance organizations are decentralized, flexible, dynamic, open, and "naturalistic" systems, whereas Tayloristic organizations are centralized, rigid, static, closed, and "machine-like." Performance Management has made extensive use of the systems theory concept of feedback. Feedback has become one of the most important means for calculating the relation of inputs and outputs, for evaluating whether performance is "on target" or whether those targets must be altered, and for making changes to improve organizational efficiency. Finally, sociotechnical systems theory, with its stress on technical subsystems, further generalizes the concept of performance. Organizational performance can be understood as composed of both social and technological performances. The importance of this social-technical interface lies at the heart of a third model guiding Performance Management.

DECISION-MAKING: PROCESSING IT

Taylor developed Scientific Management at the turn of the twentieth century, a time of massive industrialization that would lead to widespread introduction of assembly-line production in the United States. His "task-management" approach greatly expanded management's role in the performance of traditional tasks and also grafted itself onto the new emerging tasks. Traditional rules of thumb transmitted orally from worker to worker were to be replaced by rational methods communicated to employees by managers using written instructions and precise recordkeeping. By contrast, Performance Management has fully emerged in the US during a time of relative deindustrialization and a corresponding development of an economy based on services and information. The decline—or rather, the expatriation—of the steel and manufacturing industries, once almost synonymous with the US economy, has cut a rusty gash across the countryside. Since the early 1970s, US firms of all sorts have sought less expensive labor pools and less restrictive regulation in Latin America and the Asian Pacific rim. While the industrially based economy has declined in the US, another has arisen, that of the "service" or "information economy." Performance Management has become the organizational theory of the new information economy, and in this role it has relied heavily upon a school of management known as "information processing and decision-making" or IPDM.

As its name suggests, IPDM theorists focus on the gathering, storage, and transmission of information, and, more importantly, on the decision-making processes that depend upon it, processes that include identifying problem situations, developing possible solutions, choosing a course of action, and evaluating past decisions. Writing in 1975, E. Frank Harrison sketches this genealogy of IPDM: "Decision theory as an academic discipline is still relatively young. It is only since the Second World War that operations research, statistical analysis, and computer programming have imparted a 'scientific' aura to the process of choice and only within the last ten or fifteen years that the behavioral sciences—sociology, psychology and social psychology—have begun to contribute to the body of knowledge comprising decision theory."[50] IPDM first emerged in the 1950s, and became prominent in organizational theory during the 1970s. While its "scientific aura" makes it more of a continuation of Scientific Management than a break, IPDM theorists have made important contributions to the displacement of Taylorism and to the generalization of organizational performance. In particular, by analyzing the recordkeeping and planning activities of managers, they have helped theorize the performance of management itself.

Throughout the history of IPDM, its theorists have sought to justify their approach in terms of the rapid and fundamental changes occurring in the US economy. They have focused primarily upon the decline of blue-collar employment and the increasing importance of white-collar jobs, and significantly, they have attributed these changes in large part to technological developments. In a 1982 essay, William C. Howell discusses the corresponding changes in management strategy concerning performative efficiency.

> If, indeed, we have become a white-collar society, this suggests a shift in parameters of work behavior and therefore of human performance requirements. Although we should avoid the temptation to overgeneralize (there are, after all, still a number of very "physical" jobs), the trend is clearly away from tasks requiring people to supply or directly control **energy** and toward those requiring them to process **information**. More than anything, this trend reflects changes in our technology. Another trend, reflecting modern philosophies of management as much as technology, has spread the **decision** function to progressively lower echelons of the organization. . . . What all this means is that human productivity is becoming more and more a matter of efficient information processing and decision making. Productivity in our white-collar society is mediated by cognitive processes rather than by brute force.[51]

As we saw with human relations, IPDM seeks to empower workers at even the lowest organizational levels. And, like the sociotechnical systems approach, it conceives of human performance as intimately connected to technology. The significance of IPDM lies in the relation it draws between the diffusion of decision-making and the introduction of a technical system capable of totally transforming management. It is known as "IT"—information technology, the most important features of which are the digital computer, with its capacity to record, store, and process information, and telecommunication systems, with the ability to transmit this information around the world in seconds.

In the 1950s, Herbert Simon realized that computers would fundamentally change organizational decision making. Simon was one of IPDM's most influential theorists, and was also a leading proponent of management systems theory. In *The New Science of Management Decision* (1960), he echoed McGregor's invocation of atomic energy to characterize the transformation at hand: "My research activities during the past decade have brought me into contact with developments in the use of electronic digital computers. These computers are startling even in a world that takes atomic energy and the prospects of space travel in its stride. The computer and the new decision-making techniques associated with it are bringing changes in white-collar, executive, and professional work as momentous as those the introduction of machinery has brought to manual jobs."[52] For Simon, these new technologies would not only allow managers to improve and expand their existing decision making capabilities; they would dramatically alter these very capabilities.

In investigating the performance of management, IPDM has generalized performance to include both physical and cognitive activities, thereby greatly expanding its field of reference. At the same time, its theorists have folded back information processing and decision making over the entire field of organizational performance. Simon equates management *per se* with decision making, which he defines as comprising "four principal phases: finding occasions for making a decision, finding possible courses of action, choosing among courses of action, and evaluating past choices."[53] In the crucial third phase, he distinguishes between "programmed" and "unprogrammed" decisions. Programmed decisions involve routine situations with well-defined criteria and information channels; they thus rely upon rules and uniform processing. Unprogrammed decisions involve novel situations with unknown criteria and undefined information channels and rely upon judgment, creativity, and heuristics.[54] As diagrammed by the organizational charts of traditional, "machine" bureaucracies, only top management makes unprogrammed decisions, with programmed decisions being handled by both lower and middle management. According to Simon, however, computer technologies upset this division of labor by opening all levels to unprogrammed decision making. "At all organizational levels, as decision processes become more explicit, and as their components are more and more embedded in computer programs, decisions and the analyses that underlie them become more and more transportable. . . . Since information, goal premises and constraints derived from all sorts of organizational and extraorganizational sources can provide inputs to the analytical processes, the locus of decision making becomes even more diffuse than it has been in the past."[55]

Four decades later, Simon's predictions are especially impressive when one considers that in 1960 costly mainframe computers were only used widely by relatively few corporations and government agencies (e.g., the Department of Defense and NASA). By the mid-1970s, however, both large and medium-sized organizations widely employed such computers, and their managers were turning to decision-making theory for new management models. Today, with personal computers and communication devices ubiquitous in the workplace, the processing of words, numbers, photos, sounds, video, and other information occurs at millions upon millions of sites, while decision-making now occurs in office, in factory, in transit, and even at home.

In addition to the digital computer, IPDM has drawn upon another technology regularly utilized by systems theorists, a model we have already described as a metamodel of organizational performance: feedback devices. Again, Simon played a key role in theorizing organizational performance as feedback, drawing directly upon the engineering sciences, in particular those concerned with control devices or servomechanisms. Simon's 1957 *Models of Man* argues that "[p]owerful, and extremely general, techniques have been developed in the past decade for the analysis of electrical and mechanical control systems and servomechanisms. There are obvious analogies between such systems and the human systems, usually called production control systems, that are used to plan and schedule production in business systems."[56] After explaining feedback in terms of a thermostat, Simon turns to the production control system used to ensure that the actual output or inventory of a manufacturing process matches the input or desired optimum inventory. The difference between input and output is, again, known as the "error," which is fed back into the decision-making process of production planning. "This system obviously possesses the characteristics of a servomechanism. It is unilaterally coupled to the load and input (customers' orders and optimum inventory). It has a feedback loop: error → planned production → actual production → inventory → error. The error initiates a change in planned production in such a direction as to reduce the error."[57] As with systems theory, the goal of IPDM is less the control of existing performance than the ongoing improvement of performative efficiency.

The installation of computers and feedback devices into planning, production, storage, and consumption suggests some of the ways in which new informational processes overcode and transform traditional industrial processes, and also furthers our understanding of how Performance Management can displace or reinscribe Taylorism without replacing it. By shifting the parameters of performance from physical processes to cognitive ones, IPDM contributes to the generalization of organizational performance. Whereas managers under Scientific Management evaluated the physical actions of blue-collar workers, management's own decision-making activities have become the object of Performance Management. At the same time, IPDM attempts to break down Taylorism's strict distinction between worker and manager functions, arguing that information processing and decision making no longer occur solely from the top down. Under Performance Management, even blue-collar performance becomes a shade more white-collar as workers at all organizational levels become information processors and decision makers, a transformation seen in the widespread use today of IT in manufacturing, warehousing, and transportation industries. And despite their own assertions, the information processing and decision making theorists, along with the management systems theorists, demonstrate that organizations have not replaced the machine model of management; rather, they are overhauling the machine. Performance Management retools the industrial factory of Taylorism and supplements it with an informational system composed of feedback mechanisms, digital computers, and telecommunication networks. Rational processes are still important, but they too have been displaced by more intuitive approaches to management, such as those advocated by a fourth model of organizational performance, organizational development.

O.D. ON HIGH PERFORMANCE

Organizational development, also as known as "OD," is in many ways Performance Management's most comprehensive model of performance. OD's use of a variety of models and methods to analyze and transform the behavior of individuals and organizations is a hallmark of Performance Management. Organizational development first emerged in the 1960s, and in the 1980s it became a dominant model of organizational performance. In his 1969 text *Organizational Development*, Warren G. Bennis defined OD as a "response to change, a complex educational strategy intended to change the beliefs, attitudes, values and structure of organizations so that they can better adapt to new technologies, markets, and challenges, and the dizzying rate of change itself."[58] Initially guided by a behaviorist approach to management, OD has come to utilize many aspects of the human relations, systems theory, and IPDM models. OD seeks to create "high performance" organizations that not only respond to change, but generate personal and organizational changes in order to continuously renew themselves *as organizations*. Because it defines organizational performance as intimately connected to education and development, OD is often called *organizational learning*. OD seeks to create high performance by continuously stimulating learning at all organizational levels. Not only can individuals learn, so too can organizations.

But what is the "high performance" that organizational development seeks to produce through such continual learning? In organizational theory, synonyms of "high performance" include "excellence," "quality," and "peak performance." Peter B. Vaill, another important figure in OD and one of the first to theorize high performing systems, writes that these can be thought of as "systems that are 'doing better' than other similar systems composed of similar men, using similar technologies, pursuing similar goals, or adhering to similar standards."[59] However, Vaill offers this definition only as a preliminary clarification and goes to great lengths to emphasize that "there is no fixed definition of what shall constitute 'excellence' or 'high performance.' A high performing system will always be such for *someone*, someone whose values make him or her sensitive to and intrigued with all the nuances and complexities" of such systems.[60] *High performance* presupposes a comparative, contextual, and active evaluation of performative behavior. Though this last citation suggests that this evaluation depends upon an individual person's values, for Vaill it actually results from values collectively created and embodied. Indeed, what distinguishes OD from other management models of performance is its view that organizations can be creative and self-transformative as organizations, something they can do only by incorporating a variety of models and methods.

Because of its focus on the entire organization, OD relies heavily upon contributions from systems theory. But it also stresses the collaborative processes found in human relations, as well as the importance of information processing and decision making to organizational development in an information economy. The synthesis of all three of these models comes through in David A. Nadler's discussion of the function of feedback in organizational development. "[The] collection and feedback of data is a central part of any effective OD activity. Improving organizations through participative processes implies the need to collect data about how the organization functions at present and to give the data in some form to people in the organization so that they can work with it and ultimately use the information for problem solving."[61] Though OD is closely related to systems theory, its use of hybrid methods aims not at maintaining organizational structure, but at developing flexible adaptations to both internal and external changes. Hanna distinguishes OD from both the open systems theory and sociotechnical systems by arguing that, even when combined, they have often been unable "to escape the obsession of focusing too heavily on their internal operations and ignoring important signals from their environment."[62] He thus calls for an "Outside In" approach to designing organizations for high performance, one as sensitive to external changes as to internal ones.

As with the other models used by Performance Management, OD differentiates itself from management strategies associated with Taylorism. And because it draws upon the strengths of human relations, systems theory, and information processing and decision making to articulate its method of organizational learning, OD articulates the shift from Scientific Management to Performance Management in the most comprehensive terms. Two related, though contrasting, characterizations of high performance organizations demonstrate the open and dynamic nature of contemporary Performance Management.

The first comes from a bestselling book of organizational theory, Thomas J. Peters and Robert H. Waterman, Jr.'s *In Search of Excellence*. Writing in 1982, Peters and Waterman contend: "Business performance in the United States has deteriorated badly, at least compared to that of Japan, and sometimes to other countries—and in many cases absolutely, in terms of productivity and quality standards."[63] Their reason for this decline: the "rational model" of management, the lingering effects of Scientific Management in both organizations and the "analytic ivory towers" of business schools. According to Peters and Waterman, the overemphasis on rationality, analysis, and quantitative methodologies has produced a number of serious drawbacks in organizations, including a stress on cost reduction rather than revenue enhancement, "an abstract, heartless philosophy," a tendency for management to give only negative reinforcement, the avoidance of experimentation and risk-taking, overcomplexity and rigidity, a failure to "celebrate informality," the denigration of common values, and the hierarchical suppression of internal competition.[64]

Each of these drawbacks is countered, however, in the "search for excellence," for high performance. Peters and Waterman explicitly cite Kuhn's concept of paradigm shift to argue that a new management model is emerging.[65] Revenue growth, bold initiatives, positive reinforcements, experimentation, simplicity and flexibility, informality, shared values, and the productive use of peer pressure—these are some of the attributes of "excellence management." Their approach advocates the creation of a "strong culture"—a commonly-held set of beliefs, values, and styles to guide performance. "The top performers [i.e., excellent organizations] create a broad, uplifting, shared culture, a coherent framework with which charged-up people search for appropriate adaptations. Their ability to extract extraordinary contributions from very large numbers of people turns on the ability to create a sense of highly valued purpose."[66] Peters and Waterman argue that rationality, analysis, and quantitative methodologies do have a role in high performance organizations, but their dominance recedes as they are balanced and guided by a more intuitive, experimental, and quality-oriented management culture.

A second reading of OD's divergence from Taylorism can be found in Robert T. Golembiewski and Alan Kiepper's *High Performance and Human Costs* (1988). This text focuses on the application of organizational development practices by the Metropolitan Atlanta Rapid Transit Authority and the Department of State. Golembiewski and Kiepper outline their own vision of OD, one that also stresses the importance of "corporate cultures." The authors oppose two different structures underlying two types of cultures, "bureaucratic" and "purpose-oriented," which we can read as corresponding to the paradigms of Scientific and Performance Management.[67]

Bureaucratic Structure	Purpose-Oriented Structure
1. Authoritarian supervision	1. Supportive supervision
2. Monitoring details of performance	2. Monitoring of overall performance
3. Limitation of employee to a single or few operations in a total sequence	3. Control by an employee of a total sequence of related operations
4. Separating worker from control of work	4. Integrating worker and control of work
5. Centralizing decision making operations	5. Decentralizing decision making operation

The right side of this table shows the influence that the three other performance models have had upon organizational development. The emphasis on supportive supervision and employee-controlled operations recalls the human relations goal of collaboration and worker empowerment. The influence of systems theory comes through in the stress on overall performance and the integration of worker and control, while the decentralization of decision making processes obviously reflects the work of IPDM.

The importance which OD proponents place on culture reflects the contributions of the human relations approach, which also emphasizes the cultural dimension of organizations. Golembiewski and Kiepper distinguish their model of OD from that offered by Peters and Waterman, whose model of a strong, unifying culture they feel succumbs to the very organizational values it seeks to displace. Targeting Peters and Waterman, Golembiewski and Kiepper argue that OD should emphasize: 1) the dynamics of heterogeneous subcultures rather than the stable equilibrium of a single "strong" corporate culture; 2) the employee as an actor rather than as acted upon; 3) the limiting effects of institutions on individual learning rather than the limiting effects of individuals on the institutional status quo; 4) a multilateral stress on interactive and adaptational possibilities rather than a unilateral choice of "join or leave"; and 5) collectively desired norms rather than preexisting norms.[68] By stressing the importance of multiple subcultures, Golembiewski and Kiepper's model thus resonates strongly with that offered by human relations theorists who advocate the management and affirmation of diversity.

With its cultivation of heterogeneous models and values, organizational development can function here as another metamodel for organizational performance. It is also one of the most powerful—if diffuse—models within the Performance Management paradigm. And here we return to a matter raised earlier with respect to the valuing of diversity: the possibility that the "efficiency craze" initiated by Taylorism has itself become challenged within Performance Management. Valuing diversity may indeed lead to the diversification of values as some human relations and OD theorists contend; thus, the very value of efficiency may be challenged by other values, such as cultural diversity, creativity and innovation, learning, effectiveness, quality of worklife, organizational survival, and community citizenship. Under the multiple influence of these different values, organizational performance would then be guided according to a process similar to what Vaill calls "joint optimization." While Vaill's use of this concept refers to the simultaneous optimization of a human system and a technical system,[69] joint optimization can also be thought of as operating across several different value systems. We can thus say that the design, execution, and evaluation of organizational performance is joint optimized through a series of negotiations, trade-offs, compromises, and sacrifices between different evaluative matrices.

However, it is more accurate to say that while some organizations have diversified their cultures and joint optimized their organizations for high performance, the bottom line remains the bottom line: maximizing outputs and minimizing inputs. This is obviously true in business organizations, where the drive for profits remains, *de facto* and *de jure*, the ultimate evaluative register. Even in government and nonprofit organizations, the challenge of efficiency has become more pronounced, not less, especially amid calls to "run things like a business" and the often sudden embrace of corporate strategies such as TQM programs. In his reading of organizational theory since the Second World War, political scientist Stephen P. Waring concludes that "the theory of good business government remained essentially the same as in Taylor's day. Management experts were still shoveling the same stuff, although with at least ten new kinds of shovels."[70] As trenchant as Waring's conclusion may be, it is based on the premise that organizational theorists have still been promising to deliver a unified and value-free science of management. We have seen, however, that contemporary Performance Management theorists do not pose themselves as rational and objective scientists; indeed, what most distinguishes this organizational paradigm is that its challenge of efficiency *foregrounds* values, diversity, and creativity. Performance Management does not sell itself as a science, but as an *art* of management. Let us therefore turn to a few of its poetics and consider their paradigmatic relation to Performance Studies.

BETWEEN THEATER AND MANAGEMENT

Like Performance Studies, Performance Management is a paradigm of research whose emergence can be traced back to just after the Second World War. Similarly, its concept of performance has undergone an incessant process of generalization. Both the concept and the field of organizational performance steadily altered and expanded during the last half of the twentieth century. As theorized and applied in the US, organizational performance has been going global for quite some time, in part through the worldwide influence of US firms and business schools, in part through the American style of management found in multinational corporations, in part through the role the US plays in such organizations as the United Nations, the World Bank, and the International Monetary Fund. Yet Performance Management, like Performance Studies, is also not a unified research paradigm but rather a gathering of diverse models, discourses, and practices. Its passage to paradigm occurs through such sites as human relations, systems theory, information processing and decision making, organizational development, and more recently, the *peak performance cult* composed of theorists and practitioners of excellence, high performance, and maximum performance. All these models entail different definitions of performance, and thus they all enable different ways of generating and evaluating specific performances. Yet a specific challenge gathers together these models and guides the research of Performance Management: the challenge of efficiency, the imperative to maximize outputs and minimize inputs.

It is at the level of their respective challenges that we must distinguish Performance Management and Performance Studies, for these challenges program the reading machines of each paradigm, underwriting their strikingly different deployments, interpretations, and evaluations of "performance." Seeking out efficacious events in which social forces are embodied and transformed, Performance Studies researchers have created a field of cultural performance whose objects include such activities as ritual, theater, oral interpretations of literature, folklore, performance art, and popular entertainment. By contrast, researchers of Performance Management have sought out organizational practices of efficiency, of maximizing outputs and minimizing inputs, thereby creating a field of organizational performance that includes the manual tasks of blue-collar workers; the cognitive tasks of white-collar managers; the collaborative efforts of workers and managers in small teams, departments, and large divisions; as well as the overall coordinated activities of human and technical systems that compose entire organizations. In many ways, these fields are mutually exclusive: organizational performances occur at the center of social institutions, while cultural performances occur outside them or at their margins, their limen.

The distinction between the challenges of efficacy and efficiency is also reflected in their very different subjects of knowledge, subjects who respond, precisely, to different challenges, different callings. Those who dedicate their lives to researching and creating cultural performances operate at a wide variety of sites, sites generally located within the arts, activism, and humanities; whereas researchers and practitioners of organizational performance work in corporate, nonprofit, and governmental environments, as well as business and management schools. More importantly, individuals whose interests lie in valorizing the efficacy, transgression, and resistance of performance by and large position themselves in opposition to those whose professional investments involve studying and improving the efficiency, productivity, and "excellence" of performance. Indeed, given what I have called the liminal-norm of Performance Studies, many of its researchers might not even consider organizational performance to be performance at all, or might want to dismiss Performance Management as but the latest version of the Establishment, of normative business-as-usual.

However, it is crucial for Performance Studies researchers to resist the easy opposition of cultural and organizational performance and to instead read Performance Management both critically and creatively. Why? There are several reasons. *First*, because we are interested in the historical and material conditions of our own work, Performance Studies researchers might want to ask how it is that performance emerged in the late twentieth century both as a dominant practice of cultural resistance *and* as a dominant practice of organizational management. This questioning is especially needed since, like other organizations, art and educational institutions have for the past decade or so been subject to reorganizations, downsizings, restructurings, TQM programs, cost-effective budgeting, and other applications of Performance Management. Further, if we are interested in challenging our own assumptions and constructing a perspective on our perspective, then we might also consider why the two paradigms have, until recently, developed in almost total ignorance of one another's theorization and deployment of performance.

Second, while there is little doubt that, from the perspective of Performance Studies, our own field of objects and subjects functions—or should function—as a mutational social force, whereas that of Performance Management operates normatively, we should also recognize that norms and mutations actually occur in *both* paradigms. Though Performance Studies has focused primarily on liminal, efficacious activities, there are many cultural performances that do not challenge social norms but support and extend them, and even the most experimental forms of cultural performance, those which directly engage social norms, also create norms of their own. Moreover, academic programs of Performance Studies cannot escape, and indeed presuppose, norms concerning the recruitment, training, and evaluation of students and faculty. Conversely, as we have seen in this chapter, Performance Management conceives of itself as a transformational challenge to the rationalistic norms of Taylorism. Somewhat surprisingly, *both* paradigms have repeatedly launched critiques of the bureaucratic "Machine," though obviously from very divergent perspectives. While one can—and must—be critical of the valorization of efficiency that still dominates Performance Management, we can nonetheless affirm its role in cultivating creativity, diversity, and, more generally, workers' cultural and social concerns, for it is precisely from these valorizations that efficiency may continue to be challenged.

Third, Performance Management's concern with creativity and diversity demonstrates that Performance Studies is not the only paradigm interested in cultural performance. We can see this more clearly by turning to some models shared by both Performance Studies and Performance Management.[71]

From our readings of this citational network, it should be clear that organizational performance cannot be reduced to a metaphorical extension of theater or any other genre of cultural performance. Nor does it simply refer to another meaning of the term "performance," for not only is the literature of organizational performance as extensive as, indeed more extensive than, that of cultural performance, but further, the Performance Management paradigm has been institutionalized at far more sites than has Performance Studies. In short, between these two paradigms of performance research, there is something more than semantic differences at stake. The emergence of cultural and organizational performance concepts entails very different pragmatic deployments; their usages envelop different subjects and objects and alternative sets of models, discourses, and practices, and they partake of different, though related histories and material conditions. Thus, when cultural performance *does* appear within Performance Management, it is, to say the least, uncanny—familar, unfamilar, homey, alien—and above all, intriguing.

I will cite three examples where cultural performance has been deployed as a model by organizational theorists. The first comes from an author mentioned above, Peter B. Vaill. The significance of his use of cultural performance to model organizational performance lies in the fact that Vaill was the first organizational theorist to study "high performing systems," as far back as 1972. Seventeen years later, Vaill published *Managing as a Performing Art* (1989), which explicitly brings together organizational and cultural performance. In this text, Vaill explores the potential of theater, dance, and musical performance to provide "lessons" for creating high performance in a chaotic world environment which he depicts as "permanent white water." He says that talking about management as a science is "ridiculous," for science attempts to standardize and control variability, rather than trying to blend and harmonize it in a production, as occurs in the performing arts.[72] His justification for taking an artistic approach to organizations touches upon several aspects of Performance Management we have analyzed above: "A paradigm shift is underway, and as we reach for better ideas about what action in organization is, we have to let this transformation occur, I think, even if it takes us into some very unusual places and invites us to consider some rather offbeat ways of talking about management and leadership."[73] Vaill thus prepares his readers for his offbeat proposal:

to practice management as a performing art. His primary reason for using the performing arts as a model lies in their holistic approach: "if you think of action taking as a performing art, there is no danger that you will confuse proficiency in a component with proficiency in the rounded performance as a whole. Furthermore, you will be pushed to consider what the 'rounded performance as a whole' in fact is."[74] In commending its holistic approach, Vaill also credits theater's production process for being able to focus in on a particular function, defining it, "getting adequate resources for it, and rehearsing it until it is 'right.' "[75] This ability to combine different elements into a dynamic "rounded performance of the whole" without losing their particularities is one lesson Vaill thinks managers can learn from the performing arts in order to create and maintain high performance.

Other lessons the performing arts offer organizational theorists involve their attention to the interconnectedness of quality, process, and form. Vaill contends that "the forms *are* the art"[76] and that producing quality in chaotic circumstances depends upon continually balancing form and function. In this regard, he discusses something very few people associate with organizational performance.

> In management, you don't hear much about the pleasures to be derived from the operations of the organizations, except in one type—high-performing systems. Where members have learned to operate at high levels of quality, they take pleasure in the sheer conduct of the process and attach great importance to proper execution. The performing arts show that this pleasure in the process can occur even though "world-class quality" is not being achieved. Sousa marches are fun to play at any level of expertise. Themes of play and of personal enjoyment run all through the performing arts. And the arts prove unequivocally that these themes do not detract from getting the job done. Quite the reverse: play and enjoyment are integral to getting the job done.[77]

The high performance pleasure Vaill seeks does not simply involve harmonizing parts and wholes and balancing forms and functions. As with other OD theorists, Vaill seeks to joint optimize conflicting evaluative systems, and he believes five systems must be paid particular attention: economic, technical, communal, sociopolitical, and transcendental. To work with such different values, he calls for the evolution of an " 'on-line metaguidance system'; that is, a process that can be operated in the real time of the system for thinking about how it is doing, what its accomplishments are meaning to members, and what interventions, if any, are needed to more effectively fulfill both environmental opportunities and member feelings about doing well."[78] In one of his closing chapters, Vaill presents a dialogue among five figures who emblematize the five value categories: respectively, they are economist Adam Smith, Scientific Management theorist Frederick Taylor, human relations theorist Elton Mayo, labor leader John L. Lewis, and Transcendentalist philosopher Ralph Waldo Emerson. Though he presents the dialogue for "fun," there is little doubt that for Vaill it also "gets the job done." In fact, the dialogue embodies his calls for a metaguidance system and for using the performing arts as a model for managing organizations. For finally, the process of "managing as a performing art" means recasting the performing arts as an on-line metaguidance system for examining the assumptions and "faiths" guiding different evaluative systems.

A second work that explores connections between cultural and organizational performance is Iain L. Mangham and Michael A. Overington's *Organizations as Theater* (1987). As its title indicates, this text proposes a theatrical model of management. However, unlike Vaill, the authors use this performing art to articulate a social science approach to organizations. In this sense, they are very close to the model of performance research Schechner first proposed back in the 1960s, although the authors seem largely unaware of the Performance Studies paradigm.[79]

> While a dramaturgical approach to social science has been attractive, 'theatre' has not been developed as a general conceptual model for social science. We decided to attempt this. [. . .] Paramountly, an approach to organizations through the conceptual framing of a theatrical model allows us to use all that theatre, as a performing art, implies. It allows us to think about creativity, to consider the craft of actors playing characterizations, it provides considerations of tragedy and comedy, it suggests all the constraints of situation and history which affect any live performance, it allows for inquiry about the link between performance and what goes on backstage.[80]

Mangham and Overington present many dialogues, analyzing both theatrical and organizational scenes in order to discover how social tensions are embodied and resolved in different performances. Citing works from Shakespeare to British Leyland, they employ the theatrical metaphor in a much more sustained and systematic manner than does Vaill. In short, they develop it into an analytical tool.

Though they seem mostly oblivious to Performance Studies, Mangham and Overington are well versed in two of the authors important to its development. Specifically, they draw upon the social action theories of Kenneth Burke and Erving Goffman in order to situate their own dramaturgical approach to organizational performance, which stresses the relation of theatrical metaphors and the conceptualization of social action. "Theatre is the metaphor for studying social *action*, how it can be seen as staged and how it can be explained. In reflecting on realities by staging appearances, theatre is offering us an affective interpretation of the how, what, when, where and why of social action. It is precisely in this we can find the metaphorical resources that we want for the conceptualization of social conduct, and a further license for taking social theory, whatever its origins, into this same framework."[81] Using such an approach, long familiar to Performance Studies researchers, Mangham and Overington devote a chapter to each of the following dramaturgical dimensions of organizational performance: ritual and rehearsal processes; expressive aspects of space, setting, and clothing; actors and characterizations; interpretations of social action; and the relation of playscript and director. Though they present a social science approach to management, the authors justify their dramaturgical approach in this way: "Clearly, 'theatre' as an analytic framework permits a humanistic, artistic, and creatively playful approach to organizations which offers a resistance to heavy-handed models of systematic rationality that are 'thoughtlessly' tragic in portraying people in organizations as the victims of forces they do not understand and cannot control."[82] Mangham and Overington thus draw up their own version of the "Machine" vs. "Human" dichotomy and champion theater's humanizing potential for organizations.

One final theorist who turns to the performing arts as a management model is John Kao, whom we have cited earlier. In *Jamming: The Art and Discipline of Business Creativity* (1996), he writes: "Management is a performing art. Like teachers, like litigators, like film directors, like politicians, like generals, like coaches, the best managers have a bit of the ham in them. Or they should, if they want to build creative organizations."[83] Kao does not cite marching music or Shakespearean theater, but rather the improvisational jam session of experimental jazz, which he uses as a metaphor throughout his text. A jazz musician himself, Kao writes that a jam session "is not formless self-indulgence or organizational anarchy. The music follows an elegant grammar, a set of conventions that guide and challenge our imagination. . . . That's jamming. The management of creativity is rich in such paradoxes. It is both an art and a discipline."[84] Like Vaill, Kao stresses the need to work with different value systems, but rather than present a dialogue of thinkers, he outlines a postindustrial "idea factory." Here the improvisational mastery of "creativity management is matter of process skills as well as finding and developing a variety of spaces where *critically supportive listening* can take place."[85] Kao also justifies the need for creativity by pointing to rapid and continuing changes in the business environment, such as the increasing importance of information, worker demands for more creative jobs, and the shift to customer-oriented services. But first among his reasons for the necessity of business creativity is new technologies: "This is the age of creativity because that's where information technology wants us to go."[86]

In a chapter entitled "Cyberjamming," Kao writes that the "Internet culture is a jamming culture. It's nonhierarchical and centerless. Its forms and formalities are purely occasional, opportunistic, experimental. Like jazz, it is profoundly democratic and egalitarian."[87] As this citation suggests, Jamming presents a very optimistic view of organizational performance in the digital age. We get a more concrete picture of Kao's postindustrial factory when he compares his own personal workspace to Charlie Parker's "woodshed," the symbolic place were the Bird retreated to work on new jazz forms.

> As Charlie Parker had his "woodshed," I have my kitchen table—the Kao venture sushi bar, as one wag dubbed it. It's where I form new companies, plan conferences, prepare speeches, conceive courses; I can easily wipe it clean, and the nearly paperless table is quickly ready to support my next deal. My equipment consists of a high-end personal computer, a speaker phone, a state of the art videoconferencing system with groupware, and a high-speed Internet connection.
>
> I can do a lot with these tools. I can bring collaborators in on deals, and, as we share information, we sculpt virtual teams. Databases can be searched. Complex documents can be drafted using templates of my own design to help me organize the process of doing deals. But those instruments of business invention are only on the frontiers of usefulness: We haven't seen anything yet.[88]

Organizational performance has come a long way from Taylor's time and motion studies of pig-iron handlers, as well as from Mayo's Hawthorne experiments with bored factory workers. It now includes high-tech, high performance multitasking, the improvised cyberjamming that operates through many players and instruments. Responding to different scripts, high performance management here involves pitching and making deals, creating and dismantling organizations, and though Kao does not mention this, hiring and firing thousands and thousands of people. The happy postindustrial factory Kao champions is but one vision of the future, and though it is uncritically optimistic in its depiction and narrow in its perspective, he is no doubt correct about one thing: we haven't seen anything yet.

LIMINAUTIC FEEDBACK

Let us return once again to the challenge guiding this project: to rehearse a general theory of performance. From our readings of Performance Studies and Performance Management, we can begin to assemble some of its components. Both paradigms make use of several models of performance, as well as metamodels of the paradigms themselves. From some of these metamodels, I want to begin developing a metamodel for the general theory itself and will do so by again citing Guattari's notion of metamodelization, which entails the complication and enrichment of models rather than the simplification and reduction of heterogeneity to one general model. "What distinguishes metamodelization from modelization," he suggests, "is the way it uses terms to develop possible openings onto the virtual and onto creative processuality."[89] My task here: to develop possible openings between and within two paradigms, openings we shall explore more later.

Performance Studies and Performance Management each entails processes of creative metamodelization; that is, each generates and generalizes a variety of referential performance models, some of which also function as metamodels for both the field of objects and the paradigm itself. Such metamodels are both referential and self-referential; they refer to the performances they study and to their own performance of studying. The potential for such self-referential generalization exists in *everything*, even if it is not always actualized. Niklas Luhmann writes: "Every meaningfully grasped given must not only be fully present at a moment and thereby 'fulfill' experience or action; it must also organize self-reference, thus ensuring that, if necessary, it can be made available again in (more or less) different kinds of situations, at other points in time, with other possible partners of social communication. This re-availability is built into concrete experience and action by symbolic generalization. As availability for others, it is also, although not only, the precondition for possible communication."[90] To put this another way: to be what they are, to become present as such, actual performances presuppose their own iteration within a citational network, an archive of restored behaviors and discourses, a pool of virtual re-availability. Our general theory dips into the virtual pools of a few specific metamodels in order to reactualize them differently.

The challenge of rehearsing a general theory of performance lies in the metamodelization of different metamodelizations, the generalization of different generalizations, the processing of diverse processes that can only appear reductive to one another and to their respective citational networks. The trick lies in tracing mutant passages between these networks, passages that themselves risk becoming metaphorical flights of transcendence and/or dead-end crashes into the concrete. "Meaning is grasped, on the one hand, as full, concrete, and to this extent unrepeatable and nontransferable; yet, on the other hand, it refers to condensations as unities that make what is complex objectively or thematically attainable. In other words, symbolic generalizations stamp identities onto the flux of experience—identities in the sense of respective reductive references themselves at any given time."[91] Our challenge, then, is to create an *immanent* "meta-metamodel," to cast a signature performance from different performative fluxes, beginning here with those opened up by the displaced limen of Performance Management and Performance Studies.

The invention of a metamodel of performance begins by passing back and forth between paradigmatic components, by recombining efficacious and efficient challenges, by exploring hidden passages between their citational networks. Though we could easily start with the theatrical models shared by Performance Studies and Performance Management, I will instead initiate things by shuttling between two other important metamodels, namely, Performance Studies' rites of passage and Performance Management's feedback loops. The paradigmatic deployment of liminal rites was discussed in Chapter 1: they are an object of study, as well as a metamodel of cultural performance and the Performance Studies paradigm itself. In this chapter we have seen feedback loops deployed in Performance Management by proponents of systems theory, information processing and decision making, and organizational development. The model of feedback is also used in human relations, where an important part of the performance review process involves giving workers "feedback" by presenting and discussing their evaluations with them. Feedback loops have been used to analyze, design, and evaluate individual performance, the relation between the performance of subsystems and entire systems, and an organization's performance within its larger environment. In addition, organizational theorists and management consultants often describe themselves as "change agents" whose function includes providing valuable external feedback to organizations undergoing major reengineering or restructuring projects. Feedback is a specific performance that can affect the direction of overall performance. Thus feedback loops can be read as *mise en abîme*, as a part that represents the whole and thus "puts into abyss" an entire performance process, whether it be that of an individual or an organization. A performance about performance, feedback is thus a self-referential metamodel of the Performance Management paradigm.

Despite their many differences, rites of passage and feedback loops share some uncanny traits, and it is through these traits that I hope to reactualize some of their virtual possibilities and thereby open onto the creative processuality of performance. Both liminal rites and feedback loops are cyclical processes, and both involve exteriorization and interiorization, expulsion and incorporation. Recalling Turner and Foucault's discussions of the function of initiation rites: participants are separated from the rest of society for a certain period of time and then reincorporated back into it. One might even say that performers are output, then input—in other words, that rites of passage function as feedback loops for entire social groups. Some might object that this is to reduce liminality to a model of feedback, rather than open up its heterogeneity. However, as deployed by Turner and Schechner, *feedback already informs the theorization of liminality, though this feedback mechanism has long been turned off.* More specifically, Turner and Schechner's conceptualizations of liminality—from the particular effects of ritual upon individual performers and social structures to the more general relationship of ritual, theater, and other performative genres—regularly make use of feedback discourse and feedback diagrams to theorize the efficacy of cultural performance. While there are many examples one could cite, a few will suffice here.[92]

The first example comes from Schechner's 1977 essay "Selective Inattention," which contains a diagram depicting how social and aesthetic dramas "cross-feed" into one another. Significantly, Schechner uses this diagram in a section featuring Turner's theory of liminality. Schechner places the diagram at the section's conclusion, along with a caption that ends, "There is a flow to the relationship between social and aesthetic drama and

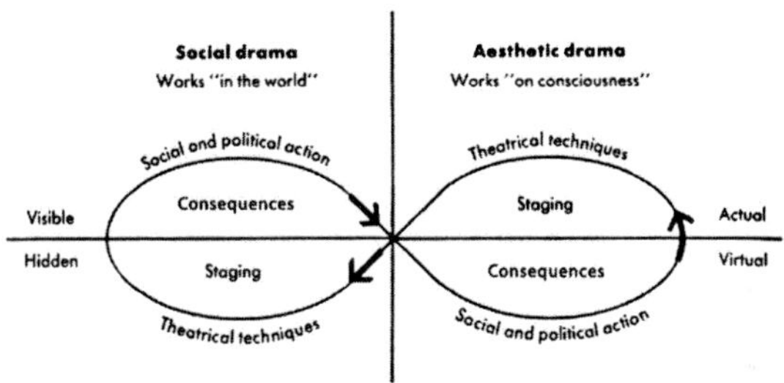

specific enactments (shows) may 'journey' from one sphere into the other, but only in the direction indicated."[93] Schechner uses feedback to theorize how Tsembaga *kaiko* dances transform destructive behavior between different groups into constructive alliances in Highlands New Guinea. "Quite unconsciously a positive feedback begins: the more splendid the displays of dancing, the stronger the alliances; the stronger the alliances, the more splendid the dancing."[94] For his part, Turner cites Schechner's loop diagram in his 1982 essay, "Social Dramas and Stories About Them." He writes that the social dramas are political processes in which "ends, means, and resources are caught up in an interdependent feedback process."[95] Regarding a Ndembu story about a drunken king beaten by his sons and comforted by his daughter, Turner comments: "Just as the story itself still makes important points about family relationships and about the stresses between sex- and age-roles, and appears to be an emic generalization, clothed in metaphor and involving the projection of innumerable specific social dramas generated by these social tensions, so does it feed back into the social process, providing it with a rhetoric, a mode of employment, and a meaning."[96] Turner stressed the need to balance social tensions, thus giving priority to negative, corrective feedback loops; for him, positive, amplifying loops lead to schismogenesis or the breakup of social groups. Schechner's analysis of the *kaiko* dance indicates that he recognizes the potential efficacy of both negative and positive feedback. Both theorists were readers of Gregory Bateson, who employed engineering concepts of feedback to theorize social conflict, play, schizophrenia, pollution, and arms races. In many ways, between theater and anthropology *there is feedback*.

Schechner employs a feedback diagram to explicate the restoration of behavior, his fundamental unit of performance, while Turner's anthropological mixing of theater and feedback also has a certain foundational dimension: Turner tells us that his mother was a successful stage actress, while his father "was an electrical (in American terms, 'electronic') engineer."[97]

Feedback, then, offers us a metamodel applicable to the invention of a general theory of performance. While in Performance Studies, feedback has been developed as a model of social efficacy, in Performance Management it has functioned as a model of organizational efficiency. More importantly, as the texts of Turner, Schechner, Vaill, Mangham and Overington, and Kao all suggest, there is feedback *between* theater and management, *between* cultural and organizational performance. One of the most important processes our readings of the two paradigms have revealed is the iterability of conceptual models, the possibility that models of performance developed in one research paradigm can be appropriated by another. Paradigmatic reading machines not only have the ability to generate, describe, and evaluate performances, they can also cite and re-site them, breaking apart the evaluative forces that bind together their discourses and practices. More importantly, they can recombine and reinscribe these forms, deploying them elsewhere while ignoring, incorporating, and/or reevaluating their previous values in new and uncanny ways. Through this iterability, mutational forces can become normative and normative forces mutational.

Between theater and management, the discourses and practices of cultural performance may enter into both mutational and normative assemblages within Performance Management. The valorimeters of efficiency remain dominant in organizations, though we have seen that the performing arts can be taken up by transformational forces that valorize creativity, cultural diversity, and the democratizing potential of new media. "If management is a performing art," writes Vaill, "the consciousness of the manager is transformed."[98] Again, such transformations can be and regularly are overcoded by demands for efficiency. Even here, we must not exclude the possibility that efficiency—the maximization of outputs and minimization of inputs—can itself produce mutational forces. Situations may arise in which this normative force becomes transformational, in which organizational efficiency becomes socially efficacious, resistant, liminal. Ecological activists, for instance, draw heavily upon the concept of efficiency in their efforts to resist industrial development and protect natural resources. Within the field of experimental performance, we can sense the miming of the workplace in such names as Growtowski's Theatre Laboratory, Warhol's Factory, and Schechner's Performance Garage, now used by Elizabeth LeCompte's Wooster Group.[99] The normative effects of efficiency cannot, of course, be so easily localized and revalorized, especially as digital media and telecommunications have multiplied the feedback between different sites.

Here we come to another reason why Performance Studies research cannot afford to ignore the Performance Management paradigm, and why a general theory is needed. After decades of decrying the sharp separation of labor and leisure in advanced industrial societies, cultural theorists and activists now face something shocking: *the separation of labor and leisure is disintegrating*, though not in the way many had hoped. Through the widespread use of beepers, cell phones, fax machines, portable computers, and handheld information devices, work activities have entered the home, the car, the street, and even the family vacation. Similarly, the emphasis on creativity, pleasure, and personal expression by Performance Management threatens the separation of labor and leisure as organizational theorists and managers attempt to infuse the workplace with elements of play, at times drawing upon the work of Bateson and Csikszentmihalyi, two theorists whose research of play and flow have been important to the study of cultural performance.

I have introduced the concept of the liminal-norm to suggest that liminality has itself become a norm in Performance Studies, one that has prevented us from recognizing and engaging other performance paradigms. As metamodel, rites of passage have directed our reading machines toward certain performance genres and steered them away from others. However, the breakdown of work and play promoted by Performance Management constitutes a significant challenge to liminality, whose theorization depends upon the distinction between labor and leisure. In "From Liminal to Liminoid, in Play, Flow, and Ritual," Turner uses the separation of work and play to distinguish the liminality of agrarian and industrial societies. In oral, agrarian societies, he argues that separate spheres of labor and leisure do not exist; thus liminal, anti-structural activities have closer connections with underlying symbolic structures. However, he defines the "leisure genres ... of symbolic forms and actions in complex, industrial societies" as liminoid,[100] writing that "the 'oid' here derives from Greek *-eidos*, a form, shape; and means 'like, resembling'; 'liminoid' *resembles* without being identical with 'liminal.' "[101] With the rise of labor and leisure as separate domains of life, genres of liminality multiplied and diversified, and their connection with structural functions weakened and became more diffuse. Thus, they became liminoid rather than liminal. Extrapolating from Turner and Schechner's use of feedback models, we can say that, in agrarian societies, feedback is strong between liminal performances and underlying social structures, whereas in industrial societies, there is little or no feedback between liminoid performances and social structures. Indeed, Schechner's call for the "ritualization of theater" can be read as an attempt to reinstall cultural feedback mechanisms in contemporary Western societies.

Given the emergence of digital societies and the increasing disintegration of work and play spheres, perhaps we need to relaunch the theory of performative liminality. Postindustrial liminality is neither liminal nor liminoid: it is instead *liminautic*. Limen remain sites of passage and transformation, but these sites are now themselves in passage, their transformations becoming networked over many different borders: geopolitical, societal, institutional, paradigmatic, generational. . . . At the turn of the twenty-first century, the citationality of discourses and practices is passing across an electronic threshold, a digital limen. Words and gestures, statements and behaviors, symbolic systems and living bodies are being recorded, archived, and recombined through multimedia communication networks. Liminal and liminoid genres are becoming cyberspatial, flighty, liminautic.

The liminautic signals the becoming-digital of both cultural and organizational performance. Between theater and management, the computer-enhanced breakdown of labor and leisure spheres creates a network of feedback and feedforward. With startling speed, forms and forces of normative efficiency appropriate those of mutational efficacy, yet are simultaneously open to rapid and radical expropriation. Forms may be seized, taken to the limit, broken apart, reassembled, remixed, left behind for dead, sniffed up later, and restored yet again. Deviations and differences may be corrected suddenly and ruthlessly or allowed to persist and slowly evolve; they may just as suddenly become amplified, enhanced, blown out of proportion. All this occurs not one time at one site for all time, but multiple times at multiple sites for some of the time. How to navigate one's way in this liminautic atmosphere? As we turn toward a third performance paradigm, let us recall Vaill's suggestion: what is needed is an online metaguidance system.

CHAPTER 3. THE EFFECTIVENESS OF TECHNOLOGICAL PERFORMANCE

THE CHALLENGE OF EFFECTIVENESS

We have cracked open the question "What is performance?" by posing another one: *which* performance? While cultural critics, artists, and activists have defined performance in terms of social efficacy, managers and organizational theorists have constructed performance as organizational efficiency. There is, however, yet another community that takes a very different perspective on performance. Rocket scientists, for instance, debate the relationship between temperature and "O-ring performance."[1] Material scientists analyze the "performance of metals" and find "aluminum-zinc alloys outperforming polymeric composites."[2] Engineers chart the "universal performance curve" of land transportation vehicles.[3] Finally, computer scientists seek to develop "high performance computing systems using scalable parallel designs and technologies capable of sustaining at least one trillion operations per second (teraops) performance."[4] All these researchers are interested not in cultural or organizational performance, but in *technological performance*.

How to read this concept of performance? Will we need some high performance device just to scan its semantic range and survey its sites of pragmatic installation? Just what is technological performance, and what is the history of its research? Tracing the development of this research poses certain difficulties, starting with the very definition of technological performance. As suggested by the above citations, the concept is used in highly technical contexts, such as technical reports and scientific articles, where writers assume their readers share a specialized language and thus understand the term "performance" without having it defined for them.

To take another example: in *Water Soluble Polymers: Beauty with Performance*, a 1986 collection of articles published by the American Chemical Society, P.A. Rey and R.G. Varsanik write that their research "focuses on the performance of polymeric flocculent in wastewater systems."[5] The difficulty: throughout their article, the authors discuss very precise yet cloudy notions of performances—such as "flocculent performance," "performance of primary clarifier," and "secondary sedimentation basin performance." The performance concept at work here is precise to chemists researching water soluble polymers, but vague to nonchemists and most likely to chemists with other specializations. Because the authors assume their readers share a set of highly technical discourses and practices, they can deploy the concept, relate it to experimental data, and reach conclusions without ever defining performance *per se*.

This paradoxical pattern of specific yet vague usage carries over to another technological performance, that of electric vehicles (EVs). In *Electric Vehicles: Technology, Performance, and Potential* (1993), we read that the "performance of EVs is now being enhanced by technical improvements in batteries." The term "performance" appears throughout the text, which includes numerous tables depicting "Performance Specifications" of existing electric vehicles, "Advancement in Performance of Permanent Magnet Materials," and the "Performance Goals in 2000 Set by Japan's EV Expansion Plan."[6] Again, however, no explicit definition of "performance" is offered. And what has occurred in this transfer from one research site to another? *The precision—and the cloudiness—of the performances has changed.* Specialists and nonspecialists alike might have trouble synthesizing the differences between the various areas of research in order to define the concept of technological performance.

The troubles multiply as the number of performance sites increases: how, for instance, do the performances of water soluble polymers and electric vehicles relate to those of aluminum-zinc alloys, O-rings, and computer systems? The pattern of precision and cloudiness extends across the field of technological performance research: the precision comes from the specific contexts of its application, while the vagueness arises from the tacit knowledge of specialists. In short, we are challenged by *the lack of an explicit and general definition of technological performance*. The lack of such a definition even among specialists is surprising, given that performance is not some marginal concept in the applied sciences. Indeed, it is central to the application of science. In her study of the *Challenger* shuttle disaster, Diane Vaughan writes that "for engineers, a design is a hypothesis to be tested. But tests only approximate reality. *The proof is in the performance."*[7]

The proof of a scientific hypothesis lies in the performance. But again, what is this performance, and why is it so rarely defined? Is it because one cannot be accurate enough in defining it? Or because one can only be *too* accurate? Or might the reason lie in the fact that performance has *no* underlying meaning, even *no* existence? Significantly, one of the few explicit definitions of technological performance that I have found makes this somewhat nihilistic claim. In *Computer Systems Performance Evaluation* (1979), Israel Borovits and Seev Neumann discuss the concept of performance as it applies to computer technologies:

> It should be noted that computer performance (or the performance of any distinguishable component) cannot be discussed but in the context of a defined application or group of applications. **Performance has no existence or meaning per se**—it must refer to a specific application. . . . It should therefore be kept firmly in mind that though it is convenient to speak of the "efficiency," "capacity," or "volume," of a system, **what is meant is its effectiveness in a given task.**[8]

"Effectiveness in a given task." This provides us an initial definition of technological performance. Other terms frequently employed as synonyms of performance are *capability, operation, function,* and *efficiency*. The performance of a technology refers to its technical effectiveness in a specific application or set of applications undertaken in a particular context. With respect to water soluble polymers used in wastewater systems, performance means clarity; with electric vehicles, it means miles per hour/recharge; with the feedback mechanisms installed in the nose-cones of guided missiles, it means accuracy. Performance means effectiveness, an effectiveness that, in most cases, must be quantified for measurement and endlessly qualified for evaluation.

Let's pause a moment to consider effectiveness in relation to the other performative values we have already investigated. While cultural researchers theorize the efficacy of performance in terms of social justice, and organizational experts scan the efficiency of performance in terms of bureaucratic economy, we can say that engineers and technicians measure the effectiveness of performances in terms of executability, the technical "carrying-out" of prescribed tasks, successful or not. At the limit, the differences between cultural efficacy, organizational efficiency, and technological effectiveness are not as clear-cut as I am suggesting here, and indeed, we will come to read how they embed or incorporate themselves within one another. At the same time, these differences are still productive, as can be felt in the respective performances of missiles, workteams, and initiation rituals.

In the previous chapter, we saw that organizational performance and its challenge of efficiency are ongoing matters of the state, specifically that of the US government, whose 1993 Government Performance and Results Act and the National Performance Review were but the latest in a series of attempts to improve its organizational efficiency. Technological performance and the challenge of effectiveness are likewise matters of the state, especially as they concern *high performance technologies*. In late 1991 the US Congress passed and President Bush signed the High Performance Computing Act. As stated in Section 3, the "purpose of this Act is to help ensure the continued leadership of the United States in high performance computing and its applications by:"

> 1. expanding Federal support for research, development, and application of high performance computing. . . .
>
> 2. improving the interagency planning and coordination of Federal research and development on high performance computing and maximizing the effectiveness of the Federal Government's high performance computing efforts.

Two years prior to the Government Performance and Results Act, this legislation put technological performance research into law. Section 4 defines high performance computing as "advanced computing, communications, and information technologies, including scientific workstations, supercomputer systems (including vector supercomputers and large scale parallel systems), high-capacity and high-speed networks, special purpose and experimental systems, and applications and systems software." Like the Government Performance and Results Act of 1993, the High Performance Computing Act of 1991 affected a wide range of federal departments and agencies; and like the later National Performance Review, a federal program was created to execute this law of performance.

To help implement the High Performance Computing Act, Congress provided the President authority to create a National High Performance Computing Program, whose function was to set goals and priorities and provide administrative oversight for enactment across different organizational sites. Backed by the President and Congress, impacting federal departments and agencies, and underwritten by nearly $3 billion, the High Performance Computing Act is technological performance research writ large.[9] Though initially passed under President Bush, the Act was quickly embraced by the Clinton administration and became the centerpiece of its much-publicized initiative to enhance this nation's computing capabilities by establishing an Information Superhighway or, as it became officially called, a National Information Infrastructure.

The 1991 Act also provided organizational and budgetary support to the High Performance Computing and Communications Initiative (HPCCI), an interagency program begun in the 1980s to facilitate the development of high performance computing and communication networks. The HPCCI has overseen a number of challenges to America, specifically *Grand Challenges*, federally funded projects that create interdisciplinary and multi-institutional teams to work on "difficult scientific problems whose solutions will yield new scientific understanding while simultaneously advancing high performance computing and communications." In addition, there are *National Challenges*, projects that "incorporate socially significant problems of national importance that can also drive the development of information infrastructures."[10] But even at this high level of research, defining technological performance still remains a challenge in itself. Thus the 1995 report *Evolving the High Performance Computing and Communications Initiative* defines high performance as "a moving target—the threshold for what is considered 'high performance' advances, as ever-increasing performance levels become more broadly available."[11] Because technological performance is itself a challenging and moving target, we will focus in on specific technologies that have guided the development of its research.

TECHNO-PERFORMANCE: FROM MISSILES TO MACINTOSHES

Because of its intense specialization, the research of technological performance is much more dispersed than that of cultural and organizational performance. Very few of its researchers seem to have reflected on the concept of performance even within their own areas of specialization, and to the best of my knowledge, no historian or philosopher of science has yet attempted to analyze the deployment of performance discourses and practices across different scientific disciplines. Nor can I identify anything in the applied sciences that corresponds to Performance Studies or Performance Management; that is, I have found no explicit attempts to articulate a paradigm of performance research, much less any intellectual histories or surveys. However, performance research has been officially institutionalized in at least one discipline, that of computer science, where today there are dozens of high performance computer centers located in the US, including:

Albuquerque High Performance Computing Center

Army High Performance Computing Research Center

Center for High Performance Computing, University of Texas

Center for Reliable and High Performance, University of Illinois at Urbana-Champaign

High Performance Computing, Naval Research and Development

High Performance Computing and Communications, Jet Propulsion Lab

High Performance Computing and Communications, University of Washington

High Performance Computing and Simulation Research Laboratory, Florida State University

High Performance Computing Group, Georgia Institute of Technology

High Performance System Software Laboratory, University of Maryland, College Park

Institute for High Performance Computing, Pennsylvania State University

Maui High Performance Computing Center

NASA High Performance Computing and Communications Program

National Consortium for High Performance Computing, University of California, San Diego

National High Performance Computing & Communications Council

NOAA High Performance Computing and Communications

Pacific-Sierra Research High Performance Computing

Utah Center for High Performance Computing

From the few usages already cited and the many more that follow, we can say that although performance has yet to receive much critical reflection, performance concepts are nonetheless widely deployed across the applied sciences, where they are routinely used to design, develop, and evaluate thousands, if not millions (or billions), of technologies. As this text may very well function as the first interdisciplinary survey of technological performance, I hope it not too imprudent to offer a name for this widely dispersed research paradigm. I propose to call it *Techno-Performance.*

Like Performance Studies and Performance Management, Techno-Performance research covers a wide variety of performative activities. It has also generalized its concept of performance over the past half-century, and we shall examine several different passages this movement of generalization has taken. In addition, despite its intense specialization, Techno-Performance has been guided by a number of models or metamodels. Significantly, one of these metamodels involves feedback devices or servomechanisms. In "Servo System Theory" (1955), Charles F. White outlines some challenges facing designers of the servomechanisms that are the heart of missile guidance systems.

> The designer is faced with demands that are basically contradictory. There is often a limitation on the servo system size, weight, and complexity, as well as on the amount of power that may be consumed in producing controlled power output during a given interval of time. At

the same time, high performance specifications of rapid response in following input commands and in reducing errors due to load variations are demanded.[12]

This citation from the field of rocket science touches upon many elements crucial to understanding the concept of technological performance, as well as the Techno-Performance paradigm. White refers to multiple *criteria* that guide the design and evaluation of these feedback systems—criteria of size, weight, complexity, energy consumption, response time, and error reduction. He does so to foreground the *contradictory demands* these criteria pose to designers, contradictions whose resolution lies in making *trade-offs* between different criteria. White also refers to *high performance specifications*, thus alluding to *standards* of performance recognized by the stakeholders of this technology, here specifically, the US military and its industrial contractors. And we also begin to see the contours of Techno-Performance, for the very *date* of this citation, the *field* from which it originates, and the *institutions* from which it takes flight—all these indicate the historical and conceptual matrix of this paradigm of performance research.

Since the 1950s, guided missiles have been a paradigmatic technology of US science. When one says that something "is not rocket science," one implicitly affirms both the complexity of aero- and astronautics and, more tacitly still, the high regard with which they are held throughout US society. This high-level commendation dates back to the early Cold War, when rocket science helped reforge the alliance between military and business interests into what Senator J. William Fulbright branded as the "military-industrial complex." The term was popularized by President Eisenhower, who presided over the complex and who used his farewell speech to warn Americans of its growing dangers. The President knew that missiles were the guiding technology of the military industrial complex; he also feared they were reducing US society to it. Stuart W. Leslie writes in *The Cold War and American Science* (1993): "As Eisenhower understood all too well, the missile was as much a symbol of postwar science as of postwar politics, evidence of what he called 'almost an insidious penetration of our own minds that the only thing this country is engaged in is weaponry and missiles.'"[13]

The missile has also been a guiding technology of Techno-Performance, a research paradigm whose formation crystallized in the atmosphere of Cold War politics and grew outward from the labs of the heavily funded military-industrial complex. "For better or worse," comments Leslie, "the Cold War redefined American science. In the decade following the Second World War, the Department of Defense (DOD) became the biggest single patron of American science."[14] The drive for sophisticated weaponry was backed by intense political and social forces. The long-running "Red Scare" legitimated unprecedented federal funding of military technologies from the 1950s through the 1980s.

> Driven by the politics of national security and by the Pentagon's belief in the competitive advantages of high technology, spending for defense research and development surpassed its wartime peak (already fifty times higher than prewar levels) by the end of the Korean War, then climbed to dizzying heights after Sputnik, reaching $5.5 billion a year by 1960. . . . The defense buildup of the 1980s actually pushed military R&D spending (in constant dollars) past the record levels of the mid-1960s.[15]

Leslie's reference here to "high technology" points back to White's use of the term "high performance." Both were launched from laboratories working with missionary fervor. Responding to political and military demands for increasingly complex weaponry, engineers and other applied scientists pushed the limits of materials, machines, and entire systems by creating higher and higher standards of technological performance: beyond "high performance" criteria there are "very high performance" and beyond them "ultra high performance" criteria.

Guided by rocket science and incubated in the atmosphere of Cold War America, the paradigm of Techno-Performance took shape around the high performance weapons developed by the military-industrial complex. I must emphasize I am not arguing that the concept of performance was first applied to technologies in the last half-century; rather, as with the cases of cultural and organizational performance, I contend that the end of the Second World War marks a decisive turning point or threshold in performance research. Over the past five decades, the concept of technological performance has become more diversified and its refinements more calculated. Scientists and technicians from different fields now design, produce, and study performances taking place at innumerable sites. It is precisely this massive deployment that defines the terrain of Techno-Performance. And simultaneous with this territorial expansion, technological performances have also become systematized and correlated with quantifiable data, a trend that supports Eugene S. Ferguson's comments on the general development of engineering during this same time: "Since World War II, the dominant trend in engineering has been away from knowledge that cannot be expressed as mathematical relationships. The art of engineering has been pushed aside in favor of the analytical 'engineering sciences,' which are higher in status and easier to teach."[16] Along with its diversification, systematization, and quantification, the concept of technological performance has also become institutionalized over the past fifty years, as evidenced in the high performance computing centers cited above.

From all these traits and others still to come, we can understand Techno-Performance as a research paradigm that took shape in Cold War America, right alongside the research of Performance Studies and Performance Management. Techno-Performance is an enormous yet amorphic paradigm, cutting across many disciplines and institutions. Though its formation crystallized around missiles and other military technologies, the paradigm now reaches far beyond them. High performance devices originally developed for weapon systems have made their way into our everyday lives, thereby generalizing the research of technological high performance beyond the military-industrial complex. Though direct technology transfers were relatively rare during the Cold War, there were some important exceptions.

In *Landmarks in Digital Computing*, Peggy A. Kidwell and Paul E. Ceruzzi point out that aeronautical computing had been analogic up until the 1960s, when "electronic digital computers reached a level of performance and reliability that surpassed their analog brethren."[17] Key to digital guidance systems was the invention of the integrated circuit, invented by engineers at Texas Instruments and Fairchild and first used extensively by the Air Force in its Minuteman II missiles.

> The Air Force order established the integrated circuit as the best of many competing ways then being proposed to shrink electronic circuits. In economists' terms, the Minuteman II contract drove the chip down the "learning curve," as manufacturers learned the art of making them in quantity. The result was that the integrated circuit, which started out as a delicate and expensive device, eventually became cheap and rugged. The revolution brought on by this sudden availability of cheap computing power is still being felt throughout modern society.[18]

We see here how high performance research can move from the military-industrial complex to more mundane sites. Integrated circuits now operate in thousands of items, ranging from cars and phones to TVs and PCs. Indeed, the computer is another paradigmatic technology of Techno-Performance research, one that has also moved from military research sites into our homes. Kenneth Flamm writes: "It is no accident that the military services largely financed the postwar development of the computer in the 1950s, for computing technology had played a pivotal role in the Allied War effort."[19] The military industrial complex drove down the learning curves necessary to manufacture certain technologies, thus making them commercially viable for nonmilitary markets. The end of the Cold War has greatly accelerated the transfer of high performance technologies into consumer and business markets, with the ARPANET's transformation into the Internet being the most visible example.[20] This dissemination of high performance research is one way that the concept of technological performance has been generalized over the past fifty years.

Both the sophistication and dissemination of high performance research make theorizing the Techno-Performance paradigm difficult, especially for someone whose training lies in the arts and humanities. However, you don't have to be a rocket scientist to understand technological performance. Nor are its many technicians exempt from the problems of defining it—far from it. As we have seen, the concept of performance lies at the heart of applied science; however, it is almost always deployed in a manner both precise and implicit. That is, performance forms part of the tacit knowledge of engineering, computer science, and many other fields scattered across the terrain of Techno-Performance, including our homes and gardens.

To set some landmarks in the vast terrain of Techno-Performance, I want to cite a list of products that, through their very names, demonstrate the extent to which performance research stretches across the applied sciences and reaches into our everyday lives. The following list is composed of consumer products whose names contain some form of the word "performance."

A.R. Musical Enterprises' Performance Plus
(musical equipment accessories)
Akiba France's Performance Sport (women's apparel)
American & Efird's Performance (thread)
Applied Research & Technology's Performance Midi
(computer software)
Aqua Pump & Products' Performance Plus (aquarium filters)
Argus Publishers' Performance Plus Video (videotapes)
Audiocontrol's Performance Match (car-stereo equipment)
Bate's Manufacturing's Performer (staplers)
Bridgestone/Firestone's Performance Poly (tires)
Caron International's Performer (yarn)
Collins & Aikman's Performance (carpets)
Combeau Industries' Performance (wallcoverings)
Corona Brushes' Performance Chinex (brushes)
Cosmair's Performing Preference (hair-care products)
Danskin's Performance Line (leotard, tights)
Diagraph's Performance (label printer)
Domco Industries' Performa (vinyl floor covering)
Downs Carpet's Performing Star (carpet)
E.R. Carpenter's Performing Primes (carpet padding)
Edelbrock's Performer-Link (automotive timing chains and gears)
Edelbrock's Performer-Plus (automotive camshaft and lifter set)
Edelbrock's Performer-RPM (automotive manifolds)

Ektelon's Performer (racquetball gloves)
ESS Laboratory's Performance (stereo equipment)
Fidelity Industries' Performance (wallcoverings)
Freud USA's Performance System (woodworking knives)
Georgia Pacific's Perfowood (hardboard)
Gexco Enterprises' Performer (tennis-racket strings)
Golden Star's Performer (mop handles)
Guilford Mills' Performance Rated (fabric)
Hancor's Performance Drain (drain panels)
Health Maintenance Program's Performance Packs
(healthcare products)
International Rotex's Performer (embossing tools)
Ionic Industries' Performer (music synthesizers)
JBL's Performance (electronic equipment)
Johnson's Carpets' Performance (carpets)
Klien Bicycle's Performance (bicycles)
Lectrosonic's Performer (wireless microphone)
Len-Dal's Performance (carpets)
Madico's Performance Tint (window film)
Maybelline's Performance 10 (nailcare product)
Maybelline's Performing Color (eyeliners)
Merisco's Performance In a Pouch (cleansing towels)
Mimetics Corporation's Performance/7 (computer software)
Moore Business Form's Performance Plus (computer diskettes)
Muelhen's Performing Care (skincare products)
NPS' Perform (roofing insulation)
O'Brien International's Performer (water skis)
Pitco Frialator's Performer (deep-fat fryers)
Quantex Carpet's Performance (carpets and rugs)
Raybestor's Performance Through Technology
(automatic transmission assemblies)
Recoton's Performer (audio antennae)
Sakate Seed America's Performax (plant seeds)
Shane Musical Products' Performance Effects (special effects)
Shane Musical Products' Performance

(musical instrument cables)
Sleek-Craft's Performance (boat trailers)
SmithKline Beecham's Perform (setting lotion)
Southern Carpet Mills' Performance (carpets and rugs)
Spring Industries' Performance Products
(home-furnishing textiles)
Spring Point's Performance Enhanced (printer toner cartridges)
Starcraft's Performance (powerboats)
Sterling Plumbing's Performa (tub and shower enclosure)
Strathmore Paper's Performance (commercial art paper)
The Coleman Co.'s Performer (personal flotation devices)
The Kawneer Company's The Performer (casement windows)
Thunderbird Products' Performance Cruiser (powerboat)
Washington Forge's Performa (cutlery)
Wilkinson Manufacturing's Performancepak (foil containers)
Wilton Industries' Performance Pans (bakeware)[21]

Bakeware, stereos, fabrics, bicycles, foil containers, plant seeds—these and the many other items listed here mark only the most literal sites of Techno-Performance research. The significance of this list lies both in its depth—some seventy brands—and its breadth—the wide diversity of product types. Though some brand names, such as Performance Line leotards and Performance musical accessories, bear a strong sense of cultural performance, the overwhelming majority do not. And there are other products not included in this list, including the Macintosh Performa, which in the early 1990s was a popular computer line manufactured by Apple Corporation. This use of "performance" to market everything from carpets and computers to mops and manifolds indicates one thing: for specialists and nonspecialists alike, *technologies perform.*

PREDICTING, MEASURING, AND EVALUATING PERFORMANCES

How are technologies made to perform? Despite the difficulties in defining performance, the concept is central to the application of science. The practice of engineering begins with a hypothesis concerning how a given technology will perform; that is, engineers start with a set of predictions. Next, the hypothesis is tested in the lab during a developmental stage using both models and prototypes. Then, the testing moves to the field, for ultimately: "The proof is in the performance."

However, such proof is not really ultimate, for operational performance can itself be used to collect measurements that are interpreted and, where anomalies are found, acted upon by engineers to refine and improve performance. This is especially the case with the NASA shuttle program which, unlike the Mercury, Gemini, and Apollo programs, involves reusable components: fuel tanks, booster rockets, and orbiters are all designed to perform again. As Vaughan says, "For the shuttle, flight was the ultimate test." However,

> Because the test of an engineering hypothesis is a comparison of its predictions with performance, experience becomes the quintessential learning device. . . . Bottlenecks, surprises, and glitches are the rule, not the exception. Designs that worked on paper have to be "debugged through use;" "corrective actions" to strengthen a weak link are the norm. This "fine-tuning" confounds interpretation of performance, muddying the causal issues.[22]

Forming hypotheses and making predictions, testing models and prototypes and operational systems, collecting and interpreting data, comparing predictions and performance, finding anomalies and debugging through use, these are all common tools of the engineering trade.[23] Especially during the developmental stage of a technology, but also during operation, a feedback loop is created between predictions and performance: performance is evaluated in terms of predictions that are then modified based on the performance and subsequently used as the basis for evaluating the next performance, and so on and so on.

The ongoing comparison of predictions and performance generates what engineers refer to as an *experience base* composed of data relating to a technology's performance history. "The frequent use of the term 'experience base' in documents and testimony conforms to the common engineering belief in performance as the ultimate design test and the importance of learning by doing in the craft of engineering."[24] In developing a technology as complex as the shuttle, NASA created a computerized system called the Marshall Problem Assessment System whose function was to track critical problems. During the developmental stage of the shuttle, "so many physical instruments were on each flight to measure performance and feed the data into the system that the workload between flights was unusually heavy. . . . The heavy instrumentation revealed many anomalies. These were important data, for they provided the first opportunity to compare engineering design predictions and test results with performance."[25]

The predictions made by designers concern the *specifications* or *specs* of performance, the quantifiable or measurable effectiveness of a given technology. Scientists call the specifications they demand or require of a technology the *criteria* of performance. (It should be noted, however, that researchers often use the terms "specifications" and "criteria" interchangeably.) Determining whether a technology performs to criteria or "meets specs" is an important step in assessing the performance of the technology in question. Such determination occurs through a *performance measurement*, which is also referred to as a *performance metric* or a *performance index*. Here quantitative information is gathered using laboratory and/or field tests to measure such performance specifications as the calculation speed of a computer processor, the energy consumption of an engine, or the resiliency of a rubber seal. The results of such measurements are commonly found in the owner's manuals of consumer items, listed under "performance specifications."

As important as it is, performance measurement is only part of a more general process called *performance evaluation, performance analysis, performance assessment*, or *performance study*. A 1995 report sponsored by the National Research Council on infrastructure performance describes "performance measurement [as] a technical component of the broader task of performance assessment, determining whether the infrastructure is meeting the community's objectives."[26] Performance analysis is the systematic and comprehensive evaluation of a technology or technological system, an evaluation that focuses not only on technical effectiveness, but also other dimensions such as safety, cost, reliability, and quality. Thus, while performance measurement determines whether a technology is currently performing to criteria, performance evaluation interprets this measurement within a wider context of interests and actions. As part of the feedback loop of prediction and performance, evaluation may include assessing current performance in light of the experience base, identifying performance trends and anomalies, and making decisions or recommendations concerning future performances. New tests may be called for or new criteria defined. Designs may be corrected, reconceived, or even scrapped altogether.

In addition to performance specifications and criteria, there are also *performance standards*. Performance standards are evaluative criteria agreed upon and recognized by members of a particular community and designed to be applicable across a wide variety of contexts. Such communities may be composed of scientists, industry workers, public policy makers, and/or the users of the technology in question. Performance standards may apply to materials or processes of construction, but increasingly they have come to be defined in relation to the actual use of a technology, to its performance in the field rather than the lab. Writing of consumer products, Lewis M. Branscomb argues that "good standards emphasize criteria for performance and leave materials and design as flexible as possible. They provide incentives for performance improvement, reduce prices by limiting variety and improving compatibility with other products, simplify the documentation problems of the buyer who can reference the standard in a purchase specification, and help the seller establish confidence in his product by using the standard's tests for performance."[27]

Performance standards also play an important role in the development and the marketing of technologies. Indeed, lack of standards constitutes one of the greatest challenges to developing and marketing new and highly innovative technologies. Erika Kress-Rogers makes this clear in her comments concerning contemporary research in the field of biosensors and "electronic noses," devices designed to detect chemical properties in foods, medicines, and the environment. She writes that at "the beginning of a development program, the performance and cost of the final instrument can rarely be predicted with absolute certainty. This means that it is difficult to definitively predict for which applications the instrument will be competitive."[28] Standards provide what is known as a *benchmark*, a set of evaluative criteria for comparing the performance of a new or modified technology to existing systems. As we shall see in a moment, however, defining such standards is very often difficult even within established industries.

In computer science, the importance of evaluating performance has given rise to a subfield called "performance analysis." This subfield addresses two basic questions: "How well is the system really performing?" and "How can we control it so as to achieve the *best possible* performance?"[29] The first question concerns performance analysis proper; the second concerns performance optimization or "tuning." In his preface to *Quantitative Analysis of Computer Systems* (1988), Clement H.C. Leung describes the specific ways computer scientists use performance analysis.

> Quantitative computer performance analysis consists of discovering and ascertaining the efficiency of a computer system; it may be, for example, concerned with the estimation of the performance behavior of systems under construction, or monitoring that of an existing one. The findings of a quantitative performance study may be used to guide decisions relating to system design, the allocation of machine resources, the acquisition of additional facilities, or the tuning of an existing configuration.[30]

Because of these functions, Leung goes on to note that "proper performance analysis is recognized to be an integral part of the professional construction and management of computer systems," thereby suggesting again how important the concept of technological performance is to the entire field of computer science. It must stressed again that, in addition to evaluating existing systems, performance analysis also contributes to the design and development of new systems as well.

Within computer performance analysis, *performance modeling* is employed in the design, testing, and evaluation of computer and communications networks, such as those which connect different components of a computer system or entirely different systems. Peter J.B. King describes three ways of measuring performance is his 1990 text, *Computer and Communication Systems Performance Modeling*. "First, the system can be built, or modified, and then measured. If the measurement is performed while a standard set of tasks is running, this technique is known as benchmarking. . . . The second approach is to build a [computer] simulation model of the system. . . . [In the third approach, a] mathematical model of the system, or parts of the system is constructed."[31] Simulation and analytical models each have their own advantages and disadvantages. Simulation can mirror fine details of system performance, but the finer the details, the longer the simulation program takes to run and the more difficult the evaluation. Analytical models, by contrast, are faster and can identify general performance principles, but do not match the real performance of the system as accurately.[32] In practice, however, "a combination of both approaches is useful," writes Leung. "Even if one ultimately decides to gauge the performance of different alternatives by means of detailed simulation modeling, analytic studies can nevertheless help to eliminate at the outset those which are clearly undesirable, thereby reducing the number of simulation models which need to be finally built."[33]

Technologies, then, are made to perform through a circular process of hypothesis and measurement, prediction and evaluation. Engineers and other applied scientists set out with a hypothesis concerning a discrete technological performance. They then design an application to meet particular performance specifications and criteria and conduct a series of experiments and tests whose results are measured and evaluated. Then, in the vast majority of cases, the entire process starts again, as the test results are fed back to create new predictions, new designs, new tests, and new results. Even the most common and apparently simple technological performances, such as those of water skis and flame-resistant carpets, are the results of intense research, research that entails the measurement, the evaluation, and, increasingly, the modeling of performance.

Computerized performance modeling is not limited to the evaluation of computers and communication networks, for it can be found across the applied sciences, potentially anywhere that involves comparing predictions and performance or monitoring and measuring an ongoing performance. Today, the use of computers to design, measure, and evaluate technological performance is increasing dramatically, and this has raised concerns about the impact that computer performance is having upon the training of applied scientists.

We have already seen that NASA employs computer systems to gather performance data about each of its shuttle missions. Similarly, the 1995 report, *Measuring and Improving Infrastructure Performance* stresses the growing importance of computerized performance analysis for evaluating municipal and regional infrastructures that handle transportation, water supply, waste, sewage, and storm water. "Increasingly powerful and cost-effective computer-based forecasting and simulation methods and new technology for measuring and monitoring system conditions have made more sophisticated approaches to assessing system performance widely available. Remote sensing, real-time monitoring, and network analysis and simulation models provide powerful new capabilities for measuring systemwide conditions and evaluating system changes."[34]

The increasing use of computers to measure and model technological performance does not resolve the underlying challenge of analyzing performance in the face of multiple and contradictory criteria. In fact, in some cases such use may even increase the difficulties: more parameters, more detailed measurements, more capabilities of real-time monitoring, and, in general, more data can make performance analysis so complex as to be unmanageable. For instance, the Marshall Problem Assessment System at NASA generated so much information about its shuttles that some engineers complained of overload.[35] Simply put, too much information about problems became a problem itself. But even with manageable dataflow and more precise measurements and modeling, computerized performance analysis can at best facilitate the handling of contradictory criteria; it cannot eliminate it altogether.

Here we approach another paradoxical aspect of technological performance. Though purportedly conceived, designed, constructed, and tested according to the rigors and methods of positivist science, the evaluation of technological performance often involves nonrigorous, intuitive techniques. This has led some computer scientists to argue that computer evaluation is not a science at all. Charles H. Sauer and K. Mani Chandy make this clear in the opening pages of their 1981 text, *Computer Systems Performance Modeling*. They stress:

> . . . **performance evaluation is an art,** not a science. This is true with measurement as well as modeling. In constructing a model, particularly in deciding which system characteristics to consider and which to ignore (it is usually impractical to consider all system characteristics), we must rely heavily on intuition and use methods which are not particularly rigorous. Unlike sciences where we strive for very precise characterizations, we must recognize that the complexity of the systems precludes great precision within practical limitations of cost and time.[36]

The idea that computer performance evaluation is an art rather than a science may surprise many artists and scientists, yet it suggests that the dualistic division of knowledge into arts and sciences is not and never has been absolute. While quantitative methods are highly valued in all sciences, the interpretation of data *as well as the valorization of quantitative methods* are themselves qualitative evaluations, not quantitative. In *Engineering and the Mind's Eye* (1992), Eugene S. Ferguson makes a similar argument with respect to engineering design, writing that "no matter how vigorously a 'science' of design may be pushed, the successful design of real things in a contingent world will always be based more on art than on science. Unquantifiable judgments and choices are the elements that determine the way a design comes together."[37]

Ferguson's comments about the art of engineering design lead us to another important observation, namely, that the use of computers within Techno-Performance research extends beyond the measurement and evaluation of given performances. The computer has become a technology that helps to *create* other technologies. With the development of computer-assisted design (CAD) programs, things no longer go back to the drawing board. Instead, they go back to the electronic desktop. In industries ranging from publishing and product design to architecture and engineering, computer technologies have radically transformed such traditional design skills as layout, drafting, cutting and pasting, and model-building. Such developments worry Ferguson, who writes that by "the 1980s, engineering curricula had shifted to analytical approaches, so visual and other sensual knowledge of the world seemed less relevant. Computer programs spewed out wonderfully rapid and precise solutions of obviously complicated problems, making it easy for students and teachers to believe that civilization had at last reached a state in which all technical problems were easily solvable."[38] In his last chapter, "Promise and Performance," Ferguson warns that analytical, mathematically oriented techniques may replace the tradition of intuitive, visually oriented design.

Such concerns may deepen as one realizes that computer technologies perform many other functions besides design and evaluation, functions that also directly affect countless other technologies. Increasingly, computers have become important to manufacturing processes, controlling manual and automated assembly lines, monitoring individual workers and teams, setting production schedules, and tracking supplies and inventories. Through the World Wide Web, companies now utilize computer networks to both advertise and market their products to consumers around the world. Finally, at the level of distribution, computerized tracking systems developed by Federal Express and emulated by other delivery companies provide firms unprecedented control over product distribution.

The computer, like the guided missile, is a metamodel of Techno-Performance. Both computer and missile research have created higher and higher standards of performance, and both are recognized by society as pushing the envelope of US science and technology. However, while the guided missile has functioned primarily as an emblem of high performance research and has spun off other technological performances, the computer's versatility—its ability to facilitate the design, testing, evaluation, manufacture, and distribution of countless other products—makes it a veritable *metatechnology*. The computer's performance overcodes and inscribes almost all others, for the computer helps produce other technological performances. In short, its performance helps create other performances. In doing so, the computer, more than any other contemporary technology, is helping to expand and consolidate the terrain of Techno-Performance research.

SATISFICIAL RITUALS

In studying the effectiveness of technologies, engineers and other applied scientists discuss performance in terms of the *behaviors, sensitivities, characteristics,* or *properties* which the technologies exhibit in a given context. Spatially, these behaviors may be exhibited in a laboratory or "in the field" or both; temporally, they may be analyzed during a technology's developmental or operational phase, although these phases are not always easy to distinguish. Even the spatial difference of lab and field may be blurred. When Vaughan says that for the shuttle, "flight was the ultimate test," the implication is this: the world has become a test site.

Earlier I stated that one way that the concept of technological performance has been generalized has been through the dissemination of high performance military research into nonmilitary markets. That the world has become a site for testing suggests another movement of generalization. We can understand this second movement by reading from a 1972 text entitled *Product Quality, Performance, and Cost: A Report and Recommendations Based on a Symposium and Workshops Arranged by the National Academy of Engineering*. In the wake of the 1960s' consumer movement led by Ralph Nader, this symposium and its related workshops brought together engineers, manufacturers, consumer advocates, and policy makers to examine issues surrounding the design, testing, and evaluation of consumer products.

This gathering of different groups itself indicates that predicting, measuring, and evaluating performances are not just matters for the engineers and scientists who design and test technologies. In one of the report's essays, Lewis M. Branscomb writes that "criteria for performance and value rest on sophisticated engineering considerations cast in a social context of real people who use, and misuse, the products made by industry."[39] Discussion comments reprinted in the report suggest that this broad contextual approach had not always been used in the testing and evaluation of products, but had evolved over decades. Gunnar A. Hambraeus of the Royal Swedish Academy of Engineering Science comments that "we have, in 50 years, moved from the nuts-and-bolts standards to intermediate standards and safety standards and, finally, to performance standards and information standards."[40] Similarly, Robert W. Peach, a manager of quality assurance at Sears, Roebuck and Company, states: "Our laboratory began—and continued for years—as a product-testing function, with full confidence that such testing would provide assurance that products that we sold would be of high quality. Today, our efforts can best be described as a systems approach toward assuring customer satisfaction through a carefully developed partnership between retailer and manufacturer."[41]

The discussion comments reprinted in *Product Quality, Performance, and Cost* strongly suggest that, concomitant with the emergence of this systems-oriented approach, the community of stakeholders has grown from engineers and scientists to include manufacturers and retailers and, ultimately, consumers and users. The 1990s, in fact, has seen the rise of new design approaches that foreground the nonspecialized user rather than the specialized designer.[42] George H. Stevens and Emily F. Stevens, a pair of computer scientists writing in 1995, suggest that if "there is a philosophy associated with effective design, it is one of *user-centered design*. Effective applications do not always need to dazzle eyes and ears with exotic images and sounds. They simply need to empower the user to perform, with the briefest of possible learning curves."[43] While the symposium participants commend these developments, the introduction of nonspecialists into the evaluative mix also reveals other problems. Carlos Fallon comments:

> One of the opportunities offered by this symposium is to improve the means of communication between users (most of whom appraise products in such terms as brightness, loudness, and sweetness) and producers (whose engineers think in terms of lumens, decibels, and sucrose). There is one language for what satisfies the consumer and another for the physical conditions that produce the satisfaction. This

is more than a question of terminology; it is a problem of the nonlinearity between physical properties and their effects on human beings.[44]

The nonlinearity Fallon describes here suggests the incommensurability and contradictions that exist between different forms of evaluation, different types of criteria that inform the design, marketing, and use of technologies. In such contexts, performance is often discussed as something that must be "traded off" against other factors, such as cost, safety, and ease of maintenance.

This trading-off of performance against other factors is quite common. To give an example: for audio engineers designing a low-end stereo system, increasing its sound fidelity performance may add such additional costs so as to price it out of the range of its intended consumers. On the other hand, reducing cost may decrease performance to such an extent that the system is no longer competitive even on the low-end market. Designers must therefore compromise or make trade-offs between performance and cost. Such trade-offs are actually the rule rather than the exception for both designers and consumers. Again, to cite *Product Quality, Performance, and Cost:*

The design trade-offs between performance, style, cost, safety, convenience, length of life, maintainability, and other quality factors present a multidimensional problem with many choices for both the designer and the consumer. Consumers will overemphasize one of these, such as cost, to the neglect of others, resulting in marginal performance and safety.[45]

Multidimensionsal trade-offs are crucial to the concept of technological performance, and thus to the entire paradigm of Techno-Performance. Another participant in the workshops puts it this way: "The trade-off of product performance against cost is an engineering problem. In fact, it may be *the* engineering problem, for it taxes the many facets of the engineer's capabilities, which run the gamut from individual technical competence to ingenuity, imagination, and professional ethics."[46]

Balancing performance with other factors may indeed be *the* engineering problem, or it may be just *one* of the problems requiring trade-offs. In addition to compromises with such "external" factors as cost and safety, effective performance is regularly subject to "internal" trade-offs. That is, this performance is itself multidimensional and marked by its own conflicts and compromises. As we saw in the case of guided missiles early in the Cold War, designers confront multiple and contradictory demands pertaining to the effectiveness of servomechanisms. Such contradictions remain common in the industries of weaponry and aeronautics, as J.C. Williams indicates in his 1995 discussion of high performance aerospace materials: "The selection of materials and of material conditions for lightweight structures is typically a problem bounded by multiple constraints, requiring a detailed understanding of all the materials' characteristics and all aspects of mechanical behavior."[47] As with the case of external constraints, making trade-offs with respect to effective performance is the rule rather than the exception.

Designers thus face making difficult trade-offs arising both from internal constraints pertaining to effectiveness *and* from such external constraints as cost, safety, and convenience. Such multisided, multidimensional trade-offs generate extraordinary pressures upon those closely engaged with any given technological performance. Here decision-making must take place via "bounded rationality," rationality defined more by limitations, contradiction, and paradox than by freedom, coherence, and orthodoxy. Or rather, paradox is here orthodox. And because satisfying all criteria is usually impossible, sacrifice becomes inevitable. Using a concept first coined by Herbert Simon, Vaughan writes that under such conditions, "performance is described as 'satisficing' rather than optimizing."[48] Technological performances are thus *satisficial* performances, the result of a long and open series of negotiations and compromises.

Because any given technological performance involves what we might call *satisficial rituals*, the formulation of effective performance standards is very difficult, to say the least. In fact, across a broad range of disciplines and specialties, the lack of performance standards is widely recognized and lamented, as this constellation of cites shows: Ahmed N. Tantawy, writing about high performance computer networks, stresses that "interoperationality is a necessity in heterogeneous networks. This translates into an urging [sic] need for standardization. The commercial market needs the security and safety of international standards (especially in communications!)."[49] From a research site of electric vehicles: ". . . methods for evaluating the performance of EVs and their components have not been established on an international basis. For example, even the testing methods for basic characteristics, such as a vehicle's acceleration and driving range per charge and a battery's energy density and power density, vary by country and developer."[50] From a research site of water soluble polymers: "A large number of methods have been used to assess the performance of drilling fluid additives as shale stabilizers. Unfortunately, no standard method is widely accepted in the industry."[51] And from a research site of municipal and regional infrastructures: "The committee found that there are few benchmarks or norms of performance that apply to infrastructure as a system, or even that apply comprehensively to any one type of infrastructure."[52]

We are now in a better position to understand the difficulty in defining the concept of technological performance. For nonspecialists, the term itself may only appear in contexts demarcated by highly technical sets of discourses and practices, whereas their own evaluations rely on terms from their everyday use of the technology in question. Yet within any one specialized context, the term "performance" may be so widespread and commonplace that to ask someone in the applied sciences "What is performance?" is to elicit a smile—at least at first. Then comes a very precise yet vague definition. But when the issue becomes that of implementing standards of performance, the response changes to one of great concern and urgency. Such responses point to the conflicted, even contradictory, dimensions that must be negotiated when defining the effectiveness of technological performances.

The definitional difficulties facing specialists and nonspecialists may also point to something else, namely, the expectations held by both concerning the form definitions should take. Defining the concept of technological performance even within a very specific experimental situation is difficult because *both specialist and nonspecialist expect definitions to be unified, coherent, and definitive, not multiple, contradictory, and provisional.* We expect clarity and instead we are faced with a cloud of competing characteristics and behaviors. We want to be satisfied, not make sacrifices. The skies become even cloudier as we shuttle from research site to research site. We are soon confronted with a storm of precise yet vague definitions of technological performance. Given the satisficial aspect of Techno-Performance research, it is little wonder that Borovits and Neumann preface their effective definition of performance by stating that it has no existence or meaning *per se.*

EFFECTIVENESS AND BEYOND

As with cultural and organizational performance, technological performance is a heavily contested concept. Its definition is highly contextual, even if I have defined this performance in general terms as "effectiveness in a given task," following the suggestion of Borovits and Neumann. We have seen, however, that even this definition is quite complex, for determining the effectiveness of any given technological performance involves a series of trade-offs, compromises, and satisfices among various factors. Despite the highly contextual and satisficial aspects of technological performance, researchers of Techno-Performance, like their counterparts in Performance Studies and Performance Management, have nonetheless generalized their concept of performance. This generalization has occurred through the dissemination of high performance military research into nonmilitary sites and markets, and through efforts to include consumers and users into decision-making processes concerning technological performances. I now wish to reconsider our general definition of performance-as-effectiveness, for the concept of technological performance has dramatically expanded and evolved in recent years.

A 1995 report by the National Research Council's Committee on Measuring and Improving Infrastructure Performance provides a far-reaching discussion of technological performance, as well as a definition that greatly extends and supplements our reading of this concept. Let us thus read closely from the Committee's report, *Measuring and Improving Infrastructure Performance*. The Committee explicitly addresses the concept of performance in two contiguous sections, "The Basic Concept of Performance," and "Performance Compared with Other Concepts: Need, Demand, and Benefits." These discussions are condensed and presented in the report's Executive Summary. There, in a section entitled "Defining Infrastructure Performance," we find this concise definition, framed in both general and specific terms:

> Generally speaking, performance is the carrying out of a task or fulfillment of some promise or claim, and for infrastructure this means enabling movement of goods and people, supplying clean water, disposing of wastes, and providing a variety of other services that support economic and social activities, protect public health and safety, and provide a safe environment and a sustainably high quality of life. Infrastructure is a means to other ends, and the effectiveness, efficiency, and reliability of its contribution to these other ends must ultimately be the measures of infrastructure performance.[53]

Effectiveness is central to the Committee's definition of performance. Indeed, effectiveness can be defined as "the carrying out of a task," and we have also seen that for engineers and computer scientists, the concept of performance is closely tied to the fulfillment of promises or predictions. However, in the second sentence just cited, the Committee not only uses the term "effectiveness," it also uses the terms "efficiency" and "reliability." With these two terms the Committee's definition of performance extends beyond that of Borovits and Neumann. It is also worth noting that the Committee uses "efficiency" not as a synonym of effectiveness but to refer to economic factors.

The Committee states that performance is composed of three separate functions or dimensions. Performance "may be defined as a function of *effectiveness, reliability,* and *cost.*"[54] With this definition, the Committee generalizes the concept of technological performance to include factors which we have seen other researchers contrast to it, factors that had to be negotiated and traded off against performance-as-effectiveness. Reliability, cost, and several other factors are here incorporated within an expanded concept of performance. However, this generalization by no means reduces the complexity of evaluating infrastructure performance. The Committee writes that the "three principal dimensions of performance are each, in turn, complex and multifaceted, typically requiring several measures to indicate how well infrastructure is performing."[55] Let us focus in on each dimension, noting as we do the extraordinary reach of the Committee's concept of technological performance.

By framing their discussion of performance in terms of the carrying out of a task and the fulfillment of a promise, the Committee confirms that effectiveness is the primary dimension of technological performance. Their definition of effectiveness, however, touches upon several other important factors as well: "Effectiveness, or the ability of the system to provide the services the community expects, is generally described by 1) capacity and delivery of services, 2) quality of services delivered, 3) the system's compliance with regulatory concerns, and 4) the system's broad impact on the community."[56] Thus, beyond the technical ability to provide and deliver expected services, effectiveness here includes factors which others might seek to trade off with performance, namely, quality, regulatory compliance, and social impact.

Such a generalizing movement also informs the Committee's discussion of reliability, which it defines as "the likelihood that infrastructure effectiveness will be maintained over an extended period of time or the probability that service will be available at least at specified levels throughout the design life of the infrastructure."[57] The Committee also states that other measures of reliable performance include "engineering safety factors, anticipated frequencies of recurrence (e.g., the '100-year flood'), or bases of identifying peak load (e.g., the '100th busiest hour')."[58] We see that while reliability is explicitly defined in terms of effectiveness, it also includes factors which could conceivably be negotiated against effectiveness (e.g., safety).

Finally, the Committee includes under its definition of performance the function of cost, whose basic elements are described as "initial construction or replacement cost (also called investment cost) and the recurring expenditures for operations and maintenance that will be required throughout the facility's or system's service life."[59] We recall that the trade-off between performance and cost is considered by some to be *the* engineering problem. Here, considerations of cost have been fully integrated within performance. The Committee later states that its definition of performance "is most closely allied with cost-effectiveness analysis."[60] Trade-offs between cost and effectiveness are still necessary, though now both are considered dimensions of performance. Further, the Committee's discussion extends beyond total costs to include issues relating to scheduling and budgeting. The Committee writes that "the questions of when money is spent, by whom, and from what budgets often have a great impact on the decisions that are ultimately made."[61]

Capacity and delivery of service, quality, regulatory compliance, social impact, reliability, safety, frequency of recurrence, peak-load capacity, investment and maintenance costs, scheduling and budgeting of expenditures—such are the complex contours of this concept of technological performance. Needless to say, the Committee's definition is far more explicit, far more theoretical, and far more general than any we have encountered to this point. For the Committee, "performance at the most detailed level of concern is related ultimately to higher levels."[62] And yet this general definition does not reduce the complexity and specificity of performance. Like Borovits and Neumann, the Committee is wary of ever defining it definitively. And like the participants of the symposium on product performance, they stress both the multidimensional nature of performance evaluation and the necessity of including many different stakeholders in the process. In fact, the Committee understands effectiveness as primarily a *political* matter, rather than a scientific one, while also recognizing the satisificial nature of technological performance.

> In our society, the answer to the question of "How effective. . . .?" is often determined in the political process not by scientific analysis. This is as it should be, but a number of factors make the political process somewhat cumbersome in determining acceptable performance. Regardless of how the decision is made, it is meant to represent how members of the public would individually make the acceptable performance decision. The collective decision is meant to reflect both judgments and perceptions of each person and their values. Different individuals, however, may have widely varying judgments and perceptions and very diverse values. There are no simple solutions to the collective decision in such a case. Such decisions cannot please everyone.[63]

For our purposes—the rehearsal of a general theory of performance—the most significant aspect of this 1995 report is that its discussion of technological performance indicates that organizational and cultural performance have already become important to Techno-Performance research. Its strong emphasis on decision-making processes points to the organizational dimension of technological performance, while the Committee's stress on community input suggests that social factors also play a significant role. I will now investigate further the liminautic feedback circuits between technological and organizational performance research and then turn to those installed between the study of technological and cultural performance.

SOCIOLOGIES OF TECHNOLOGIES

The social dimension of technological performances is not external to some realm of pure technology. While one can compose readings that focus on the technical history of a particular device or system, this can only be done by disconnecting the technology from the social forces that help to produce it. Before any production, before there is a high performance missile, computer, or transit system, there are only projects, and projected technologies are more social than technological, more fantastic than objective. As sociologist Bruno Latour writes, "By definition, a technological project is a fiction, since at the outset it does not exist. . . . In the beginning, there is no distinction between projects and objects. The two circulate from office to office in the form of paper, plans, departmental memos, speeches, scale models, and occasional synopses."[64] Only gradually does a technological performance become sedimented into a real object; its initiation and development are social and organizational. Many projects remain fictions without ever being realized.

The generalization of technological performance, its expansion to include technical and social dimensions, coincides with the growing interest of sociologists in technological projects, in particular, in the organizational processes that surround, nourish, and sometimes terminate them. Over the past two decades, there has emerged a "sociology of technology" or "science studies" movement, one that has produced detailed sociological and cultural analyses of specific technical systems. Reading from two of these studies, we can refine our understanding of Techno-Performance and its expansion into society, while also reflecting upon our own reading of this paradigm.

Latour's recent text, *ARAMIS or the Love of Technology* (1996) is one such sociology of technology. As the title suggests, it delves into the heart of a sociotechnical system. This experimental text studies an infrastructural performance that, after nearly two decades of research and investments totaling over 150 million francs, remains a fiction to this day. Latour's object of study is a French self-guided rail system called ARAMIS (an acronym for *Agencement en Rames Automatisées de Modules Indépendants dans les Stations*, "arrangement in automated trains of independent modules in stations").[65] But ARAMIS never made it out of the research station: after it had survived as a highly publicized pet project of the Mitterand government, the project was unceremoniously canceled by the Chirac government in 1987. But the story is even more complicated than these partisan politics suggest, so to trace the demise of a project that gained a little reality only to lose it completely, Latour writes a theoretical tale, what he calls a "scientifiction."[66] To compose his *ARAMIS*, he frames his research documents and interview transcripts within a fictive scene of research, crafting a tale that is part detective novel, part love story, part sociology textbook. The prologue is entitled "Who Killed ARAMIS?", the epilogue "ARAMIS Unloved," while the plot in between matches up a studious young engineer and a sardonic professor of sociology.

Our interest here lies in Latour's reading of the social dimension of technological projects and his suggestions on how to best to study it. Paradoxically, he finds that even after a project enters development, social forces predominate over technical ones. "The more a technological project progresses, the more the role of technology decreases, in relative terms: such is the paradox of development."[67] As we might expect from our reading of infrastructure performance, it is the interactions of multiple stakeholders and not just technical factors that guide or derail a project's development. And as we have learned from several other cites, the entire process is marked by trade-offs and satisfices. Latour finds that compromises between different stakeholders are absolutely necessary for any technological project to become an object. "The only way to increase a project's reality is to compromise, to accept sociotechnological compromises."[68] Development via sociotechnological compromise—in our terms, sociotechnical satisficing—entails transferring or translating a project from a specific site to broader, more general ones. Yet "to translate is to betray: ambiguity is part of translation."[69] A project that stays on paper or in the lab remains just that: a project. "The only thing a technological project cannot do is implement itself without placing *itself* in a broader context. If it refuses to contextualize itself, it may remain technologically perfect, but unreal."[70] Starting out as an obscure transportation project in the late 1960s, ARAMIS was subsequently transferred through a host of institutional contexts; at its grandest stop, it was hailed by supporters as paradigmatic of France's technological capabilities. Yet once it lost contextual support, once it ran out of *love*, ARAMIS died.

Latour's analysis refines our understanding of the difficulties in reading the performance of even a single technology, as well as the challenge of scanning an entire paradigm of Techno-Performance. The very development of a technology requires that it pass through diverse sites, changing and altering its performance under the pressures of different sociotechnical criteria. Latour created his scientifiction precisely to track such transformations, giving it flexible contours: "A fiction with 'variable geometry': this is what needs to be invented, if we are to track the variations of a technological project that has the potential to become an object."[71] Similarly, our own reading machine has been transmuted by its passage through the various citations collected here, only in our case we have been moving at high speeds across distant sites in order to theorize the concept of technological performance and the paradigm of Techno-Performance.

To focus in more sharply on the paradigmatic infrastructure of technological performance research, let us now switch tracks and take as our guide someone cited in ARAMIS. The citation occurs within an American *mise en scène*, a 1965 Senate hearing on Personal Rapid Transit systems. As should be evident by now, Latour's project not only calls for the use of artistic practices, but is itself an artistic experiment. In it, a Senator Don MacKenzie makes a brief, cameo appearance. His first words are, "But Professor. . . ."[72] This senator is a scientifictional character, and Latour has taken his name and figure from another sociologist of technology, Donald MacKenzie. It is to this researcher's work that we now turn.

Donald MacKenzie is the author of several sociologies of technologies, including *Inventing Accuracy: A Historical Sociology of Nuclear Missile Guidance* (1990). This text focuses on missile guidance systems, but MacKenzie's aim is even wider: "In studying guidance, we are of course examining but a single aspect of the processes of the creation of nuclear weapons technology. But my aim in studying guidance has been to throw light on these processes more generally."[73] MacKenzie's reading machine, like ours, thus involves a movement of generalization that takes off from specific sites. His interest lies in the invention of accuracy, specifically, the invention of nuclear missiles whose effective performance can not only rain down on large cities, but can strike individual missile silos and command centers. In other words, such missiles are not just accurate, they are *extremely* accurate. In the early 1960s, US and Soviet ICBMs were accurate within 2 nautical miles (5220 yards); by 1980, their estimated accuracy was around 0.13 nautical mile—about 250 yards.[74] MacKenzie's question: how was such extraordinary accuracy achieved?

Though MacKenzie does not attempt a scientifiction, his text provides important material for our own reading of Techno-Performance. The guiding thesis of *Inventing Accuracy* is that extremely accurate missile performance does not result from some "natural" evolution of guidance technology. "Rather it is the product of a complex process of conflict and collaboration between a range of social actors including ambitious, energetic technologists, laboratories and corporations, and political and military leaders and the organizations they head. The invention of accuracy has fueled, and has itself been fueled by, the cold war. It has been a shaping force, but has itself been shaped."[75] The emphasis here on conflict and collaboration recalls the satisficial rituals discussed above, and as with the studies by Latour and the Committee on Measuring and Improving Infrastructure Performance, MacKenzie's approach is sociotechnical. For him a "technology is not just social up to the point of invention and self-sustaining thereafter. Its conditions of possibility are always social."[76]

We have returned to the technological performance from whence we started, that of guided missiles, which we have also cited as paradigmatic of Techno-Performance research. Guided by rocket science, this research paradigm crystallized within the military-industrial complex of Cold War America, and MacKenzie's study sheds light on this complex and, more generally, upon the role of social institutions in technological change.

> To talk of the "institutionalization" of a pattern of technological change means several things. First, it indicates the existence of a relatively stable organizational framework within which the technological change takes place. . . . Second, institutionalization implies the channeling of resources to support this organizational framework and its activities. . . . [Third, it indicates] the credibility of the prophe-

> cy that is at its core. Organizations are created and sustained, and resources flow, to the extent that it is believed that the predicted change in technology will become, or at least has a chance to become, a reality.[77]

MacKenzie's analysis focuses on specific military and corporate institutions, as well as key individuals who invented the devices at the heart of extremely accurate missiles, namely, inertial or self-contained guidance mechanisms. The pattern of technological change he tracks concerns these specialized, high performance mechanisms. Our concern, however, is with a much broader change: the emergence of a research paradigm that, though guided by rocket science, extends far beyond it. America's military-industrial complex provided the organizational framework and resources for the consolidation of Techno-Performance research at the end of the Second World War, as well as the legitimating prophecy that not only could high performance weapon projects become reality, but they also would be essential to defeating Communism.

The technosociologies of both Latour and MacKenzie reveal the social dimension of any technological project. In addition, their specific objects of study—a rapid transit system and guided nuclear missiles—show how the performance of such technologies can become a matter of the state. Evaluation of these technologies becomes highly complex, as their assessment grows to include not only engineers and technicians, but also bureaucrats, politicians, and even the national public. In Chapter 4 we will examine what such complex evaluation entails.

For now, let us examine further the wider social dimension of guided missiles. We have already described their role within the military-industrial complex and, more generally, the Techno-Performance paradigm. Let us briefly consider their impact in US society at large. To improve the accuracy of my own reading machine: the expansion of Techno-Performance research over the past five decades has relied not on the military-industrial complex but more precisely on what Senator William J. Fulbright eventually came to call the "military-industrial-academic complex."[78] This inclusion of the academy is crucial to understanding the importance of technological performance research in American society. Stuart Leslie writes that prior to the Second World War, the US military had forged only limited alliances with university researchers, these being primarily in aeronautics. But such partnerships increased dramatically during the war, and rather than end or reduce them after the Allied victory, "the military, shaken out of its traditional complacency by the wonder weapons of the war—radar, the proximity fuse, solid fuel rockets, and of course the atomic bomb—and by the power of the contract to deliver them, was willing and able to prolong the wartime pattern of cooperative research. General Dwight Eisenhower drew up detailed plans for extending the partnership of science, industry, and the military into the postwar world."[79] Thus, the number of high performance research sites further increased during the Cold War and drew heavily on researchers employed in universities.

More significantly, research conducted by the military-industrial-academic complex or, for short, the *MIA complex*, has in no way been limited to the laboratories of the Army, Navy, and Air Force, nor those of military contractors. Research universities were themselves targeted as sites for expanding the MIA complex and its Big Science projects.

> "Big Science" was one of the hallmarks of the scientific enterprise in the postwar period, and one whose genesis and destiny was closely tied to the fortunes of the national security state. But it was not only at Los Alamos, Oak Ridge, and Lawrence Livermore or at Lockheed, General Electric and MITRE that American science was being transformed, but also in the individual classrooms and laboratories where the people who would one day work in those institutions were being trained.[80]

The expansion of the MIA complex to include educational sites is another way to read the term "Big Science," which more commonly refers to large-scale, heavily funded research projects.[81] The massive expansion of Big Science into the university ensured that even those who did not wind up working on military projects were also influenced by the MIA complex, for its projects "virtually redefined what it meant to be a scientist or an engineer."[82] In short, the Big Science of the MIA complex reshaped entire disciplines of research and training.

Moreover, the growth of Big Science did not stop at the college level. In the wake of the Soviet *Sputnik* launch in October 1957, the MIA complex reached down into elementary and high schools. The December 1957 issue of *The Science Teacher* contained an article entitled "Children, Put Away Your Sputniks," which lamented that the "time for discussing sputniks will probably never come" to most American school childern because they are "without a respectable science program."[83] Military, political, and social concerns over the *Sputnik* launch and the perceived "missile gap" between the US and the USSR led Congress to pass the National Defense Education Act of 1958, which provided $900 million for education. Both the Act and the funding were unprecedented in American history. Barbara Barksdale Clowse writes that the "sputnik crisis transformed the politics of federal aid to education; it altered the terms of the debate and temporarily neutralized much of the opposition. The cold war rivalry seemed to dictate that the nation mobilized her brainpower, including schoolchildren and undergraduate and graduate students, on an emergency basis."[84] The full-blown emergence of Techno-Performance must be read as a response to a full-blown national emergency.

The post-*Sputnik* mobilization of brainpower and the National Defense Education Act initiated large-scale federal funding to education, and the government's decades-long emphasis on high performance technologies altered the nation's education system by privileging the physical sciences over both the social sciences and the humanities. With respect to advanced research, Leslie states that "the long-term costs only gradually became apparent in academic programs and corporate products so skewed toward the cutting-edge performance of military technology that they had nothing to give to the civilian economy."[85] As we have seen, however, high performance technologies and, even more importantly, the research and educational practices associated with them have trickled down from the MIA complex into our everyday lives. Conversely, the expansion of the military-industrial-academic complex was itself socially legitimated for decades by nationwide fears of Communist takeover and global annihilation. In the wake of the Cold War, new fears become necessary—terrorists, "rogue" nations, and info-wars. At its limits, a sociology of Techno-Performance would entail an ongoing study of American society itself, while calculating the opportunity costs associated with the MIA complex may be an impossible task.

BETWEEN THEATER AND THE LAB

Perhaps one of the most striking cultural paradoxes of the late twentieth century was that while many practitioners, critics, and scholars sadly observed theater's precipitous decline as an art form, it nonetheless continued to provide vibrant and supple models for studying and producing events *outside* the theater. Within the paradigm of Performance Studies, for instance, theater has been developed into an analytical tool by anthropologists, psychologists, and sociologists to study the social efficacy of performative forms. Similarly, in Performance Management, organizational theorists have used theater as both a metaphor and an analytical tool for studying organizations and for developing more innovative and efficient performances. Everyday life, rituals, business meetings, organizations themselves—all have been theorized "as" theater. However, it may still come as a surprise that behaviors and sites associated with technological performance have also been studied as theater. In this section, I will briefly discuss two such research projects.

We have seen that the generalization of technological performance has occurred in part through the inclusion of consumers and users into the design and evaluation of technologies. This approach has become known as user-oriented design, and it has led to attempts to use the performing arts as a model in the design of technologies. In *Computers as Theatre* (1993), Brenda Laurel argues that the design and development of human–computer interfaces cannot be left up to engineers and computer scientists alone. "A scientific approach still dominates the design of human–computer interaction today. Such disciplines as cognitive psychology, ergonomics, and optics have been drawn in to support computer scientists in the task of designing interfaces for their applications."[86] Countering this scientific dominance, she argues that the focus on interface design and interface metaphors must be redirected to what she calls "designing experience." Laurel writes that "designing human–computer experience isn't about building a better desktop. It's about creating imaginary worlds that have a special relationship to reality—worlds in which we can extend, amplify, and enrich our own capabilities to think, feel, and act. . . . [T]he theatrical domain can help us in this task."[87] In this computers-as-theater approach, technologies are defined not as scientific tools but as artistic mediums. At the same time, scientific methodologies are not discarded but are instead supplemented by the more intuitive methods of the performing arts.

Laurel's strategy consists of theorizing human–computer interaction (HCI) in terms of theatrical representation, specifically the aesthetics found in Aristotle's *Poetics*. She systematically translates Aristotle's six dramatic elements (spectacle, melody, language, character, thought, and plot), and four causes (material, formal, efficient, and teleological) into the realm of interface design. Thus, for instance, spectacle and melody within HCI translate, respectively, into the "sensory dimensions of the action being represented" by the computer and the "pleasurable perception of pattern in sensory phenomena."[88] Obviously, from a cultural performance perspective, the most significant transformation introduced here is the inclusion of both human and computer actors in the realm of aesthetic experience. For Laurel, coherency of action and the resulting cathartic pleasure define the criteria of any human–computer interaction. Significantly, she also suggests that in the future, some interactions might lead to experiences found in ritual contexts. "I think we can someday have Dionysian experiences in virtual reality, and that they will be experiences of the most intimate and powerful kind. But to do so we must breathe life into our tools. Our creative force must be manifest, not as an *artifact* but as a *collaborator*—an extension of ourselves embodied in our systems."[89]

Elsewhere I have discussed Laurel's project to conceptualize computers as theater in relation to both virtual reality technologies and recent works of the performance artist Laurie Anderson.[90] While I have questioned her selection of Aristotle's *Poetics* as the most relevant model of theater for her purposes, her allusion above to Dionysian rituals points in the direction of other research: the exploration of other forms of cultural performance as models of HCI, including experimental theater, popular entertainments, and performance art. And indeed, in 1995 there emerged a new media company in New York City's Silicon Alley called SiteSpecific. Drawing on backgrounds in the performing arts, its founders sought to create site-specific performance on the World Wide Web and explicitly cited 1970s performance art as a model for their approach. Similarly, one of the most successful programs on the market today for creating interactive multimedia is MacroMedia's

Director, which incorporates "stages," "scenes," and other theatrical metaphors into its interface. These developments confirm Laurel's basic intuition that cultural performance offers powerful models for human–computer interactions.

A second and very different use of theater as a conceptual model within the sciences can be found in Robert P. Crease's *The Play of Nature: Experimentation as Performance* (1993). Although Crease, a philosopher of science, focuses primarily on basic rather than applied science (e.g., physics rather than engineering), his theorization of experimentation is applicable to both and, further, he pays close attention to the role played by laboratory technologies in the production of "performances." "The laboratory, like the theatre, is a special place where special things are learned. But those special things can be learned only because the laboratory has been specially constructed to execute and witness particular kinds of actions."[91] He frames his project by arguing that philosophers of science have neglected experimentation and focused instead almost entirely on theory. In doing so, they have tended to reinforce a "mythical account" of experimentation, in which theorists are seen as visionaries of eternal truths and experimenters as merely confirmers of their insights. This myth is linked "with a general view of science as principally a body of information rather than practices,"[92] a positivist view that has been criticized on the grounds that such truths are historically and socially constructed. Crease's work is clearly sympathetic with this critique; however, he does not believe that the phenomena disclosed in experiments can be reduced to social epiphenomena. Paraphrasing Marx, he writes that "human beings make science, but not any way they please. The fact they 'make' science means the presence of social factors is irreducible; the fact it is 'not any way they please' means invariants are involved. A principal task of contemporary philosophy of science, in my view, is to create a model of this interaction."[93]

The model Crease proposes of the interaction between physical invariants and social factors is the performing arts and, in particular, theater. Though he at times refers to musical performance, he uses theater to develop an argumentative analogy, a "more or less point-by-point comparison between scientific experimentation and theatrical performance."[94] For him, what experiments produce are phenomenological performances. "Performance is first of all an execution of an action in the world which is a *presentation* of a phenomenon; that action is related to a *representation* (for example, a text, script, scenario, or book), using a semiotic system (such as a language, a scheme of notation, a mathematical system); finally, a performance springs from and is presented to a suitably prepared local (historically and culturally bound) community which *recognizes* new phenomena in it."[95] Crease's philosophical framework for this experimentation-as-performance analogy is hermeneutical phenomenology, which combines Edmund Husserl's phenomenology of invariant structures and Martin Heidegger's hermeneutical insight that phenomena only appear through historically determined practices of interpretation.[96] This framework informs Crease's title, *The Play of Nature*. "Play is here meant in the sense of an infinite, ceaseless activity that exhibits a myriad of forms in as many situations. Yet this play is not chaotic or random, but governed by patterned, discoverable constraints."[97]

To demonstrate the saliency of his rigorously playful analogy, Crease first theorizes the experimental hall as a theatrical space in which phenomena are presented: "The hall has been constructed specifically for the purpose of facilitating the performance and witnessing a specific kind of action therein. It is a *theatron*, or place for enacting and seeing a performance; better still, given that the stage is everywhere and the *audience*. . . . as it were on the outskirts, an *amphi-theatron*."[98] Technological performance is crucial in this laboratory theater, for "advances in the technology of experimentation make possible greater performance capabilities."[99] Crease then argues that theories must be understood in relation to the primacy of performance. In this light, theories are representational scripts. "A theory, we might say, *scripts* a phenomenon."[100] The privileging of representation over presentation in traditional philosophy of science corresponds to the hierarchization of theory over experimentation in science and text over *mise en scène* in traditional theater studies, aligning Crease's critical gesture with early Performance Studies research which challenged the primacy of the text.[101] Yet Crease also develops an analogy between the production of theatrical performances and production which goes into scientific experimentation—namely, the politics and economics of research funding, environmental regulations, and the logistics of securing lab time—a perspective with much affinity to what I have called "postexplosion" Performance Studies. In the end, Crease defines performance in terms of the presencing of invariants and production in terms of the social context in which they appear, thereby addressing the concerns of both positivists and social constructivists. "Like the general analogy between the sciences and the theatrical arts of which it is a part, the analogy with production helps guide development of a language with which to speak about experimental activity that enables one to assign a place both to the cultural and historical contexts that influence experimental activity (and which, for instance, are studied by social constructivists) and at the same time to the invariants that show through such contexts in that activity (on which positivists and scientists themselves rightly place so much emphasis)."[102]

In terms of our general theory, the texts of Laurel and Crease operate within the liminautic feedback of technological and cultural performance. They develop their argumentative analogies of "X-as-theater" not as superficial metaphors but as analytical tools that pass from one field of performance to another. And though each targets a different X, a different site of research activity, each turns to one of the founding metamodels of cultural performance. Laurel and Crease create their theatrical analogies to stress the importance of subjective experience and creativity within areas long dominated by values of objectivity and rational methodology. In this regard, the development of cultural performance analogies to theorize human–computer interactions and laboratory experimentation can be connected both to the contention that engineering design is an art due to the nonquantifiable judgments involved there, as well as to arguments that the evaluation of computer systems is also an art because it relies on intuitive and nonrigorous methods. Further, we can begin to sense the applicability of cultural performance models in understanding the decision-making processes guiding the design, construction, and evaluation of technological performances that range from consumer products to public infrastructure systems. Indeed, the cast of different stakeholders or social actors participating in any technological performance, the dramatic conflicts that arise from their different frames of evaluation, the necessity of playing out and resolving these conflicts—all this portends the ritual satisficing of efficacy, efficiency, and effectiveness. This reading looms just over the horizon.

LIMINAUTIC TRAJECTORIES

Our rehearsal of a general theory of performance has thus far focused on three fields of performance—cultural, organizational, and technological. At the same time, I have attempted to track the emergence of their corresponding research paradigms, Performance Studies, Performance Management, and Techno-Performance. In preparation for the next stage of our rehearsal process, let us now investigate some of their interrelationships.

Each field is structured and guided by a different challenge, a different set of criteria for creating and evaluating performances. Cultural performance, as produced and studied by Performance Studies researchers, entails the embodiment of symbolic structures in living behavior and, crucially, the transformation of these structures through discourses and practices of transgression, resistance, and mutation. The challenge is thus one of social efficacy. Organizational performance, as designed and reviewed by Performance Management researchers, consists of tasks and strategies for maximizing an organization's output and minimizing its input; these tasks and strategies are both human and technological. The challenge here is one of organizational efficiency. Technological performance, as engineered and evaluated by Techno-Performance researchers, refers to the behaviors and properties that technologies exhibit while executing specific tasks in specific contexts. Here the challenge is defined in terms of technical effectiveness. Efficacy, efficiency, and effectiveness are thus the respective valorimeters of the three performance paradigms.

In discussing these paradigms of performance research, I have focused on the specific historical and institutional contexts in which each emerged. Performance Studies is the youngest and, not surprisingly, the least institutionalized of the three paradigms. Though the concept of cultural performance owes much to theater history, the emergence of interdisciplinary Performance Studies research begins in the 1950s and comes of age in the United States during the political and social unrest of the 1960s and early 1970s. Significantly, the formal institutionalization of Performance Studies begins in the United States in 1980 and continues through the long decade of Reaganomics, neo-conservative social policies, and the development of new forms of mediated cultural resistance. The concept of organizational performance dates back at least to the early twentieth century. However, Performance Management emerges after the Second World War, when managers and organizational theorists inaugurated what would eventually become a paradigm shift away from the rational model of Scientific Management. The institutionalized study of Performance Management extends across every conceivable type of organization, though its most formalized study occurs in business and management schools. The rise of this performance paradigm coincides with the emergence of the service/information economy. The concept of technological performance also extends back prior to the Second World War, but because I have found little or no historical reflection upon it, its earlier history awaits more research and construction. I have attempted here to track the postwar emergence of an interdisciplinary paradigm which I call "Techno-Performance." Spearheaded by research into high performance missiles and computer systems, Techno-Performance has been institutionalized in the United States for a half-century, starting in its military-industrial-academic complex and then branching out into the production and marketing of common consumer products.

The trajectories of these paradigms are unique, yet they are nonetheless entwined. Their different passages to paradigm twist around one another, at times forming oppositions, at times alliances, but for many decades functioning largely in ignorance of each other's performance research. Here I want to draw attention to certain patterns that connect Performance Studies, Performance Management, and Techno-Performance. Perhaps what is most striking—and momentous—is that all three paradigms unfold within a particular historical formation whose coordinates first emerge in Cold War America but are today graphing themselves around a multicultural, multinational, and multimediated world. This global performative matrix will be explored momentarily. Here, however, I wish to entertain some other striking structural and processual affinities between the three performance paradigms.

If our readings thus far have demonstrated nothing else, they have shown that performance is a heavily contested concept no matter whether one is discussing cultural, organizational, or technological behaviors. To put this another way: though each paradigm's concept of performance differs markedly from the other two, the paradigms are similar in that each devotes much time and effort to interpreting, debating, and contesting the semantic definition and pragmatic deployment of performance within its particular field of inquiry. Each paradigm is dedicated in its own way to posing and reposing the question "What is performance?" while at the same time resisting any overarching definition. Part of this ongoing questioning results from the fact that each paradigm valorizes process over product and structuration over structure. Across the paradigms, performance is a moving target, for it is defined as a dynamic event, not a static entity. Yet these events have been relatively discrete, that is, they are largely taken as disconnected from one another.

The intense focus of their respective investigations no doubt contributes to the fact that the different performance paradigms operated for decades in almost total ignorance of each other's performance research. Such ignorance comes as no surprise, given the increasing specialization of knowledge and research over the course of the twentieth century. It is therefore important to stress that by supplementing the question "What is performance?" with the question "Which performance?" other types of performance come into play, as do new avenues of comparative analysis that allow one to better study the forms and functions of performance within any given paradigm of research.

Another affinity between Performance Studies, Performance Management, and Techno-Performance may be surprising at first but, upon reflection, understandable: all three paradigms valorize the testing and contesting of norms. Performance Studies scholars have come to privilege those cultural performances that transgress and/or resist the dominant norms of a given social situation: this has become the defining trait of "liminality." Performance Management theorists and managers, while using very different discourse, likewise stress the continual overcoming of organizational limitations: thus they use terms such as "managing creativity," "affirming diversity," and "thinking outside the box." For their part, engineers and scientists of Techno-Performance design and produce highly experimental phenomena in both their laboratories and the field in order to test the limits of materials and systems: thus, the terms "cutting-edge" and "risk-taking" are commonly used to describe these technological performances.

Obviously, the norms tested and contested within each paradigm are not only quite divergent, the different testings would no doubt be subject to very different evaluations within the other performance paradigms. From the perspective of Performance Studies, "thinking outside the box" might be deemed normative because of its institutional inscription. Some Techno-Performance researchers might also scoff at "thinking outside the box," especially when it impacts the funding or organization of their own research, while also finding liminality to be either merely entertaining or irrelevant or both. Alternatively, some Performance Management researchers might agree with this evaluation of liminality, while also dismissing cutting-edge technologies as unnecessarily wasteful or costly. On the other hand, certain performance researchers might sense and affirm the mutational forces operating in all three paradigms and seek to explore ways to connect and extend them.

While the three paradigms have each resisted attempts to articulate an overarching definition of performance and have instead stressed its highly contextual and processual character, they have all nonetheless generalized their respective performance concepts. That is, although individual researchers in each paradigm conduct detailed research of specific performances, the collective, decades-long extension of performance concepts across different sites of practice and the theorization of this deployment have *de facto* contributed to movements of generalization within each paradigm. In short, all three paradigms share an affinity for generalization.[103] This generalization has generally occurred in at least four specific ways: 1) through the introduction of new objects of inquiry, i.e., new cultural activities, new organizational practices, and new technical phenomena; 2) by the emergence of new methods of inquiry, e.g., deconstruction, systems theory, and computer modeling; 3) by the development of metaphors into interdisciplinary analytical tools, as evidenced in all three paradigms by the extraordinary resiliency of theater; and 4) through the entrance of new subjects of inquiry, i.e., members of groups long marginalized or excluded from conducting performance research, whose entry brings with it new objects, methods, and/or metaphors. Over the past three decades especially, new objects, methods, metaphors, and subjects have entered into all three performance paradigms, often contesting existing norms and definitions and diverting yet nonetheless contributing to their movements of conceptual generalization.

Our general theory is itself a generalization directed, in part, by these movements of generalization. The paradigmatic passages have relied upon specific metamodels, performances that have served as models for the fields and for the paradigms themselves. Likewise, the metamodel of the general theory is partially composed from components of specific paradigmatic models. In Chapter 1, liminal rites of passage emerged as a metamodel of Performance Studies, while Chapter 2 showed that feedback served this function in Performance Management. What of Techno-Performance? Given its lack of paradigmatic self-reflection, identifying a metamodel for Techno-Performance is difficult. However, in light of the role which the MIA complex has played in the paradigm's development and, further, the role which rocket science has played within this complex and within American society at large, the missile stands as one of the most emblematic models of Techno-Performance. Though it's not all rocket science, the development of technological performance research since the Second World War cannot be thought without citing high performance missiles, missiles that range from the V-2, the Red Stone, the Delta and Saturn V to the contemporary Stinger, Scuds, and Tomahawks. In the vapor trail and spin-offs of all these missiles has arisen the paradigm of Techno-Performance.

From the perspective of our general theory, there are thus three meta-models of performance: rites of passage, feedback loops, and missiles. My selection of the missile here is in some sense strategic, as it will help us compose an online metaguidance device, one capable of navigating beyond the terrains of paradigmatic performances. "Although it is like stating the obvious," states Charles White, "one is led to say that missiles could not perform without guidance."[104] Missiles are already inscribed within the liminautic circuits that operate between rites of passage and feedback, for missile guidance systems depend upon feedback devices known as servomechanisms or servos. Further, the "guided missile may be thought of as a large servo system comprising many small servo mechanisms."[105] In other words, a guided missile is a feedback device. With its target being the desired output, information about the missile's current speed and position is inputed into its servomechanism, deviations between input and output calculated and signaled to the navigation system, and corrections made again and again to its flight path. MacKenzie's input puts the output into perspective: "Look out the window of the room in which you are now sitting. Focus on a tree or building about a hundred yards or meters away. Imagine a circle with your room at its center and that object on its edge. That circle defines the accuracy of the most modern U.S. strategic missiles."[106]

There is a strange loop connecting the metamodels of rites of passage, feedback, and missiles, and through it, the paradigms of Performance Studies, Performance Management, and Techno-Performance and their respective challenges of efficacy, efficiency, and effectiveness. This loop defines the twisted and broken trajectory our metamodelization will take from here on out. We have thus far limited ourselves to moving between paradigms of cultural, organizational, and technological performance, but now our general theory must attempt other flights of generalization and thereby risk some gestures of transcendence and metalanguage. Yet our metamodel must also touch down time and again in order to map the rocky stratum on which these paradigms have built themselves. Things won't be as straightforward as sending up a missile and bringing it down on a predetermined target.

Our mission is to relaunch the general theory. Again, our passage involves what is called a strange loop. In certain eccentric circles, strange loops are distinguished from feedback loops in that they violate system boundaries, while feedback loops respect such limits and norms. Douglas Hofstadter provides some direction here: "The 'Strange Loop' phenomenon occurs whenever, by moving upwards (or downwards) through the levels of some hierarchical system, we unexpectedly find ourselves right back where we started."[107] The path we trace passes through a tangled hierarchy of performance, an unstable system with interconnected levels of performative specificity and generality. It is an odd hierarchy, one marked by iterative patterns of order and chaos, by blind flights and queer characters, and by a number of dramatic surprises. "A Tangled Hierarchy occurs when what you presume are clean hierarchical levels take you by surprise and fold back in a hierarchy-violating way. The surprise element is important; it is the reason I call Strange Loops 'strange.' "[108] Let us loop back, then, toward our point of departure, the challenging ends of *Perform or Else*, only this time we'll make use of a scientifictional craft, one whose mission is to scan the age of global performance.

PART II:
THE AGE OF GLOBAL PERFORMANCE

I REMEMBER WHEN WE WERE GOING TO GO INTO OUTER SPACE.
I REMEMBER WHEN THE PRESIDENT SAID WE WERE GOING TO LOOK FOR THINGS IN OUTER SPACE.
AND I REMEMBER THE WAY THE ASTRONAUTS TALKED AND THE WAY EVERYBODY WAS WATCHING BECAUSE THERE WAS A CHANCE THAT THEY WOULD BURN UP ON THE LAUNCHING PAD OR THAT THE ROCKET WOULD TAKE OFF FROM CAPE CANAVERAL AND LAND IN FORT LAUDERDALE FIVE MINUTES LATER BY MISTAKE.
AND NOW WE'RE NOT EVEN TRYING TO GET THAT FAR.
NOW IT'S MORE LIKE THE BUS.
NOW IT'S MORE LIKE THEY GO UP JUST HIGH ENOUGH TO GET A GOOD VIEW.
THEY AIM THE CAMERA BACK DOWN. THEY DON'T AIM THE CAMERA UP.
AND THEN THEY TAKE PICTURES AND COME RIGHT BACK TO DEVELOP THEM.
THAT'S WHAT IT'S LIKE NOW. NOW THAT'S WHAT IT'S LIKE.

Laurie Anderson, 1984

CHAPTER 4. CHALLENGER LECTURE MACHINE

In rehearsing a general theory of performance, I have articulated a number of challenges: Performance Studies' challenge of social efficacy, Performance Management's challenge of organizational efficiency, Techno-Performance's challenge of technological effectiveness, and, more generally, the challenge to perform—or else. In addition, I have articulated this entire project as, precisely, a challenge and have done so with an eye toward the metamodelization of the general theory itself, something that has been guiding my lecture machine from afar for quite some time.

On the morning of 28 January 1986, I stood at a lectern teaching freshman writing at the University of Florida. I was a graduate student, and it was my first year teaching. One hundred and thirty-five miles to the southeast, at Kennedy Space Center, another teacher was about to give the lesson of her life. On this bitterly cold morning (there had been a freak Florida freeze the night before), Teacher-in-Space Christa McAuliffe sat aboard NASA's space shuttle *Challenger*, which had begun launch sequence for mission 51-L. The sky was clear, the airwaves open. That freezing morning at Kennedy, it was not one teacher going into space—if we make this judgment affirmatively, it was an entire world of teachers. Lifting off at 11:38 EST, *Challenger* carried with it a crew of seven Americans: Commander Richard Scobee, Pilot Michael Smith, Mission Specialists Ronald McNair, Ellison Onizuka, and Judy Resnick, and Payload Specialists Gregory Jarvis and Christa McAuliffe. From the perspectives of our three performance paradigms, *Challenger* 51-L promised to be a high performance mission.

From a technological perspective, the shuttle embodied an unprecedented design. While plans for space "ferries" date back to German rocket science of the 1940s,[1] NASA's shuttle was the world's first fully operational, reusable space craft, and its construction required the testing and evaluation of millions of individual components. The shuttle was the latest embodiment of a series of high performance space vehicles designed by NASA, a series that includes the *Mercury*, *Gemini*, *Apollo*, and *Skylab* missions.

Organizationally, NASA's long-standing reputation as a high performance institution was on the line. This reputation had been firmly established by NASA's response to President Kennedy's 1961 challenge to land a man on the moon before that decade's end and return him safely back to Earth. Overcoming an erratic start and the deaths of three astronauts in an on-ground fire, NASA's *Apollo* program successfully completed the first manned lunar mission in the summer of 1969. The program behind the shuttle or Space Transportation System was attempting to carry on this tradition of excellence under a new set of organizational constraints, including a tight financial budget and loss of public interest in space flight.

From a cultural perspective, this particular *Challenger* mission was to be performed by a seven-person crew that "looked like America." In addition to Scobee, Smith, and Jarvis, all three American men of European descent, the multicultural crew included the Jewish-American woman Resnick, the African-American McNair, the Japanese-Hawaiian-American Onizuka, and the Euro-American McAuliffe. The *Challenger* shuttle craft itself, it should be noted, played a leading role in democratizing the US astronaut corps. From the original *Mercury 7*, to crews of *Gemini*, *Apollo*, and *Skylab*, on to the first shuttle crews, white men *were* America's space race. But on its second flight in 1983, *Challenger* carried Sally Ride, America's first woman astronaut to go into orbit, and on its third mission took up Guion Bluford, the first African-American in space.

Challenger mission 51-L brought together cultural, organizational, and technological performances and did so in a highly publicized media campaign, one that highlighted the shuttle's performance as a teaching machine, a lecture machine. The Teacher-in-Space mission reaffirmed the close relation between the nation's space program and its post-*Sputnik* educational system. The lesson planning for this educational astronaut program ranged from presidential stage craft to booster rocket joints to sociotechnical satisficing and beyond. The pedagogical function of *Challenger* 51-L can be gleaned in the words of President Reagan, whose 1984 reelection campaign strategy against NEA-backed Walter Mondale included the establishment of the Teacher-in-Space program. In announcing this program, the President stated that "when the shuttle lifts off, all of America will be reminded of the crucial role that teachers and education play in the life of our nation. I can't think of a better lesson for our children and our country."[2]

A year later McAuliffe, a high-school history teacher from New Hampshire, was selected to give the lesson of *Challenger*. She soon entered training as a Payload Specialist and "jokingly told a fellow teacher that much of this training consisted of stern admonitions to 'never touch these switches,' but in reality her final weeks of training were exhausting."[3] The Teacher-in-Space trained to perform two tasks: the videotaping of six science demonstrations and the televised teaching of two live lessons to earthbound schoolchildren. Significantly, NASA had wanted her lessons scripted, but McAuliffe objected to this lecture format, stating the following about her upcoming performance: " 'This isn't a stage play,' she said. 'Teachers don't need speeches. All they need is a lesson plan and their students. It's worked for ages on Earth, and there's no reason why it shouldn't work up here.' "[4] Although NASA provided the content of her teaching (she was a history teacher assigned to give science lessons), McAuliffe's resistance to the scripted lecture machine paid off: the space agency relented on the format, and she planned to give informal lessons from outer space, lessons she and the crew rehearsed repeatedly.

But students here on Earth never saw McAuliffe's lessons, for seventy-three seconds after lift-off, *Challenger's* external fuel tank exploded in the Florida sky. With a mile-high flash and a long plunging fall to the sea, the mission ended with the deaths of the Teacher-in-Space and her six crew-mates, with the loss of spaceship *Challenger*, with its twisting smoketrail disintegrating across the upper atmosphere. In an instant replayed around the world, Challenger became a high performance disaster, one from which many other lessons have been drawn.

The Presidential Commission appointed by Ronald Reagan to investigate the accident found that, technically speaking, the disaster was caused by the failure of a "high performance field joint" on the right Solid Rocket Booster; more specifically, a rubber "O-ring" had failed to properly seal the joint. However, the Commission's conclusion primarily addressed NASA's organizational performance, citing its "flawed decision-making process."[5] The US House of Representatives' Committee on Science and Technology later reviewed the disaster and concentrated its findings on the shuttle's technological performance, blaming less the organizational procedures than the individual engineers and managers who had known about the O-rings' anomalous performance in cold weather and yet "failed to act decisively."[6] Yet organizational theorist Howard E. McCurdy has concluded that the "NASA experience suggests that three forces work against the maintenance of a high performance culture in government: a volatile political environment, the long-term trend toward an increasing administrative burden in the government as a whole, and the natural processes of aging, fed by the inevitable expansion and contraction that government bureaus go through."[7] For his part, statistician and information designer Edward R. Tufte has argued that if the engineers had visualized their data properly, "no one would have dared to risk the *Challenger* in such cold weather."[8] Addressing the wider cultural fallout of the disaster, feminist critic Constance Penley has connected the post-disaster "ritual effort to find and reconstitute the body of the woman and the spaceship" to the "omnipresence of fantasmatic thought" in both popular culture and empirical science.[9] And folklorist Elizabeth Radin Simons has found that about half of the sick jokes told by schoolchildren after the accident targeted the Teacher-in-Space. One joke echoed McAuliffe's own account of her "never touch these switches" training: "What were Christa McAuliffe's last words?" "What's this button for?"[10] From such sick *Challenger* jokes, Simons draws this conclusion: the nation's educational system is perceived by the public as "failing everywhere from the cities to the suburbs and everyone from the slow learner to the gifted, from the majority to the minority."[11]

The lessons from *Challenger* I wish to consider here involve reading it as a metamodel of the general theory of performance, one that incorporates components of the metamodels of Performance Studies, Performance Management, and Techno-Performance and, further, uses their respective movements of generalization as boosters for an even more general trajectory. The lessons proffered here are tentative, not definitive, and they are concerned primarily with our theory of performance, not with the shuttle disaster *per se*. Important insights into the disaster will certainly emerge, but I am reading *Challenger* as a vehicle of metamodelization, one that will bring together many different dimensions of performance without, however, reducing them to one single model. Indeed, it is the diverse performances housed in a certain genealogy of Challengers that will henceforth guide our general theory.

Specifically, over the next seven chapters, I want to theorize the performances stored or incorporated within the figure of "challenger" in order to: 1) demonstrate the ways in which cultural, organizational, and technological performances can embed themselves within one another; 2) situate the performance paradigms within an onto-historical formation of power and knowledge; 3) theorize the relationship between challenging and performance; and 4) speculate on the future of performative resistance. To these ends, we will relaunch the general theory by tracking *Challenger* as a high performance lecture machine. The twists and turns of its passage will transform our metamodel and our general theory, giving them a pronounced scientifictional character, one marked and unmarked by a certain variable geometry.

The launch pad of our metamodel is a text we have cited earlier, the reading of *Challenger* offered by sociologist Diane Vaughan. Vaughan's *The Challenger Launch Decision* focuses not on the shuttle crew, but on the workgroup responsible for the performance of the joints that connect and separate the segments of the Solid Rocket Boosters (SRBs). It was one of these joints that the infamous rubber O-rings failed to seal on that cold

January morning in 1986. Our interest in Vaughan's research stems not only from the fact that she studies *Challenger*, but more importantly, that she concludes the disaster resulted from "performance pressure" that affected the SRB workgroup. This pressure arose from the combined effects of three different imperatives, imperatives she argues hindered the workgroup's decision-making process. To put this another way: the group members worked under multiple challenges to perform—or else. Significantly, these three imperatives correspond to our challenges of cultural, organizational, and technological performance. Thus, in terms of our project, *Vaughan's text will be read as an uncanny textbook for the general theory of performance.* It is not the only possible textbook by any means, but by presenting multi-paradigmatic performance research, it demonstrates the applicability of the general theory and opens one avenue for future elaboration.

Like the works of Bruno Latour and Donald MacKenzie, *The Challenger Launch Decision* is a sociology of a technology. Vaughan's research focuses on the decision-making processes that informed the design, testing, and construction of the shuttle's SRB joint, as well as its failed performance. She casts her project as a "historical ethnography"—historical in that her object of study is a series of past events, ethnographic in that she focuses on the culture of the SRB workgroup and, to a lesser extent, on the larger political forces that contributed to their actions. In researching her historical ethnography of an astronautical technology, Vaughan conducted extensive interviews while also drawing upon the writings of an ethnographer well-known within Performance Studies, Clifford Geertz, and his concept of "thick description."[12] Reporting on the male-dominated, techno-organizational culture of NASA, she writes that "to convey another culture, the ethnographer must write in 'thick description' that retrieves and interprets what was said and done at the microscopic level of everyday life."[13] By carefully reading how Vaughan uses this methodology to study the NASA *Challenger*, we can understand the ways in which technological, organizational, and cultural performances can become embedded within one another.

The extent of technological performance within the shuttle can be gauged by the frequency with which the term "performance" appears in Vaughan's thick description of engineering discourse. She cites such terms as "O-ring performance," "putty performance," "joint performance," "SRB performance," "shuttle performance," and "mission performance." From rubber seals to rocket engines to the entire assemblage of boosters, fuel tank, and orbiter, *everything* that comprises *Challenger* was an object of Techno-Performance research. This point is stressed by one of Vaughan's primary interview subjects, Larry Wear, a Solid Rocket Motor Manager at the Marshall Space Flight Center in Huntsville, Alabama. Wear puts the shuttle's technological performance this way: "The performance that you are requiring of everything in that vehicle is top notch. . . . It is a high performance flying machine. It's a high performance re-entry body. It's a high performance landing device. Everything in it is a high performance tool and it has elements of risk all the way through."[14]

Such Techno-Performance discourse was the *lingua franca* of the SRB workgroup, of which Wear was an important member. The workgroup consisted of engineers and managers who worked either at Marshall or at Morton Thiokol, the company contracted by NASA to manufacture the booster rockets. It must be stressed that the workgroup's managers were themselves engineers who had entered management positions only after years of training and experience in laboratory environments. The managers, like the engineers they supervised, worked at the lower levels of the NASA hierarchy (Levels III and IV) and were closely involved with the performance of the booster joints, joints whose problems of erosion and breakdown had been known since the mid-1970s.[15] From this involvement of engineers and managers, Vaughan argues, a distinct culture emerged, that of a scientific paradigm.

> As the Level III and IV Marshall and Thiokol managers and engineers assigned to work on the SRB joints interacted about booster joint performance, they developed norms, values, and procedures that constituted a scientific paradigm. That paradigm supported a belief that was central to their worldview: the belief in redundancy [i.e., if one O-ring seal failed, a second would back it up]. It developed incrementally, the product of learning by doing. It was based on operating standards consisting of numerous ad hoc judgments and assumptions that they developed in daily engineering practice.[16]

Innovative design, multiple evaluative criteria, the creation of models and methods of analysis, laboratory and field tests, contested standards, and sociotechnical compromises—all the elements of technological performance we encountered in the previous chapter are found in Vaughan's reading of the SRB workgroup. If the $3 billion High Performance Computing Act of 1991 is Techno-Performance writ large, the SRB workgroup is that paradigm writ small: "Although the workgroup's scientific paradigm is hardly of the scope of the scientific communities and dominant paradigms described in Kuhn's path-breaking *The Structure of Scientific Revolutions*, it is Kuhn in microcosm."[17] Given that the shuttle has over one million parts, we can imagine sociotechnical studies of hundreds if not thousands of other microcosmic paradigms at work on the shuttle craft.

The micro-Techno-Performance paradigm that crystallized around the booster joints also embodied the larger technical culture associated with NASA's famous "can do" spirit, its aggressive attitude for meeting technological challenges. "'Can do,'" writes Vaughan, "was shorthand for 'Give us a challenge and we can accomplish it.'"[18] Ground zero for "can do" was Marshall Space Flight Center. Marshall emerged from the Army Ballistic Missile Agency, which was started after the Second World War with a staff of 120 engineers expatriated from Germany to Huntsville (leading some Americans to tag this Southern town "Hunsville"). Marshall was officially opened by NASA in 1960, and its first director was Wernher Von Braun, the rocket scientist who helped develop the V-2 missile used by the Nazis against London and Antwerp during the war. Once stateside, "Von Braun and his associates inculcated the technical exactitudes, superior knowledge and expertise, mandated hands-on strategies, awareness of risk and failure, and open communication that gave Marshall its original technical culture. . . . It was Marshall's strong research culture, together with the pioneering rocketry successes that resulted, that was the origin of NASA's legendary 'can do' attitude identified with the Apollo Program."[19] This legendary "can do" attitude thus embodies the technological challenge of performative effectiveness.

With this challenging, "can do" spirit guiding its technological performance, NASA successfully responded to one American President's challenge to go to the moon, and it was with this attitude that the SRB workgroup approached the unprecedented challenge of deviant joint performance. "Test results indicated that SRB joint deviated from performance predicted by design. Because no precedent existed for the joint design, no precedent existed for responding to the problem."[20] On several occasions the workgroup's post-flight examination and on-ground testing of the joints found erosion of the rubber O-rings designed to seal the joints. These findings raised serious challenges. "Each time a signal of potential danger occurred, it challenged the scientific paradigm and the cultural construction of risk that was its product."[21] However, tests and calculations made by the workgroup indicated that such erosion, though unexpected and thus deviant, did not pose a serious enough risk to warrant totally redesigning the joint. Instead, further study was planned and minor design alternations made that allowed for better monitoring of joint performance. Such decision-making processes produced what Vaughan describes as the "normalization of deviance," whereby repeated instances of deviant technological performance gradually led to a change in the predicted performance, and thus in what the workgroup considered to be normal performance.[22] In short, under the technical challenge to perform—or else, deviant performance gradually became normalized through its own repetition.

Immersed as it was in an exacting technical culture, the SRB workgroup was simultaneously part of NASA's organizational performance. The NASA organization had changed significantly since its heady race to the moon under Von Braun's guidance. In the 1960s NASA had received massive federal funding and prided itself not only on employing the best and brightest engineers, but also on creating a high performance organization that could point to many successful projects: *Mercury*, *Gemini*, and *Apollo*. By the time of the shuttle missions in the 1980s, however, the NASA organization had been transformed.[23] Part of this transformation had to do with the nature of the shuttle program itself. Though the shuttle utilized cutting-edge technology, the very uniqueness of the space craft—its reusability—also made the shuttle program a routine though highly complex project. Instead of producing a series of unique and expendable space craft, NASA now created and maintained a small and efficient fleet of recyclable vehicles. Efficiency was crucial, for the US financial crisis of the early 1970s, brought on by a costly war in Vietnam, the OPEC oil embargo, and a global recession, had led President Nixon to drastically scale back NASA's projects. Two of the planned *Apollo* moon landings were cancelled outright, and the space shuttle, whose originally planned function was to transport astronauts to a space station for orbital launches to Mars,[24] soon found itself with a severely truncated and somewhat unglamorous mission. Manned missions to Mars were put on indefinite hold, leaving the shuttle to function as a utility space bus for astronauts to conduct military and scientific space research. Nonetheless, the "Space Transportation System was an idea whose time had come: not only was it visionary, but the shuttle's reusability promised cost effectiveness."[25] Cost effectiveness, as we have seen, is another term for organizational efficiency.

By the mid-1980s, NASA had thus reinvented its organizational performance. Its mission was no longer the heroic endeavor of rocketing astronauts to other heavenly bodies, but the more mundane task of making space flight routine and, at the same time, efficient. And while NASA had once conducted the majority of its research internally, the shuttle's complex technological challenges, coupled with the demand for greater efficiency, forced NASA to rely increasingly on outside contractors, which in turn added new organizational challenges. In addition, after the early *Apollo* successes, Von Braun retired as Marshall's director in 1971, and in 1974 William Lucas took over, bringing with him a strikingly different management style. Vaughan describes the change in this way: "Saddled with a vastly more complex Marshall organizational structure and apparently lacking Von Braun's charisma and skill at maintaining personal contact with people at different levels in the Marshall hierarchy, Lucas relied on hierarchy and formal mechanisms to transfer information. He insisted on bureaucratic accountability for monitoring and controlling internal operations."[26] The result of all these changes: a much thicker layer of bureaucratic accountability was folded over on top of the original technical culture. Technological performance became deeply embedded in organizational performance.

Vaughan's historical ethnography analyzes the technical and organizational dimensions of the SRB workgroup as a culture. From our perspective, the clearest instances of what we have called cultural performance can be found in the formal presentations the workgroup made of their research activities. Operating within NASA's organizational structure required the workgroup to submit their technical recommendations to "adversarial challenges" posed within a multileveled, overlapping review procedure known as the Flight Readiness Review or FRR process. The performative dimension of these presentations comes through in Larry Wear's account of the Marshall Center Board FFR, the final Level III review prior to Level II review. I cite Wear's account at length, for he explicitly and repeatedly comments upon the dramatic and challenging character of these briefings.

> The Center Board would be held in a **humongous conference room that looks like an auditorium**. It's an open meeting. There might be one hundred—one hundred and fifty people there. Be a whole raft of people who weren't going to ask you any questions. . . . **It's a great drama**. Sometimes people give very informative, very interesting presentations. **That's drama in a way**. And it's an adversarial process. I think there are some people who have, what's the word, there is a word for when you enjoy someone else's punishment . . . masochistic, they are masochistic. You know, come in and watch Larry Wear or Larry Mulloy [another Marshall project manager] or Thiokol take a whipping from the Board. **There are people who I think actually come to watch that element.**
>
> It's serious work. There are reputations at stake, not just individuals, but the Center itself. . . . You don't leave the Center to give a significant briefing unless the Center's senior management is aware of what you're doing, and that Board was a means of doing it. **He [Lucas] was looking after the institution's image and his own**. One reason is because he becomes a member of this thing, as it gets on up higher. He doesn't want to go to the high-level board and sit there and then be embarrassed by what his people are saying.
>
> There are standards to be upheld. **He challenges the technical information**. We have this saying, "only one-chart deep." You can't go to the Board knowing only your [engineering] charts. Lucas and the Board ask very hard questions, going into details much deeper than what's presented to them in the charts. You've got to be able to answer any question. **And he challenges the style of the presentation**. He [Lucas] requires you to present the things up to the standards of Marshall Space Flight Center, and I heard him say several times, he'd stop something and he'd turn to the man's boss, and he'd say, "Jim, I just don't believe this represents the standards of this Center, do you?" Of course, Jim would say, "No, sir, I certainly don't." And that meant the briefing is not crisp enough.
>
> It is intense information. It's important information. It's important from the standpoint of whether the vehicle is going to fly and its danger and the national assets. This is a billion dollar program, and national assets are involved. In a lot of ways, **you always thought the future of the Center hinges on whether we do right or don't do right.** You know, it is not an insignificant affair. For one thing, human life is

> involved. For that reason alone. But also the image of the Center is at stake. The continuance of the program is at stake. If you lose this program, you know, we lose 8,000 jobs. **It is a high, important, dramatic situation**. There's big money at stake. There's your job at stake. There's national prestige, prestige of the Center, all those things are at stake. **So it's a lot of pressure**.[27]

The "humongous" room, the "whipping from the Board," Wear's confusion between masochism and sadism, the challenges over information and style, the understated invocation of formal standards and the concern with personal and institutional images amid matters of life and death, the entire high-pressure drama played out before "a whole raft of people"—this scene channels the plays of Genet, the novels of Kafka, the films of Terry Gilliam. In a frighteningly absurd fashion, it stages the demand to perform—or else while also suggesting the role these reviews played within Marshall. Vaughan writes that "the FRR process had ritualistic, ceremonial properties" and characterizes the Marshall Center Board FRR as "the quintessential embodiment of Marshall culture."[28] Combining Wear's fine account and Vaughan's thick description, we might file the FRR presentations somewhere between theater and ritual.

The Marshall Center Board FRR is an exemplary and chilling production of the challenge to perform—or else, and it gathers together many dramaturgical elements of our rehearsal process. It is, shall we say, a quasi-quintessential embodiment of our general theory. First, the FRR reveals the *embedding* of cultural, organizational, and technological performances. A bureaucratic performance (Level II Flight Readiness Review) concerning a technical performance (of the solid rocket booster) becomes played out as a cultural performance ("a great drama"). Second, the FRR functions as a *metametamodel* of performance, combining key elements of metamodels found in Performance Studies, Techno-Performance, and Performance Management. Together, the FRR-as-ritual and the solid booster rocket form an organizational feedback loop, for the shuttle's "physical condition and performance from one launch was critical input in the FRR for the next. The effect was a continuous feedback loop, joining one launch decision and its outcome to the next."[29] Third, in the Flight Readiness Review process, the *adversarial challenges* of efficacy, efficiency, and effectiveness—each one multi-dimensional and contested—come together to enframe and challenge one another. Vaughan writes that the "challenges raised in FRR drove [the engineers] back to the labs for further research."[30] The stakes of this multi-paradigmatic performance are immense: human lives, the national assets of the shuttle and its payload, a billion-dollar program, thousands of jobs, the reputations of individuals, institutions, and an entire nation—all are at risk in this challenge of challenges. And, indeed, all were lost or severely damaged when *Challenger* disintegrated in the atmosphere off the Florida coast.

In demonstrating the ways in which cultural, organizational, and technological performances can be incorporated within one other, Vaughan's historical ethnography reveals the manner in which the resulting "challenge of challenges" creates powerful pressures on all those involved, pressures Wear himself cites in his account of the FRR process. These are pressures to perform—or else. The SRB workgroup, Vaughan writes, struggled to perform under "three cultural imperatives: 1) bureaucratic accountability—following rules and procedures for decision making and relaying information up the hierarchy, 2) political accountability—meeting the schedule by getting the necessary flight qualification work done in time for the Center Board, and 3) original technical culture, being able to support work group recommendations and conclusions with data, engineering analysis, and technical rationale that were responsive to every conceivable question."[31] While the bureaucratic and technical imperatives she identifies obviously correspond to our challenges of organizational efficiency and technological effectiveness, the political imperative may at first seem far removed from the challenge of social efficacy, especially since Vaughan also describes it as the "business ideology of production."[32] Yet the political imperative/business ideology she analyzes reflects the pressures put upon NASA by its outside funders and supporters, as well as its detractors. As a federal agency, NASA must account for itself to Congress, the President, the press, and, ultimately, the American public.

Launch delays, cost overruns, mission problems—the political accountability of the space agency is calculated on a cultural ledger, for such debits can affect NASA's image and legitimacy within US society at large. Thus: "Top NASA administrators were absorbed with 'myth managing': attaining legitimacy (and thus resources) by projecting and living up to a cultural image of routine, economical spaceflight."[33] Here cultural performance operates at a macro level, as distinguished from the micro level of individual FRR presentations. In the face of public criticism, growing lack of interest in space travel, and declining support for its costly missions, NASA has developed sophisticated public-relations campaigns over the past two decades in order to "manage" the organization's cultural image. To ensure continued public support and funding, NASA has cultivated popular interest in particular missions. These efforts have ranged from promotionals featuring the original *Star Trek* cast members to the highly publicized 1997 Mars lander mission that, combining precise flight scheduling and a taste for apple pie, managed to land a robotic vehicle on Mars *on the Fourth of July*. With respect to the *Challenger* 51-L mission, in addition to the widely covered Teacher-in-Space program and the impression that the seven astronauts "looked like America," there were rumors that President Reagan planned to speak to the orbiting crew as part of his State of the Union Address.

The imperative of political accountability described by Vaughan thus corresponds to our challenge of social efficacy, thereby allowing us to align her three imperatives with our three paradigmatic challenges. Cultural, organizational, and technological challenges were operative in different ways at different times for the SRB workgroup, but they came to a fateful culmination the night before the *Challenger* launch. With meteorologists forecasting an unusually hard freeze that night in central Florida, Thiokol engineers were concerned about O-ring performance and requested a last-minute Flight Readiness Review. They feared the extremely low temperatures could reduce the O-rings' resiliency, thereby preventing them from sealing the joint properly and possibly triggering a catastrophe. This *ad hoc* FRR lies at the center of Vaughan's thick description, or rather serves as bookends for her study: she opens her text with its *mise en scène* and returns to it near the end. Unlike the public, face-to-face briefing described above, this last-ditch FRR was a small teleconference held between engineers and managers located at three sites, Marshall, Kennedy Space Center, and Morton Thiokol-Wasatch in Utah. The fateful decision-making process regarding the *Challenger* launch unfolded as a virtual, multimedia performance. Verbal presentations and ensuing discussion occurred over phone lines; hastily prepared charts were faxed to the widely dispersed participants; and additional information was made available via computer network.

This *ad hoc* performance was also a high-pressure, multiparadigmatic event. As in the Marshall Center Board FRR, challenges of technical effectiveness, organizational efficiency, and social efficacy came together to produce tremendous tensions, which Vaughan characterizes as "performance pressure." She writes that "the tone of the meeting was set outside the teleconference by political elites who took actions that added political accountability and bureaucratic accountability to NASA's original technical culture. These imperatives trickled down to NASA managers who, experiencing performance pressure, openly expressed their frustrations about upholding these standards."[34] Some of the Thiokol engineers most familiar with O-ring performance recommended delaying the launch until temperature conditions improved. However, as their arguments concerning the correlation between O-ring resiliency and temperature variation were not supported with appropriate research data, but instead relied on observation and the intuition that rubber hardens when cold, they were challenged by NASA engineers and managers as not being scientifically rigorous. NASA also found inconsistencies in Thiokol's verbal presentation and visual charts, and, further, wanted to know why such a correlation had not been reported before. As the performance pressure mounted, Marshall's Larry Mulloy pointedly asked, "My God, Thiokol, when do you want me to launch, next April?"[35]

Under the increasing performance pressures of effectiveness, efficiency, and efficacy, the SRB workgroup faced a multidimensional challenge to perform—or else. The contested issue of deviant joint performance created the necessity of joint optimization, the demand to compromise between conflicting evaluative frameworks. After suspending the teleconference for thirty minutes to confer among themselves offline, the Thiokol engineers reversed their initial recommendation and supported the scheduled launch for the next morning. NASA officials, seeking documentation of the decision-making process, asked the Thiokol engineers to put their recommendation in writing and sign it.

The rest is history, the media's instant replay having inscribed the *Challenger* explosion deep within our memory banks: "The image retained by the American public is a billowing cloud of smoke, from which emerged two white fingers tracing diverging paths of the Solid Rocket Boosters across the sky."[36] Today we can read this cloud of smoke as a trace, one that resulted from a long series of compromises—or better still, one that programs an ongoing performance of ritual satisficing.

As a textbook of the general theory outlined here, *The Challenger Launch Decision* demonstrates how the fields of cultural, organizational, and technological performance, while separated by different histories and research paradigms, can and do overlap and feed back into one another. To say that they totally converge into a unified performance would be inaccurate, for the challenges posed by each remain distinct and, at times, diverge sharply from one another. Nonetheless, through joint optimization and satisificing, the challenges of effectiveness, efficacy, and effectiveness can be negotiated, decisions can be made, and actions taken.

Further, as a metamodel of the general theory, Challenger lecture machine offers us lessons about the close affinity between performance and challenging. As we've seen in previous chapters, the discourse of challenging operates within the paradigms of Performance Studies, Performance Management, and Techno-Performance. Vaughan's analysis of the three imperatives that produced performance pressure on the SRB workgroup reveals that challenging played an important role in the decision-making process leading up to the *Challenger* launch. The pre-accident adversarial challenges posed by the FRR—the challenging of technical data, bureaucratic protocols, and presentational styles—as well as those posed by the subsequent Presidential Commission and House Committee that investigated the accident, all indicate not only that the shuttle was a high performance vehicle, but that the performance history of *Challenger* was also permeated by cultural, organizational, and technological challenges.

In fact, we can say that challenging was the performative norm of *Challenger*, and Vaughan concludes that, far from deviating from multidimensional challenges, the SRB workgroup actually conformed to them. "We saw how the performance pressure at Marshall mandated conformity to all three cultural imperatives, and that the workgroup did, in fact, conform to all three."[37] This conclusion differs significantly from the findings of the Presidential Commission and House Committee assigned to investigate the

Challenger accident, and here we must consider the performance of Vaughan's historical ethnography. Not only does she find challenges operating within the *Challenger* launch decision, she defines the function of her *own text* as a challenge. "This book challenges conventional interpretations," she writes. It functions as a "revisionist account" that contests other previous readings of the events leading up to the disaster.[38] Vaughan also notes that these interpretations had shaped her initial assumptions about the accident and then goes on to describe how her research process presented a number of challenges along the way: "I made discovery after discovery that challenged key aspects of the case on which my beginning assumptions were based."[39] In other words, challenges operate within her text both at the level of object (the performance of *Challenger* and the three imperatives guiding the SRB workgroup) and at a metalevel (the performance of Vaughan's research and of the conclusions based upon this research).

If a cloud of smoke makes up our memory of the lost vehicle, an odd pattern of challenges and performances haunts our general theory. We have encountered numerous challenges within the three paradigms of performance research. In turn, I have named *Challenger* as a metamodel of the general theory and, reading Vaughan, cited challenges that informed its ill-fated performance. I have noted that she positions herself as a researcher who, challenged by her findings, also acts as a challenger of other interpretations of *Challenger*. And, lest anyone forget, I have initiated my own text by posing a challenge, both to my readers and to myself.

Why all these challenges? Throughout my research of performance, I have been *surprised* by all the challenges unearthed in performance—and all the performances stowed away in *Challenger*. At times, I have been awed by this uncanny affinity between performance and challenging. From the concrete and specific performances surrounding *Challenger* to the paradigms of Performance Studies, Performance Management, and Techno-Performance, to even higher levels of abstraction and generality, performance and challenging appear to be closely linked, gathered together, bound up in a sort of joint performance-challenge. Today, no matter at which site I start rehearsing the general theory, this performance-challenge recurs.

How to read the recurrence of challenges within our general theory of performance? Is this some kind of trick or ruse? Shuttling between theory and practice, between generalizations and specifications, our trajectory is marked by chance associations, idiosyncratic passages that connect disparate sites by reciting and displacing a singular performance-challenge. Such chances and idiosyncracies are key to the process of metamodelization. "There must be a trick to the train of thought, a recursive formula," writes mathematician Stanislaw Ulam, commenting on the nature of associative thought. "A group of neurons starts working automatically, sometimes without external impulse. It is a kind of iterative process with a growing pattern. It wanders about in the brain, and the way it happens must depend on the memory of similar patterns."[40] In our case, the patterns cut across different networks—individual and sociotechnical, ontological and historical, memorable and futural. To track the iteration of these patterns, our reading must now move into high orbit, thereby getting another perspective on the paradigms of cultural, organizational, and technological performance. We must aim for a different level of generality, one drawn by a moving constellation of cites. To this end, let us continue the dramaturgy of Challenger lecture machine.

CHAPTER 5. CHALLENGING FORTH: THE POWER OF PERFORMANCE

On 18 November 1955, in the main auditorium of the Technische Hochschule in Munich, Martin Heidegger gave a lecture concerning the question of technology. Over his long career, Heidegger earned quite a reputation as a lecturer, one that was so famous, so infamous, that he would, in effect, come to hide the signatures carved into his lecture machine. Hans-Georg Gadamer, who studied with him in the 1920s, recalls the dramatic arrival of the young Heidegger at the Marburg University: "One can hardly portray Heidegger's arrival in Marburg dramatically enough—not that he tried to make a sensation. His entrance into the lecture hall did betray a sense of self-assurance and a consciousness of his own impact, but what was truly characteristic of his person and his teaching was that he became completely absorbed in his work, and that his work shone forth. With him, lecturing became something altogether new."[1] Over the next decade, or so however, his lectures would shine forth in the darkest of places, the MIA complex of the German Third Reich. We will loop back to this complex later, and for now read on from Heidegger's 1955 lecture.

The text Heidegger delivered in Munich that year has since been translated and published as the lead essay of the book *The Question Concerning Technology and Other Essays*. The questions raised in and by this text will help us articulate further the affinity between performance and challenging, for Heidegger connects the question concerning technology to a particular revealing of truth, an ordering of knowledge that challenges forth the world.

We will first try to track the challenging posed by Heidegger and connect it to our readings of performance, those of Techno-Performance, Performance Management, and Performance Studies. We will then pick up on other readings, other philosophical tracks that take on the *power of performance.*

What is the question concerning technology? For Heidegger, it is a question concerning the essence of technology, an essence that "is by no means anything technological."[2] Instead of answering the question by defining the essence of technology as an instrument or as a human activity, Heidegger responds: "Technology is a way of revealing. If we heed to this, then another whole realm for the essence of technology will open itself up to us. It is the realm of revealing, i.e., of truth."[3] Such truth must not be understood as the correspondence of a representation to an objective or subjective reality, nor as the adequation of elements within a formal system such as logic or mathematics. Heidegger instead approaches truth as *aletheia*, as *poiesis*, as a revealing or bringing-forth that also conceals. Yet he also makes this call: modern technology's mode of revealing is not authentic, it's a fallen call, a hail that fails, a revealing of *eidos* that conceals the concealing of *aletheia.*

Our interest lies in this inauthentic call, and not only or even primarily because it pertains to Techno-Performance's challenge of effectiveness. There is a more profound, if trickier, challenge that draws us on while also repelling us with its call: Heidegger names the inauthentic revealing *Herausfordern* or "challenging forth." Challenging calls forth the world in a particular way. "The revealing that rules in modern technology is a challenging [*Herausfordern*], which puts to nature the unreasonable demand that it supply energy that can be extracted and stored as such."[4] Instead of channeling the authentic bringing-forth of sky and earth, gods and man, modern technology instead challenges forth nature's energies and orders them into reality as "standing reserve," as objects on call to subjects who are themselves called forth as challengers. Translator William Lovitt provides this note on Heidegger's term: "*Herausfordern* means to challenge, to call forth or summon to action, to demand positively, to provoke. It is composed of the verb *forden* (to demand, to summon, to challenge) and the adverbial prefixes *her*- (hither) and *aus*- (out)."[5] Although Lovitt does not draw attention to it, his translation of *Herausfordern* as "challenging" and "challenging forth" also bears with it the sense of inauthenticity, for "challenge" comes from the Latin *calumniare* (to accuse falsely), and is also related to *calvī* (to deceive) and *calumnia* (trickery).

Challenging forth is for Heidegger the inauthentic revealing carried out by modern science and industry, both of which challenge the earth by setting upon it. "This setting-upon that challenges forth the energies of nature is an expediting [*Förden*], and in two ways. It expedites in that it unlocks and exposes. Yet that expediting is always itself directed from the beginning toward furthering something else, i.e., toward driving on to the maximum yield at the minimum expense."[6] In other words, challenging forth also entails the call to maximize output and minimize input, the very challenge of organizational efficiency that guides Performance Management. But challenging forth extends far beyond this research paradigm. Indeed, for Heidegger challenging helps to define the modern age since Descartes, an era he names in another essay in *The Question of Technology*, "The Age of the World Picture." "The fundamental event of the modern age is the conquest of the world as picture. The word 'picture' [*Bild*] now means the structured image [*Gebild*] that is the creature of man's producing which represents and sets before. In such a producing, man contends for the position in which he can be that particular being who gives the measure and draws up the guidelines for everything that is."[7] In the modern age, the world is challenged forth as a picture, as an object of representational knowledge, and humans become the subject of this challenging knowledge. "It is no wonder," writes Heidegger, "that humanism first arises where the world becomes a picture."[8] The challenging forth of the world, then, is not limited to science and industry, for Heidegger defines humanism as a "moral-aesthetic anthropology" and anthropology as "that philosophical interpretation of man which explains and evaluates whatever is, in its entirety, from the standpoint of man and in relation to man."[9]

As a mode of bringing forth that extends from techno-science to industry to anthropology, challenging forth provides us a certain framework for gathering together the paradigmatic challenges of effectiveness, efficiency, and efficacy, as well as the many other challenges ordering our general theory. Challenging forth is precisely a framing, an ordering: "We now name that challenging claim which gathers man thither to order the self-revealing as standing reserve: *'Ge-stell'* [Enframing]."[10] Heidegger defines Enframing as an "ordaining of destining," a sending forth that puts humans on the way to truth. It is a dangerous passage, for "the destining of revealing is as such, in every one of its modes, and therefore necessarily, *danger*. . . . Yet when destining reigns in the mode of Enframing, it is the supreme danger."[11] Why? Because in it, man "stands so decisively in attendance on the challenging forth of Enframing that he does not apprehend Enframing as a claim, that he fails to see himself as the one spoken to, and hence also fails in every way to hear in what respect he ek-sists."[12] The supreme danger of this challenging call is that humans risk missing the authentic call, the call of truth as *poiesis*, "the call of a more primal truth."[13]

At the end of his question concerning technology, Heidegger gathers together the call of challenging forth and the call of *poiesis* into a stellar constellation. In doing so, he draws us skyward in our Challenger lecture machine, which thus far consists of a disastrous space ship named *Challenger* and a dangerous mode of revealing called "challenging forth." Heidegger stargazing: "When we look into the ambiguous essence of technology, we behold the constellation, the stellar course of the mystery. The question concerning technology is the question concerning the constellation in which revealing and concealing, in which the coming to presence of truth, comes to pass."[14] The mystery refers to a line cited from Hölderlin: "But where the danger is, grows/The saving power also." For Heidegger, the saving power comes in the turning of modern technology toward a more profound sense of *techne*. "Once there was a time when the bringing-forth of the true into the beautiful was called *techne*. And the *poiesis* of the fine arts also was called *techne*."[15] In the danger of challenging forth grows the saving power of *poiesis*. How to make the turn, how to pass from one to the other?

> Because the essence of technology is nothing technological, essential reflection upon technology and decisive confrontation with it must happen in a realm that is, on the one hand, akin to the essence of technology and, on the other, fundamentally different from it.
>
> Such a realm is art.[16]

The distinctions here between *techne* and technology, between the calls of *poiesis* and challenging forth, between the danger of revealing and the supreme danger of Enframing, between science and art, all these distinctions are part of a bipolar constellation whose coordinates extend beyond the texts of Heidegger. From afar, these coordinates guide the critical challenges regularly launched by those in the arts and humanities against science and technology. They also guide the challenges posed by those within the sciences who seek to recast their own activities in terms of intuition and creativity, as well as efforts of organizational theorists and managers to challenge the rationality of Scientific Management.

Around the oppositions of this challenging constellation grows the multivalent power of performance. The spectacular development of performance concepts over the past half century, the movements of generalization in such divergent areas as technology, management, and culture, the patterns of joint performance-challenges—all these suggest that *the world is being challenged forth to perform—or else.*

How can I make such a call? How can one trained to study performance as a transgressive, resistant force of social efficacy come to connect it to challenging forth, as well as to the challenges of technological effectiveness and organizational efficiency? I stress that I am not trying to reduce cultural performance and the challenge of social efficacy to these other challenges. Nor am I denying the mutational potential of cultural performance. I am instead suggesting that cultural performance and its efficacy cannot be thought outside the generalization of certain performance concepts in the humanities and social sciences and, further, that this conceptualization process has an onto-historical relationship to the generalization of other performance concepts and to the institutionalization of other paradigms of performance research. If today we can readily locate performance in the production of culture worldwide, this has not always been the case; nor has it always been possible to measure the performance of public infrastructures or to reengineer entire organizations for peak performance. Sixty years ago, these performances were largely unthinkable; today, not only is each thinkable, we can also cite rituals of sociotechnical satisficing that incorporate elements of cultural, organizational, and technological performance. What makes such multiparadigmatic performances possible, and what challenges me to speculate on the link between performance and challenging forth, is a more powerful movement of generalization than those undertaken by Performance Studies, Performance Management, and Techno-Performance, a movement that at once incorporates and passes beyond all these paradigms.

I call this more general movement the *power of performance*. To theorize this performative power within our rehearsal process, I will first present some dramaturgical research, for I am not the first person to theorize power as performance. In other words, we'll put in a call for conceptual backup, as this power has been analyzed by several important and well-known cultural theorists. Indeed, what is perhaps most striking about the power of performance is that it was first theorized a half century ago, and more striking still, this powerful call was left on hold for so long.

In 1955, the same year as Heidegger's challenging lecture in Munich, another German philosopher published a text across the Atlantic in the United States. The text was entitled *Eros and Civilization: A Philosophical Inquiry into Freud*. Its author, Herbert Marcuse, had been a student of Heidegger before joining the Frankfurt Institute of Social Research (better known as the Frankfurt School). In 1934 he left Germany for exile to the US, where he would come to live, teach, and write. In *Eros and Civilization*, Marcuse argues that a radically historical sociology forms a hidden trend in Freudian psychoanalysis, and articulating it, he sets out to analyze the reality principle that dominates modern civilization. Writing in the United States, in English, in 1955, Marcuse called this repressive principle the "performance principle:"

> . . . in our attempt to elucidate the scope and the limits of the prevalent repressiveness in contemporary civilization, we shall have to describe it in terms of the specific reality principle that has governed the origins and the growth of this civilization. We designate it as **performance principle** in order to emphasize that under its rule society is stratified according to the competitive economic performances of its members. It is clearly not the only historical reality principle: other modes of societal organization not merely prevailed in primitive cultures but also survived into the modern period.[17]

The performance principle is the reality principle guiding what Marcuse will later call "one-dimensional societies," advanced industrial societies whose dominant social stratification consists of labor.[18] In concise and explicit terms, he defines performance *as alienated labor*. "Men do not live their own lives but perform pre-established functions. While they work, they do not fulfill their own needs and faculties but work in *alienation*."[19] The performance principle entails the repressive sublimation of human desire, for in contemporary society "libido is diverted for socially useful performances in which the individual works for himself only in so far as he works for the apparatus, engaged in activities that mostly do not coincide with his own faculties and desires."[20] Marcuse argues that the performance principle extends far beyond the sphere of labor. He speaks of the pleasurable yet repressive desublimation encouraged by mass culture in the spheres of leisure and private life.

In societies stratified by the performance principle, individuals work and live only to enact performances dictated by others, performances normalized according to the dictates of expediency and efficiency. For Marcuse, such performances are closely tied to modern technology, a connection he explored years earlier in his essay, "Some Social Implications of Modern Technology." In this 1941 text, Marcuse analyzes the pervasiveness of performance in society while explicitly connecting it to technology, which he defines not only as the totality of instruments characterizing "the machine age," but more importantly, as a mode of social relationships, "an instrument for control and domination."[21] Performance is the name for that mode of social domination which corresponds to the apparatus of modern technology. The mechanisms of this performance are not the raw exercise of physical power, but the more subtle control of psychic desire, the rational transformation of individual desire into the socially defined desire to fit in, to get along, to conform to the pattern of the apparatus. Marcuse outlines the technological origins of this power of performance as well as its extension into all of society. "The 'mechanics of conformity' spread from the technological to the social order; they govern the performances not only in the factories and shops, but also in the offices, schools, assemblies and, finally, in the realm of relaxation and entertainment."[22]

Within our general theory, this last citation, written more than half a century ago, provides an extraordinarily prescient reading of the power formation underlying the fields of technological, organizational, and cultural performance. At the same time, "Some Social Implications of Modern Technology" bears the traits of its inscription, the signs of its time, and these help us understand Marcuse's theorization of the power of performance. Early in the essay, he cites National Socialism as a striking example of a highly rationalized, mechanized, and efficient economy in the service of totalitarian oppression. However, he goes on to predict that "it will fall before that power which proves to be more efficient than fascism."[23] Though he does not explicitly attribute this more efficient power to the United States, Marcuse does criticize certain experiments in organizational management that were explored in this country, including those found in Taylor's Scientific

Management and in J. Burham's 1941 *The Managerial Revolution*, a post-Tayloristic text. Along similar lines, Marcuse dismisses vocational training programs that focus on the psychological and personal aspects of workers. "The 'human side' of the employee and the concern for his personal aptitudes and habits play an important role in the total mobilization of the private sphere for mass production and mass culture."[24] Marcuse thus draws a clear connection between the doomed "technocracy" of the Third Reich and two forms of organizational performance found in the US, Scientific Management and what would become Performance Management. Within a larger historical perspective, he also argues that the critical, individualist rationality which arose in the sixteenth and seventeenth centuries is now succumbing to the effects of modern technology. "Under the impact of this apparatus, individualistic rationality has been transformed into technological rationality. It is by no means confined to objects of large scale enterprises but characterizes the pervasive mode of thought and even the manifold forms of protest and rebellion."[25] He calls this mode of thought "technological rationality," and it will form the defining characteristic of what he later called the "one-dimensional man."

Marcuse's analysis of performance is important to us for several reasons. First, the fact that in 1941, seven years after arriving in the US, he recognized the role of performance within a "mechanics of conformity" and then in 1955 developed a full-blown theory of the performance principle suggests that the Second World War marks a sort of initiation rite of performativity within the United States. The rite was reiterated at innumerable sites. As we have seen, it was shortly after the war that Performance Studies, Performance Management, and Techno-Performance began to crystallize as paradigms of research in the US, though at different rates of formalization and different sites of pragmatic deployment. Second, reading Marcuse's early theorization of performance as the groundwork for his later theory of the performance principle, we can begin to understand the ways in which performance functions as a formation of power: as a mode of domination, the performance principle extends a certain technological rationality and economic alienation into all social organizations and, through mass culture, into leisure activities and private life. Third, though we have noted its emergence in the wake of the Second World War, Marcuse also situates the power of performance within a wider historical perspective. For him, its technological rationality is an outgrowth and displacement of the critical, individualistic rationality that blossomed into the European Enlightenment. The performance principle thus strikes at the core of modern individual subjectivity while also extending itself throughout society. For Marcuse, performative power is both psychological and social. It dominates every aspect of individual and social life: work, education, entertainment, sexuality, even individual protest and rebellion become standardized performances that conform to highly normative social demands.

Given the radical politics of Marcuse's performance theory, there is little wonder that it has never played much of a role within the paradigms of Performance Management and Techno-Performance. It does come as a surprise, however, that the performance principle has been largely, if not totally, absent from the reading machines of Performance Studies. Marcuse was, after all, something of a guiding figure of 1960s radicalism—Angela Davis, Frederic Jameson, and Stanley Aronowitz were all his students. In the US, he was probably the most widely read theorist associated with the Frankfurt School prior to the translation, publication, and profuse reading of Walter Benjamin's texts. Perhaps Marcuse's omission from the canon of cultural performance literature can be understood by turning to another prominent theorist who has also analyzed the power of performance. Significantly, though his name is well-known within Performance Studies, his theory of normative performance has also largely escaped our critical scanners.

I refer here to Jean-François Lyotard and, specifically, to his 1979 text *The Postmodern Condition: A Report on Knowledge*. This report was presented to the Conseil des Universités of the Quebec government at the request of its president. Translated into English in 1984, it has since become one of the most influential texts on postmodernity. Lyotard opens the text by stating his "working hypothesis:" "the status of knowledge is altered as societies enter what is known as the postindustrial age and cultures enter what is known as the postmodern age. This transition has been under way since at least the end of the 1950s."[26] Lyotard's interest lies in how this knowledge legitimates itself, and also how this legitimation relates to the broader question of social bonds. "Knowledge and power are simply two sides of the same question: who decides what knowledge is, and who knows what needs to be decided?"[27] My interest lies in Lyotard's answers to these questions, for they involve performance.

While Marcuse theorizes performance in terms of Freud's reality principle, Lyotard defines it through Wittgenstein's language games. Language games are categories of utterances defined by specific rules that guide their usage, and Lyotard seeks to place such games within a general field of social agonistics. "There are many language games—a heterogeneity of language particles. They only give rise to institutions in patches."

> The decision makers, however, attempt to manage these clouds of sociality according to input/output matrices, following a logic which implies that their matrices are commensurable and that the whole is determinable. They allocate our lives for the growth of power. In matters of social justice and of scientific truth alike, the legitimation of that power is based on its optimizing the system's performance—efficiency.[28]

Lyotard names the language game that has come to dominate both knowledge and social bonds since the 1950s with a single word: "performativity." Performativity is legitimation defined as the maximization of a system's output and the minimization of its input. It normalizes activities by optimizing a system's performance. Under this mode of performative legitimation, other language games are allowed—narration, speculation, jokes, etc.—but they must be calculable in terms of system optimization, even if only to be evaluated as inefficient or dysfunctional. For Lyotard, performativity replaces the traditional goals of knowledge, truth and/or liberation, and one could call performativity a metalanguage game, except that a part of the postmodern condition, one I will call the "performativity condition," entails that performativity operates through a plurality of localized and temporary situations. Continuing the text cited above, Lyotard writes: "The application of this criterion to all of our language games necessarily implies a certain level of terror, whether soft or hard: be operational (that is, commensurable) or disappear."[29] In other words: perform—or else.

The highly contextual aspect of the performativity condition can best be understood in relation to the modern mode of legitimation it displaces, what Lyotard calls "grand narratives." These grand narratives include "the dialectics of Spirit, the hermeneutics of meaning, the emancipation of the rational or working subject, or the creation of wealth,"[30] in short, the modernist projects of Hegel, Heidegger, Marx, and Smith. Lyotard, like Marcuse, points to the close relation of performance and technology; yet writing some twenty-five years later, he focuses on digital computers, machines whose binary codes allow the rapid and widespread calculation of inputs and outputs. The hegemony of computers and the diversity of language games seal the fate of grand narratives and thus of modernity. Lyotard, "simplifying to the extreme," defines the *"postmodern* as incredulity toward metanarratives. . . . The narrative function is losing its functors, its great hero, its great dangers, its great voyages, its great goal."[31] The result is delegitimation: the decline of philosophy and revolutionary politics, the crisis of representation and of the university, and the replacement of universal metalanguages by a plurality of discrete systems.

With respect to the decline of epistemological metanarratives, the performativity condition is postmodern; but in relation to social bonds it displays its modernity and its cynicism, which consists in acting as though such a metadiscourse does exist and playing the game of efficiency without challenging the rules or metaprescriptions that define not only the moves, but also who can play. Here Lyotard addresses what we have seen Robert Crease call the production of laboratory experiments. For Lyotard, performative research emerges as a result of the reciprocity of science, technology, and capital: science requires proof, proof requires technology, and technology requires capital—thus the "criterion of performance is explicitly invoked by the authorities to justify their refusal to subsidize certain research centers."[32] Likewise, performative education emerges when the university student's goal of "learning a philosophy of life" is replaced by "learning a job skill." The university lecture machine thus contributes to improving the performance of social systems by training competent, noncritical workers: performativity's "general effect is to subordinate the institutions of higher learning to the existing powers."[33] In short, under the social bonds of a performativity condition that cynically seeks to regulate diverse and incommensurable language games, knowledge ceases to be either true or false and becomes instead optimal or suboptimal.

In different ways, Marcuse and Lyotard each theorize performance not as a radical, transformative force in contemporary society, but as a mode of power. Significantly, each of these two theorists left their mark on a particular generation of cultural scholars, Marcuse in the 1960s, Lyotard in the 1980s. Though he does not cite *Eros and Civilization*, Lyotard does at one point use the term "performativity principle." He also supports my contention that Marcuse's analyses indicate that performative power emerges around the Second World War. Though Lyotard's text does not locate the emergence of performativity in the United States, he cites many American researchers, including Daniel Bell, Ihab Hassan, and Erving Goffman, as well as US labor statistics showing the increased importance of information in the workplace. In addition, Marcuse and Lyotard both define the power of performance with reference to capital, technology, and organizations. While Lyotard stresses digital decision-making rather than industrial factory work, he and Marcuse both theorize performance in terms of techno-efficiency, which we can characterize as the alliance of technological and organizational performance. Just as important, both also theorize performative power as a threat to the modern subject of knowledge, though here the major differences between their theories emerge. Lyotard explicitly criticizes the Frankfurt School for relying on the notion of autonomous, free subjects who have become alienated by social forces and thus must be emancipated.[34] In short, Lyotard reads the Frankfurt School's critical theory as a modernist, representational project. Conversely, his own theory of postmodernism and his call for paralogical experiments have been criticized by Jürgen Habermas, Frederic Jameson, David Harvey and others as foreclosing the possibility of consensual politics. For us, however, what is most important is the fact that Marcuse and Lyotard each contribute to our general theory by defining performance as a formation of power arising in the wake of the Second World War. Each characterizes performative power primarily in terms of economic and technological efficiency, though neither restricts its effects to the applied sciences or corporate organizations. Instead, performance operates throughout certain societies as a distinct mode of power and knowledge.

There is one other striking consistency between the performance theories of Marcuse and Lyotard, one that reveals the workings of performative power within the Performance Studies paradigm: like Marcuse's performance principle, Lyotard's concept of performative legitimation has been largely missed by cultural performance theorists. Not that Lyotard's *Postmodern Condition* has been overlooked, far from it. In fact, theorists analyzing postmodern performance art have often cited this text, but they tend to do so without addressing the normativity of performance, much less its terror. I'll cite two examples. In the aptly titled text *Postmodernism and Performance* (1994), Nick Kaye cites *The Postmodern Condition* to distinguish modern and postmodern knowledge, but he does so without mentioning the concept of performativity, which is, as we've just seen, the defining characteristic of postmodern knowledge. Instead, Kaye quickly shifts to Lyotard's distinction between discourse and figure in order to concentrate on aesthetic concerns.[35] More recently, Marvin Carlson also discusses postmodern performance art using Lyotard's *Postmodern Condition*. Unlike Kaye, Carlson does cite performative legitimation. However, he defines performativity as "activity that allows the operation of improvisatory experimentation based on the perceived needs and felt desires of the unique situation,"[36] a reading that greatly understates its normative valences and, in effect, conflates performativity with paralogy, another mode of legitimation which Lyotard suggests can contest it.[37] I must stress that Kaye and Carlson are performance scholars whose work I admire. Indeed, what I find most intriguing is that such insightful authors can bring together postmodern performance and *The Postmodern Condition* without discussing the normativity of performativity, for in many ways, performativity *is* the postmodern condition. My point is not to criticize Kaye and Carlson, but rather to suggest that their readings of Lyotard are produced by our paradigmatic lecture machine, that is, by interpretative and evaluative mechanisms that have also programmed the decades-long nonreading of Marcuse's performance principle.

If Lyotard's theory of performativity has been missed not only by two scholars but by an entire generation of cultural performance researchers, and if Marcuse's performance principle has been off our scanners for more than two generations, these omissions are less a question of hasty reading by individual scholars and more a matter of our institutional reading machines being out of tune and technically blind to the feedback of performative power circuits. Perhaps it takes a certain nose to sense the power of performance. That Marcuse and Lyotard's performance theories have been cited oddly or not at all results, I think, from the fact that each analyzes performance as a normative process, while Performance Studies researchers most interested in cultural politics have, until recently, theorized performance almost exclusively as mutational, resistant, transgressive. Somewhat like the *Challenger* SRB workgroup, we have unwittingly and perhaps unavoidably normalized deviation, and through repetition our very competencies have generated a certain structural incompetency with respect to other discourses and practices of performance. The paradigm's liminal-norm, while enabling us to theorize transgressive and resistant performance and our own contested situation as a paradigm, has simultaneously prevented us from sensing the power of performance, not to mention the joint performance-challenges of Performance Management and Techno-Performance. Or to put things yet another way: *the liminal-norm is itself an effect of performative power,* one that has prevented us from addressing the onto-historical forces that connect Performance Studies to other performances. Paradoxically, our attentiveness to liminal performance has kept us out of the loop with respect to the performativity of power and, in doing so, has limited our liminality.

This liminal-norm is starting to break down. The disciplinary seals separating the paradigms are eroding under the pressure of certain citational forces, though these seals have never really been failsafe. The erosion can perhaps best be felt in the impact which the works of Judith Butler have had upon Performance Studies. Even here, however, the reading pattern just cited initially guided the reception of her work among many cultural performance scholars. We have seen that Turner and Schechner theorized performative genres as liminal, that is, as "in between" times/spaces in which social norms are broken apart, turned upside-down, and played with. What Butler creates in the time and space of numerous articles and a handful of books is a theory that poses performativity not only as marginal, transgressive or resistant, but also as a dominant and punitive form of power, one which both generates and constrains human subjects. In short, she theorizes both the transgressivity and the normativity of performative genres. If Turner's centrality lies in his theory of performative liminality, Butler's subversiveness lies in her theory of performative normativity.

Unlike Marcuse and Lyotard, whose performance concepts critically engage those of Performance Management and Techno-Performance, Butler directly addresses the concept of performance articulated by Performance Studies, and she does so by citing both Turner and Schechner. In the first section of her 1990 article "Performative Acts and Gender Constitution," she writes that "the acts by which gender is constituted bear similarities to performative acts within theatrical contexts."[38] While Turner and Schechner use theatrical action in order to theorize liminal and potentially transgressive performances, Butler takes another route, toward an analysis of compulsory heterosexual norms: "as a strategy of survival within compulsory systems, gender is a performance with clearly punitive consequences. Discrete genders are part of what 'humanizes' individuals within contemporary culture: indeed, we regularly punish those who fail to do their gender right."[39] This punitive performance is not expressive; it does not exteriorize an interior substance, identity, or essence; instead, gender emerges from performances that disguise their constitutive role. Gendered subjectivity is itself constituted through compulsory performances of social norms. "From a feminist point of view, one might try to reconceive the gendered body as the legacy of sedimented acts rather than a predetermined or foreclosed structure, essence or fact, whether natural, cultural, or linguistic."[40] Through repeated performances, these norms become sedimented *as* (and not in) gendered bodies.

In order to flesh out her performative reading of gender, Butler turns to anthropological discourse and, of particular interest here, to Turner's theory of ritual. But she does so with a twist. Reiterating the importance for feminism of a theatrically based theory of social action, she asks:

> In what senses, then, is gender an act? As anthropologist Victor Turner suggests in his studies of ritual social drama, social action requires a performance which is **repeated**. This repetition is at once a reenactment and reexperiencing of a set of meanings already socially established; it is the mundane and ritualized form of their legitimation. When this conception of social performance is applied to gender, it is clear that although there are individual bodies that enact these significations by becoming stylized into gendered modes, this "action" is immediately public as well.[41]

Why do I say that Butler turns to Turner with a twist? Because her reading explores gender issues recognized as important but not systematically pursued by him. The twist, however, comes not only in Butler's application of social drama to gender, but also in her reading of Turner's ritual. Ritual for him is sacred, not mundane or profane. Further, Butler writes that Turner's research "suggests [. . .] that social action requires a performance which is *repeated*." Her emphasis on repetition is most suggestive, for while repetition is certainly at work in any ritual, Turner's theory does not explicitly focus on it. Indeed, Butler reads ritual performance in a manner from which he might turn away: as compulsory routine.[42] Let us note that Turner also opposes ritual to "technological routine." He minimizes the repetitive valences of ritual, and this citationality is precisely what interests Butler most. Rather than simply repeat the familar reading of liminal ritual as transgressive, however, she actively reads (reinscribes) Turner's theory of social drama as a theory of normativity. By pushing the pedal on performative citationality, Butler allows us to see how his theory of ritual can be generalized to understand both transgressive and normative performance.

Shortly after her discussion of Turner, Butler cites Schechner while distilling the differences of theatrical and social acts. She cautiously suggests that "gender performances in non-theatrical contexts are governed by more clearly punitive and regulatory social conventions" than those in theatrical contexts.[43] Her citation of Schechner then comes in a passage that could itself be read as a script:

> Indeed, the sight of a transvestite onstage can compel pleasure and applause while the sight of the same transvestite on the seat next to us on

> the bus can compel fear, rage, even violence. . . . On the street or in the bus, the act becomes dangerous, if it does, precisely because there are no theatrical conventions to delimit the purely imaginary character of the act, indeed, on the street or in the bus, there is no presumption that the act is distinct from a reality; the disquieting effect of the act is that there are no conventions that facilitate making this separation. Clearly, there is theatre which attempts to contest or, indeed, break down those conventions that demarcate the imaginary from the real (Richard Schechner brings this out quite clearly in **Between Theatre and Anthropology**).[44]

In citing Schechner, Butler theorizes the transgressive aspects of performance, writing that the transvestite on the shuttle bus "challenges, at least implicitly, the distinction between appearance and reality."[45] In light of these citations of Turner and Schechner, let me repose the liminal-norm this way: liminality can be theorized not only in terms of a time/space of antistructural play, but also in terms of a time/space of structural normalization. Further, the subjunctive mood of the "as if," used by Schechner and others to theorize liminality, must be understood not in opposition to an indicative mood of "it is," but as intimately related to an *imperative* mood which commands "it must be." Perform—or else: the liminal-norm is a *command performance*.

Butler explains the political stakes of performative citation in *Gender Trouble: Feminism and the Subversion of Identity* (1990). We see here the ways in which performative power operates through the process of signification. "The subject is not *determined* by the rules through which it is generated because signification is *not a founding act, but rather a regulated process of repetition* that both conceals itself and enforces its rules precisely through substantializing effects. In a sense, all signification takes place with the orbit of the compulsion to repeat; 'agency,' then, is to be located within the possibility of a variation on that repetition."[46] Acts become sedimented precisely through the orbit of their historical repetition and desedimented through, shall we say, exorbitant variations on such repetitions, variations which, however, also nonetheless involve repetition, citation, rehearsal, and parody. Thus, the "task is not whether to repeat, but how to repeat or, indeed, to repeat and, through a radical proliferation of gender, *to displace* the very gender norms that enable the repetition itself."[47] Butler uses drag performance to theorize how parody can operate to repeat and displace gender norms. Since both normative sedimentation and transgressive desedimentation involve repetitive performances, Butler warns that parody is not inherently subversive. Drag may further sediment gender identities by repeating and reinforcing the orbit of hegemonic significations, while at other times destabilizing those very significations through exorbitant, hyperbolic repetitions that give rise to political resignifications.

After the publication and enthuasiastic reception of *Gender Trouble*, Butler offered some corrections to her readers, corrections that entail a certain rewriting of the relation between performance and performativity. The performance theory of *Gender Trouble* is itself reread and resignified in her 1993 article "Critically Queer." Here Butler returns to the question of gender performativity and drag, now stressing the *discursivity* of performatives. "Performative acts are forms of authoritative speech: most performatives, for instance, are statements which, in the uttering, also perform a certain action and exercise a binding power."[48] Significantly, she turns to the effects of her own discourse, namely the theory of subversive gender parody posed in *Gender Trouble*. Butler asks: "If gender is a mimetic effect, is it therefore a choice or a dispensable artifice? If not, how did this reading of *Gender Trouble* emerge?"[49] She offers two reasons for this misapprehension, while also suggesting there may be others. First, she says that she herself cited "drag as an example of performativity (taken then, by some, to be *exemplary*, that is, *the* example of performativity)."[50] Second, with the "growing queer movement . . . the publicization of theatrical agency has become quite central."[51] If I may offer a third and closely related reason for the misreading of Butler's theory of performativity: given the numerous critical theories that articulate performance as transgressive and/or resistant cultural practices, many readers may have passed too quickly over Butler's stress on performativity as both normative and punitive and instead installed her work within more conventional, i.e., "radical," readings of performance. In short, their readings may have been governed by the liminal-norm.

The essay "Critically Queer" also contains a certain breakup of the close alliance between theatrical performance and performativity that Butler forged in *Gender Trouble*. If there she sought to theorize performativity via performance, in this essay she also emphasizes performativity *contra* performance. Elaborating her corrective reading, she now clearly distinguishes performativity from performance and does so in a paragraph entirely italicized.

> *In no sense can it be concluded that the part of gender that is performed is therefore the "truth" of gender; performance as bounded "act" is distinguished from performativity insofar as the latter consists in a reiteraton of norms which precede, constrain, and exceed the performer and in that sense cannot be taken as the fabrication of the performer's "will" or "choice"; further, what is "performed" works to conceal, if not to disavow, what remains opaque, unconscious, un-performable. The reduction of performativity to performance would be a mistake.*[52]

This passage calls for comment. Butler is obviously not referring to the ritualized performance she reads in Turner, wherein performance always already entails a citational process. Instead, she defines performance as an act in the here-and-now, that is, as a presence, one bounded in the will of the performer. This resignification of "performance," in turn, involves a resignification of "performative:" opening her essay by citing Eve Sedgwick's reading of J.L. Austin, Butler makes it clear that she now wishes to distinguish embodied performances from discursive performatives, to transfer performance from theatrical to discursive contexts.

Butler's theory of punitive performativity is a crucial contribution to our general theory. In addition to theorizing performance as both normative and transgressive, her work also distinguishes the discursive and the embodied dimensions of performativity. As we have just seen, she even warns that performative must not be reduced to performance. However, in the version of "Critically Queer" published in *Bodies that Matter: On the Discursive Limits of "Sex"* (1993), Butler also points to their possible convergence. "It may seem [. . .] that there is a difference between the embodying or performing of gender norms and the performative use of discourse. Are these two different senses of 'performativity,' or do they converge as modes of citationality in which the compulsory character of certain social imperatives becomes subject to a more promising deregulation?"[53] Here Butler's use of the term "performance," while retaining the sense of embodiment, also restores the repetition she earlier read in Turner's theory of social drama. We can link this insistence on repetition to Schechner's restoration of behavior, the theory that all performances are rehearsed, recited, reactualized. Thus gender, and more generally, all subject formation, entail a normative ensemble of restored behaviors and discourses, a mundane yet punitive regime of *performances* and *performatives*, a sedimented stratum of acts and words always already repeated for the *n*th time. By suggesting that discursive performatives and embodied performances are both modes of citationality, Butler gestures toward the possibility of a general theory that could account for their convergence. What I am calling the power of performance is one such theory.

Let me rehearse this theory of power once again (and not for the last time) by splicing together some film clips from our dramaturgical readings. Marcuse's performance principle provides an establishing shot of performative power. In comprehensive terms, he defines performance as the standardization of society according to norms of techno-economic efficiency. His socio-psychoanalytic reading focuses on the alienation of individual desire, and Marcuse's models of rational subjectivity and repressive power lead him to cast performative power as rather monolithic and homogeneous in its effects. Lyotard, however, delivers an alternative establishing shot of performative power with his theory that modern grand narratives have been displaced by input/output matrices. In addition, by drawing attention to the plurality of contemporary language games, he provides mid-range shots that capture the ways in which performative legitimation depends upon multiple and localized demands to perform—or else. We should note here that Lyotard explicitly aligns performativity with Austin's concept of the performative, arguing that the "two meanings are not far apart. Austin's performative realizes the optimal performance."[54] With a last bit of discontinuity editing, we can read Butler's texts as offering close-up shots of the power of performance, shots that engage Marcuse's own close-ups of alienated performance. Her detailed analysis uncovers the micro-operations of discourses and practices in the constitution of gender, sexuality, and subjectivity itself. Butler also lets us into the archive of performativity by arguing that all performances, spoken or enacted, are real only because they reel off and on from a general matrix of citationality.

This theory rehearsal, with its cutting back and forth between different theoretical set ups, suggests that discursive performatives and embodied performances are the building blocks of an immense onto-historical production, one which we will soon explore as the *performance stratum.* Performatives and performances form the basic tactical units, the BTUs of a power/knowledge formation that is a half-century old and growing more powerful and knowledgeable every day. At the crack of millennia, performativity guides innumerable processes, ranging from the intricacies of class, race, ethnic, gender, and sexual identification to the large-scale installations of technologies, organizations, and cultures. "Perform—or else" is a challenge made in the USA and now restoring itself worldwide through innumerable circuits. That's one reason I prefaced our current theory rehearsal with Heidegger's call of challenging forth and his age of the world picture, for performance is going global, *fast.* I have restaged our theory as a moving picture so as to evoke this speculative possibility: the age of the world picture is becoming *an age of global performance.*

Challenging is the fundamental tonality of this transformation without foundation; it is the affective dimension of the performance stratum, the shifting element of its "perform—or else." Accordingly, the age of global performance is not only populated by high performers, peak performers, star performers, performers who challenge forth themselves and others, but also by the performatively challenged, those who cannot perform up to spec: the mentally challenged, the physically challenged, the economically challenged, the digitally challenged, the stylistically challenged, and even the liminally challenged. Perform—or else: there is no performance without challenge, without claims and contestations, demands and accusations, field tests and identity checks, as well as the occasional untimely dare.

And no performance untouched by the calamity of *calumnia.* The call of the performance stratum is not monotonal but polytonal; it is composed of multitudes of challenges, of contests and force relations that produce different performances, different machinations of performatives and performances, of words and bodies that challenge, mime, and trick out one another. Challenger challenging challenger. The challenges of efficacy, efficiency, and effectiveness are among the most insistent calls cast across the emerging performance stratum. Each is produced by a reading machine, a sociotechnical arrangement of discourses and practices that guides and is guided by different movements of generalization and appropriation, as well as by diverse specifications, enactments, applications, breakdowns, and reboots. As productions of performance, the paradigms of Performance Studies, Performance Management, and Techno-Performance have helped to actualize the forces of normativity and mutation that criss-cross the performance stratum. Their research has already given us preliminary mappings of the performance stratum. But to read this formation in greater depth and detail, to get even more concrete and at the same time even more abstract about the power of performance, we must attend yet another lecture. We must introduce yet another Challenger, one whose theory of stratification may at first bore us deeply, but which will with luck put the age of performance in sharper focus.

CHAPTER 6. PROFESSOR CHALLENGER AND THE PERFORMANCE STRATUM

On the third of *A Thousand Plateaus*, the same Professor Challenger "who made the Earth scream with his pain machine, as described by Arthur Conan Doyle, gave a lecture mixing several textbooks on geology and biology in a fashion befitting his simian disposition. He explained that the Earth—the Deterritorialized, the Glacial, the giant Molecule—is a body without organs."[1] However, for Gilles Deleuze and Félix Guattari, the producers of this scene of fictive theory, the primary question at hand is not, for the time being, an Artaudian body without organs, but rather the strata that crystallize and form upon it. Challenger continues: "Strata are Layers, Belts. They consist in giving form to matters, of imprisoning intensities or locking singularities into systems of resonance and redundancy, of producing on the body of the earth molecules large and small and organizing them into molar aggregates."[2] The professor lecturing here is a scientifictional character, one Deleuze and Guattari have cast from the sci-fi stories of a writer named Doyle, who, after he had created, killed, and resurrected a detective named Holmes, spent his later years channeling a gay scientist in the name of "Challenger."[3] Deleuze and Guattari recast this professor to lecture within their own writing machine, and they do so for a singular purpose: to conduct a "stratoanalysis," a reading of stratification processes in rocks and organs and subjects. Simultaneously, their reading is also a demonstration of destratification, the creative breakdown and erosion of systems and forms.

I have signed on to this lecture machine to initiate a stratoanalysis of performance, and Professor Challenger performs here as an online metaguidance device. The third of *A Thousand Plateaus* is called "10,000 B.C.: The Geology of Morals (Who Does the Earth Think It Is?)." The text mixes together many others, including Nietzsche's *Genealogy of Morals*, Doyle's short story "When the World Screamed," as well as a textbook on geology. The *topos*, the site and topic, of the lesson is stratification. "Challenger quoted a sentence he said he came across in a geology textbook. He said we needed to learn it by heart because we would only be in a position to understand it later on: 'A surface of stratification is a more compact plane of consistency lying between two layers.' The layers are the strata. . . . In effect, the body without organs is itself the plane of consistency, which becomes compact or thickens at the level of the strata."[4] Stratification proceeds through a double process which consists of 1) the sedimentation or layering of flows and submolecular elements into molecular forms, and 2) the folding or compounding of these forms into molar compounds and functions. This "double articulation" takes place through a process of territorialization or appropriation that creates a "form of content" which then enters into a process of encoding or linearization that produces a "form of expression." In the formation of geological strata, for instance, sandstone and schist settle to form a layer of sediment, the form of content; this layer then stabilizes and hardens, forming the structure of sedimentary rock, the form of expression. Strata are thus always double, with forms of content and expression composing, respectively, the substratum and metastratum of a particular stratum.

But Professor Challenger is interested in much more than rocks: his theory of stratification is a general theory covering inorganic, organic, and human realms. To stress the general yet differentiated nature of stratification, Challenger contends that "God is a Lobster, or a double pincer, a double bind. Not only do strata come at least in pairs, but in a different way each stratum is double (it itself has several layers)."[5] Not only are strata composed of a substratum and metastratum, but an entire, doubly articulated stratum may itself serve as substratum or metastratum in another stratification. In this way, there are strata within strata within strata. The Professor suggests that the earth has thickened into three general belts of strata: geological, biological, and anthropomorphic or, respectively, the inorganic, the organic, and the human. These belts build upon and are enfolded and embedded within one other, and each is itself multiple and divided. For instance, the geological stratum contains crystalline, physicochemical, and geological strata proper, while the biological stratum contains levels of morphogenesis, cellular chemistry, and genetics. The anthropomorphic stratum is the most complex, as it is generated by the double articulation of an alloplastic content, practices that bring about "modifications in the external world" and a linguistic expression, discourses that operate with "symbols that are comprehensible, transmittable, and modifiable from outside."[6]

Our general theory of performance unfolds on this third stratum, for it is here that performance must first be situated. Our own stratoanalysis might be called "2001 A.D.: The Geology of Performance (Who Does IT Think It Is?)," and its drilling and boring is directed by Professor Challenger, who suggests that we "follow Foucault in his exemplary analysis."[7] We begin by citing *Foucault*, Deleuze's booklength study of this genealogist of power/knowledge. *Foucault* is itself a stratoanalysis, a diagrammatic digging of force relations and knowledge forms. Deleuze writes that "strata are historical formations, positivities or empiricities. As 'sedimentary beds' they are made from things and words, from seeing and speaking, from the visible and the sayable, from bands of visibility and fields of readability, from contents and expressions."[8] One such stratum is the disciplinary formation theorized by Foucault in *Discipline and Punish*. Here Foucault analyzes the historical formation of eighteenth- and nineteenth-century Western Europe, which he argues was modeled on a particular regime of statements and visibilities, specifically, "the legal register of justice and the extra-legal register of discipline."[9] As the power regime that displaced the formation of torture found in sovereign societies, discipline actualized itself through the juxtaposition of two forms of knowledge: the discursive statements of penal law and the concrete mechanisms of surveillance exemplified in Jeremy Bentham's panopticon. "In effect," Foucault writes, "the great continuity of the carceral system throughout the law and its sentences gives a sort of legal sanction to the disciplinary mechanisms."[10] To read the extent of disciplinary power and knowledge, he documents its normalizing effects within discourses and practices far beyond the prison, such as those of hospitals, factories, and schools. Foucault concludes his text by writing that it "must serve as a historical background to various studies of the power of normalization and the formation of knowledge in modern society."[11] And, indeed, his reading of discipline has subsequently served as background to many studies of power and knowledge.

While some theorists have applied Foucault's reading of discipline directly to contemporary society, others have dismissed it as inadequate to today's power arrangements. Rather than quickly embrace or dismiss Foucault's model of discipline, let us take a cue from Deleuze, who stresses that "what Foucault recognized as well was the transience of this model." In "Postscript on the Societies of Control," Deleuze writes that "the disciplines underwent a crisis to the benefit of new forces that were gradually instituted and which accelerated after World War II: a disciplinary society was what we already no longer were, what we had ceased to be."[12] Deleuze contends that we now live within a different stratum, one which he names (citing Burroughs) "societies of control." Yet in light of our readings of Marcuse, Lyotard, and Butler, of the NEA 4, the NPR, and the MIA complex, in light of these and many other citations, let us deviate a bit from Deleuze and call things another way: we're living, dying, on the tip of a massive formation that I call the *performance stratum*. Or, to cast this thought in the form of a speculative analogy:

> **Performance will be to the twentieth and twenty-first centuries what discipline was to the eighteenth and nineteenth: an onto-historical formation of power and knowledge.**

Though it obviously draws upon and recombines other knowledge forms and power forces, the performance stratum coalesced in the United States in the wake of the Second World War, and its effects have been going global for some time, expanding especially fast with the thaw of the Cold War, the breakup of the Soviet Union, and the subsequent expansion of global capital markets in a postcolonial world. Perhaps the most forceful indicator that performance is a contemporary yet futural formation of power and knowledge lies not in the passing of the Government Performance and Results Act, nor in the existence of numerous High Performance Computing Centers, nor in the establishment of an organization called "Performance Studies international." Rather, the most telling evidence of the performance stratum might be how easily we can understand statements and practices as, respectively, *performatives* and *performances*.

Performatives and performances are the building blocks of the performance stratum. They are, respectively, its forms of expression and content, and as such, they are the statements and visibilities that compose the age of global performance. "An 'age' does not pre-exist the statements which express it, nor the visibilities which fill it," writes Deleuze in *Foucault*. "These are two essential aspects: on the one hand each stratum or historical formation implies a distribution of the visible and the articulable which acts upon itself; on the other, from one stratum to the next there is a variation in the distribution, because visibility itself changes in style, while the statements themselves change their system."[13] Performatives and performances are our system and our style, our ways of saying and seeing. As distributions of language and light, they are the emergent forms through which things are said and seen. Performance Studies, Performance Management, Techno-Performance, these and other research paradigms join and seal together different collections of practices and discourses, different combinations of performances and performatives. The subject and object fields of these paradigms stretch across the stratum whose building blocks they have also helped to solidify. But more powerfully, more generally than these paradigms, performatives and performances are in the midst of becoming the onto-historical conditions for saying and seeing anything at all. "Everything is performative," "everything is performance"—what is most striking about these sweeping generalizations is that their ontological exaggeration carries a historical precision.

And we can be even sharper: the truth of everything emerges through the cracked and uneven joints that bind together performatives and performances. Words and acts are not joined in a harmonious ring, but are sealed together through ongoing contests and struggles. "Truth is defined neither by conformity or common form, nor by correspondence between the two forms. There is a disjunction between speaking and seeing, between the visible and the articulable: 'what we see never lies in what we say,' and vice versa. . . . The archive, the audiovisual is disjunctive."[14] The audiovisual archive can be plugged into what we have been calling the citational network. From this network emerge different arrangements of words and things, of discourses and practices whose ongoing battles produce subjects and objects alike. "The image of a battle signifies precisely that there is no isomorphism. The two heterogeneous forms comprise a condition and a conditioned element, light and visibilities, language and statements."[15] Channeling Professor Challenger, let's make like a lobster and doubly articulate the age of global performance writ small:

Performances are territorializations of flows and unformed matters
into sensible bodies,
while performatives are encodings of these bodies
into articulable subjects and objects.

Performance-performative forms a single, cracked block of stratification, with the embodied performance comprising as a rule the substratum or determined element and the discursive performative functioning as the metastratum or determining element. "The statement has primacy by virtue of the spontaneity of its conditions (language) which give it a determining form, while the visible element, by virtue of the receptivity of its condition (light), merely has the form of the determinable."[16] This distinction between spontaneity and receptivity is crucial to understanding the power of performance, but it must not be understood as corresponding to active and passive essences. As heterogeneous forms of knowledge, discursive performatives and embodied performances presuppose each other, and because these forms do not conform or correspond, their integration must be understood at another level, that of force relations, i.e., power.

While the performance stratum generates an archive of knowledge-forms, it is also enveloped by an emergent diagram of power-forces, forces that are not stratified into discourses and practices but instead consist of affective strategies, micro-arrangements of normativities and mutations. Normative relations of force, forces of law and order, are what construct and seal together the heterogeneous forms of performatives and performances. Mutational forces, on the other hand, forces of deviation, transgression, and resistance, break these seals apart and erode the forms of knowledge. Here the spontaneity of statements and receptivity of visibilities refer, respectively, to *the power to affect* and *the power to be affected.* "In each formation there is a form of receptivity that constitutes the visible element, and a form of spontaneity that constitutes the articulable element. Of course, these two forms do not coincide with the aspects of force or the two sorts of affects, the receptivity of power's ability to be affected and the spontaneity of power's ability to affect. But the two forms are derived from these affects, and find in them their 'internal conditions.' "[17] The diagram of forces functions as the *a priori* element of the audiovisual archive of forms, and its agitations give rise to the diagram's atmospheric quality.

Like the contested relation between performances and performatives, the relations between normative and mutational forces and between archive and diagram are stormy and contentious. Though outside the strata of knowledge-forms, the atmospheric element of power-forces is nonetheless historical. The power of performance is virtual and unstable; yet its relations of force only actualize and stabilize themselves through the stratification of performances and performatives, through the formation of embodied practices and linguistic discourses. "This is the paradoxical character of the *a priori* element, a microagitation. For the forces in the relation are inseparable from the variations in their relations or their distances from one another. In brief, forces are in a perpetual state of evolution; *there is an emergence of forces which doubles history,* or rather envelops it, according to the Nietzschean conception."[18] The truths found in gestures and voices carry with them distinctive tonalities of affect. In disciplinary institutions, the formal categories of truth include "to make educated," "to make rehabilitated," and "to make healthy," while among their affective categories are "to allocate," "to classify," "to compose."[19] It is perhaps too early to define the formal categories of truth that characterize the emergent performance stratum. However, our readings of the three performance paradigms and the *Challenger* SRB workgroup suggest that these categories already include "to make efficacious," "to make efficient," and "to make effective." And the affective categories of performative power, the powers to affect and to be affected, what atmospheric tonalities envelop the performance stratum? Do they not include "to challenge" and "to be challenged"?

The battles of performances and performatives, the microagitation of their *a priori* element, these effect the challenging forth of the world writ large and small. The blocks of words and acts produced by the different paradigms may appear unrelated, as if cast about by a series of violent storms. Yet they have come to form a sedimented layer of stratification, one whose deposits have been laid down for decades, if not longer. The blocks are connected, recast, and bound together in another role as this layer folds back upon itself and their microagitations begin to function within a matrix of power-forces that surrounds and permeates the performance stratum.

Let us explore this stratum in another way. As with the case of the performance paradigms, a comparative analysis will enable us to generate different perspectives on this formation whose diverse power arrangements are most subtle and complex. Our launch sequence thus reinitiates itself here with a geology lesson on performance.

Before embarking on this reading, however, some preliminary remarks are called for. As should be readily apparent, I am not casting performance as a "good" thing and discipline as a "bad" one. Their relationship must not and, indeed, cannot be evaluated in this way, for performance and discipline are themselves two different evaluative regimes, each with its own criteria, its own norms, its own deviations. Nor am I posing performance in opposition to discipline; rather, performance is, in part, a displacement of discipline, a breaking-down, transformation, and reinscription of its discourses and practices within an entirely different milieu of forces, one that generates statements and visibilities unimaginable within disciplinary societies of the eighteenth and nineteenth centuries. Finally, though performance is displacing discipline, it has not replaced it. The performance stratum is futural, still under construction, and discipline, though in decline, remains operational, especially in industrializing societies but also in postindustrial ones, where it provides auxiliary power to the emerging performativity.

With these remarks in place, I will take some core samples of the emerging performance stratum. I will do so by differentiating discipline and performance in terms of seven layers or belts of stratification. Here, then, is the geology of performance.

1. *Subjects and objects.* The stratum of discipline attempts to construct and solidify highly centered, unified human subjects and highly stable fields of objects. As the onto-historical formation of the Enlightenment and its modern institutions, discipline was the power source behind what Marcuse calls individual rationality. But its power did not corrupt an already present subjective truth and objective reality; rather discipline constitutes this truth and reality. It is the representational production of the real. Deleuze writes: "Power 'produces reality' before it represses. Equally, it produces truth before it ideologizes, abstracts, or masks."[20] Discipline underwrites the modern legitimation of knowledge and social bonds via such grand narratives as Reason, Progress, Liberation, and Revolution, and it actualizes these metanarratives through its many institutions.

The performance stratum, by contrast, constructs and proliferates decentered subjectivities and highly unstable object fields. Just as discipline's subjectivity and objectivity do not preexist its power arrangements, *performative subjects and objects do not perform as much as they are performed.* As Butler stresses, there is no agent behind performance; rather agency is itself an effect of performative citationality. These effects are multiple and diverse: though Marcuse stressed the homogenizing effects of the performance principle's technological rationality, performativity has also contributed to the diversification of subject positions, to the creation of what Donna Haraway calls "fractured identities."[21] Across the performance stratum, hybrid, hyphenated subjects rapidly emerge and immerge, passing through a variety of subject positions and switching quickly between innumerable language games. Multitasking, channel-surfing, attention-deficit disorders: these portend the emergence of fractal, (n-1) dimensional subjectivities. Indeed, in the US, the social construction of identity and the plurality of subject positions is becoming readily apparent to individuals and society alike, so much so that ideological critiques of "natural identity" will become increasingly ineffective. It may well be that theories of social constructivism are already in the process of becoming an ideology in need of deconstruction (along with the concept of ideology itself).

Similarly, the constructedness of even the most "natural" of objects is also becoming readily apparent in performative societies. Through mass media and mass education, we "know" that theoretical research and computer modeling constitutes the scientific knowledge of subatomic particles and distant celestial bodies. More down to earth, we also "know" that vegetables come from "the market," or rather, from far-flung, capital-intensive farms of agribusiness, from labor-intensive fields of organic farmers, or simply from the supermarket. The patently artificial nature of nature was recognized in the late nineteenth century by Oscar Wilde and other decadent writers. More recently, Jean Baudrillard has analyzed the power of simulacra in the late twentieth century, focusing much of his analysis on the United States. In this country, critiques targeting the historical construction of objective knowledge have entered into public debates concerning the multiculturalism of workplaces, classrooms, and museums. Knowledge on the performance stratum, then, is characterized by simulation rather than representation, by the instability of subjects and objects, and by the playing and contesting of diverse language games—which, make no mistake, can be deadly serious.

2. *Geopolitics.* Though Foucault theorized the early formation of discipline within eighteenth-century Western European nations, disciplinary statements and practices were simultaneously transplanted around the world in seedling form through their colonial institutions. Discipline took different forms in different colonies, battling and mixing with indigenous power arrangements and at times reverting to the discourses and practices of torture in these encounters. Nonetheless, through institutions such as governments, armies, businesses, hospitals, churches, schools, and prisons, disciplinary mechanisms were exported by European states. These states administered their colonies from afar through their own domestic disciplinary organizations, and yet these organizations were also subtly transformed through these very encounters. Discipline, in short, was the stratum of European colonialism, both of its economic and political racism as well as its ethnocentric altruism. Significantly, some of these colonial

disciplinary institutions, especially the university and military, later came to play crucial roles in nationalist liberation movements of the Third World.

By contrast, the performance stratum's initial formation occurred in the United States of the mid-twentieth century, and its statements and visibilities have since been disseminated around the postcolonial world with the demise of the European imperial powers, an extracted Cold War, the rise and decline of Third World, and the growing hegemonies of American politics, economics, military might, and cultural media. With the fall of the Soviet Union in 1989, the overseas recessions of the mid-1990s, and the intense growth of the American economy during this same decade, this hegemony has strengthened tremendously. The performative network now includes numerous alliances effectively directed by the US and, just as significantly, by such media as American and American-style film, music, television, and, more recently, Internet services (e.g., AOL and AOL-Japan).[22] However, and this is crucial, performance cannot be reduced to the power vested within and exercised by any individual nation state, including that of the United States. Though in some sense "made in the USA" during the Cold War, the performance stratum extends far beyond this place and time, and given its networked distribution of power, it is not guided solely by the US government or its MIA complex. This state and complex are but a few of the most obvious relay stations of performative power. Other stations include supranational organizations (e.g., the United Nations, the International Monetary Fund, the World Bank, The World Trade Organization, NATO, the European Union), numerous regional trade alliances (e.g., NAFTA, OPEC), multinational corporations and NGOs (non-government organizations such as relief and refugee agencies).

On a more molecular level, Marcuse's and Butler's analyses demonstrate that performative effects are also generated far below such molar institutions as nation states and large-scale organizations. The power of performance operates through social stratifications such as gender, sexual, ethnic, racial, class, and religious identity, where blocks of performatives and performances constitute different subject positions within different language games. And here we come to an ambiguous possibility: while the power figures of discipline have been almost exclusively white European men, those of performance may be much more diverse. The emergence of postcolonial nations, the increasing importance of cultural differences for both social groups and global markets, and the emergence of women and people of color as astronauts, managers, politicians, and media stars, all suggest that the performance stratum will eventually be populated by culturally diverse power figures. Taking all these developments together, we can foresee that in the age of global performance, *the integration of diversity will be supplemented by the diversification of integration.*

3. *Economics.* The stratum of discipline is inseparable from modern, commodity-based capitalism. Though it is punctuated by periods of deep

crisis, the accumulation of capital during times of expansion is comparatively stable, with the value of money being tied to a common gold standard. Disciplinary labor, too, is relatively stable in its form, with skills and production techniques evolving rather slowly. Labor is also collectively organized, as evidenced by the establishment, consolidation, and militant growth of national labor unions. Further, capital and labor are both concentrated in the enclosed space of the factory, a panoptic institution that is at once emblem, product, and producer of the industrial revolution. This industrialization was centered in Western Europe and North America, and though its raw materials were imported from colonial lands, factory labor was provided locally, while finished commodities were both consumed locally and sold abroad.

By contrast, the performance stratum cannot be thought outside of postmodern, information-based capitalism. Here again, it must be stressed that performativity is in the process of displacing forms of discipline: nationally oriented, industrially based capital and labor have not disappeared, but they are rapidly being restructured by global capital and labor forces and reinscribed within digital infrastructures. We can identify three phases in the emergence of this information economy.

The period 1945 to 1972, a period of unprecedented economic growth sometimes referred to as "Fordism," can be read as an initial, transitional phase. Industrialization and mass production surged in the US and, later, in the nations of Western Europe and Japan, whose economies were rebuilt after the war with massive US support. Growth was steady and robust, and the accumulation of capital remained very stable. At the same time, labor militancy subsided as unions and management entered into cooperative, long-term contracts. In terms of organizational, technological, and cultural performance, Fordism can be defined as rapid industrial expansion carried out by the more socially conscious practices of Performance Management, the full-blown emergence of consumer culture, and the investment in high technology systems. Information technologies in the US and elsewhere were only beginning to become available to nonmilitary institutions.

In the early 1970s, however, a number of crises occurred that dramatically affected capitalist economies, crises that have helped to shape the stratum's current contours. Among the most significant events were the 1973 OPEC oil embargo and the breakdown of the 1944 Bretton Woods Agreements in 1971, a breakdown that contributed to the global restructuring of financial markets, the uncoupling of the US dollar from the gold standard, and the emergence of global capital markets. David Harvey writes that the "new financial systems put in place since 1972 have changed the balance of forces at work in global capitalism, giving much more autonomy to the banking and financial systems relative to corporate, state, and personal financing."[23] A post-Fordist, high performance capitalism has since emerged, one that is socially unstable and multinationally incorporated. North America and Western Europe have been deindustrializing and becoming wired for the past two decades, installing computerized networks at home and abroad while exporting production processes and entire factories to Latin America and Pacific Asia, thereby accelerating industrialization in these regions. With this dispersion of capital and production, labor has become increasingly "disorganized." As Scott Lash and John Urry argue, the number of blue-collar jobs in the West has decreased in both absolute and relative terms, and this has been accompanied by the decline of collective bargaining and national, class-based political action.[24] Worldwide, geographically stable labor forces have given way to massive waves of internal and external migration. In postindustrial societies, worker expectations of decades-long or life-long job security have been replaced by constant fears of downsizing and outsourcing, as well as the insecurity of permanent part-time and flex-time positions offering little or no health and retirement benefits. Workers in newly industrializing countries, many of them women and children, may initially welcome factory employment yet many inevitably come to suffer under the harshest of conditions: the prohibition of labor unions, the absence of environmental protection laws, long hours, hazardous work environments, and even forced labor.

Since the early 1990s, a third economic phase has taken shape. With the breakup of the Soviet Union and the fall of Communist governments in Eastern Europe, capitalism has claimed a global victory. The win has been ambiguous, to say the least. New market economies have struggled to establish themselves in Russia and its former satellites, often failing to deliver basic goods and services once provided by the state. In Asia and the Pacific, once vibrant economies experienced severe recessions, high unemployment, and capital flight. South American and African economies maintain higher expectations than realization, and higher levels still of foreign debt. Yet a new global economy has emerged, led by the extraordinary growth of the US economy, more specifically, its information economy, by the formation of new economic alliances, such as NAFTA, the European Union, and the World Trade Organization, and by a dizzying number of mergers and strategic alliances across far-flung borders, industries, and markets. Capitalizing on the reform and/or repeal of Bretton Woods and other Depression-era economic measures, the accumulation of capital has become hyperflexible and hypermobile; capital is now able to enter and exit markets around the world with dazzling speed. Deleuze characterizes the current global economy as "a capitalism of higher-order production. It no longer buys raw materials and no longer sells the finished products: it buys finished products or assembles parts. What it wants to sell is services and what it wants to buy is stocks. This is no longer a capitalism for production but for the product, which is to say, for being sold and marketed. Thus it is essentially dispersive, and the factory has given way to the corporation."[25] Institutionally, the culturally attuned practices of Performance Management have matured alongside the installation of information technologies within schools, businesses, public arenas, and private spaces. As services have become more "human," capital has become fully hardwired to IT and through this convergence, more "democratized." Through aggressive pension and investment plans, legions have collectively entered the stock market, while others experiment with radically new financial instruments, such as online and day-trading services. More and more people are turbo-charging the speculative feedback loop, using information technologies to invest in information technologies. From millions of desktops, cell phones, and hand-held devices, capital is now able to move between markets in a matter of hours, minutes, or even seconds. The society of the spectacle is fast becoming the society of speculation.

4. *Knowledge production.* We have already studied some of the differences between modern and postmodern knowledge. Let us investigate closer the infrastructure of their production. In disciplinary societies, knowledge still went by the book. That is, the medium of the printed, alphabetic book structured not only the transmission of disciplinary knowledge, but also its generation, storage, and reception. As the grammatological readings of Derrida, Ulmer, and Ronell have shown, the book and its alphabetic writing must be read as the medium of a profound ethnocentrism, one governed by the linear, logocentric traditions of Western thought.[26] On the disciplinary stratum, the university was ground zero for alphabetic knowledge production, though this production was limited to a relatively elite segment of the population.

The performance stratum is characterized by numerous developments in knowledge production. After the Second World War, enrollment in the alphabetic lecture machine increased dramatically around the world. In the US, the GI Bill brought African-Americans, Jews, and the working and middle classes into the university in large numbers. Increasingly, these institutions also became co-educational, and women in unprecedented numbers began earning degrees, not just in traditional disciplines such as education and nursing, but in a wide array of fields once the exclusive domain of men. Overseas, Third World nations made universal literacy a prominent if not fully realizable goal. Its successes have often been striking. Eric Hobsbawm observes that "whether or not mass literacy was general, the demand for places in secondary and especially in higher education multiplied at an extraordinary rate. . . . [By the 1980s] in educationally ambitious countries, students formed upward of 2.5 per cent of the *total* population—men, women, and children—or even, in exceptional cases, above 3 per cent."[27]

Coinciding with this diversification and growth of student bodies around the world has been a rebuilding of the student desktop. As the millennium turns, knowledge is increasingly generated, stored, distributed, and received via computers and telecommunication networks. Books, lessons, lectures, curricula, research—the entire university machine is going online. One implication is easy to read: if universal literacy is ever achieved, it will occur through electronic interfaces. In its grammatological face-off with word processors, databases, desktop publishing, and online sales and distribution, the book finds itself reinscribed within these new information media: alphabetic writing remains, but its dominance fades as it becomes but one element of hypertextual multimedia. Does this portend the death of the ABC lecture machine, of its rituals, its performances, its lecterns? Lyotard's forecast: "It does not seem absolutely necessary that the medium be a lecture delivered by a teacher in front of silent students, with questions reserved from sections or 'practical work' sessions run by an assistant. To the extent that learning is translatable into computer language and the traditional teacher is replaceable by memory banks, didactics can be entrusted to machines linking traditional memory banks (libraries, etc.) and computer data banks to intelligent terminals placed at the students' disposal."[28]

If we face the passing of the alphabetic lectern, the emerging high performance lecture machine operates via lesson creep. The production of formal knowledge, once situated so securely in the schools and universities of disciplinary societies, now extends far beyond these institutions. On the performance stratum, education is no longer something one undertakes as a child and completes as a young adult: it is fast becoming a lifelong activity. Deleuze writes that *"perpetual training* tends to replace the school, and continuous control to replace the examination. Which is the surest way of delivering the school over to the corporation."[29] And of delivering the corporation over to the school. As universities expand their continuing-education curricula, high performance companies strive to become learning organizations in which individuals and entire organizations continually reinvent themselves in response to changes in their environment. Here again, information technology serves as a crucial catalyst for this learned diffusion. The Bluebook of the High Performance Computing and Communications Initiative lists "life-long learning" as one attribute of what it calls "High-Performance Living."

On the performance stratum, then, the educational lecture machine is not only becoming democratized and digitized: along with performance itself, it is becoming assigned throughout one's personal and social life. Perpetual learning, high performance living: this is yet another way of reading the term "lecture machine." With performativity, life becomes one long continuing ed program. Max Weber once characterized the university as that bureaucracy which trains people to work in other bureaucracies; today, the university lecture machine is a dispersed mechanism whose lessons are dispensed whenever and wherever there is performance—that is, everywhere and everywhen.

5. *Media archives.* Across the entire disciplinary stratum of eighteenth- and nineteenth-century Europe, the audiovisual archiving of statements and practices proceeded primarily through the alphabetic book with its chap-

ters, lists, and tables and through such graphic techniques as painting, engraving, diagrams, and, later, photography—in addition, of course, to storytelling, theater, and other performative genres that rehearse and restore behavior through the medium of the human body. Foucault's archeologies of the clinic and prison concentrate on how discourses and visibilities constructed modern bodies and normalized subjects within an enclosed space and a serialized time. Disciplinary training, the citational inscription of modern bodies and voices, was a long and gradual process that unfolded within relatively stable physical architectures. Further, the passage from one institution to another was regulated and well-marked, as their archives were widely separated and sealed off from one another in time and space. Discourses and practices therefore evolved and circulated slowly in comparison with those of performative societies.[30]

Across the performance stratum, audiovisual archiving increasingly occurs through multimedia networks. Its citational network is programmed less and less by the book and increasingly by the metatechnology of the computer. Quite literally, the computer has incorporated a wide range of information technologies including the book itself, as well as the post, photography, telephony, film, television, typewriter, radio, video, compact disc, copy machine, fax, and an astonishing array of artistic media and scientific instruments. The very notion of an archive has come undone. Friedrich Kittler argues that Foucault's methodological techniques led him to uncritically privilege alphabetic inscription, effectively reducing the archive to a library. "Archeologies of the present," Kittler writes, "must also take into account data storage, transmission, and calculation in technological media."[31]

The networked computer culminates a process that has been underway since the invention of photography and phonography: *the radical transformation of the citational network of discourses and practices.* Kittler has analyzed two "writing systems" or discourse networks: that of 1800, with its Romantic poetry and handwriting manuals; and that of 1900, with its psychophysical experiments, typewriters, and gramophones. A third system, which we might call cite.net 2000, is characterized by information science, guided missiles, and digital computers. This network has been installing itself for decades, incorporating other technologies and techniques into its encrypted digital codes. Transcribed into such codes, statements and visibilities circulate across distances with speeds unprecedented in world history. Electronic digital encoding of discourses and practices enables them to be recorded, played back, and edited in new and uncanny ways. Schechner states: "Already the past fifty years are available on film, tape, and disc. Almost everything we do these days is not only done but kept on film, tape, and disc. We have strong ways of getting, keeping, transmitting and recalling behavior. We live in a time when traditions can die in life, be preserved archivally as behaviors, and later restored."[32]

The effect of IT (information technology) upon the circulation of performatives and performances has already been profound, and it helps to account for the fractured identities and the simulated realities dispersed across the performance stratum. More profoundly than the transportation revolutions of commercial air flight and national highway systems in the 1950s, contemporary IT and mass media such as satellite TV and CDs put audiovisual archives into hypertransit, bringing them in contact with bodies and voices across spatiotemporalities unimaginable a century ago: in a matter of seconds, words and gestures pass between continents as well as generations, restoring behaviors and discourses while reinscribing them within multiple rehearsal processes.

6. *Desire*. Discipline produced a segmentation of desire, creating a libidinal subject whose destiny passed through a series of lecture machines: family, church, school, military, factory, government. . . . In short, desire proceeded via a series of institutionalized rites of passage. Discipline's enclosed space and serialized time captured the productive force of desire and made it Progress itself, segmenting flows and intensities into genders, sects, disciplines, armies, classes, races, and nationalities. The respective discourses and practices achieved the stratification of disciplined minds and bodies, minds and bodies evaluated according to a complex set of bifurcating norms. A subject was either male or female, Christian or non-believer, educated or ignorant, soldier or civilian, bourgeois or proletarian, civilized or savage. At the same time, a subject's position was determinable within a big picture or overarching narrative. But most importantly, in the stratification of disciplinary subjectivity, desire was not simply repressed: it was first constructed as something that *could* be repressed, negated, alienated. As Foucault makes clear in the first volume of *The History of Sexuality*, and as Deleuze and Guattari reiterate in so many places, the desire of modern capitalism is an Oedipalized desire, a desire robbed of its positivities, its productivities, its connectivities, and instead molded into a lack forever returning within an economy of loss and scarcity.

Performativity, by contrast, generates a networked desire, the simulated control of libidinal subjectivities whose paths mingle, collide, and transform one another. "Enclosures are *molds*, distinct castings, but controls are *modulations*, like a self-deforming cast that will continuously change from one moment to the other, or like a sieve whose mesh will transmute from point to point."[33] Performative desire is not molded by a series of distinct disciplinary mechanisms but constantly modulated through a disjunctive network of competing matrices. As suggested by the *Challenger* crew and workgroup, the atmosphere is complex, highly pressurized by challenges and counterchallenges to perform efficiently one moment, effectively another, and efficaciously the next. More generally: even though disciplinary mechanisms are still operational, their institutional forms and functions have been so radically displaced that their terrains have begun to overlap, their codes mix, their limen erode. The breakdown of extended families, the half-life of their nuclear replacement, the mutual incorporation of school and business and military, the collusion between unions and management and government, the multiculturalism of multinational corporations, the "coverage" of all this by mass multimedia technologies—these events index the performative displacement of disciplinary mechanisms in the West. Yet the disintegrative effects of performance have also begun to be felt around the world. Audiovisual archives of different cultures, institutions, and time periods are now being patched into one another, and in the resulting recombinant network, one desiring-machine challenges forth another, and another, and another.

It is precisely because the stratification of desire proceeds through a network of overlapping evaluative grids that the performance stratum generates fractal subjects, unstable objects, and rituals of sociotechnical satisficing. The channel surf of multiheaded reading machines helps generate the diversification of integration: not only are the talking heads of power becoming culturally diverse, the installation of power has become dispersed, nomadic, virtual. Normalization proceeds not through distinct mechanisms that one at a time segment and slowly mold a repressive desire. Instead it operates through embedded and mobile matrices whose shifting patterns modulate an "excessive" desire, making flows of intensity shuttle quickly between different grids, challenging desire to multitask, innovate, and indeed *exceed* itself, driving desire across different thresholds in order to test those limits themselves. More and more, desire on the performance stratum is becoming undisciplined—*it performs.*

7. *Power mechanisms.* Disciplinary power, according to Foucault, functions continuously and in a decentralized manner through distinct institutions that cluster around bodies of the subjected; whereas the power regime which discipline displaced, that of torture, functions discontinuously and radiates from a single center, the body of a sovereign. Unlike both disciplinary and sovereign power, performative power operates as a polyrhythmic network. Discontinuously continuous, continually discontinuous, it incessantly breaks down and starts up again as its widely dispersed command and control centers function at times in alliance, at times in conflict, sporadically fluctuating between incommensurable chaos and patterns of ordered complexity. In what William Bogard calls the "simulation of surveillance," even resistance can become normative. "In the ultimate ploy, the system counters resistance not with any moral imperative or forceful repression but with the pleasure of resistance itself—to limits, finalities, boundaries. No pain, no suffering, just a delusion of matter over everything final, the hypnotic, integrated satisfactions of the screen and the code. No limits, no worries. Rather, be the limit, be the end."[34]

This possibility was described a half century ago by Marcuse, who, we recall, wrote that under the performance principle, the apparatus "characterizes even the manifold forms of protest and rebellion." In contrast to discipline's normative rites of liminal passage, the performance stratum provokes us with an alluring array of liminal-norms: go the limit, play the margin, be the other. Discipline's enclosed space is being transformed into a networked space or rather a network of divergent spacings, while its serialized passage of time (school, army, work, hospital) is becoming a polyrhythmic time, an undulating current of temporal interference (lifelong learning). "We are dealing first of all with a kind of hyperpanoptics—instead of architectures of control, walls and floor and viewing locations, we need to talk about cyberarchitectures, digital structures, and environments; instead of orderings of space and time, virtual space-times and the coding conventions for displaying them onscreen; instead of visibilities and temporal series, about virtual light, programmed images, and cyberloops."[35] It is the spatiotemporality of differing, deference, differance. Here and there, now and then, performative power surges through every body and no body: it makes multiple, even incompatible, challenges upon everyone, yet it cannot be readily located in anyone or any one group, for in contrast to discipline and torture, the power of performance generates both physical and digital bodies. With the rise of IT, everybody becomes haunted by electronic bodies stored in multiple databases. *Everybody.*

Some might object that only those with high-tech jobs, e-mail, credit cards, bank accounts, telephones, etc., have such digital bodies, and that there are millions upon millions of people living without electricity, much less computers, credit cards, and AOL accounts. Yet this objection focuses solely on the subjects of performative knowledge. If instead one takes into account decades of demographic research by economists, social workers, health officials, and relief workers, as well as the databases currently maintained by financial agencies, trading alliances, governments, defense agencies, corporations, NGOs, research institutes, and universities, then one quickly realizes that even those—or rather, *especially* those—living in impoverished isolation have long been objects of performative power and knowledge. You don't have to be a rocket scientist to be targeted by a nuclear warhead, nor be a programmer to have life-and-death decisions made on your digital account.

Resampling these seven geological belts, we can say that the performance stratum is the power matrix of the New World Order, an order in which disorder is put to work, where bodies perform both physically and digitally, where new and multiple agents are maintained by audiovisual archives and transformed by liminautic power circuits. The most striking aspect of performative power is that it actually encourages transformation, innovation, even transgression and perversion. No longer objects of discipline, we now perform, multitask, do our own thing. This last aspect of performance is especially troubling, for it reveals the libidinal infrastructure of contemporary domination. Deleuze, reading Foucault, writes that strata coalesce around relatively rare performative statements or "order-words." The order-word of the performance stratum?

Perform—or else

Just how far have we read beyond the *Forbes* cover bearing this headline? Let us rescan this cover as a block of the performance stratum, a fragment of its underground formation. Between headline and headjerk, there is a challenging forth and a challenged forth, a double articulation of expression and content, discursive performative and embodied performance. Moreover, this doubling occurs doubly, once as depicted *in* the ad, between word and image, once as effected *by* the ad, between the magazine and its readers. The challenge "Perform—or else" is directed not just to the executive on the cover but potentially to anyone who picks up this *Forbes*. Together, these doublings produce a powerful interpolation, a challenging forth of performers that is more sudden and gripping than any Vaudevillian hook.

How might one challenge this challenge, or more generally, how might one challenge challenging itself? Our lecture machine cites and recites the challenge "Perform—or else," displacing it through numerous reading machines, connecting it to different sites in order to make it pass into something else. From the throttling front cover of *Forbes*, to the exigencies of efficacy, efficiency, and effectiveness and the destiny of *Herausfordern*, the challenge of performance calls up a future that is already under construction. Perhaps by chance, this future world is pictured on the back cover of this very same issue of *Forbes*, where we find yet another geological fragment, one that frames the stratum in an uncanny perspective, like that seen by a craft sailing high overhead.

PART III. PERFUMANCE

SHIP TEST WITH PIECES ARRANGED
FOR SUBJECT TO PLACE IN FRAME

FLIGHT CONTROLLERS ARE LOOKING VERY CAREFULLY AT THE SITUATION. OBVIOUSLY A MAJOR MALFUNCTION. WE HAVE A REPORT FROM THE FLIGHT DYNAMICS OFFICER THAT THE VEHICLE HAS EXPLODED. THE FLIGHT DIRECTOR CONFIRMS THAT. WE ARE LOOKING AT CHECKING WITH THE RECOVERY FORCES TO SEE WHAT CAN BE DONE AT THIS POINT. CONTINGENCY PROCEDURES ARE IN EFFECT. WE WILL REPORT MORE AS WE HAVE INFORMATION AVAILABLE. AGAIN, I REPEAT, WE HAVE A REPORT RELAYED THROUGH THE FLIGHT DYNAMICS OFFICER THAT THE VEHICLE HAS EXPLODED.

Mission Control, 28 January, 1986

CHAPTER 7. PROFESSOR CHALLENGER AND THE DISINTEGRATION MACHINE

With his Assyrian beard and prodigious voice, Professor Challenger was known to shock audiences with his exorbitant remarks and gestures. Lecturing before a large crowd gathered in Doyle's short story "When the World Screamed," the professor introduces one of his most daring experiments by stating that " 'the whole matter is very fully and lucidly discussed in my forthcoming volume upon the earth, which I may describe with all due modesty as one of the epoch-making books of the world's history. (General interruption and cries of "Get down to the facts!" "What are we here for?" "Is this a practical joke?").' "[1] Challenger, a brilliant if eccentric scientist, is unaffiliated with any university, and in this experiment he seeks to contact the earth itself, which he proclaims to be a living entity. As he explains to the story's narrator, "a self-styled expert in artesian boring," the earth is modeled on " 'a sea urchin—a common echinus.' " Holding one of these creatures in his massive simian hands, the professor continues, " 'Nature repeats itself in many forms regardless of the size. This echinus is a model, a prototype, of the world.' "Just as the sea urchin gets its nourishment from the water surrounding it, so too the " 'earth browses upon a circular path in the fields of space, and as it moves the ether is continually pouring through it and providing its vitality.' "[2]

To field test his model, Professor Challenger has enlisted the boring expert, a Mr. Peerless Jones, and contracted him to operate a special drill bit as part of a public experiment. Challenger seeks to drill home his theory by digging some eight miles down into the earth's strata. He has already passed through "the sallow lower chalk, the coffee-colored Hastings beds, the lighter Ashburnham beds, the dark carboniferous clays, and then,gleaming in the electric light, bands and bands of jet-black, sparkling coal alternating with rings of clay."[3] And indeed, as predicted by his theory, at the shaft's bottom he has found something truly amazing: a moist, palpitating flesh whose surface glistens under the light, gray and gelatinous. It is this surface that the professor plans to harpoon with the expert's incisive bit—and to do so in the name of Challenger. "'I propose to let the earth know that there is at least one person, George Edward Challenger, who calls for attention—who, indeed, insists upon attention. It is certainly the first intimation it has ever had of the sort.'"[4] For this audacious experiment—which is nothing less than the challenging forth of the world—the professor has gathered together a large number of his peers (assuming, that is, that he has any). There are heads of learned societies, members of Parliament and the royal family, as well as his most adamant critics, those representing the popular press. Challenger has invited them all out from the city of London and seated them around a huge hole he's dug largely for himself. As the experiment is about to commence, however, something utterly astonishing unfolds eight miles down. Framed in a special apparatus, the peerless bit hangs ready for its plunge—yet by "some strange telepathy the old planet seemed to know that an unheard-of liberty was about to be attempted. The exposed surface was like a boiling pot. Great gray bubbles rose and burst with a crackling report. The air spaces and vacuoles below the skin separated and coalesced in an agitated activity. . . . A heavy smell made the air hardly fit for human lungs."[5]

Amidst this fetid atmosphere, let us summarize the general theory of performance. Its site presents a tangled hierarchy, one that consists of at least three levels. Starting with the most abstract: performance is **an onto-historical formation of power and knowledge**, an emergent diagram of power forces that envelops a stratum of knowledge forms whose crystallization began in the mid-twentieth century. Though it initially took shape in Cold War America, this performance stratum is becoming a global formation, one that is multicultural, multinational, and multimediated in its effects. Stretching across this immense stratum are **contested paradigms of performance research**, paradigms that gather and compose a wide variety of "events,""activities,"and "behaviors" into specific fields of performance. From initiation rites to constructions of race and gender, from assembly lines to virtual boardrooms, from guided missiles to electronic noses, these paradigmatic performances have helped shape the very stratum on which they operate. Each paradigm is guided by its own reading machine, its own set of presuppositions and infrastructures through which it works around the clock and around the globe to archive and seal together particular collections of discourses and practices. At the most concrete level, **discursive performatives and embodied performances** are forms of knowledge that challenge forth the world according to different relations of force, making it perform in the name of technological effectiveness, organizational efficiency, social efficacy, and many other performative valorimeters. At the turn of the twenty-first century, the paradigms are coming into contact more and more, and as their citational networks become hyperlinked, their respective performatives and performances break apart and recombine in a highly charged, highly pressurized milieu.

This atmosphere insists upon our attention, indeed dares us to give some sense of it within our general theory. Reading the stars, the clouds, the bubbling entrails of planet Earth—these all forecast an age of global performance, an epochal event currently initiating its end(s). In these remaining chapters, we continue our dramaturgical reading of Challenger in order to approach *destratification*, the atmospheric disintegration of the performance stratum. Our mission is to trace the pattern of challenger-performance into "the plane of consistency or Body without Organs, in other words, the unformed, unorganized, nonstratified or destratified body and all its flows: subatomic particles and submolecular particles, pure intensities, prevital and prephysical free singularities."[6] With its digging of strata and its smell of earthy fumes, Professor Challenger's experiment gives us an opportunity to remount our lecture machine, even at the risk of it cracking apart at the seams.

The age of global performance harbors new forms of normativity, new bodies and practices, new voices and discourses. We have only begun to scratch the surface of the stratum. We can see the wire frame model of its world, but very little of its surface has been rendered in any detail. The core samples taken above merely hint at the algorithms shaping its structure and history. The stratum's high performance programming remains under incessant testing and revision, with future releases incoming at an alarming rate. Nonetheless, we have picked up some patterns of its sedimentation and folding, and if we're on target in suggesting that power and knowledge are becoming mobile to the point of nomadic, diverse to the point of eccentric, and networked to the point of all cursors—then it's absolutely imperative for us to ask how emerging patterns of destratification affect processes of performative resistance.

To approach resistance in terms of destratification, we will begin by examining the latter in terms of machinic processes of recursion and communication, and then try to characterize the machinic element proper to the emerging performance stratum. In subsequent chapters, we engage strategies of performative resistance passing through the three levels of our general theory. At the level of performatives and performances, we explore catachrestic uses of language and catastrophic restorations of behavior. At the level of sociotechnical systems, we take up multi-paradigmatic, polytonal collaboration. Finally, at the level of onto-historical formations, our reading turns to "minor" histories and "minor" anachronisms. Time and again, we'll make reference to our lecture machine.

What is a lecture machine? Which one? you might ask. In the course of our readings, "lecture machine" has been turned in a variety of ways—as a simple lectern or prop for reading, as a synecdoche for a university reading machine and its displacement in other institutions, and, more generally, as an interpretative machine that processes both discourses and practices. In particular, we have of late deployed the lecture machine as a metamodel for our general theory, engaging and disengaging a number of performances. Let us now tune our machine a bit finer. We have seen that Heidegger reads technology not as an instrument or human activity, but as a way of revealing, a *poesis*. Deleuze and Guattari propose a different scanning with their incisive notion of the machine, writing that the "object is no longer to compare humans and machines in order to evaluate the correspondences, the extensions, the possible or impossible substitutions of the one for the other, but to bring them into communication in order to show how humans *are a component part* of the machine, or combine with something else to constitute a machine. The other thing can be a tool, or even an animal, or other humans. We are not using a metaphor, however, when we speak of machines: *humans constitute a machine* as soon as this nature is communicated by recurrence to the ensemble of which they form a part under specific conditions."[7] Not a metaphor, not an extension of the human body, not a prosthetic device, not a human activity, this machine performs as *generalized technology*, a *technopoesis* that does not return to *physis*, to Nature, to God, to Man, to Being. Such machinic performances do not return. They recur, intermittently, in patterns of stratification and destratification.

Recurrence refers to the ability of machinic assemblages to operate across different systems, to bring diverse elements and processes into communication through sheer repetition. To paraphrase the professor, *difference repeats itself in many forms regardless of the size*. Such repetitions repeat themselves across different scales, generating and degenerating patterns within patterns, creating a strange looping or entangling of citational networks. Recurrent, machinic performances can operate with or without technologies in the classical sense and also with or without human agents. Machines arise on all levels of strata; or rather, geological, biological, and social strata can themselves be understood as evidence of machinic processes. Manuel De Landa writes: "In a very real sense, reality is a *single matter-energy* undergoing phase transitions of various kinds, with each new layer of accumulated 'stuff' simply enriching the reservoir of nonlinear dynamics and nonlinear processes."[8] A winter storm is a machine, as is a cold virus. At the anthropomorphic level, Deleuze and Guattari cite ergonomics as coming closest to their notion of machine because it is concerned not with the coadaptation of humans and machines, but with "recurrent communication within systems made up of men and machines. . . . The human-horse-bow forms a nomadic war machine under the conditions of the steppe. Men form a labor machine under the bureaucratic conditions of the great empires."[9] On the performance stratum, the field of human–computer interaction is ground zero for the emergence of a new and powerful machine, the feedback and feedforward of world culture, transnational organization, and global information technology. Guattari writes of the age of planetary computerization: "Subjectivity today remains under the massive control of apparatuses of power and knowledge, thus consigning technical, scientific, and artistic innovations to the service of the most reactionary and retrograde forms of sociality. In spite of that, other modalities of subjective production—processual and singularizing ones—are conceivable."[10] This last point bears elaboration: the age of global performance gives rise to extraordinary processes of stratification as well as massively singular flights of destratification. The recursive patterns of machinic performances can thus be normative or mutational.

The variable geometry of Challenger lecture machine is produced by recursive patterns of stratification and destratification. As metamodel, Challenger takes on many shapes and takes off in many *sens* or directions. It repeats itself differently in multiple forms, forms themselves determined, by chance, through differential relations of force. Lifting off from lectures rehearsed but never performed by the teacher in spaceship *Challenger*, our reading studies the ways in which technological, organizational, and cultural performances embed themselves within one another, and further, the ways their challenges of effectiveness, efficiency, and efficacy can create intense pressures on those who must perform—or else. Switching channels to Heidegger's lecture on technology, the reading machine tracks the question of *Herausfordern* in order to resituate these challenges within the power circuits of performance. These challenges and many others, indeed challenging *per se*, are all caught up in the challenging-forth of the earth, the bringing forth of *physis* in the age of the world picture. Speculatively, we are entering an age of global performance, an age in which the entire world is challenged forth to perform. To explore the power of performance, our machine plays back readings of the performance principle, performative legitimation, and punitive performativity. Maneuvering our way across *A Thousand Plateaus*, we attend Professor Challenger's stratoanalytic lecture on rocks and organisms and societies. The professor's double pincer movement serves as a heuristic model for theorizing the performance stratum, an onto-historical formation whose stratifications of performatives and performances are coming to define our postindustrial, postcolonial, and postmodern world.

Here the machine sputters and gasps, then abruptly takes off again, dredging up fragments of strata while processing them all in a seemingly random fashion. Passages of high theory suddenly find themselves violated by crude and dirty images from the underworld. Cites are recited and miscited. Almost on cue, the "audience rather sulkily denounced the numerous misunderstandings, misinterpretations, and even misappropriations in the professor's presentation, despite the authorities he had appealed to, calling them his 'friends.' Even the Dogons. . . . And things would presently get even worse. The professor cynically congratulated himself on taking his pleasure from behind, but the offspring always turned out to be runts and wens, bits and pieces, if not stupid vulgarizations. Besides, the professor was not a geologist or a biologist, he was not even a linguist, ethnologist, or psychoanalyst; what his specialty had been was long since forgotten."[11] Disgusted by this incompetent, *a tergo* performance, most of the audience bolts, storms away from the careening lectern. "To keep the last of the audience from leaving, Challenger imagined a particularly epistemological dialogue of the dead, in puppet theater style."[12]

Channeling *Foucault*: Deleuze sets the stage with a sketchy yet precise diagram of the relation between world and atmosphere, strata and the non-stratified. It is a drawing he might well have doodled while in seance with Doyle, for it also scans as a diagram of Professor Challenger's boring experiment, his daring attempt to contact the earth by drilling the depths of its strata. Here is Deleuze's diagram, along with bits and pieces of Foucault's great fiction.

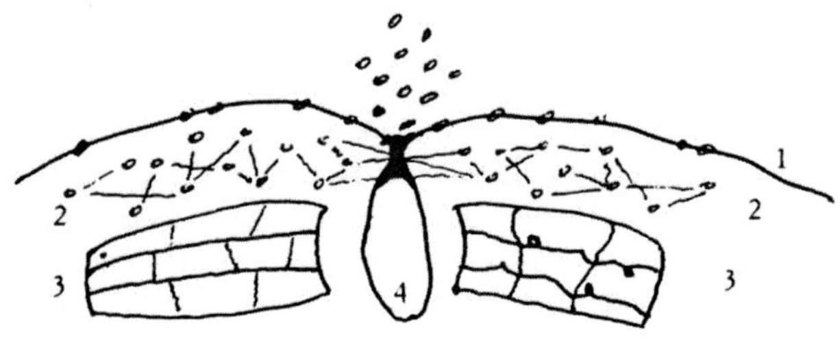

1. Line of the outside
2. Strategic Zone
3. Strata
4. Fold (zone of subjectivation)

"I have never written anything but fictions . . . " But never has fiction produced such truth and reality. How could we narrate Foucault's great fiction? The world is made up of superimposed surfaces, archives or strata. The world is thus knowledge. But strata are crossed by a central fissure that separates on the one hand the visual scenes, and on the other the sound curves. . . . We immerse ourselves from stratum to stratum, from band to band; we cross the surfaces, scenes and curves; we follow the fissure, in order to reach an interior of the world. . . . But at the same time we try to climb above the strata in order to reach an outside, an atmospheric element, a "non-stratified substance". . . .

The informal outside is a battle, a turbulent, stormy zone where particular points are tossed about. . . . Each atmospheric state in this zone corresponds to a diagram of forces or particular features which are taken up by relations: a strategy. If strata are of the earth, then a strategy belongs to the air or the ocean.[13]

Destratification begins by boring deep into the performance stratum in order to follow the fissures, the disjunctive joints between performances and performatives, paradigm and paradigm, stratum and stratum. It is by eroding the seals between different belts and layers that the process of destratification unfolds, and by amplifying the cracks and flows that we begin to approach a nonstratified atmosphere. Professor Challenger, again reciting the geology textbook: " 'A surface of stratification is a more compact plane of consistency lying between two layers.' The layers are the strata. . . . In effect, the body without organs is itself the plane of consistency, which becomes compact or thickens at the level of the strata."[14] Crucial here, and also echoed in the diagram above, is the suggestion that at certain points *the outside is folded inside*, the destratified atmosphere churns not only at the external margins of strata, but also within them, at their very core.

To get at this from another angle: forces of mutation vie with forces of normativity not only at the external limen of subjective, sociotechnical, and onto-historical strata, but also deep inside them, at their internal limen. Systems theorist Niklas Luhmann posits that any system is defined less by the border that separates it from its environment than by an internalized, self-referential description of this very same border: "systems must create and employ a description of themselves; they must at least be able to use the difference between system and environment within themselves, for orientation and as a principle for creating information. Therefore self-referential closure is possible only in an environment, only under ecological conditions. The environment is a necessary correlate of self-referential operations because these out of all operations cannot operate under the premise of solipsism. . . . The (subsequently classical) distinction between 'closed' and 'open' systems is replaced by the question of how self-referential closure can create openness."[15]

Through processes of self-referentiality, the limen between inside and outside recurs within the system, giving it its sense of stability and completion with respect to the alterity of the outside environment. In order to be what it is, a system must be other. Yet because self-referentiality incorporates alterity deep inside the system, it simultaneously creates a pocket within it: the very process of self-referentiality that generates a system's coherence also renders it systematically unstable, incomplete, disoriented. The outside, turned inside, can turn the inside out. In reference to self-referential linguistic systems, Douglas Hofstadter comments that the "fascinating thing is that any such system digs its own hole; the system's own richness brings about its own downfall. The downfall occurs essentially because the system is powerful enough to have self-referential sentences. . . . Once this ability for self-reference is attained, the system has a hole which is tailor-made for itself; the hole takes the features of the system into account and uses them against the system."[16] Such destabilizing, self-referential holes pockmark the emerging performance stratum, acting as disintegrating machines that erode the seals between discourses and practices, that bore their way across diverse paradigms, and that, more rarely, trace mutant passages to other onto-historical strata. It is through these and other oddly tailored pockets that strata destratify, norms deviate, hierarchies entangle, and general theories generally degenerate.[17]

Across the performance stratum, it is "within" such destabilizing holes that recurrent communication occurs across diverse systems. Yet in another way, these pocket holes precede any system, any stratum. In the nonstratified atmosphere, they open as eyes of autoproductive storms, chaotic gatherings of forces and non-stratified substances where systems first commune or refer with themselves, where structures evolve and devolve through iteration. Violent storms, virulent viruses, vagrant desires—entire worlds are initiated and destroyed via the permutations of holey alterity. Patterns of repetition and differentiation generate strange attractors for the self-organization of structures. In chaos theory, the self-organization of systems within chaotic milieus is often called autopoesis or autoproduction. Guattari nicknames it "chaosmosis," chaotic transformation, transformative chaos, a name suggesting that the auto- of autopoesis and autoproduction is wrecked from the get-go. In *Chaosmosis: An Ethico-Aesthetic Paradigm*, he distinguishes machines from structures by differentiating their respective mechanisms of autopoesis and feedback. The difference is a matter of eternal life and a certain desire of death. "This autopoetic node in the machine is what separates and differentiates it from structure and gives it value. Structure implies feedback loops, it puts into play a concept of totalization that it itself masters. It is occupied with inputs and outputs whose purpose is to make the structure function according to a principle of eternal return. It is haunted by a desire for eternity. The machine, on the contrary, is shaped by a desire for abolition. Its emergence is doubled with breakdown, catastrophe—the menace of death. It possesses a supplement: a dimension of alterity which it develops from different forms."[18] Structures are defined by the normalization of mutant forces, by the calculation of inputs and outputs, that is, by the guidance devices of performative optimization, while machines follow a vagrant itinerary, twisting their way through a series of strange loops and turning forces inside out. It is a recurrent passage with no guarantee of return.

While we can say that structural performances tend to integrate while machinic performances tend to disintegrate, we must also add that *each tends toward the other.* Stratification and destratification are not opposed to one another, for both are haunted by alterity. Structural systems may attempt to master difference, but self-referential incorporation opens them to catastrophe. And likewise, though machines are in tune with radical alterity, they also run the risk of sedimenting, folding, and stratifying into structures. Our general theory, for example, fluctuates between totalizing structures that generalize and integrate performance and disintegrating machines that particularize and disseminate it. Who, or what, is Challenger? Which Challenger? Challenger names an errant performance, a shuttling between stratum and atmosphere, earth and sky, geology and the weather.

The atmosphere insists on our attention. But how to get a finer sense of it? While the performance stratum's visible and discursive forms, its performances and performatives, command our eyes and ears, the dispersed dimension of forces must be sensed otherwise: " . . . *there is an emergence of forces which doubles history,* or rather envelops it, according to the Nietzschean conception."[19] Nietzsche ridiculed the historians of his time for trying to reduce life to knowledge, suggesting instead that life was itself imbued with a dimension foreign to the forms of knowledge. "Every living thing needs to be surrounded by an atmosphere, a mysterious circle of mist: if one robs it of this veil, if one condemns a religion, an art, a genius to orbit as a star without an atmosphere: then one should not wonder about its rapidly becoming withered, hard, and barren."[20]

In contrast to the certainties of knowledge-forms, this mysterious circle of mist is composed of "instincts and powerful illusion." Its truths are different from those of the historical forms it surrounds. They are untimely, out of season, and can appear a bit foolish. Of his own destiny, the philosopher writes:

> I do not want to be a saint, rather even a buffoon. . . . Perhaps I am a buffoon. . . . And nonetheless, or rather *not* nonetheless—for there has hitherto been nothing more mendacious than saints—the truth speaks out of me.—But my truth is *dreadful*: for hitherto the *lie* has been called truth.—*Revaluation of all values*: this is my supreme formula for an act of supreme coming-to-oneself on the part of mankind which in me has become flesh and genius. It is my fate to have to be the first to *discover* the truth, in that I was first to sense—*smell*—the lie as lie. . . . My genius is in my nostrils.[21]

For us, the revaluation of values starts by shifting our senses from specific paradigms (and the values of efficacy, efficiency, or effectiveness) to a more general stratum of performance (the decisive satisficing of multiple values), and then from the forms of knowledge to the forces of power—from stratum to atmosphere. Yet this requires not only a shift of senses, but a shift *in* senses. Sight and hearing, according to Hegel, constitute the theoretical senses, in that they provide the critical distance between subject and object that is necessary for the formation of objective knowledge. Their predominance in Western philosophy, science, and art stretches from the *eidos* and *logos* of Plato through the idea and logic of Descartes to the imaginary and symbolic orders of Lacan. It is within and against this tradition that Nietzsche turns his nose, even turning it against himself at times. Reflecting back on the political indifference of his first book, *The Birth of Tragedy,* he comments that it "smells offensively Hegelian, it is in only a few formulas infected with the cadaverous perfume of Schopenhauer."[22]

With its arrangements of power-forces and affective strategies, the atmosphere of flows and nonstratified substances is not so much seen or heard as smelled, sniffed out, traced by nasal passages. Smell, like taste, is a chemical or proximity sense. It entails the disintegration of forms, the mixing of subjects and objects. Significantly, Marcuse argues that the immediacy associated with smell is incompatible with the performance principle. He theorizes the performance principle in terms of "surplus-repression,"[24] defined as "the restrictions necessitated by social domination. This is distinguished from (basic) *repression*: the 'modifications' of the instincts necessary for the perpetuation of the human race in civilization."[23] To clarify this distinction, Marcuse follows his nose and turns to "the vicissitudes of the 'proximity senses' (smell and taste) [which] provide a good example of the interrelation between basic repression and surplus-repression."[24] With respect to the former, Marcuse cites Freud's observation that the coprophilic elements of human instinct, that is, the human *love of crap*, particularly its scent, became incompatible with aesthetic ideas. This incompatibility, Freud writes, dates "probably since the time when man developed an upright posture and so removed his organ of smell from the ground."[25]

In short, the basic repression of the organ of smell is closely associated with *homo erectus*, with a certain becoming human. In standing up, we lost our noses, so to speak. The loss of nasal pleasures/disgusts, their sublimation within not only aesthetic but also moral ideation, defines basic repression. Moving to surplus-repression, Marcuse continues: "There is, however, another aspect to the subduing of the proximity senses in civilization: they succumb to the rigidly enforced taboos on too intense bodily pleasures. . . . Smell and taste give, as it were, unsublimated pleasure *per se* (and unrepressed disgust). They relate (and separate) individuals immediately, without the generalized and conventionalized forms of consciousness, morality, aesthetics. Such immediacy is incompatible with the effectiveness of organized *domination*."[26] In relation to smell, basic repression and surplus-repression build on each other: basic repression occurs at the intersection of geology and biology (the organism's relation to the earth), while surplus-repression occurs at the intersection of biology and social psychology (the organism's relation to a particular society). Radical desublimation via the nose would thus entail passages cutting across the anthropomorphic, organic, and inorganic.

The study of the ways in which different societies train and restrain the nose has commenced. In *The Foul and the Fragrant*, Alain Corbin analyzes the disciplining of smell in eighteenth- and nineteenth-century France, while in *Aroma*, Classen, Howes, and Synnott attempt a broader survey of smell, tracking it across different cultures and historical epochs. Our focus here is slightly different, in that we're not only concerned with how different historical formations structure the realm of odor but also with how the nose points toward an element that disorders such strata, a chemical or even alchemical element. More specifically, we are interested in the atmosphere or diagram of forces that doubles the performance stratum. Unlike this formation, where forms of discourse and practice are constructed and maintained, in the atmosphere of forces performatives and performances dissolve, disintegrate, become elemental. We're thus interested not only in the order, but also the odor of things and words.

A funky milieu comprises the fourth level of our general theory, though "level" is imprecise here precisely because this atmosphere imbues and disorders the other three levels, those of performatives-performances, performance paradigms, and performance stratum. What, then, to call this queer element of the general theory? Let us name it—***Perfumance***: the citational mist of any and all performances. ***Perfumance***: the incessant (dis)embodying-(mis)naming of performance. ***Perfumance***: passing through the liminautics of Performance Studies, Performance Management, and Techno-Performance. ***Perfumance***: the (dis)integration of the performance stratum. ***Perfumance***: the becoming-mutational of normative forces, the becoming-normative of mutant forces. ***Perfumance***: the odor of things and words, the sweat of bodies, the perfume of discourse. ***Perfumance***: the ruse of a general theory.

Something other than a grand theory, our reading of perfumance partakes of petite theoretical fictions in order to allude to the intra-extra-performative, the inside out of the performance stratum, that which escapes the orbits of its discourses and practices, the centrifugal force of its research paradigms, the gravity of its onto-historical formation. Carrying the scent of exteriority, perfumance haunts the stratum's interior with odors emitted by certain incorporated remains, in this case, the perfumed remains of an errant cast of challengers.

In the last of Doyle's sci-fi stories, Professor Challenger makes contact with the perfumative element. The text is titled "The Disintegration Machine," and in it the professor pays a visit to a strange inventor named Theodor Nemor. He has come to examine a prototype of Theodor's latest invention, Nemor's Disintegrator. The inventor explains to the professor how the electrical poles of his machine create vibratory currents, currents capable of disintegrating forms into molecular mist and, if need be, reintegrating them again. He then tells Challenger of the powerful payload his disintegration machine will bring forth once in full production.

> "We will suppose that one pole was in one small vessel and one in another; a battleship between them would simply vanish into molecules. So also a column of troops."
>
> "And you have sold this secret as a monopoly to a single European power?"
>
> "Yes, sir, I have. When the money is paid over they shall have such power as no nation ever had yet. You don't even now see the full possibilities if placed in capable hands—hands which did not fear to wield the weapon which they held. They are immeasurable."[27]

Doyle penned the Challenger sci-fi texts late in life, using them to explore and promote his personal involvement with astronomy, spiritualism, as well as the politics of research. "The Disintegration Machine" calls attention to many contemporary currents, not only those that pass through Nemor's invention, but also those of the military-industrial-academic complex of post-First World War Europe. (Across the Atlantic, the US government had just initiated evaluating its recruits' performance on the Army Mental Test.) Within this atmosphere, Doyle crafted his Challenger stories. The entire sci-fi series operates in a very different manner from the author's more celebrated detective series, for their two protagonists present contrasting styles of research. While Sherlock Holmes proceeds by detached logic, critical analysis, and orderly investigation, Professor Challenger's research is characterized by sensual affect, creative invention, and exuberant experimentation.

In "The Disintegration Machine," however, it is one mad scientist facing another. Professor Challenger is highly skeptical of Theodor's invention and rudely questions the logic and analogics on which it is based. In response, the inventor proposes a test and dares Challenger to personally take part in a demonstration of the prototype, a machine that oddly resembles an electric chair with its zinc base, its burnished copper cap, and a slotted control handle mounted on one side. "'Nemor's Disintegrator,' said this strange man, waving his hand toward the machine. 'This is the model which is destined to be famous, as altering the balance of power among the nations. Who holds this rules the world. Now, Professor Challenger, you have, if I may say so, treated me with some lack of courtesy and consideration in this matter. Will you dare to sit upon that chair and to allow me to demonstrate upon your own body the capabilities of the new force?' "[28] There's a slight pause, then Challenger seats himself in the chair. The handle's clicked—

CHAPTER 8. THE CATACHRISTENING OF HMS CHALLENGER

In December, 1872, HMS *Challenger* and a crew of researchers set out on a voyage around the world. Their mission: to chart the ocean floor, to fathom its depths, to challenge forth its mysteries. The mission was an extraordinary project, combining scientific research, military might, and highly idiosyncratic adventures. Over the next three and a half years, *Challenger* navigated the oceans, collecting samples and cataloguing hundreds upon hundreds of species of underwater plants and animals. Along the way, it helped to launch modern, large-scale scientific research. "To understand the importance of this moment—and of course it was not really a single moment, but an event which serves as an icon for a process that was occurring at that time—we need to understand its context which is the triumphalism of late Victorian science. Here we see the Challenger Expedition of 1872-1876, under the leadership of Sir Charles Wyville Thomson, as the world's first foray into big science. The Expedition was the Apollo Program, the Human Genome Project, the Hubble Space Telescope of its day."[1]

HMS *Challenger* was originally a corvette, a small warship, but researchers at the University of Edinburgh and the Royal Society persuaded the British Navy to convert the vessel into a floating laboratory for undersea exploration. Erik Linklater describes the ship and the nature of its passage: "*Challenger* was a three-masted, square rigged, wooden ship of 2,300 tons displacement and some 200 feet over all. Officially described as a steam corvette, she had an engine of rather more than 1,200 horsepower, but was still essentially a sailing ship; for on a voyage designed for searching the depths of the sea she could not order her course from coaling station to coaling station, but used wind and canvas to make her passages, and kept her steam-engine for dredging, for harbour work, and emergencies that had to be anticipated though they could not be foreseen. All but two of her seventeen guns were removed, and in the space that they and the ammunition had occupied, laboratories and workrooms were built, storage for trawls and dredges and the specimens they would collect. The ship became, in effect, a many-celled, seaworthy and sea-faring department of the Royal Society. . . . "[2] It became, in effect, a nautical lecture machine.

HMS *Challenger* remains one of science's most famous research vessels. In addition to being the first modern Big Science project, the voyage of *Challenger*—and the research it generated—helped to establish the science of oceanography. Much of the ship's research is recorded in an enormous reading apparatus: an illustrated, fifty-volume report published by one of the crew's most celebrated scientists, an itinerant researcher by the name of John Murray. For Linklater, his was not a model performance for most students today. "For students of the present day it may be advisable to add that his habits, as a student, should not be regarded as a model of undergraduate behavior unless the contemporary student, who reads of him, possesses that sort of genius which is instinctive, devoted to an issue that is the confluence of several related issues, and has inherited physical robustitude, an exceptional self-assurance, and an uncommon aptitude for getting his own way and reaping, from science and his own shrewdness, a large profit. . . . At the University of Edinburgh he showed no respect for the tedious discipline of examinations, no wish to acquire the decorations of degrees, but worked at any subject which interested him." As a result of his efforts and his success in publishing the *Report on the Scientific Results of the Exploring Voyage of HMS Challenger*, the name "John Murray" became closely associated with that of "Challenger."[3]

Through a series of recursive twists, HMS *Challenger* functions as the nominal source of our *Challenger* perfumance. Its name moves from site to site, tacking between one performance and another. HMS *Challenger* is famous both for its ambitious mission and for its contributions to science, and no doubt it was for such reasons that NASA named its third operational shuttle craft after it. (Ironically, the 1986 *Challenger* explosion produced one of the largest undersea salvage operations in history, with naval ships, small submarines, and even shrimp boats contributing to the search for *Challenger* and crew. Because the salvage operation focused primarily on the crew cabin and the right booster rocket, much of this *Challenger* remains today on the bottom of the Atlantic. The rest was buried in a large hole.) As for Professor Challenger, he too owes his name to HMS *Challenger*. Doyle studied at the University of Edinburgh from 1876 to 1881, the years immediately following the ship's celebrated voyage. As Edinburgh had been instrumental in conceiving the exploration in the first place, its successes were especially celebrated there. Further, as a medical student, Doyle studied with several of the *Challenger* scientists. Based on this pedagogical experience and the ship's reputation, he named his volatile professor "Challenger." We have seen that, in one particularly daring experiment, Professor Challenger attempts to challenge forth the earth, and this research provides a tangential link with Professor Heidegger's questioning of technology. A more substantial connection (assuming substantiality has any relevance at all in perfumance) can be made with the Challenger of Deleuze and Guattari, whose schizoanalytic professor channels the character created by Doyle some seventy years earlier.[4]

We are tracking the ways in which words and things come together, how performance-performative blocks are joined and jointed to one another, how, for instance, "Challenger" and a collection of challengers become bound up with one another at different times and places. We're thus tracking the ways in which words and things crack and break apart. Our lecture machine performs as a sometimes irreverent referencing device, one that processes different forms of reference. And as its name is itself "Challenger," it's a self-referential machine as well, one bored out by many passages of alterity and difference. The trajectory of *Challenger* from ocean to science fiction to hermeneutics to stratoanalysis to outer space, this itinerant passage suggests the effects of perfumance upon performance, of forces upon onto-historical forms. One can perhaps only suggest or allude to such effects, as perfumance eludes presentation and representation. As a dimension of differential forces that doubles and troubles history and being, perfumance cannot be directly shown or told in established forms of knowledge. However, it may be sensed indirectly through its pressure and impact on these stratifications. Perfumance is atmospheric, it's funky, it smells a bit odd. Far from being homogeneous, however, this atmosphere thickens and disperses at different times and places; its condensations and disseminations make perfumance radically heterogeneous, so radically heterogeneous that homogeneity may be produced as one of its effects. One can easily argue that, over and over and over, all I'm really showing and telling is Challenger, Challenger, Challenger. *Yes*—and yet who, or what, is Challenger? Challenger is this singularly multiple passage, this line of flight through an oddly scented atmosphere. (Other passages are certainly possible—and indeed encouraged.)

Let's try to get a better sense of the destratifying potential of perfumance. Though there are innumerable effects we could study, we shall concentrate on performative resistance and do so by focusing on the three levels that help to compose the general theory: performance stratum, performance paradigms, and discursive performatives-embodied performances. In this section we begin with the latter, and do so by elaborating further on matters of referentiality and self-referentiality.

Over the past two decades, referentiality and self-referentiality have come under intense scrutiny through a renewed interest in Austin's theory of performative speech acts. Austin's self-described revolution in linguistics overturned the notion that language simply "constates" or reports on reality. Performatives are not informational reports, but actions, events, doings. Today, performative utterances are understood to be crucial to the construction of reality, a construction that is sociotechnically *ordered*. To bring out this ordering of language, Deleuze and Guattari employ the concept of "order-word," which they define using an example of a schoolhouse. "When the schoolmistress instructs her students on a rule of grammar or arithmetic, she is not informing them, any more than she is informing herself when she questions a student. She does not so much instruct as 'insign,' give orders or commands. . . . The compulsory educational machine does not communicate information; it imposes upon the child semiotic coordinates possessing all of the dual foundations of grammar (masculine-feminine, singular-plural, noun-verb, subject of the statement-subject of enunciation, etc.) The elementary unit of language—the statement—is the order-word."[5]

Order-words are performatives, but understood machinically, in terms of processes of recursive communication. While Austin cites direct discourse as the paragon of the performative (more specifically, the first-person singular, with one of his examples being "I name this ship the *Queen Elizabeth*"), he also explicitly excludes the third person and indirect discourse from his analysis. By contrast, Deleuze and Guattari's theory of order-words subverts this ordering and gives precedence to indirect discourse, the third person, even to hearsay. "We believe that narrative consists not in communicating what one has seen but in transmitting what one has heard, what someone else said to you. Hearsay. . . . Language is not content to go from a first party to a second party, from one who has seen to one who has not, but necessarily goes from a second party to a third, neither of whom has seen. It is in this sense that language is the transmission of the word as order-word. . . . "[6] The order-words passing between "you" and "me" are always already received, recircuited and detoured by him and her, them and it.

At the same time, this passage from statement to generalized hearsay situates performatives not in the presence of individual subjects, but rather in the perfumative force of citational networking, in the incessant archiving, transformation, and transmission of statements and practices. Austin pointed toward this dimension when he distinguished the forms of constatives and performatives from the forces of locution and illocution. In Lecture XII of *How to Do Things with Words*, he suggests that the "doctrine of the performative/constative distinction stands to the doctrine of locutionary and illocutionary acts in the total speech act as the *special* theory to the *general* theory."[7] But while Austin sought to ground the performative and the illocutionary in subjective presence, Deleuze and Guattari move instead toward collective assemblages of enunciation, utterance machines irreducible to subjective or intersubjective relations because what they produce are fields of subjectivity. Engaging Benveniste's attempt to ground performative self-referentiality within intersubjective communication, they counter that the "performative itself is explained by the illocutionary, not the opposite. It is the illocutionary that constitutes the nondiscursive or implicit presuppositions. And the illocutionary is in turn explained by collective assemblages of enunciation, by juridical acts or equivalents of juridical acts, which far from depending on subjectification proceedings or assignations of subjects in language, in fact determine their distribution."[8]

The crucial point here is that performative referentiality and self-referentiality, the binding of words and acts to each other and themselves, always involve a radical alterity, an otherness irreducible to other subjects in that it also entails machinic relations between assemblages of expressions and contents. A collective assemblage of enunciation, of expression, is always coupled with a "*machinic assemblage* of bodies," "using the word 'body' in the broadest sense, as applying to any formed content."[9] As we have seen, such couplings are not harmonic correspondences; rather, assemblages of words and bodies are sealed together through relations of power-forces. It is the effect of this atmosphere that both joins and seals knowledge-forms—and erodes and breaks them apart.

We can outline some initial strategies for destratifying performative utterances: one must dig into the implicit presuppositions that underlie discursive statements while exploring creative lines of flight. One such path of analysis and creativity has been opened by Butler's research into the performativity of queer discourse. It is a twisted passage, one she calls "resignification." Strategically, it involves troubling the sedimented presuppositions that govern language. In the version of "Critically Queer" published in *Bodies That Matter*, she takes up the term "queer" by citing a theatrical source, asking "how is it that a term that signaled degradation has been turned—'refunctioned' in the Brechtian sense—to signify a new and affirmative set of meanings?"[10] She then proceeds to analyze how the homophobic term "queer" has entered a process of collective contestation and resignification. In doing so, Butler affirms her hand in the creative resignification of "queer" by shifting suddenly from its substantive to its verbal form (a shift that might be bottled as an essence of her performance): "If the term 'queer' is to be a site of collective contestation, the point of departure for a set of historical reflections and futural imagings, it will have to remain that which it is, in the present, never fully owned, but always and only redeployed, *twisted, queered* from a prior usage and in the direction of urgent and expanding political purposes."[11] Critically redirecting "queer," Butler not only analyzes how this term has been refunctioned, she also invents resignification as a queering or twisting of discourse, something she herself performs textually.

Shifting now to the term "performance," you can sense the current drift of our reading machine: within Performance Studies, Butler has in effect challenged the sedimented signification of "performative" as referring primarily to oppositional cultural practices and sought to queer the term so that it also refers to normative practices and discourses. One might protest that such queering amounts to a misuse of language. "Surely, Butler's performative refers to something else!" "It's linguistic rather than embodied!" "It means normativity as much as subversion!" "Couldn't she use another term!?" Rather than attempting to justify her use of this term by reciting *Gender Trouble's* alliance of theatrical performance and performativity, let us entertain the thought that it *is* a misuse, and that this misuse is itself a strategy of resignification, of queering, of destratification. Butler theorizes the political dimension of such normative misuse in another chapter of *Bodies That Matter*, one that engages the discursive performativity of naming. Summarizing Saul Kripke and Slavoj Zizek's theories of referentiality, she writes: "It is Kripke's position to argue that the name fixes the referent, and Zizek's to say that the name promises a referent that can never arrive, foreclosed as the unattainable real."[12] Butler instead argues that the referent is neither fixed nor foreclosed, but produced through the differentiation of proper and improper usage. However, "the instability of that distinguishing border between the proper and the catachrestic calls into question the ostensive function of the proper name."[13]

If the referent emerges in the unstable limen of proper and catachrestic usage, then Butler's resignification involves a strategic use of catachresis, which Merriam-Webster defines as "the misuse of words: as a: the use of the wrong word for the context b: the use of a forced figure of speech, esp.

one that involves or seems to involve strong paradox." Thus, while she commends Zizek's work on the politics of the sign because it connects the question of the unsymbolizable to minoritarian social groups, Butler seeks to theorize referentiality not in terms of negation, lack, and a universalized Real, but instead through an affirmation of the historic and symbolic possibilities uncorked by a politics of catachrestic naming. "Here it seems that what is called 'the referent' depends essentially on those catachrestic acts of speech that either fail to refer or refer in the wrong way. It is in this sense that political signifiers that fail to describe, fail to refer, indicate less the 'loss' of the object—a position that nevertheless secures the referent even if as a lost referent—than the loss of the loss, to rework that Hegelian formulation. If referentiality is itself the effect of a policing of the linguistic constraints on proper usage, then the possibility of referentiality is contested by the catachrestic use of speech that insists on using proper names improperly, that expands or defiles the very domain of the proper."[14] Catachresis troubles such property rights and is crucial to the futural imagings that Butler calls for, to the affirmative resignification of "queer," as well as "women," "race," "class," and, as I am arguing here, of the "genus" of "performance."

There's trouble at the limen of performance, and if Butler isn't the only trouble-maker, her *Gender Trouble* remains something of a script for coming to or getting at the end(s) of its liminal-norms. Transcribing her title from English to French and back, we can read it again and generate "*genre* trouble," for *genre* translates both as gender and genre. I am gambling with the French that deconstructing the performativity of gender has everything to do with subverting not only the genders but also the genres, and indeed, the genealogies, generation(s), gens, and genus of performance. Troubling one troubles them all. As Derrida shows in "The Law of Genre," marking genre involves a citation and displacement of borders. The law or clause that genres cannot be mixed only emerges out of the law of genre, the troubling clause that the mark of belonging does not belong, that property rights involve writs of impropriety. This citation and displacement of borders, of limen, opens the gates to the generation and degeneration of genre. Derrida is at the gates, writing with this outlaw law of genre: "The clause or floodgate [*'écluse'*] of genre declasses what it allows to be classed. It tolls the knell [*'glas'*] of genealogy or of genericity, which it however also brings forth to the light of day. Putting to death the very thing that it engenders, it cuts a strange figure; a formless form, it remains nearly invisible, it neither sees the day nor brings itself to light. Without it, neither genre nor literature come to light, but as soon as there is this blinking of the eye, this clause or this floodgate of genre, at the very moment that a genre or a literature is broached, at that very moment, degenerescence has begun, the end begins. The end begins, this is a citation. Maybe a citation."[15] We should note here that Derrida's essay includes a discussion and topological diagram of a pocket of "invagination," a catastrophic *topos* where generic limits fold themselves inside out.

Maybe the end(s) of performance will have been its catachrestic initiation, the relaunching of its rites and writs, the displacement of its sites and cites of passage. Exploring the implicit presuppositions of propriety and the "improper" holes that mark contemporary citational networks is but one strategy of destratification, yet the catachrestics practiced by Butler and Derrida highlight the social efficacy of what many have dismissed as mere frivolity and wordplay. "There is nothing outside the text" means precisely this: there is nothing outside repetition, difference, life-death rehearsal. One can generalize genre trouble catachrestically. Derrida initiates such a reading in the opening pages of *Glas*. In the first "judas hole" or inset text bored into its Genet column, he cites a dictionary definition of "catachresis" ("Trope wherein a word is diverted from its proper sense and is taken up in common language to designate another thing . . . . Musical term. Harsh and unfamiliar dissonance"), which is immediately followed by that of another, "catafalque" ("Platform raised as an honor, in the middle of a church, to receive the coffin or effigy of a deceased. . . . According to Du Cange, *cata* derives from the Low Latin *catus*, a war machine called *cat* after the animal"), and another, "cataglottism" ("Term from ancient literature. The use of abstruse terms").[16] In short, Derrida's reading of catachresis is itself catachrestic, and throughout *Glas* he employs this improper approach in his affirmative deconstruction of Hegel and Genet. This deconstruction includes a reading of their signatures, the *mise en abîme* or placing into abyss of their proper names both within their respective works and without. "Hegel" gives rise to *aigle* (eagle), angel and the angle these figures take in speculative dialectics, while the reading of "Jean Genet," the name of an author who flaunts his signature, elicits *genet* (horse) and *gênet* (a flower), as well as generosity, gender, genre, genus, genitals, generic, genetics, generation, genius, gentleness, genesis, Gentile, John the Baptist, genealogy, generalization, and even a "general theory of the ruse."[17]

Puns, acronyms, anagrams, numerologies, alliterations, rebuses—such are the anagrammatical possibilities cracked open by generalized catachresis. In our ruse of a general theory, the strategy of what I will call *catachristening*, (catastrophic naming) engages the interminable death and birth of performative referentiality; it names "itself" by channeling the machinic generation and degeneration of genre, the comings and goings of the machinic phylum. The name becomes an event: catachristening is the detonation of discursive alterity through holes of autopoetic self-referentiality. Its catastrophic effects register the inherent ability of performatives to fail and misfire, and, in misfiring, to link up with other referents, other contents, other performances.

Among catatchristening's signature traits is antonomasia, the movement between proper and common names, the confusion of species and genus, generality and specificity. Reference becomes jammed, short-circuited; proper names fall into common use, the profane turns sacred, only to risk being double-crossed later. Words and acts become disoriented and reoriented by machinic repetition, the echoing death knell (*glas*) of naming. Christa McAuliffe, christenings, Christ, crystallization, Christmas, catachresis—the catachristening of performatives and performances "takes place" across networks of iterability, alterability, citationality. At its limit, catachristening not only erodes the seals binding performatives and performances, it also breaks apart these forms themselves. Word becomes cry, body becomes elemental, their particles and subparticles mix, become imperceptible, recombine in other processes and assemblages. NASA *Challenger* channels HMS *Challenger* channels Professor Challenger channels . . . [18]

Though we began by looking at statements, we could have easily started at the other end of the performative-performance block, for practices, like discourses, are always already worked over by forces of destratification. "Both forms of content and forms of expression are inseparable from a movement of deterritorialization that carries them away. Both expression and content are more or less deterritorialized, relatively deterritorialized, according to the particular state of their form. In this respect, one cannot posit a primacy of expression over content, or content over expression."[19] And elsewhere, Deleuze and Guattari suggest that stratification proceeds from content to expression, while with destratification the process tends to be reversed.

Within Performance Studies, significantly more attention has been given to practices than to discourses, practices such as gender parody and postcolonial mimicry. These and other processes of cultural exappropriation all tap into the deterritorializing potential sedimented within normative forms of embodiment. These processes do so by foregrounding the citationality of the most lively, original, and present of performances. In his reading of Mardi Gras performances and their place within "the circum-Atlantic world," a world created by the circulation of diverse bodies and practices between Europe, Africa, and the Americas, Joseph Roach defines performance as "the transformation of experience through the renewal of its cultural forms."[20] Roach is interested in the relation of identity and memory, and he focuses part of his attention on the New Orleans Jazz Funeral, in which a solemn funeral service is followed by a festive procession and burial with music. He traces the roots of this performance back to African "celebrations of death founded on religious belief in the participation of ancestral spirits in the world of the present. . . . Such a performance event opens up, with its formal repetitions, a space for play."[21] Such spaces of play, Roach argues, must be understood in terms of collective social memory rather than official history. "In opposition to the official voice of history, which, like Aeneas looking back on the pillar of smoke, has tended to emphasize the cultural annihilations of the diaspora, the voice of collective memory, which derives from performance, speaks of the stubborn reinventiveness of restored behavior."[22]

The distinction to be made, then, is not between an originally present performance which has been lost and a cultural reinvention of performance through repetition, but between two repetitions: on the one hand, the normative repetition of traditional mimesis, which tends to erase differences and anomalies in order to create the *appearance* of a unified, coherent, and originary presence, and, on the other, the mutational repetition of countermimesis or countermimicry, in which repetition is exaggerated to the point that differences proliferate and disseminate themselves. Rebecca Schneider discusses countermimicry in reference to the work of the Native American performance group Spiderwoman: "On the one hand, it is a repetition of the technique of mimesis upon the dominant culture that has mimicked them (as if to say, you've doubled me now I'll double you back). But on the other hand, it is a significant historical counter-analysis, a doubling back as in a retracing of steps to expose something secreted, erased, silenced along the way. . . . Counter-mimicry, vigilant repetition, and the painful irruption of 'real stuff.' "[23]

The analyses of Roach and Schneider reveal that cultural identity and the presence of performance emerge from repetition and difference. Again, there are two types of repetition, one normative, one mutational. Unfortunately—or rather *not* unfortunately—each repetition repeats the other. Thus there are actually at least *four* repetitions: the mimetic repetition "of" presence, the counter-mimetic repetition of difference, the mimetic repetition of counter-mimesis, and the counter-mimetic repetition of traditional mimesis. These four repetitions entail, respectively, processes of propriation (the normative formation of forms from forces), expropriation (the mutational deformation of forms by forces), appropriation (the becoming normative of mutational forces), and exappropriation (the becoming mutational of normative forces). It is by moving through this citational matrix that things repeat themselves differently, that patterns of stratification and destratification emerge and immerge.

The paradox that presence and identity are actually effects of repetition and difference has been theorized extensively by Schechner, and also by Derrida. Schechner puts things very concisely: "Performance means: never for the first time. It means: for the second to the *n*th time. Performance is 'twice-behaved behavior.' "[24] For him, all performance is "restored behavior." "Restored behavior is living behavior treated as a film director treats a strip of film. These strips of behavior can be rearranged or reconstructed; they are independent of the causal systems (social, psychological, technological) that brought them into existence. *They have a life of their own.* The original 'truth' or 'source' of the behavior may be lost, ignored, or contradicted—even while this truth or source is apparently being honored and observed. How the strip of behavior was made, found, or developed may be unknown or concealed; elaborated; distorted by myth or tradition."[25] Restored behavior is performance understood in terms of iterability, repetition, even arche-writing.

Though some might contest this reading, restored behavior shares an uncanny affinity with Derrida's generalized writing, which also entails an essential break with (and *within*) origins and causal systems. In "Signature, Event, Context," a reading of Austin's performative in terms of the iterability of generalized writing, Derrida stresses: "This is the possibility on which I wish to insist: the possibility of extraction and of citational grafting which belongs to the structure of every mark, spoken or written, and which constitutes every mark as writing *even before and outside every horizon of semiolinguistic communication*; as writing, that is, as a possibility of functioning cut off, at a certain point, from its 'original' meaning and from its belonging to a saturable and constraining context. Every sign, linguistic or nonlinguistic, spoken or written (in the usual sense of this opposition), as a small or large unity, can be *cited*, put between citation marks; thereby it can break with every given context, and engender infinitely new contexts in an absolutely unsaturable fashion."[26]

The event of performances, the doing of performatives, these take off from the launch pad of citational networking. We can extend their entwined trajectories even further. The restoration of behavior is to embodied performances what catachristening is to discursive performatives: a strategy of destratification, a turning inside out of performative power, the opening of a mutant hole of self-referentiality within sedimented and enfolded strata. Though the term "restoration" may suggest that a once-present behavior is now being revitalized, we must reiterate that all performance is rehearsed "for the second to the *n*th time." But to underscore the disruptive, destabilizing potential of this generalized citationality, let us catachristen the restoration of behavior within our own reading machine and henceforth tag it the *catastoration* of behavior.

As a process ongoing since (before) the start, catastoration treats embodied processes as raw material for creating something else. "Originating as a process, used in the process of rehearsal to make a new process, a performance, the strips of behavior are not themselves process, but things, items, 'material.' "[27] Any arrangement of forces and processes, small or large, can be seized, "put between citation marks," and reinscribed elsewhere and elsewhen. Such catastorations do not befall a pre-existing, self-present performance; rather, performance only comes into existence, only becomes present to itself, through iterability. Such "originary" repetition generates surprising effects. Cut off from the original context, the reinscribed forces and processes are released within a new context, where they begin to function in entirely different ways. And yet, the cut is not clean, it's not clear-cut, for reinscription opens a hole of self-referentiality that incorporates the alterity of the original context within the new one. Likewise, this original context is always already contaminated by the potential of such reinscription. This is why no context is absolutely original, saturable, or self-contained. Entire contexts can themselves be cited and displaced within new contexts, and, in fact, this is precisely how the process of contextualization proceeds. What would a site specific performance be that could not be cited?

A perfume? A perfumance?

Up to this point we have concentrated on strategies of destratification within the anthropomorphic strata. Yet catastoration occurs within and across other strata as well. One of Schechner's most provocative analyses concerns animal ritualizations and behavioral displays. Drawing on the work of ethologist Irenaus Eibl-Eibesfedt, he describes how a particular behavior, such as a shake of the tail or a nod of the head, can be displaced into another.

1. Behavior changes function.
2. Movements become independent of their original causes and develop their own releasing mechanisms.
3. These movements are exaggerated and at the same time simplified; they frequently freeze into postures; they become rhythmic and repetitive.
4. Conspicuous body parts develop such as the peacock's tail and the moose's horns. These body parts become important parts in behavioral displays.[28]

It must be stressed that such catastorations of behavior entail machinic processes that operate self-referentially across a network of complex systems: biological, behavioral, environmental, etc. From our perspective, the display of a peacock's tail opens up a hole of autopoesis. It functions as a signature event not only for a particular peacock, but also for other peacocks as well as other species.

Deleuze and Guattari offer a striking example of how such machinic performances can even occur across different kingdoms. Bridging the animal and vegetable kingdoms, for instance, wasps and orchids enter into a machinic becoming which they call a "rhizome." "The orchid deterritorializes by forming an image, a tracing of the wasp; but the wasp reterritorializes on that image. The wasp is nevertheless deterritorialized, becoming a piece in the orchid's reproductive apparatus. But it reterritorializes the orchid by transporting its pollen. Wasp and orchid, as heterogeneous elements, form a rhizome."[29] This double becoming obviously occurs not only across a particular pair of wasp and orchid, but also across generational pairings of wasps and orchids. Their evolutionary paths entwine, with an orchid species taking on a particular wasp's shape and a wasp species developing highly specialized organs for collecting the nectar of a specific orchid. (We might also note that the orchid's fragrance plays an essential role in this cross-kingdom performance.) Double deterritorializations or destratifications go far beyond imitation as traditionally understood: "something else entirely is going on: not imitation at all but a capture of a code, surplus value of code, an increase in valence, a veritable becoming, a becoming-wasp of the orchid and a becoming-orchid of the wasp. Each of these becomings brings about the deterritorialization of one term and the reterritorialization of the other; the two becomings interlink and form relays in a circulation of intensities pushing the deterritorialization ever further. There is neither imitation nor resemblance, only an exploding of two heterogeneous series on the line of flight composed by a common rhizome that can no longer be attributed to or subjugated by anything signifying."[30] The passage is produced by a veritable wasp-orchid machine; it is the trace of the machinic phylum, the living-dead, the *genre machinic*.

We can cite many cases of double destratification between humans and animals. Freud's Wolf Man becoming-wolf and Gregor Samsa becoming-insect in Kafka's "The Metamorphosis" are two cases analyzed in depth by Deleuze and Guattari.[31] Let us read of yet another case, that of the Chicken Woman, the becoming-chicken found in Linda Montano's performances of the late 1960s and early 1970s. Significantly, the first performance of Montano's Chicken Woman occurred within a university context, the artist's MFA show in sculpture at the University of Wisconsin. "On May 20, 1969 I had my MFA show on the roof of the art department and throughout the city of Madison. . . . All the other graduate students in Madison were constructing gigantic, minimal objects and I couldn't keep up with them. I was scared and felt out of place in sculpture and graduate school. I often visited the agriculture school and saw chickens there. . . . they became my totem."[32] Scared, she created *The Chicken Show*.

According to Montano, *The Chicken Show* was composed of seven elements: 1. She placed three chicken wire cages in a gallery and put three chickens in each, rotating them between the different cages over several days. 2. Montano hung nine hand-tinted photos of chickens inside the building. 3. Throughout the show, she played a chicken video. 4. A month prior to the event, she posted a phone number around Madison and when people called in, they heard the sounds of chickens on the answering machine. 5. During the show itself, Montano drove around the city playing chicken sounds on a loudspeaker. 6. She distributed chicken posters and vacuum-formed chicken parts. 7. At the end of the show, she gave the nine chickens to the art department's janitor, who in turn started a chicken farm. Montano comments on the creative forces unleashed by this multimedia performance: "Once I decided that I could show chickens in the gallery, all kinds of creative ideas began to flow. The chicken show taught me how to laugh—plus I became the Chicken Woman."[33] Faced with her fellow students' gigantic, static sculptures, she instead created a living environment, a performance installation. She and the chickens merged in a creative line of flight, with the chickens becoming deterritorialized from their agricultural surroundings and reterritorialized within an artistic context, and Montano becoming deterritorialized from her sculpture and graduate school existence and reterritorialized as a performance artist-chicken-woman.

The emergence of Chicken Woman is machinic autopoesis writ small, autoproduction within a milieu of conflicting forces, creation of a mutant creativity, an iterative invention of alterity. Faced with the challenge of being scared, being chicken, Montano becomes chicken and learns to laugh. The Chicken Woman takes on a life of its own. Montano becomes part of a woman-chicken machine that operates far beyond her MFA show. Over the next five years, she performed numerous Chicken Woman events, incorporating chickens into her lifework, using them as occasions for personal transformation: live chickens, taped chickens, chicken sculptures, a chicken costume with feathers and wings, and a large collection of chicken anecdotes gathered from relatives and friends, like this one from a fellow named Howard Fried. "I was a fried chicken freak when I was a little kid. One time we went to Florida and everytime we stopped we had fried chicken. I had southern fried chicken with hash browns. I particularly remember our dinner in the Skyline Drive."[34]

Recursion, self-referentiality, communication across diverse systems, citational networking—these processes can be found in Montano's Chicken Woman performances. As with the catachristening of discourse, the catastoration of behavior erodes the seals between practices and discourses, cracking up forms of knowledge and reinscribing their elements within new machines. In *The Story of My Life* (1973), Montano walked uphill on a treadmill for three hours. She told her life story while playing recorded bird sounds and wearing a "permanent smiling device" on her face. This Chicken Woman performance was, in effect, a multimedia, smiley-faced lecture machine. Significantly, Montano attributes the resulting transformation of her walking talking performance to its physical repetition. This is the lesson of *The Story of My Life*. "After walking for three hours on the treadmill, going uphill, I felt psychically and physically expanded and when I got off the machine I couldn't stop walking because my legs were programmed to move. I was very surprised by this and decided if I could change myself physically by means of repetition, then maybe I could change old fears by repeating the action that seemed fearful (talking). As a result I later sat in front of a video camera and practiced talking for months."[35] We see here that though a process of destratification may begin on one side of the performative-performance block, it will inevitably affect the other side as well. As a line of flight not from but *into* her fright, Montano's becoming-chicken initiates itself with a particular form of content (an embodied performance with chickens). Yet this mutant passage also drags along in its wake forms of expression (discursive performatives, the naming of "Chicken Woman," imperatives to talk and give an account of oneself), leading to the double deterritorialization of body and word, chicken and human, walking and clucking.

On the level of performances and performatives, such two-sided, double-headed becomings characterize perfumative destratification. Again, performances are territorializations of flows and unformed matters into visible bodies, while performatives are the simultaneous encoding of these bodies into articulable subjects and objects. Catachristenings and catastorations alter the *sens* or direction of territorialization and encoding, displacing knowledge-forms into passages of multiple becoming. These becomings are machinic in nature and must be approached not so much in terms of a particular being or set of beings that enter into a process of becoming, nor as a becoming that culminates in one or several beings; rather being is an effect of becoming, just as strata are effects of atmospherics, forms effects of forces, and presence an effect of citational networking. To repeat all this differently: "Multiplicity is the inseparable manifestation, essential transformation, and constant symptom of unity. Multiplicity is the affirmation of unity; becoming is the affirmation of being. The affirmation of becoming is itself being, the affirmation of multiplicity is itself one."[36]

One or multiple Challengers? Yes—

Poised behind the lectern, which at times doubled as the helm of a cruiser, Professor Challenger paused amidst a particularly twisting passage. Gazing off into space, he reflected on the geology of performance, as well as the meteorology of his perfumance: from warships and shuttles to core samples and underwater currents and on to the becomings of flora and fauna, things were coming together and blowing apart at the same time. Looking up, he peered out into the audience and cracked a smile at the faces fading like so many stars into oblivion. "Most of the audience had left. . . . The only ones left were the mathematicians, accustomed to other follies, along with a few astrologers, archaeologists, and scattered individuals. Challenger, moreover, had changed since the beginning of his talk. His voice had become hoarser, broken occasionally by an apish cough."[37] The professor continued his lesson. He lectured on and on, navigating quickly from strata to strata, cite to cite, directed by who knows what guidance device. "Challenger wanted to go faster and faster. No one was left, but he went on anyway. The change in his voice, and in his appearance, was growing more and more pronounced. Something animalistic in him had begun to speak when he started talking about human beings. You still couldn't put your finger on it, but Challenger seemed to be deterritorializing on the spot."[38] The clock in the hall started spinning backwards, then forwards, as fumes of olibanum filled the space, choking all within it. “We had to summarize before we lost our voice. Challenger was finishing up. His voice had become unbearably shrill. He was suffocating. His hands were becoming elongated pincers that had become incapable of grasping anything but could still vaguely point to things. Some kind of matter seemed to be pouring out of the double mask, the two heads; it was impossible to tell whether it was getting thicker or more watery. Some of the audience had returned, but only shadows and prowlers. ‘You hear that? It’s an animal’s voice.’ ”[39] Posed behind the lectern, Challenger was cracking up.

CHAPTER 9. PROFESSOR RUTHERFORD AND GAY SCI FI

It was getting late. Arthur Conan Doyle reflected back on his life and adventures, recalling at one point his years of study at Edinburgh and, in particular, the dazzling lectures given there by a young professor of physiology. Doyle was especially taken by the lecturer's behavioral displays. "Most vividly of all there stands out in my memory the squat figure of Professor Rutherford with his Assyrian beard, his prodigious voice, his enormous chest and his singular manner. He fascinated us and awed us." His was a model performance, one that Doyle relaunched in sci-fi fashion: "I have endeavoured to reproduce some of his peculiarities in the fictitious character of Professor Challenger."[1]

If HMS *Challenger* sets sail as the nominal source for the catachristening of Challenger, Professor Rutherford stands in as the primal body of its catastoration. We are most interested in the professor's lessons concerning research and teaching. By nearly all accounts, William Rutherford, Professor and Chair of Physiology at the University of Edinburgh, performed brilliantly at the lectern. Many other students besides Doyle wrote of the impact his meticulous demonstrations had on their studies, and from the shelves of the University Library one can still read copies of notes taken during his classes. His lectures were legendary. In his memoirs, Doyle writes that even when this professor's desk stood vacant, the lecture machine could still emit explosive lessons, for Rutherford "would sometimes start his lectures before he reached the classroom, so that we would hear a booming voice saying: 'There are valves in the veins,' or some other information, when his desk was still empty."[2]

Professor Rutherford was fondly remembered by many students, and thanks to Doyle's science fiction his figure haunts the outrageous remarks and extravagant gestures of Professor Challenger—the Challenger of Doyle, of Deleuze and Guattari, and still others. Yet William Rutherford's name remains largely forgotten within the annals of science. This eclipse can perhaps be explained by the fact that to this day much of his research remains highly controversial. Rutherford was among the first vivisectionists, those whose cutting-edge experiments were performed on living organisms. Over the years, canines, crustaceans, and many other creatures were laid out upon his laboratory table. There were cries and outcries. In Victorian Britain, and on the Continent as well, the emerging practice of vivisection received intense moral condemnation from both scientists and the general public. Rutherford and other researchers were attacked in person and print and made to appear before a Royal Commission set up to investigate their incisive techniques. In the wake of this Commission, Parliament passed the Cruelty to Animals Act of 1876. Rutherford subsequently put his research on hold for several years, and when it later recommenced, he sought out less controversial subjects. This included research on the ear, "his so-called 'telephone-theory,' now discounted,"[3] and "Cause of the retardation of the pulse which follows artificial or voluntary closure of the nostrils in the rabbit." The professor, it should be noted, was an inventor as well. A contemporary engraving shows him holding the freezing microtome, a device he invented for freezing and slicing tissues into razor-thin samples. On the workbench next to him in the engraving there rests a large crab, whose left pincer Rutherford gently lifts with his fingers.

"My nose is freezing."

The scandal produced by his vivisection experiments may account for Rutherford's posthumous eclipse in the history of science. However, in a

1986 essay, "Conan Doyle's 'Challenger' Unchampioned," Stewart Richards has noted that other vivisectionists of the time have long since entered the canon of British physiology. Investigating the institutional forgetting of Rutherford, Richards also considers whether lack of support from university and professional peers contributed to his eclipse. Again he finds that other Victorian scientists operated under similar constraints and still gained lasting recognition for their work. So to champion the unchampioned Challenger, Richards distills another dimension of Rutherford's archival fall, a more intimate scandal that involved his reading machine.

It was an affair of gross indecency, for Rutherford's machine at Edinburgh was, it appears, queer. Though a formal inquiry did not make this finding official, chances are that the star lecturer's peculiarities were those of a gay scientist. Richards writes: "it seems that Rutherford was decidedly a 'character,' with an affected voice, exaggerated mannerisms, and plagued by a constitution prone to nervous breakdown; he was probably a homosexual."[4] Like the Challenger roaming *A Thousand Plateaus*, this professor may well have taken his pleasure from behind. Indeed, Rutherford's troubles apparently started behind his lectern, site of suffering and gaiety.

> [T]he problem began in 1886 when Rutherford publicly accused his assistant, H.H. Ashdown, of making phallic signs at him during a lecture. The ensuing trouble led to a long enquiry that ran into 1888, when the University Court decided that Rutherford had been ill, had now recovered, and that he was so valuable to the University that his services should be retained. There were evidently other isolated episodes in which Rutherford was reputed to have made sexual advances to members of his staff or students, or to have accused them of doing so to him.[5]

From the Royal Commission and University Court to the judgment of history and test of time, Rutherford's passage was a gradual decline. In the 1890s things really began to break down, and the fading of legacy set in. Citing the Victorian indignation at all things "abnormal," Richards reads the exposure of Rutherford's homosexuality, "which has nothing to do with genuine qualitative estimates of his science," as the "deeper and more potent reason" behind his fall from the annals of physiology. *Ecce homo*: "Had Rutherford not suffered the misfortune of sexual proclivities at the time almost universally condemned as 'abnormal,' not to say repugnant, his reputation as a major minor pioneer in late Victorian physiology would long ago have been secure. That he did so suffer guaranteed that the initial, and readily intelligible, embarrassment of the late 1880s was nurtured in an atmosphere of contrived silence to yield, year by year, a dismissive and overbearing prejudice that ever since has effectively obscured his true importance."[6]

The trajectory of Professor Rutherford's lecture machine cuts across the strata of Victorian discipline. During his life, his research activities earned him renown and rebuke in the scientific community, as well as controversy in the British press and courts, while his teaching activities earned him renown and other pleasures at the lectern, as well as the humiliation of a sexual scandal. That Rutherford's name has subsequently been passed over in the history of science while his gestures live on in sci-fi crypts, this breakdown and dispersion of word and body suggests the manner in which one passes into the atmosphere of forces and intensities. Voice becomes cry, body elemental, who or what remains, recurs, perfumes . . .

Our current lesson plan follows the scents of destratification, only now we're tracing them through paradigms of performance research and, more generally, at the level of sociotechnical systems. Again, there are innumerable strategies one might track, but let's start out from the trail of catachristening and catastoration. The perfumative effects they produce at the micro-level of discourses and practices recur, repeat themselves differently, at the scale of institutions, with their audiovisual archives, their fields of subjects and objects, and their discrete pragmatic installations. Destratification here not only affects performances and performatives, but also sociotechnic assemblages—groups, collectivities, organizations, research paradigms, and all their various infrastructures—whose components become dislodged and refunctioned as parts of a machinic, autopoetic invention. As words and acts enter holes of alterity, they drag in with them other processual elements, bits and pieces of the systems that they occupy. Latent affiliations and cryptic incorporations between different systems suddenly come to fore. As bits and pieces of processes detach from their respective systems, as released flows and matters self-organize, they recur across different scales of alterity. If conditions are just so, a network of major performances goes utterly minor.

"Major" and "minor" are terms introduced by Deleuze and Guattari to distinguish normative and mutational processes in art, science, and society at large. A major art, a major science, a major language is one that dominates a given field or tradition. The major is filled with Great Works, Great Men, Great Events. The minor, however, works within but also against the major. In theorizing the minor literature of Kafka, for instance, Deleuze and Guattari investigate: 1) how Kafka deterritorializes the major languages used in his native Czechoslovakia, experimenting with their contents and expressions and pushing their sense into new and strange intensities; 2) how such experimentation is necessary but insufficient if it does not connect to a larger political immediacy; and 3) how Kafka's writing functions not so much as a social critique but as a "relay for a revolutionary machine-to-come," as a collective assemblage of enunciation already in contact with the future.[7] They go on to argue that Kafka's minor literature constitutes *"another science,"* and in *A Thousand Plateaus*, they extend the notion of minor to scientific research. A minor science is nomadic, eccentric; it is neither a technology nor a proper, "royal" science.

> 1. First of all, it uses a hydraulic model, rather than being a theory of solids treating fluids as a special case. . . .
>
> 2. The model in question is one of becoming and heterogeneity, as opposed to the stable, the eternal, the identical, the constant. It is a 'paradox' to make becoming itself the model, and no longer a secondary characteristic, a copy. . . .
>
> 3. One no longer goes from the straight line to its parallels, in a lamellar or laminar flow, but from a curvilinear declination to the formation of spirals and vortices on an inclined plane. . . .
>
> 4. Finally, the model is problematic, rather than theorematic: figures are considered only from the viewpoint of the *affections* that befall them: sections, ablations, adjunctions, projections. One does not go by specific differences from a genus to its species, or by deduction from a stable essence to the properties deriving from it, but rather from a problem to the accidents that condition and resolve it.[8]

Because the paradigms of performance research stretch across and beyond the arts and sciences, the traits just enumerated here and above are all pertinent to distinguishing major and minor performances. Let's flesh out this distinction by linking it up with some others already introduced—those between structure and machine, form and force, being and becoming.

Major performances occur within structures or systems, where they are directed by determinable goals, such as the survival of the system, the "minimaxing" of inputs and outputs, and the controlled transgression of borders, limen, and other distinctions of inside and out, proper and improper. They thus tend to focus on form, insuring the presence of forms, the maintenance of good form, and the filling in and distribution of forms of all kinds. Major performances propriate and appropriate, they turn mutational forces normative and, in turn, forces into forms. They are performances of being that can only feed back or transform themselves into another being.

Minor performances, alternatively, are produced within machines of becoming. The direction they take is itinerant, flighty, a random walk in the circuits of citational networking. It's not that minor performances are totally out of control; rather, they're guided in another way: they're remote-controlled by patterns of recursive mutation. In a minor performance, seemingly unrelated components and widely dispersed processes are expropriated and become caught up in a machine of becoming. Loopholes of self-referentiality start networking together, at times falling into or being blown out of one another, all the while creating an entangled hierarchy of forces and currents. The borders and limen of different systems are not simply transgressed; they become realigned both in relation to one another and, more radically, to the outside inside of the performance stratum. Forms, structures, and systems disintegrate, normative forces mutate, everything repeats itself otherwise in a strange and singular manner—these are among the signature traits of a minor performance.

Yes—and yet. There's another way to read this distinction of major and minor, one that twists things around in a peculiar manner. Rather than neatly lining up major and minor under the distinctions of structure and machine, form and force, being and becoming—and thereby risking a fall into oppositional binaries—we might instead use the distinction of major and minor to draw and quarter these very oppositions. To put this in more graphic terms, instead of aligning major with structure and minor with machine, like so

structure/machine

major/minor

we can instead draw up the distinction of structure and machine vertically and then bisect them horizontally with the distinction of major and minor:

structure machine

major

minor

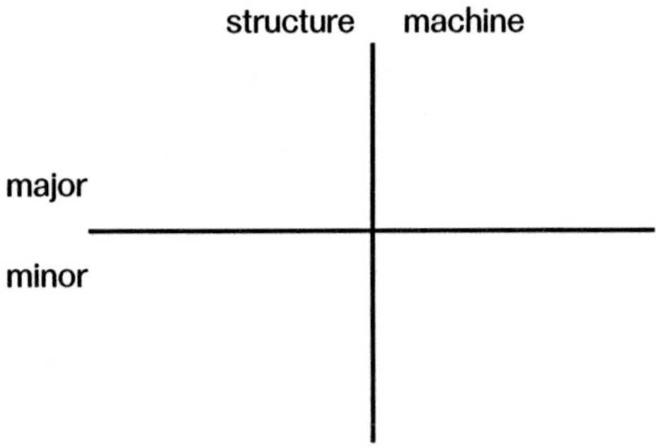

Drawn and quartered in this way, the distinctions divide and multiply, and we can begin to sense differences between major and minor structures, major and minor machines, major and minor forms, major and minor forces, major and minor beings, major and minor becomings.[9] Further dividing and multiplying: in addition to structures and machines, there is the becoming-structure of machines and the becoming-machine of structures; in addition to forms and forces, there is the becoming-form of forces and the becoming-force of forms; and so on. Further still: while we can track and differentiate major and minor performances, we must say that each may become the other. There's a becoming-major of minor performance and a becoming-minor of major performance. Major, minor, major minor, and minor major.

"Roger."

Perhaps some encased studies are called for here from Challenger's cargo bay. NASA *Challenger* 51-L can be read as a major performance, one in which deviations in technical, cultural, and organizational performance were methodically analyzed and normalized through repetition. Attempts to challenge the norms of NASA's Flight Readiness Review by introducing research based on intuition—another hallmark of minor science—were blocked by the FRR process and by the workgroup members themselves. By contrast, Montano's Chicken Woman constitutes a minor performance: the deviations from the norms of graduate school were not blocked off but continued to proliferate, and Montano extended her self-transformations into works exploring women, spirituality, and the relation of art and life, even going so far as establishing an Art/Life Institute—in effect, a minor institution. Professor Rutherford's lecture machine, however, stands as a minor performance gone bad, gone major, and eventually, gone down a disastrous black hole. Due to a complex arrangement of forces, its connection to a political immediacy—a nexus of animal rights, research protocols, and homosexuality—was juridicially dissected, while any attempt to generate a collective assemblage of enunciation and a machinic assemblage of bodies did not prevent a crash-and-burn ending. Lastly, Doyle's shift from medicine and detective mysteries to sci-fi stories can be read as a major performance gone minor: decades after his lessons at Edinburgh, the well-respected medical doctor and creator of Sherlock Holmes began writing his sci fi series, becoming so taken with his new character that he started performing as Professor Challenger, donning makeup and costume and channeling the peculiarities of his self-professed model, Professor Rutherford. Wearing an Assyrian beard and affecting a singular manner, Doyle appeared repeatedly as Challenger in order to champion and promote his science fiction stories, stories that engaged such topics as astronomy, spiritualism, and the political dimensions of research. At times, Doyle-Challenger played jokes on unsuspecting colleagues, and it is even reported that his wife Jean had to fight off his attempts to perform as this character in bed.[10]

On the level of sociotechnical systems, destratification proceeds through the production of minor performances. We have thus far used "perfumance" to designate the atmosphere of forces that surrounds the performance stratum; we shall now also call a particular minor performance *a* perfumance.

"You know, I think these visors are cold from being outside and are fogging up. Here's the pocket checklist."

1. A perfumance is a displaced, disjointed performance, a minor performance that breaks with the sociotechnical system producing it and enters into recursive communication from other systems, thereby displacing their discourses and practices as well as their systemic limits. There is a certain gaiety to perfumance. Cranking up a reading of Jean Tinguely's sculptures, Deleuze and Guattari describe the workings of a joyful, deterritorializing machine. "A machine brings into play several simultaneous structures which it pervades. The first structure includes at least one element that is not operational in relation to it, but only in relation to a second structure. It is this interplay which Tinguely presents as being essentially joyful, that ensures the process of deterritorialization of the machine, as well as the position of the mechanic as the most deterritorialized part of the machine."[11] This last point is crucial: in a perfumance, one does not simply perform as an actor, engineer, manager, etc. One perfumes, disintegrates, becomes other via a machinic process of invention, intervention, in(ter)vention. Such perfumances can emerge anywhere, anytime, for the perfumative dimension pervades every contemporary sociotechnical system, from the most intimate to the most public of relations. Perfumance—it is the id, the other, the iterability of any and all performance, its machinic unconscious, as it were. Deleuze and Guattari distinguish between social technical machines and desiring-machines in the following manner: "Desiring-machines are not in our heads, in our imagination, they are *inside the social and technical machines themselves*. Our relationship with machines is not a relationship of invention or of imitation; we are not the cerebral fathers nor the disci-

plined sons of the machine. It is a relationship of peopling: we populate the social technical machines with desiring-machines, and we have no alternative. We are obliged to say at the same time: social technical machines are only conglomerates of desiring-machines under molar conditions that are historically determined; desiring-machines are social and technical machines restored to their determinant molecular conditions."[12] Sociotechnical systems are desiring-machines that have become stratified; they are perfumances sedimented and enfolded into the territories and codes of a major performance. Conversely, desiring-machines are deterritorialized sociotechnical systems, systems whose words and actions have become decoded and deterritorialized, whose performances have become minor, become joyful, become perfumative. The two performances presuppose one another, cite one another, for "desiring-machines are indeed the same as technical and social machines, but they are their unconscious, as it were; they manifest and mobilize the investments of desire that 'correspond' to the conscious or preconscious investments of interest, politics, and the technology of a specific social field."[13] In sociotechnical systems, desire performs; in desiring-machines, it perfumes. Machinic desire is not limited to the psyches of individuals, nor to a society's superstructure; rather, it pervades all social and technical fields, where it serves as our libidinal infrastructure. (Again, who does IT think it is?)

2. With respect to the performance paradigms—and a nod to Professor Rutherford—the joyful invention of a minor performance might best be characterized as what Nietzsche called "gay science," a certain alliance of thought and laughter, rigor and levity, the profound and the ridiculous. It is an alliance that differs remarkably from the gravity that attracts and weighs down the major arts and sciences, making thought into a clunky pain machine. "In the great majority, the intellect is a clumsy, gloomy, creaking machine that is difficult to start," writes Nietzsche in *The Gay Science*. "They call it 'taking the matter *seriously*' when they want to work with this machine and think well. How burdensome they must find good thinking! The lovely human beast always seems to lose its good spirits when it thinks well; it becomes 'serious.' And 'where laughter and gaiety are found, thinking does not amount to anything': that is the prejudice of this serious beast against all 'gay science.' — Well then, let us prove that this is a prejudice."[14] In perfumance, laughter becomes a sensor for conducting multiparadigmatic research (though it is not the only one by any means). A perfumative machine is characteristically nimble, light, and joyful. It dances on table legs. The coming together of discourses and practices from different performance paradigms creates countless incongruities, odd paradoxes, and even outright absurdities—and from this gathering there intermittently arises a certain nonsensical sense, a non-sense that may explode in laughter. Nietzsche writes that science "may still be better known for its power of depriving man of his joys and making him colder, more like a statue, more

stoic. But it may yet be found to be the *great dispenser of pain.* And then its counterforce might be found at the same time: its immense capacity for making new galaxies of joy flare up."[15]

3. Nonsense is essential to the sense, the gay scents, of a perfumance. If there's no nonsense in one's work, then one has not gone far enough in engaging the logic and common sense—the formal presuppositions and informal prejudices—underlying one's training and research. In short, one has left untouched the inner workings of one's own reading machine. In saying-doing nonsense, however, one is already caught up in a sort of meta-learning. As Susan Stewart observes: "To engage in nonsense, one must already have the ability to learn about learning; nonsense not only engages this ability, nonsense itself may be seen as an exploration of the parameters of contexts of learning."[16] In a related though different way than comparative analysis, nonsense provides an angle on one's sense of being. If one is only serious about one's discourses and practices, if one never laughs with them or at them, or, more seriously still, never *laughs at oneself,* then one has closed off an immense affective realm of experience and learning. "To laugh at oneself," Nietzsche writes, "as one would have to laugh in order to laugh *out of the whole truth*—to do that even the best so far lacked sufficient sense for the truth, and the most gifted had too little genius for that. Even laughter may yet have a future."[17] A century later, Craig Saper, reading Barthes—himself a writerly reader of Nietzsche—proposes laughter as a methodology. Saper calls for the creation of "artificial mythologies," Barthesian inventions that use laughter not only to critique cultural myths, but to dissolve metalanguages, including that of critique itself. "If we dismiss [Barthes'] laugh, we miss the chance to understand his strategy to dissolve any metalanguage the moment it constitutes itself. That is, he engages in *bathmology,* a statement with a series of interpretations ranging from the naive to the ironic. His laugh teaches the reader to listen not only to what the writer says but also to the texture, tone, and *bathos* of his humor."[18] There are some thoughts that require laughter in order to be thought at all, and perfumance is one of them.

4. When it comes to the intimacies of perfumance and gay science, not just any laughter will do: there is an affirmative, active laughter and a negative, reactive laughter, even if mastering their differences will remain an impossible task. (For fun, one might say that sociotechnical systems labor to produce negative laugh tracks, while desiring-machines activate affirmative tracks.) In "Ulysses Gramophone," a lecture that navigates around laughter, performativity, and the *yes* in Joyce's *Ulysses,* Derrida explores the double tonality of two "yes-laughters," laughters tainted with the poison-remedy scent of the *pharmakon.* One is a negative yes-laughter, a mournful laugh that "takes joy in hypernmesic mastery and in spinning spiderwebs that defy all other possible mastery. . . . Even in its resignation to phantasm, this yes-laughter reaffirms control of a subjectivity that draws together

everything as it draws itself together, or as it delegates itself to the name."[19] Here one always gets the last laugh, laughs best, laughs at the other. But this negative yes-laughter is also "joyously ventriloquised by a completely different music, very close to the vowels of a completely different song. I hear this too, very close to the other one, as the yes-laughter of a gift without debt, light affirmation, almost amnesic, of a gift or an abandoned event, which in classical language is called 'the work,' a lost signature without a proper name."[20] The abandoned event and lost signature Derrida speaks of can be read, respectively, as catastoration and catachristening, as performances and performatives whose presence (and absence) emerge via traces of differential repetition, repetition that always allows one laughter to trail off into another. Let me hazard this thought: in *Ulysses*, these different *yes-laughters* shuttle between a joyful Joyce and a Joyceless joy. Derrida poses laughter as a fundamental, "quasi-transcendental" tonality, one that cannot be exhausted by knowledge or hermeneutics. Similarly, he approaches *yes* as a "pre-performative" force that is prior to any affirmation or negation, to any signature, event, or context: "*yes* is the transcendental condition of all performative dimensions. A promise, an oath, an order, a commitment always implies a *yes*, I sign. The *I* of *I sign* says *yes* and says *yes* to itself, even if it signs a simulacrum. Any event brought about by a performative mark, any writing in the widest sense of the word, involves a *yes*, whether this be phenomenalized or not, that is, verbalized or adverbalized as such."[21] Far from forming a closed, narcissistic loop, this *yes, I sign* installs difference into all acts and words, all systems and paradigms: it is self-referential alterity that returns neither to an auto- or self, but is always already received and sent on. "Yes, the condition of any signature and of any performative, addresses itself to some other which it does not constitute, and it can only begin by *asking* the other, in response to a request that has always already been made, *to ask it* to say *yes*. Time appears as a result of this singular anachrony."[22] With affirmative yes-laughter, the other laughs anachronistically, laughs first, at last and last, at first. Because the gramophony of *yes* operates between and beyond the eyes and ears, between and beyond the *eidos* and *logos* of knowledge and truth, Derrida calls *yes* the "perfume of discourse." "I could (and I thought about it for a while) have turned this paper into a treatise on perfumes—that is on the *pharmakon*—and I could have called it *On the perfumative in 'Ulysses.'*" [23]

5. One might be tempted to say that perfumance counters the challenging tonality of performance with the tonality of laughter, but what's really at stake are at least two tonalities of challenging, two tonalities of laughter. The question becomes: how do these tonalities reverberate within our general theory? Cultural performance, organizational performance, technological performance, embodied performance, discursive performative, performance stratum—these are the main concepts composing our theory. Perfumance,

however, is not a concept; rather it can be thought of in terms of what Gregory Ulmer calls a "puncept." While concepts are organized in terms of signifieds, puncepts follow the materialities of signifiers, the tonalities of affects, the traces of differance.[24] Our reading has tracked the generation and generalization of performance concepts within a number of fields, including anthropology, computer science, engineering, linguistics, organizational theory, philosophy, sociology, and theater. While the performance stratum is an attempt to generalize these generalizations and gather them together into one concept, this attempt fails, or rather, degenerates by necessity, for the pragmatic arrangement of forces that underwrites all these performance concepts cannot itself be conceptualized. Not only are its forces and intensities too diverse, too dispersed, too disseminated, but perfumance is anachronistic, untimely; if anything, *it belongs to the future*. More accurately: perfumance emits emissions of the future. Significantly, Ulmer explores punceptual laughter as the tonality of a futural, post-conceptual thought, one that he reads in Derrida's perfumative writings. "Against the emphasis on utterance as a performative *enunciation*, Derrida imagines comprehension in terms of the *annunciation* as it is couched in the apocalyptic mode, in the Biblical tradition of apocalyptic prophecy and forecasts. To perform writing in terms of *annunciation*, for a mind listening with a psychoanalytic or dialogical ear, requires a shift away from signifieds to tone."[25] Such a prophetic ear produces visions, just as the eye of the visionary begins to hear things, and this eye-ear and ear-eye both become nose, become perfumative, anachronistically, challenger challenging challenger, laughter laughing at laughter.

6. One faces many tests in thinking and linking perfumance and gay science, among them learning to laugh at knowledge and at oneself, learning to learn through nonsense, and crosstraining one's eyes and ears to catch a scent of the future. Another test pertains to the relation of gay science and the queer theory that has given so much to the study of cultural performance in the last decade, a decade perhaps destined to be called "the *other* gay '90s." Is gay science queer, queer theory gay? In his 1974 introduction to *The Gay Science*, translator Walter Kaufmann perhaps foresaw such a question, writing that "it is no accident that the homosexuals as well as Nietzsche opted for 'gay' rather than 'cheerful.' 'Gay science,' unlike 'cheerful science,' has overtones of a light-hearted defiance of convention; it suggests Nietzsche's 'immoralism' and his 'revaluation of values.' "[26] However, though he mentions other, "superficial," similarities between Nietzsche and gays—"Nietzsche says some very unkind things about women, and he extols friendship and the Greeks"—Kaufmann hopes his readers will not draw too strong a connection between the two: "it is hoped that the title of this book will not be misconstrued as implying that Nietzsche was homosexual or that the book deals with homosexuality."[27] Nonetheless, a number of theorists—lesbian, gay, and straight—have

of late drawn upon this thinker who philosophizes with a hammer (not a sledgehammer, but the small instrument for striking tuning forks—and idols). Judith Butler, for one, tags her project as a critical genealogy of gender, while also issuing this charge in *Gender Trouble*: "The challenge for rethinking gender categories outside of the metaphysics of substance will have to consider the relevance of Nietzsche's claim in *On the Genealogy of Morals* that 'there is no "being" behind doing, effecting, becoming; "the doer" is merely a fiction added to the deed—the deed is everything.' "[28] Indeed, for their part, Lisa Duggan and Kathleen McHugh hammer the gaiety button in their manifesto for a "fem(me) science." "Make no mistake about it, fem(me) science is a joke, a howl of laughter that would ridicule and demolish any notion of the feminine that takes itself seriously. Fem(me) science calls for a revaluation of all feminine values; it aims not to explain, or instruct, but to evoke and provoke those passions frequently seething under controlled, objective and didactic prose."[29] Fem(me) science, queer theory, gay science—tracing the genealogical affinities of these research programs requires imaging a science that is not substantiated by a subjectivity or objectivity, that is not substantiated by any thing at all, but instead is active without being appropriative and passive without being appropriated, a science, in short, that gaily challenges science itself.

7. In "The Test Drive," a high perfumance reading of *The Gay Science*, Avital Ronell has also picked up on the homophonic emissions between gays and gay science, as well as Kaufmann's wary reading of their relationship. Rather than warding off this association or chastising Kaufmann for doing so, Ronell reads him generously (thinking as thanking *à la* Heidegger) and affirms the connection: gay science is a question of gaiety in all its senses, including that of "alternative lifestyles." "In this context 'gay,' as Walter Kaufmann is careful to point out, does not necessarily mean 'homosexual,' though such rights of nonreproductive association by pleasure and thought pattern, are certainly extended by the terms of the contract that Nietzsche draws up."[30] This contract, binding across remote area codes, leads Ronell to pose these provocative questions: "What is a science that predicates itself on gaiety without losing its quality of being a science? And how does Nietzsche open the channels of a scientificity that, without compromising the rigor of inquiry, would allow for the inventiveness of science fiction, experimental art and, above all, a highly stylized existence?"[31] The inventiveness, experimentation, and stylizations of Nietzsche's gay science are all caught up in a scientificity whose current contours we've encountered at several test sites, including those of NASA *Challenger*, the Techno-Performance paradigm, and Heidegger's questioning of technology. This scientificity is an onto-historical issue, for like the technology with which it dominates, it is not only historically inscribed, but also forms "an ever elusive and yet at the same time tremendously potent force field," one that

calls forth our being. "Our being has been mobilized by the various technologies in ways that are beginning to receive serious attention in the fields of ontology, ethics, political theory, cybernetics, and artificial intelligence." And—

> Yet there is something that belongs neither inside nor outside any of these fields but has nonetheless infiltrated their very core—something, indeed, that Nietzsche's Gay Sci first articulated. Nietzsche variously motivates the scientific premises of his work by terms that indicate the activities of testing, which include experimentation, trial, hypothetical positing, retrial, and more testing. If anything, Gay Sci signals to us today the extent to which our rapport to the world has undergone considerable mutation by means of our adherence to the imperatives of testing.[32]

Seeping out from within the deepest, most obscure cracks of the performance stratum, perfumance "is" the test drive, "is" the performance principle, "is" the challenging-forth of the world to perform—or else. Or rather, it's all these things *read another way, read with a certain laughter, a certain joy, a certain gaiety.*

And herein lies one of the trickiest challenges of all—at least for someone trained in the arts, humanities, and/or various schools of cultural criticism—and that is to read the incessant testing found in science and technology not only as an object of critique, not only as an activity to question and negate, but also as a performance *that can and must be affirmed.* This is the most daunting test of contemporary gay science. "Testing, which our Daseins encounter every day in the form of SAT, GRE, HIV, MCATS, FDA, cosmetics, engines, stress, and arms testing 1-2-3-broadcast systems, and testing your love, testing your friendship, in a word, testing the brakes—was located by Nietzsche mainly in the eternal joy of becoming."[33] Is this some kind of joke? Becoming-testy? *Affirm* the test drive? But think about it: to oppose art and science, technique and technology, creativity and analytics, isn't this among the most comfortable of positions, the most major of presuppositions? To make matters trickier: doesn't critique, even critique of critique, entail putting something to the test, not just once and for all, but again and again? And even trickier still: aren't the most active of artists and activists precisely those who experiment with their materials, their coalitions, their lives—who put them all to a certain test? In the age of global performance, all the world becomes a test site. As Ronell calls it, "testing marks an ever new relation between forces."[34] Thus the *calumnia*, the trickery, of challenging challenging itself: to negate *and* affirm this worldwide test pattern.

"T minus 6 minutes and the orbiter test conductor has given pilot Mike Smith the 'go' to perform the auxiliary power unit [APU] prestart. He has reported back

that prestart is complete. T minus 5 minutes and 30 seconds and counting, and Mission Control has transmitted the signal to start the on-board flight recorders."

One might begin with some minor performance testing, reading "performance" itself as a puncept, one whose perfumative atmosphere makes itself up with the scents and sensibilities of other performance concepts. Cultural performance, for instance, is permeated by organizational and technological performances, as well as by financial, medical, and educational performances. All senses of performance harbor diverse forces and potentialities, for these meanings are nothing other than forces that have been captured and stratified by various lecture machines. Ulmer suggests that one needn't "choose between the different meanings of key terms, but compose by using all the meanings (write the paradigm [of meanings])."[35] Similarly: create a perfumance using all the paradigms of performance research.[36] Rather than champion a properly contested sense of performance and leave untouched the norms that produce and take it to the limit, seek instead to develop sensibilities with researchers from other paradigms, and not just at their margins but also deep within their strata. For all sociotechnical systems, all groups, all paradigms harbor both normative and mutational forces, though in different arrangements. It takes a certain nose to distinguish them.

The challenge lies in channeling mutational forces across the entire performance stratum, releasing desires and intensities from contexts that constrain them, creating perfumances that test the modulations of performative power. Factory workers, information processors, middle managers, top executives, civil engineers, chemists, computer scientists, rocket scientists, doctors, trainers, athletes, stock brokers, financial analysts, teachers, administrators, school children—*anyone* who knows *anything* about *any performance*—these are potential allies. Such alliances are crucial to operating across different territories of the performance stratum. We can take some guidance from Critical Art Ensemble, who calls for countering nomadic power mechanisms through acts of electronic civil disobedience, acts carried out by small cells that draw upon different knowledges and skills. "The cell must be organic; that is, it must consist of interrelated parts working together to form a whole that is greater than the sum of its parts. To be effective, the schism between knowledge and technical ability in the cell must be closed. A shared political perspective should be the glue that binds the parts, rather than interdependence through need. Avoid consensus through similarity of skills, since in order to be useful, different skills must be represented. Activist, theorist, artist, hacker, and even a lawyer would be a good combination of talents—knowledge and practice should mix." And one shouldn't dismiss the bureaucrat either, for "the authoritarian fetish for efficiency is an ally that cannot be underestimated."[37] It is precisely by mixing paradigms and juxtaposing performances and performatives that one distills a perfumance of minor test patterns, a joyful scientifiction, *a gay sci fi.*

"T minus 5 minutes."

But let's not kid ourselves too much—or too little: experimental research can be dangerous, for becoming puts one's being on the line. The *calumnia* can calumniate. Catastrophic risks may be run, whether one experiments collaboratively or individually. In the case of Nietzsche, the gay '90s were hardly all fun and games. In late 1888, early 1889, he launched into a final test flight, taking off on a passage of ecstasy and pain, his suffering become gay, his gaiety becoming insufferable. Nietzsche spent the 1890s shuttling from sanatorium to *die Sorge* of his mother and sister, and passed away in the century's last year, 1900, which we commonly read as the first of another. Perhaps by chance, a second gay scientist had been booked on a hauntingly similar flight. Across the Channel, Professor Rutherford's lectern was again empty, but now silent as well. After decades of cutting-edge experiments, after years of scandal and creeping infamy, the major minor professor of physiology suffered a major breakdown. While Nietzsche's life-experiments took manic flight, Rutherford suffered a depressive dive. He left the university and entered an asylum. He managed to continue some research for a time, but his world was eventually consumed by wave upon wave of depression. The bad weather set in, and the blue waves deepened into black. William Rutherford passed away in 1899, "and (despite the official records indicating that he died of influenza) may well have taken his own life."[38] Richards bases this reading on Rutherford's epitaph. Penned by the Professor himself, it reads *"nec sorte nec fato,"* neither chance nor fate.

Why such disastrous flights? Why so many downed test pilots? Stateside, on the emerging performance stratum, we could cite the crash sites of Pollack and Bird, Joplin and Hendrix, Basquiat and Cobain, and on and on and on. In their studies of the minor arts and sciences, Deleuze and Guattari cite the efforts of Artaud, Woolf, and other experimenters who constructed amazing desiring-machines and yet passed through black holes so twisted and mangled that they crashed—sometimes repeatedly, sometimes fatally. "What happened? Were you cautious enough? Not wisdom, caution. In doses. As a rule immanent to experimentation: injections of caution. . . . Mimic the strata. You don't reach the BwO, and its plane of consistency, by wildly destratifying. . . ."[39] Even if you destratify performatives and performances, even if you connect up your machine with other system operators and channel a collective assemblage of annunciation, all this is no guarantee that things will take off and go down smoothly. The passage can get very treacherous, either precipitously or in shorter and shorter gradations. At any point, the blue sky of an autopoetic hole can go black, and "instead of opening up the deterritorialized assemblage onto something else, it may produce an effect of closure, as if the aggregate had fallen into and continues to spin in a kind of black hole."[40] Recursion can turn sinister, becoming a curse. The flight hardens into a missile, a shell. Suddenly, a hole—and everything passing through it—gets plugged.

It's not only solo flights that can wind up in a heap of flesh and wreckage. Small crews and large social groups can crash; whole nations can plunge into a deadly nosedive, taking down peoples and histories and leaving a sickly vapor trail cutting across not one but multiple strata. Sadly, there are many such crash sites we could cite, far too many from the last century alone. Let's approach one of the most pungent and ghastly, one that marks an initiation of sorts for the performance stratum. From its veils is launched a rocketing lectern.

In 1928, following the removal of his former professor and mentor Edmund Husserl, Martin Heidegger accepted the vacant chair of philosophy at his *alma mater*, the University of Freiburg. He had a phone installed in the office as he finetuned his lecture machine to better receive the call of Being. In April 1933, three months after Hitler became Chancellor of the Weimar Republic, Heidegger was elected the University's Rector. That May he joined the National Socialist party. His lectern had begun to resemble the *Führer's* podium. In the Nazi military-industrial-academic complex, lecturing again became something altogether new. "Suddenly words like *Kampf*, 'military service,' and 'the destiny of the German *Volk*' appeared alongside 'science' and 'Being' in Heidegger's addresses."[41] The calls to the Rector intensified. As Heidegger later recounted, "someone from the top command of the Storm Trooper University Bureau, SA section leader Baumann called me up."[42] In her telephone-theory of this scene (we've been reading from *The Telephone Book*), Ronell poses this lucid question: "Simply asked, what is the status of a philosophy, or rather a *thinking*, that doesn't permit one to distinguish with surety between the call of conscience and the call of the Storm Trooper?"[43] How could someone who posed the sending of Being to Daseins as the most authentic of calls have answered the call of the Nazi MIA complex? What called and challenged forth the thinker of calling and challenging forth?

The deconstructive reading of this scene, far from attempting to disconnect these calls and challenges, traces the ways their transmissions are connected and grounded onto-historically. While Ronell picks up and picks apart Heidegger's telephony, Derrida has addressed the risky question of spirit (*Geist*) in the philosopher's *Rectorship Address*. Here Heidegger defines spirit as the will to essence and science, thereby getting caught up in the historical and metaphysical currents he elsewhere warns against. But in the *Address*, "this risk is not just a risk run. If its program seems diabolical, it is because, *without there being anything fortuitous in this*, it capitalizes on the worst, that is on both evils at once: the sanctioning of nazism, and the gesture that is still metaphysical."[44] Heidegger's address upon taking the rectorship was titled "The Self-Affirmation of the German University." According to Derrida, what guided Heidegger's conduct at this critical juncture, what called him forth to lead the German university's self-affirmation and put it in service to the Third Reich, can be read in a certain command or order-word that appears in the very opening of his address. That word is *Führung* (ordering, leading, conducting, guiding).

The Rector speaks: "To take over the rectorship is to oblige oneself to guide this high school spiritually [*die Verpflichtung zur gestigen Führung dieser hohen Schule*]. Those who follow, masters and pupils, owe their existence and their strength only to a true common rootedness in the essence of the German university. But this essence comes to the clarity, the rank and the power which are its own only if first of all and at all times the guides [*Führer*] are themselves guided—guided by the inflexibility of this spiritual mission, the constraining nature of which imprints the destiny of the German people with its specific historical character."[45] Derrida writes: "Self-affirmation, first of all, would be impossible, would not be heard, would not be what it is if it were not of the order of spirit, spirit's very order. The word 'order' designating both the value of command, of leading, duction or conduction, the *Führung*, and the value of mission: sending, an order given. Self-affirmation *wants* to be . . . the affirmation of spirit through *Führung*. This is a spiritual conducting, of course, but the *Führer*, the guide—here the Rector—says he can only lead if he is himself led by the inflexibility of an order, the rigor or even the *directive* rigidity of a mission (*Auftrag*)."[46] *Führers*, guides, leaders, conductors, directors, rectors—such posts made up the Nazi hierarchy of command and control, a system whose spiritual mission was guided by the *Führer* of *Führers*, Adolf Hitler. Through his lectures and speeches of the early 1930s, Heidegger helped secure the phone lines between a risky reading of Nietzschean affirmation and the answering of orders, directions, and calls for being (a) Nazi.

Elsewhere Derrida has tracked the ontological trajectory of Heidegger's call in terms of rocket science and the posting of letters, writing that the "emission or sending of Being is not the firing of a missile or the posting of a missive, but I do not believe it is possible, in the last analysis, to *think* the one without the other."[47] There were many other experimenters called up by the Nazis—artists, philosophers, postal workers, and scientists alike. For instance, the Third Reich's telephone book also contained the names of Eugen Sänger and Irene Bredt, a husband-and-wife team of rocket scientists. Together, Sänger and Bredt designed a low-orbiting vessel named the *Silverbird*, a version of which they rechristened and proposed to the German *Luftwaffe* as the *Amerika Bomber*. This craft was designed to make a special delivery: its mission was to lift off from Germany, attain an altitude of 100 miles, and "then commence its series of aerodynamic skip-glides across the upper atmosphere, delivering its 660 pounds of bombs on New York City, and slowly decelerating to settle in the lower atmosphere. Near the end of its flight, it would enter a continuous descending glide and eventually land some 12,000 miles from its launch site."[48] If it had been built, the *Amerika Bomber* would have been the first space shuttle, predating *Challenger* and its companion ships by well over three decades. The *Luftwaffe* did not take up the *Amerika Bomber* project, however, though the Third Reich did employ and deploy armies of rocket scientists, many of whom were later reassigned east and west to design the high performance missiles and spacecraft of the US and USSR.[49]

Perhaps this is the time and place to translate "performance" into German and back again. In technical and organizational contexts the term "performance" has lately begun to enter the German language intact in its English form, yet "performance" in the theatrical sense is still often translated as *Aufführung*. The verb "perform" can be translated as *aufführen*, composed of *auf-* (up, upward) and *führen* (to lead, to guide). In other words, the semantics and pragmatics of "performance" is in communication with the discursive network of *Führung* and *Führer*. Translating back into English, we can get some sense of this translatory network in the phrases "to mount a production" and "put up a show." I am not arguing, however, that performance is somehow inherently fascistic, that its diverse passages are all directed by Nazi calls of *Führung*. Rather, I want to suggest that these and innumerable other translations of "performance" are always already at work helping to produce the age of global performance. To read them, we must increasingly attune ourselves to the meanings and valences of "performance" in languages other than English—and to the practices embodying them, as well as the systems that seal together these words and acts. One can imagine, and indeed foresee, readings of the ways in which "performance" has been deployed in various languages, how and when it has been translated into different tongues, where and when it has been left untranslated, and in all cases, how "performance" has come to referentially construct diverse bodies around the world. To take yet another example: though etymologists trace "performance" back to the Old French *parformer*, a variant of the Latin *parfornir*, contemporary translators face great difficulties in translating our "performance" into French. Possible translations include *representation* and *spectacle*, two terms heavily loaded with theoretical significance—and possibilities. Translating back into English, perhaps we might start reading Guy Debord's *La Société du Spectacle* as *The Society of Performance.*[50]

These excursions into German and French are but two passages cutting across the tip of a massive performative iceberg, a submerged body of performances that has been shaped by centuries of struggles and forces and that is in no way limited to North America and Western Europe. The age of global performance emerges from innumerable stratifications and erosions, from trial runs and wrecked ruins, from bits of life and death that have come to serve as its substratum. It is built upon individuals and peoples, upon memories and dreams, on the crusts of shifting continents, atop the rubble of cities and cultures and the vestiges of defunct empires and failed revolutions. It is built upon the remnants of an Old World's disciplinary mechanisms, its outmoded modes of power/knowledge, its history of violent campaigns directed toward even older worlds. Taking all these sites as its launch pad, performance takes off with a new mission, a new world order, one of computerized experimentation, of optimizing and satisificing, of testing and exceeding limits and limen, of boldly going where no one's gone before: a world that faces tomorrow as yet another day to perform—or else.

One must not turn one's back on these crash sites, nor feel secure in one's critical distance from all their odors; instead, one must keep them under one's nose, taking flight not away from the stratum, *but straight into it.* "Lodge yourself on a stratum, experiment with the opportunities it offers, find an advantageous place on it, find potential movements of deterritorialization, possible lines of flight, experience them, produce flows of conjunctions here and there, try out continuums of intensities segment by segment, have a small plot of new land at all times."[51] Crash is perhaps inevitable, and yet "the black hole is a machine effect in assemblages and has a complex relation to other effects. It may be necessary for the release of innovative processes that they first fall into a catastrophic black hole: stases of inhibition are associated with the release of crossroad behaviors."[52] One must, in all senses, experiment with experience, taking discretionary lessons from what survives—lives on—disaster.

The countdown recommenced. There was static on the line, massive feedback and garbled transmissions. The lecturer was trying to recap before she lost the linkup or wandered into some stinking trap. Destratification of sociotechnical systems: Perfumance insinuates itself at this level by cutting across multiple structures. It gives rise to gay sci fi experiments, minor art and science projects whose strategies include the catachristening and catastoration of discourses and practices, and a light, hammering laughter—all this injected with large hits of discretionary caution. Here the lecturer cited a philosopher on the perfumative and the pharmakological. "The *pharmakon* introduces and harbors death. It makes the corpse presentable, masks it, makes it up, perfumes it with its essence. . . . *Pharmakon* is also a word for perfume. A perfume without essence."[53] A nonessential essence, perfumance resides not so much within paradigms, performances, or performatives, but in the outside inside them. Under its influence, the joints binding discourses and practices erode, as do the seals separating different archives and power set-ups. As mutational forces are released from their stratifications, as limits and limen give way, iterability erupts recursively across all affected systems. A gesture, a tone, a singular manner, such discrete elements emerge as parts of a mutant desiring-machine, one that channels multiple situations and struggles. In a minor performance, machinic elements self-organize, their mutational forces enter into new and dynamic constellations. Across the performance stratum, these constellations generate a plateau of recursive intensities, a pattern of differential repetition that cuts across diverse systems. Resistant perfumances operate by critique and displacement, negation and affirmation. Creative processes do not so much become objects of critical analysis as much as critical analyses become part of a machinic creativity. A "yes," a "no"—and always—"and yet." "There's a price to be paid by the experimental player," Ronell writes. "One cannot remain detached from the activity but finds oneself subject to morphing." Someone—or something—is calling and challenging you out of yourself. "Unknowable, and as yet unseen, something within us could come from the future because we are molting and the gay science has pledged itself in so many ways to the future."[54]

Maybe it's a dark and beautiful creature on the line, a gay scientist in her own way, and she's just dying to go out. A vessel driven to cruising. Her corset is riveted tight, real tight, so tight that it's coming apart at the seams. She's starting to crack and her flesh wants out. She needs to get naked, but she knows the score (she's been down deep), and she's willing to take some risks, though with discretion, of course. Her thoughts, like her claws, are sharp and ready. "Because a female lobster mates only just after she sheds her corsetlike shell, it is a time when she is most vulnerable to attack from predators. In order to ensure a successful encounter between these potential cannibals, lobster society has evolved a complex courtship ritual. When she is ready to molt, the female lobster approaches a male's den (usually the largest male in the neighborhood). She wafts a 'sex perfume' called a *pheromone* in his direction. He responds by fanning the water with his swimmerets, permeating his apartment with her scent. He emerges from his den with his claws raised. She responds with a brief boxing match or by turning away. Either attitude seems to work to convince the male of her amorous intentions. They enter the den together."[55]

(Static—then a slight pause.)

Onizuka: " . . . Kind of cold this morning."

Smith: "Up here, Ellison, the sun's shining in."[56]

CHAPTER 10. JANE CHALLENGER, DISASTRONAUT

There remains one last Challenger stowed away on our lecture machine, though its recursive mission always leaves the hatch open for others. This Challenger is "Jane Challenger, the red-haired journalist who had become legendary covering the last gasps of the present worldwide economic order." The fiery reporter was moving quickly, "without displaying the slightest sign of disgust as she passed through the halls of these five-star hotels in Geneva."[1] But Challenger, who roams a recent novel by Brazilian writer Márcio Souza, was in fact thoroughly disgusted by the Geneva conference on Third World debt, an event she was covering for the British magazine *New Economist*. She was stupefied by the contrast between the scholars' and bureaucrats' grave public lectures and their happy, off-the-record remarks, and also by the lack of any conclusive resolution to the problems at hand. She had to get away. "She wanted to spend a weekend in the most distant place possible. Some place that was really far away, on another continent." As it happened, however, she was so out of it at the travel agency that "she didn't pay attention to the name of the place when the agent presented the plan to her. . . . That same night she was on a jet, crossing the Atlantic Ocean, without knowing exactly what she was doing. She fell into a deep sleep, and when she woke up, she saw they were flying over a carpet of forest that lost itself in the horizon. She began to feel uneasy when the airplane made a long and smooth turn over the dark waters of an enormous river and came down for a landing."[2] Having booked a blind flight, Challenger's taken off across the waves and now is about to touch down on a jungle plateau, a sweltering region populated with walking, talking anachronisms.

By neither chance nor fate, Challenger has flown to Amazonia, more precisely, to Manaus, Brazil, a place she's sworn never to go near. Though she's never been there before, she knows the place only too well, for her grandfather "Professor Challenger came back from there speaking of dinosaurs. Jane's father, Dr. Challenger, Jr., returned from those wild lands swearing to have pacified authentic Amazons, tribal precursors to today's feminists."[3] Professor Challenger traveled to the region in Doyle's 1911 sci-fi novel *The Lost World.* In 1990, Jane Challenger makes the trip in *O Fim Do Terceiro Mundo*, Márcio Souza's long-delayed sequel to Doyle's adventure story, a sequel translated and published in English in 1993 as *Lost World II: The End of the Third World.* Souza is also a writer well acquainted with the mad atmosphere of Manaus, for he was born there. Now an internationally recognized novelist, he has worked as Director of Brazil's National Book Department and promoted Brazilian literature around the globe. In *Lost World II*, he immerses the Challenger adventures in a fetid cauldron, mixing elements of magical realism and Doyle's sci fi with the currents and undercurrents of postcolonial, postmodern reflexivity.

Citing and displacing Doyle's novel, Souza reflects on the role of the Latin American writer in contemporary world literature and ruminates on the Third World's fate in an age of telecommunications, advanced capitalism, and ecological nightmares. He does so by channeling the specter of Doyle—and Challenger. Somewhere between the real and the fictive, he recounts an interview with an English journalist by the name of Virginia Challenger—"Exactly: Challenger! According to her business card." He tells her of another epoch, another age of challenging: "I remember a time when to come to a place like the Amazon River region was to experience the realm of adventure and the unknown. Lands like Amazonia were challenges, but challenges with human stature, not statistics of catastrophes. In that epoch, each travel account could be an amazement, a collection of marvels that celebrated the diversity of civilizations, the face of tenacity. These adventurers risked everything because they offered up their very lives, and upon their return, safe and worn-out by the difficulties of their trips, they communicated to us their deep-rooted belief in the daily enchantment of city life. The West was a slate roof, a good and well-served table, breakfast eaten without a care to the sound of wind in the beefwood trees. Now it all comes down to a moral crisis."[4]

Thus Souza's adventure commences. He intertwines the story of Jane Challenger and global crises with tales of his own worldly travels, framing himself as a character at conferences and speaking engagements, and along the way telling stories of his deviant craft. A great reader of world literature, Souza writes admiringly of the way that German writers faced the task of literary experimentation after the Second World War, writers such as

Heinrich Boll: "For a writer like him, trained in the Catholic Rhine tradition, it was disheartening to acknowledge that his language had been transformed into a stinking quagmire and this generation of writers had their work cut out for them. In order to realize their dreams as artists, they would have to do nothing less than reinvent the German language."[5] Souza writes this while recounting a conversation he had with Boll: he's telling a story and writing about storytelling, boring a hole of self-referential alterity deep into his text. To read *Lost World II* is also to read its writing, to operate its machinery while taking it apart and making it do something else. Word and act turn each other inside out, outside in, languages and worlds circling around in a dizzying pattern. It is a perfumance of minor literatures. The story of Boll leads to another, this one about an American writer crucial to Souza's own literary development. "It was Kurt Vonnegut, Jr. . . . I know now that Vonnegut pointed the way to another approach for a writer to deal with his language. While Boll worked with a German contaminated by the Nazi gang, Vonnegut wrote in the sandy terrain of the mass media in which the English language had been transformed. . . . During the sixties, he was the author most read by young people; they realized that he had taken their tame English and turned it inside out, that Puritan English, smelling of the sixteenth century, full of pious interjections. He set about equipping it with the language of the millions of voiceless people. And he did it with an ingenious alchemy, becoming at the same time a highly intelligent and concise writer."[6]

In terms of our gay sci fi, Souza's discussions of Boll and Vonnegut function as directions for mounting a minor performance. Writing at the intersection of Portugese and English, Souza intervenes in World Lit through a hybridized text, one that mixes styles, genres, and languages. He targets the *word* and *world* of "challenger," a name given to ships and spaceships, to contenders of sports titles and political seats, and less commonly to stratoanalysts and gay scientists. "Challenger" is a legendary name written across the bow, so to speak, of countless missions. Souza writes that "legends are a poetic transformation of something that really took place. And in the Challengers' case, what had happened involved such detail, one could hardly call them familial legends. They more closely resembled a curse."[7]

Challenger forms a vast and maddening project, the challenging forth of earth and sky, strata and the destratified. "X challenges Y." Imagine writing the genealogy of this simple statement, of its embodiment across diverse sites, of these words become worlds become words over and over—imagine this and you can begin to get a sense of the challenge challenged up here: to cite, iterate, transmute the curse of Challenger across time and space.

Doyle's lesser-known sci-fi stories constitute a legendary gift (though Souza might say this gift is precisely the curse): tales of exploration and conquest, of environmental disaster and mass death, of living dinosaurs and geological experimentation. Embodying and engaging the curse of Challenger, Souza's adventures roam across history and the world, from indigenous tribes to capitalist returns, from planetary destruction to Amazonian astronauts, from world conferences to a cosmic sex scene between a god and a mortal, a woman by the name of Jane Challenger. At times, *Lost World II* takes up the marginalization of Brazilian Portuguese and the exclusion of Quebecois from the realm of "Latin American literature." At times it charts the steady displacement of storytelling by novels and of novels by mass media. At times it criticizes the patronization of the Third World by the First, at times the scapegoating of the First by the Third. And suspended over everything there hangs a diminished heavenly body, a comet dimmed by the challenging forth of the world. Jane wonders about this degradation as she's led astray by a wealthy Brazilian businessman (or is it she that's taking this minor god for a very wild ride?). Looking up, she speculates: "Who knows if comets, in their nocturnal splendors, weren't prophesying this: the irreparable loss of the ability to feel awe. Could there be anything more terrible? Without the power of awe, humanity would be as lost as a king without a throne, as hopeless as a medieval burg facing the plague. But, on the other hand, how can one be awestruck by these cosmic visits when they appear so much more grandiose in the mass media than they do on earth, overshadowed by the neon lights of the big cities?"[8] The challenge threatens to overwhelm the challenger, as does the tale its teller. The writer is tempted to abandon ship. "Jane Challenger's intriguing narrative remained hanging on the phosphorous green monitor. I stored the diskettes, stopped working on the novel for several months, and for some reason, felt the temptation to back out of it."[9]

Our reading machine has disappeared from the screen intermittently, having been restored, lost, and relaunched countless times. Through this interrupted passage, its geometry has molted into seven scientifictions, vagrant musings guided by a small crew of challengers. Of late, HMS *Challenger* and gay scientist Rutherford have served as metaguidance devices for destratifying performances-performatives and sociotechnical systems. With yet another challenger restoring herself through various databanks, we maneuver toward the performance stratum itself, that futural formation whose effects we started to sense a while back and whose network of autopoetic holes we are again attempting to navigate.

Recounting the core samples taken earlier: 1) The performance stratum produces fractal subjects and objects that are articulated through simulation rather than representation and legitimated in terms of system optimization rather than grand narratives. 2) Geopolitically, performativity is coming to order the postcolonial, post-Cold War world, a world in which the integration of diversity is being supplemented by the diversification of integration. 3) Economically, performance is inseparable from advanced capitalism, defined by high-tech information industries, the decline of organized labor, the rise of performance management, and the flexible accumulation of hyperspeculative capital. 4) Knowledge production dramatically increases worldwide; not only does it reach more and more people, formal learning and research increasingly occurs through computers and telecommunication networks and extends far beyond traditional educational institutions. 5) The alphabetic archive of discourses and practices is being transformed by information technologies that allow for the multimedia archiving and recombinant processing of words and acts, as well as their "real-time" worldwide distribution. 6) Desire on the performance stratum is pushed to excess rather than repressed; instead of being sequentially segmented and molded by discrete institutions, its flows are intermittently channeled and modulated through multiple, overlapping evaluative grids. 7) Performative power is nomadic: its dispersed command and control systems generate networks of spaces, pluralities of temporalities, and more troubling still, multivalent pressures not only to adapt and conform, but at certain times and places, to transgress, resist, and test the limits of these very systems. Perform—or else: this is the order-word of glocalized stratification.

Perfumance is an odor-word for surviving its effects. Thus our interest in the perfumance of Jane Challenger and the lessons buried in her legendary adventures. Our current mission: to investigate the effects of generalized citationality on onto-historical strata, to track the crack-up of being in the becoming of forces, and to do all this by tracing the emission of history in the legends and fables of Challenger. While Professor Challenger found dinosaurs on a jungle plateau and Dr. Challenger, Jr. a tribe of Amazons, Jane Challenger makes another untimely discovery, one she reveals upon returning to London to her reluctant sidekick, a journalist named Lester who keeps a framed picture of Engels atop his writing desk.

> "Now examine these papers," she ordered.
>
> They were photocopies of microfilms. They all bore the mark of the British Museum stamp. Lester looked through them, little by little acquiring an interest. Each page documented the official bookkeeping of a British firm from the first industrial revolution. Old records of the eighteenth century.
>
> "Interesting, isn't it?" she commented excitedly.
>
> "Very," he responded vaguely.
>
> "And if, just by chance, you were to find one of the entrepreneurs in the flesh?"
>
> "What entrepreneurs?"
>
> "For example, the owner of this woolen mill in Warwick." She pointed at one of the pages.
>
> "This one? But the woolen mill is from . . . from 1798!"

> "Exactly, Lester. And if you were to find an entrepreneur from 1798 alive?"
>
> "I would have good reason to doubt my sanity."
>
> "Well, I found one of these specimens."
>
> "Oh, please Jane," he protested.
>
> "And not only one, I found a good number of them. A whole economy. A lost world."[10]

What on earth has Challenger unearthed? "' . . . *she discovered that there still exist—reasonably healthy and well fed—species of capitalists considered extinct in England since the eighteenth century.*'" [11]

The Challenger curse is anachronistic, out of joint, temporally fucked up, and to underscore this untimely malediction, Souza titles one of his chapters with this warning: "Never Risk Your Neck for an Economic Anachronism." Writing *O Fim Do Terceiro Mundo* in the late 1980s, Souza is alluding to the anachronism that pervaded the rhetoric and policies of Prime Minister Thatcher of Great Britain, President Reagan of the United States, and a whole generation of neoliberal economists, New Right politicians, and multinational CEOs, a generation that looked back with nostalgia to Adam Smith, or rather, to a certain reading of him. They championed the "invisible hand" that purportedly guides economic markets, using it to justify laissez faire government and the division of labor. At the same time, they totally ignored Smith's own warnings about the social dangers of unbridled corporate activity. "Adam Smith's praise of division of labor is well known," writes Noam Chomsky, "but not his denunciation of its inhuman effects, which will turn working people into objects 'as stupid and ignorant as it is possible for a human creature to be.'"[12] Championing the glories of global performance and ignoring its traumatic effects, putting profits over people, over the environment, over the entire planet—such are the workings of neoliberalism's invisible hand job.

How then to read the anachronistic curse of Challenger, not just the adventures of grandfather, father, and daughter, but also the disasters that haunt so many other challengers, cloaking them all in a ghastly aura? Should we attempt to disperse this cloud by reviving a grand narrative or two—that of Progress or Revolution, for instance—in order to correct the anachronisms and reset the historical clock by defining what's proper to our epoch, what befits our episteme? And haven't I offered such a definition of the performance stratum? Yes, one can read the seven belts of stratification as a taxonomy of our era, or lay them out in a table to contrast the epochs of performance and discipline. I have staged such a reading for I do not think that an understanding of performative power and knowledge can do without it. At the same time: No, I prefaced my earlier comparative analysis of performance and discipline by stressing that the two strata are not opposed, that performance displaces discipline, and discipline, though crumbling, is still operative. The break between them will never be a clean one. In addition, any historical reading of the performance stratum must draw on the historical imagination—the imaginary invention of History—that consolidated itself in what we now can call the age of discipline. As Derrida writes in *The Archeology of the Frivolous* (a title that suggests a certain gay reading of Foucault): "The imaginary of one episteme is the terrain and the condition for the upsurging of the general theory of epistemes which alone would make the table, the finite code, and taxonomy its determining norm."[13] Thus the difficulty, long posed by critically minded historians, of making general statements about a particular epoch, of demarcating where one period leaves off and another begins, and, in general, of defining what's proper to any age whatsoever.

And yet I'd like to offer this hypothesis: what's proper to the performance stratum is its heightened sense of temporal impropriety. That is, what's historically specific about the age of global performance is its flagrant anachronisms, its glaring mix of forms and traditions from past and present. Consider the experience base on which it draws: centuries of historical research; the mechanical reproduction and now the digital storage, processing, and transmission of words and deeds; the explosion of cultural, scientific, and organizational research; the proliferation of fractal subjects and objects; the worldwide release of postcolonial and post-Cold War energies—all these contribute not to the end of history, but rather to its multiplication and division, its generative and degenerative recombination. Some historians and cultural critics have decried such anachronisms as empty postmodern pastiche, as a hodge-podge of simulations that cover over the reality of authentic historical processes. But instead of relying on the opposition of the historical and the anachronistic, instead of championing one and cursing the other, let's give some thought to the possibilities of major and minor histories, major and minor anachronisms, as well as the becomings and begoings of one and an other.

From such a perspective, performativity does indeed produce reactive, major anachronisms, including neoliberal economics, jingoistic nationalisms, and Disneyfied multiculturalisms. Yet, when need be, its performers can also seize the moment and regenerate the very grandest of narratives: Progress, Liberation, and even their own version of Revolution (e.g., the 1994 Republican Revolution led by Newt Gingrich). Just because performativity can be defined as the death of grand narratives doesn't mean these can't come back to haunt us—they may haunt us interminably. Performative power is multivalent and polyrhythmic, its stratifications should not be reduced to either the anachronistic or the historical.

Testing the limits of performative competencies, minor histories—such as those produced by Diane Vaughan and Bruno Latour, Michael Taussig and Anna Deavere Smith—are key to destratifying sociotechnical systems and dislodging their blocks of performances-performatives. Such histories provide an understanding of their solidification and breakdown, as well as those of other onto-historical strata. Even grand narratives may still have a role to play if inscribed and passed on with care—and a certain carefree air—as the stuff of minor history. Similarly, rather than decry the gross anachronisms of postmodernity, we might retool their effects for other experiments, such as sending up time machines into the outer reaches of the perfumance atmosphere. Maddening syntheses, errant juxtapositions, time-travels and space-outs—these characterize the passages opened by minor anachronistics. "The present has been shattered into a thousand shards," writes Critical Art Ensemble, "all of which require different strategies for resistance. Now more than ever, an anarchist epistemology should be adopted, one that leads to situational knowledge. It must be one that tolerates research and exploration within any time or spatial zone. Resistance cannot be carried out from the safety zone of a single bunker. Those who are able must be free to move through time by any means necessary."[14] As Johannes Fabian suggests elsewhere, the time has come to supplement geopolitics with chronopolitics.[15]

As a mode of experimental resistance, perfumance engages the emerging performance stratum with minor histories and minor anachronisms. While major histories tell grand, linear, straight narratives of Great Men and Great Events, minor histories emit petite, nonlinear, gay stories (often told straightfaced) of the nobodies and nonevents crammed down in the cracks of onto-historical strata. And while major anachronisms nostalgiate upon some golden age and attempt to escape the present into a bright and shiny city, minor anachronisms recombine machinic elements from past and present, using them to tune in test patterns from the future. The signals picked up on are broken and garbled, interrupted by blasts of static and bathed in faint murmurs and the grainy snow of figures blowing in over from the horizon. Perfumances rehearse the future, or more precisely, cite it in anticipation with catachristenings, catastorations, and gay sci-fi projects, all of them performing as parts of a collective assemblage of annunciation, a minor lecture machine. *"I have sensed the future, and it is perfumed."* It is not a question of representing some fragrant garden, some balmy utopia without pain and injustice; what's at issue is not a representation but a monstration (monstrous showing), not an enunciation but an annunciation, the forewarning of a power/knowledge system whose effects are already online.

In a minor manner, *Lost World II* takes shape as a monstrous anachronism. From a dinosaur-green monitor, it displays a radar scan of our near future, a scenario transmitted from the nearness of an even more distant age. The end of the Third World, the fate of Amazonia and planet earth are all forecast through a futural figure: Sir Wallace Kxalendjer, a researcher who arrives from another millennium. He is "the last descendant of a notable line of trailblazers, energetic people, willful almost to the point of audacity;

he is very proud of having family roots reaching back to the industrial age and of belonging to a family that became legendary at the end of the last millennium."[16] Kxalendjer, whose name bears traces of gramophonic mutation and continental drift, is what we would call a stratoanalyst, a boring expert. A "brilliant ethno-archaeologist," his research includes the geology of ancient ruins and past injustices. "Any public information terminal had records of his latest work, a magnificent report on his excavations in South Africa and a surprising study on an exotic culture of the twentieth century known as 'apartheid,' including the bitter polemic that it generated."[17] Dr. Kxalendjer's subsequent research takes him to the area formerly known as Manaus. There he becomes Director of the Department of General Research at the University of the Amazonian Protectorate, a position that "had been vacant since the death of the former director, an entomologist who had been devoured alive by army ants."[18] In the far-off future, the Amazonia is still ruled by armies of insects and humans, though there have been some cataclysmic disruptions.

Kxalendjer arrives in Jane Challenger's adventure via a process of "temporal immersion." It is from a far-out time zone that we get a trace of the future, a future far closer to us than to him, a trace bearing the scent of clear-cut forests and quarantined peoples, of floods and plagues and madness and death. The MIA complex is not missing in all this action, nor is a particular type of challenge.

> The final destruction of the rain forest, which took place between 2012 and 2017, prompted by the post ecologists and the large urban demographic explosion coming at the end of the twentieth century, resulted in the appearance of new environmental factors. The temperature of the planet continued rising at the rate of one degree per year, and in the month of August, it easily reached 150 degrees Fahrenheit. Violent storms occurred all year long, causing rivers to pour over their banks, hindering air navigation even for the few suborbital lines that serviced the two urban centers in the area that were still reasonably inhabited, both of which had been designed as research centers and were under military command.
>
> Around 2020 there were outbreaks of deadly epidemics known as the green plague, which were caused by mutant arboreal viruses. Those were the times of anguish and horror for all the human inhabitants of the region. The victims of this highly contagious disease would become crazed, lose all muscle control, and die hours after the onset of the initial symptoms. When first carriers of the disease were discovered in other parts of the world, the military council regime took a drastic step and, in spite of a great uproar in the scientific community, declared a quarantine throughout the Protectorate. The indiscriminate extermination of all the inhabitants of the region followed, until 90 percent of the population had disappeared, a total of

> twenty-five million victims, which left the area practically unoccupied and isolated.
>
> Even after a vaccine had been discovered in 2050, the act of living there was a kind of technological challenge.[19]

Centuries later, the entire Amazon region remains sealed off, and travel is highly restricted by the authorities. But Kxalendjer receives permission to conduct research deep into the region, and he quickly organizes an expedition. Like the Challengers before him, he soon discovers something that leaves him utterly transformed, though what exactly happens remains clouded in mystery.

Reports indicate that "a small caravan, led by a patrol of sanitroops, set out in the direction of the Protectorate. Nothing more is known regarding the expedition nor what transpired there, and the council authorities insist on maintaining secrecy in spite of the protests reiterated by the government in London along with the World Parliament. The only thing known is that Dr. Kxalendjer suffered some kind of shock; perhaps he witnessed some frightening event, some dreaded horror capable of rocking his strong constitution. And that part of the planet, blanketed in mystery and kept apart by the authoritarian system of the Protectorate, could contain something truly monstrous."[20] Legend has it that some native peoples somehow survived the ecological disaster and continue to live on under extraordinary circumstances, though this could be not confirmed as "observation satellites weren't able to penetrate the perennial blanket of clouds that had covered the region for more than two centuries."[21]

Nonetheless, when Kxalendjer returns, and indeed, for long after, he endlessly repeats the words " 'Manaus! Manaus! Maaanaaauuusssh!' "—the name not only of a city, but also of "an indigenous tribe extinct since the eighteenth century of the last millennium." Significantly, in the late twentieth century, Jane Challenger meets up with a small group of indigenous people, natives " 'from the largest tribe that exists around here, the tribe of those who no longer have any tribe left.' " These natives, a woman and three men, work in Manaus' office buildings as cleaners and technicians. They practice a corrosive form of electronic resistance, scouring computer components with Brillo pads and sometimes pouring "sodium bicarbonate on the solid-state components." They are forever on the move. " 'We never stay in one neighborhood for long,' the woman said. 'We are nomads; we aren't able to stay in any one place for long,' said the other man."[22] Challenger and nomads, Kxalendjer and neoliberal dinosaurs, all come together around the good ship *Leviathan*, a vessel hosting a gathering of multinational executives and journalists who, unbeknownst to them, have been targeted for bombing by a group of militants named the Jihad Jívaros.

The curse of Challenger is as much a thing of the future as of the past. Connecting Professor Rutherford, Professor and Jane Challenger, the futural Kxalendjer and beyond, its performance is already long-running and may very well be sold out far, far in advance. Its perfumance, however, belongs without belonging to a time without time. It is a queer event, one that's always already over—and over—and yet always already not yet. Incited outside, incipit catachristening, impending catastoration—the eventless event of perfumance. Haunting the multiplication and division of history, double-timing being as an untimely Dopplegänger, perfumance partakes of the *disaster* of which Maurice Blanchot writes. "We are on the edge of disaster without being able to situate it in the future; it is rather always past, and yet we are on the edge or under the threat, all formulations which would imply the future—that which is yet to come—if the disaster were not that which does not come, that which has put a stop to every arrival. To think the disaster (if this is possible, and it is not possible inasmuch as we suspect that the disaster is thought) is to have no longer any future in which to think it."[23] The thought, the disaster, the "event" of perfumance is the inside out of past, present, and future. It is time turned on itself, sheer repetition, the singular anachrony of iterability/alterity which makes and breaks each moment, over and over—interminably terminal repetition. "Let us remember. Repetition: nonreligious repetition, neither mournful nor nostalgic, the undesired return. Repetition: the ultimate over and over, general collapse, destruction of the present."[24]

Shadowing the performances of Rutherford and Challenger, darkening the missions of Heidegger and the *Challenger* shuttle, of Jane Challenger and Wallace Kxalendjer too, a fingery cloud cut its way across different strata of history and being. Cast within its shadow, a troupe of performers wander about as *disastronauts*, as errant challengers destined to roam

**UNDER THE SIGN OF A PARADOX
THAT SEEMS MORE LIKE
A PAINFUL COMEDY OF ERRORS**[25]

playing itself out across innumerable sites. Souza situates the legend of Amazonia, of the Third World, the lost world too, under this paradoxical sign. It dangles from the rearview mirror of our own reading machine, for this craft is itself disastronautic, its passages twist and turn from crash site to crash site, cracking up all along the way. If I have cast resistant perfumance in terms of gay sci fi, it should be clear from our readings that perfumative laughter is not some escape from "serious" matters of politics, history, and ontology. Sick jokes, gallows humor, the cackle of vultures and the gasp of worldwide witnesses—these suggest the *bathos* of our disastronautic flight.

The perfumance of Jane Challenger exposes a deepening crack in the performance stratum. It is a crack of self-referentiality, the abyssal iterability of all performances and performatives, all performance paradigms, and indeed of the formation's own christening and initiation. The performance stratum has been in rehearsal for centuries, if not longer, and may take centuries to emerge fully (if it ever really does, for it will always be haunted by alterity). Nonetheless, its recombinant formation is already producing novel forms of power, for performativity draws not only on the disciplinary mechanisms of Western Europe and its colonial empires but also on traditions overrun and marginalized by this colonialism, as well as on those few cultures that somehow long managed to evade its formal control (e.g., China and Japan). It even draws upon modes of resistance developed to counter discipline.

This last point bears reiteration. Because generalized citationality "ensures" the alterability of words and acts and sociotechnical systems, *the mutations of one age may become the norms of another*. Manuel De Landa articulates this possibility with the following hypothesis: "the creation of *novel* hierarchical structures through restratification is performed by the most destratified element of the *previous* phase."[26] This possibility helps clarify the caution expressed here concerning too heavy a reliance on theories and practices of liminality, a caution that informs the remark that the integration of diversity will be supplemented by the diversification of integration. Liminality, disintegration, diversification, fragmentation: while these may harbor forces of resistance and mutation, they may also carry forces of reaction and normalization. This is why their study carries such risks, for the most incisive experiments operate at the very point where norms become mutant, which is also the point where mutations become normative. The site to study is thus not only the centrality of formal norms, not only the liminality of aberrant transgressions, but also the interface of the between and the center, the paradoxical place where one turns into the other—the place of liminal-norms. A place like Manaus, perhaps. As Souza's minor god Pietro Pietra, Jr. wonders to himself: "Just how does one define a native of Amazonia, . . . if everything is in bits and pieces? It would be like trying to reconstruct a building that collapsed in an earthquake without any blueprint. But perhaps the issue of having an identity isn't so important after all; on the other hand, it could be that the so-called Amazonian identity is the fragmentation itself. A paradox!"[27]

The paradox: fragmentation can become an identity, disintegration can serve an integrating function. Thus the necessity—and chance—of reading the relation between identity and fragmentation, integration and disintegration, sameness and difference not as oppositions, but as fluctuating patterns of appropriation and exappropriation, as dynamic rhythms of forces that recur across different strata. What rhythms mark us, what patterns repeat themselves differently in this "here and now"? In *The Age of Extremes: A History of the World 1914–1991*, historian Eric Hobsbawm situates himself in the future in order to look back upon the last decades of the twentieth century, and in doing so, he identifies a pattern of disintegration and integration that connects the 1980s and 1990s back to an earlier time.

Hobsbawm writes in 1994: "Not for the first time, the combination of intellectual nullity with strong, even desperate mass emotion, was politically powerful in times of crisis, insecurity, and—over large parts of the globe—disintegrating states and institutions. Like the movements of inter-war resentment which had generated fascism, the religio-political protests of the Third World and the hunger for a secure identity and social order in a disintegrating world (the call for 'community' was habitually joined with the call for 'law and order') provided the humus in which effective political forces could grow. These in turn could overthrow old regimes and become new ones."[28]

At the level of onto-historical formations, perfumance pervades the contemporary landscape with temporal overload, chronochronic feedback and feedforward, the short-circuiting of past, present, and future. As an effect of iterability, the self-referential emergence of the performance stratum presupposes recursion with other strata. It is precisely such patterns that the strategy of disastronautics attempts to distill with its minor histories and minor anachronisms. Without reducing one formation to another, without posing a transcendence of history, the task becomes tuning in the rhythms and breaks that repeat themselves differently across various strata. The challenge: not only to recognize that one experiences history from the perspective of the present, but to plug into emergent forces in order to generate untimely perspectives on this very perspective, perspectives that multiply and divide the present, rattling it to and fro.

Perhaps the most uncanny scanner of such patterns and perspectives—and one who, like Marx, has been deployed posthumously by the most vicious of political regimes—was Nietzsche, a thinker who traversed past, present, and future as one destined to a series of random walks. Such wanderings were crucial to his gay science project. In *The Gay Science*, he writes of his approach to the morality of his own time: "If one would like to see our European morality for once as it looks from a distance, and if one would like to measure it against other moralities, past and future, then one has to proceed like a wanderer who wants to know how high the towers in a town are: he *leaves* the town."[29]

Nietzsche's own wanderings did not last long, and they were frequently characterized by brief, sudden immersions into the deep. In seeking to displace the coldness of objective science with the warm sunlight of gay sci, he also undertook untimely passages that plunged him into freezing cold waters—and then yanked him out just as quickly. These sudden dips mark the rhythms of Nietzsche's thought, the quick beat of his bathoscopic reading machine. "I approach deep problems like cold baths: quickly into them and quickly out again. That one does not get to the depths that way, not deep enough, is the superstition of those afraid of the water, the enemies of cold water; they speak without experience. The freezing cold makes one swift."[30] Let us recall how perfumance is distinguished from the performance strata, how its flows and waves of forces differ from the sedimentations and foldings of forms. One does not take hold of waves, one does not grasp their ebbs and flows; instead one plunges in and out, becomes swept up in their currents and recurrence.

Wandering passages, sudden immersions into the deepest of problems—such maneuvers are part of the rehearsal process for minor anachronisms, temporal immersion, disastronautic flight. In addition to meandering walks and freezing cold baths, Nietzsche had a nose for the perfumative element. Across different epochs and cultures, the recurrence of forces caught his *Nase* time and again. Though we've already cited this uncanny sensibility, we have yet to follow Nietzsche's passage through our own time, that is, his walks and dips into the emerging performance stratum. Yet pass through he did, and it was a trail-blazing journey, one whose pathmarkers can be glimpsed in the texts of Marcuse, Lyotard, and Butler, all three theorists of performative power, all three readers of Nietzsche.

We pick up the scent of Nietzsche's untimely passage in the second edition of *The Gay Science*, in its supplementary Book Five, in a forecasting segment titled "How things will become ever more 'artistic' in Europe." Though elsewhere he often and enthusiastically affirms the artist, the creator, the player of masks, the quotation marks here around "artistic" tip us off: something's up, Nietzsche's taking a different tack, one directed toward what we have cited earlier as major art. The writer of *The Birth of Tragedy* and *Dithyrambs of Dionysus* now takes aim at actors, at role-playing, and yes, even and especially at performance, "good performance." Significantly, the performance he targets mixes the theatrical and the occupational, and in doing so, uses and abuses its performers. The prophetic section begins:

> Even today, in our time of transition when so many factors cease to compel men, the care to make a living still compels almost all male Europeans to adopt a particular role, their so-called occupation. A few retain the freedom, a merely apparent freedom, to choose this role for themselves: for most men it is chosen. The result is rather strange. As they attain a more advanced age, almost all Europeans confound themselves with their role; they become the victims of their own "good performance."[31]

This passage does not demarcate the transitional time in which Nietzsche senses this confounding performance, but Nietzsche begins Book Five (subtitled "We Fearless Ones") by defining the "meaning of our cheerfulness," namely, "God is dead," "the belief in the Christian god has become unbelievable," though he adds that this great event is so distant that even its tiding has not yet arrived (elsewhere he gives an ETA of three centuries). The death of God triggers a certain loss of spiritual control. As the helm passes to humans, they are increasingly called upon to make their living by occupying new roles, by becoming good performers: "whenever a human being begins to discover how he is playing a role and how he *can* be an actor, he *becomes* an actor."[32]

What Nietzsche senses in "good performance," what he seems to fear even as he proclaims his fearlessness, is something that anticipates Marcuse's performance principle, Lyotard's performativity, and Butler's punitive performatives. What catches his nose is an emergent power, one in which humans fall victim to their own roles, their own acts, their own performances. Though Nietzsche initially ascribes this "good performance" to Europeans, specifically to European males, he proceeds to place it in a much wider perspective, connecting it to a certain "cocky faith" found in democratic ages. He sniffs out this faith in the distant past, as well as in an emerging culture, one that's already growing dominant in his contemporary Europe. These are, respectively, "the Athenian faith that first becomes noticeable in the Periclean age, the faith of the Americans today that is more and more becoming the European faith as well: The individual becomes convinced that he can do just about anything and *can manage almost any role*, and everybody experiments with himself, improvises, makes new experiments, enjoys his experiments; and all nature ceases and becomes art."[33] Playing their roles to the hilt, taking command of any and all situations, improvising and experimenting with themselves and the world, humans are becoming overwhelmed by the artistry of their own performance. This overpowering performance is not restricted to male Europeans, for it comes from overseas, from America, and is tied to its cocky democratic spirit. In a later section that addresses the "problem of the actor," Nietzsche analyzes other "'artistic'" cases: the buffoonery of the lower classes, the controlled histrionics of diplomats, the cultural adaptability of Jews, the expertise of the "'man of letters,'" and, finally, the artistry of women, who, he writes, "'put on something' even when they take off everything."[34]

But precisely what does Nietzsche sense in this all-too-American performance, what is it that really catches his nose? Surprisingly, it is *an inability to create*, an incapacity to build as an architect does, to plan, to organize, to construct a future that spans millennia. "The strength to build becomes paralyzed; the courage to make plans that encompass the distant future is discouraged; those with a genius for organization become scarce: who would still dare to undertake projects that require thousands of years for their completion? For what is dying out is the fundamental faith that would enable us to calculate, to promise, to anticipate the future in plans of such scope, and to sacrifice the future to them—namely, the faith that man has a value and meaning only insofar as he is a *stone in a great edifice*; and to that end he must be *solid* first of all, a 'stone'—and above all not an actor!"[35]

Again, these passages run counter to many others, both in this text and elsewhere, in which Nietzsche affirms the artist, the actor, the experimenter. Here familiar masks and motifs are cast in different perspectives, thereby revealing the strong countercurrents at work in *The Gay Science*. In the depths of certain sections, levity gives way to something weighty, play is abandoned for calculation, and the mysterious mist settles into a great and solid edifice. What is affirmed here is not what we've been calling destratification but rather a certain stratification, a minor stratification perhaps, but perhaps not, the formation and solidification of a stone. The currents shaping and tearing at this rocky spur can be sensed throughout *The Gay Science*, but they're especially powerful in Book Five, for between its writing and that of the previous four books, Nietzsche has written *Thus Spake Zarathustra, Beyond Good and Evil,* and *The Genealogy of Morals,* texts that take his thought to new heights—and new depths. Book Five solidifies certain elements of *The Gay Science*'s first four books and casts them toward the edifice of a massive, futural project, one which Nietzsche spent years planning and sketching but would never publish in his lifetime. At various times, he called this project *The Will to Power, Revaluation of All Values,* and *The Philosophy of the Future.*

When Nietzsche crashed in the late 1880s, he left behind outlines and fragments of this vast project, one with which he sought to battle all forms of reactive nihilism, including that of "'good performance.'" These fragments remain less a collapsed building than scattered bits of blueprints, tattered pieces of plans and diagrams, the rehearsal sites of his agonizing, joyful thought. Over the last century, these scraps have been arranged in numerous ways, always, inevitably, by selecting here and citing there. Our reading machine now plays back this perhaps indigestible digest. For Nietzsche, thought is an arrow whose flight takes it from epoch to epoch, where it lands as dice, falling, rolling back, and becoming cast up again as other missives. Taking up such arrows, gay science is practiced by researchers who experiment and experience the world as the will to power, which is not the will of an individual or group, not the power of human appropriation and representation, but rather the chaosmosis of forces from which subjects and objects emerge and into which they dissolve. The will to power is shaped by the passage of these forces' circuitous recurrence. The atmosphere or ocean of chaosmic forces is always already bound and bounding off in a circle, the ring of the eternal return—a figure that, like the death of God, makes its initial appearance in Nietzsche in *The Gay Science*. From our perspective, *eternal recurrence is generalized citationality played out at the levels of history and ontology; it is differential repetition recurring across time and being and beyond.* Nietzsche initially received the eternal return as a curse (one is destined to experience this moment eternally) but later sensed the necessity of affirming its chances (it might, it *must* repeat itself differently). Through this destinal chance, this chance destiny, the eternal return may be twisted, its seal broken, its center displaced. Recursion of the curse, signature—laughter—of the other. This is the mission of gay scientists: to test and reevaluate values, to hammer idols that stretch from Plato to Hegel and beyond—the valuations of being over becoming, form over force, sameness over difference, representation over simulation, logic over affect. And most importantly: to create other valorizations, draw up new tables, build new worlds, break with the history of an all-too-human being and, through rigorous cross- and countercultural training, prepare the way for man's overcoming and surpassing. "Man is a bridge. . . ." Nietzsche's apocalyptic promise: the superman is coming.

"You highest men my eyes have encountered! This is my doubt of you and my secret laughter: I think you would call my superman—*a devil!*"[36] As an impulsive bather and extempore wanderer, Nietzsche also had a nose for his "own" future. In late 1888, just weeks before his legendary collapse, he completed his last book, the heteroautobiothanatography entitled *Ecce Homo: How One Becomes What One Is.* (It would be published posthumously in 1908.) In its concluding section, "Why I am a Destiny," the same section in which he proclaims that his genius resides in his nostrils, Nietzsche issues some of his last forecasts, lasting premonitions that would haunt the twentieth century and will no doubt spook us for some time to come. In this concluding section, he speaks of secret laughter and superhuman types, as well as great politics and social explosions: "when truth steps into battle with the lie of millennia we shall have convulsions, an earthquake spasm, a transposition of valley and mountain such as has never been dreamed of. The concept of politics will have merged entirely with a war of spirits; all power structures of the old society will have been exploded—all of them are based on lies: there will be wars the like of which have never yet been seen on earth. It is only beginning with me that the earth knows *great politics.*"[37] It is difficult, if not impossible, to read these passages without thinking of the spectacular politics and traumatic wars of the past century, of its gases, guns, and missiles, its ideological and psychological battle zones, its massacres and deathcamps and mushroom clouds. Whether or not Nietzsche's forecasts rang true in these catastrophes cannot be decided, though this does not mean the question cannot be discussed and debated, recited and rehearsed. Certain is the fact that the name "Nietzsche" became associated with Nazi teachings, and in part the hammering philosopher has his sister Elisabeth and his reader Heidegger to thank for this—and also his "own" texts, including the posthumously published text on *Führers* and the future of teaching institutions, a text which Nietzsche swore never to publish, would not sign off on, a text written, incidentally, for lecture during his early and brief career as a university professor.[38]

As Nietzsche sensed better than anyone, there's no insurance policy against the posthumous workings of citational networks, nor against the *"nicht,"* the annihilations and nihilisms of "Nietzsche."[39] What he writes in his untimely meditation on Schopenhauer can easily be read of himself: " . . . he will be misunderstood and for a long time thought an ally of powers he abhors. . . ." Nietzsche's scathing ridicule of anti-Semitism and German nationalism were later edited out by Nazi readers as they went about restaging his superman in black and tan. His futural project was produced as a world historical film, a thinly veiled, darkly overcoated, far-right Reich whose editing machines took the shape of firing squads, gas chambers, and guided missiles. A century after his passing, the name "Nietzsche" still carries an explosive charge. The uncanny political currents of his lecture machine have been tapped by Derrida in his essay "Otobiographies: The Teaching of Nietzsche and the Politics of the Proper Name." Derrida writes that the "future of the Nietzschean text is not closed. But if, within the still-open contours of an era, the only politics calling itself—proclaiming itself—Nietzschean will have been a Nazi one, then this is necessarily significant and must be questioned in all of its consequences. . . . In a word, has the 'great' Nietzschean politics misfired or is it, rather, still to come in the wake of a seismic convulsion of which National Socialism or fascism will turn out to have been mere episodes?"[40]

Is Nietzsche's promise of the superman felicitous or infelicitous, has it succeeded or failed (disastrously in either case)?[41] Has the revaluation of values commenced and the curse of eternal recurrence been broken? Or have all these questions been amortized by events of the twentieth century, or, again, do they remain open queries that carry some currency in the age of global performance?

The question of Nietzsche's superman and its relation to onto-historical formations is taken up in the appendix of *Foucault*, Deleuze's reading of Foucault's great fiction of strata and the outside that cracks and disjoints them. (Again, with deepest respect to the performance stratum, we have named this outside inside "perfumance.") To his short study of Foucault, Deleuze appends an even shorter essay, titled "On the Death of Man and Superman." For Deleuze and Foucault, Nietzsche was less a prophet of the death of God and more a forecaster of the death of man. "The question that continually returns," writes Deleuze reading Foucault channeling Nietzsche, "is therefore the following: if the forces within man compose a form only by entering into a relation with forms from the outside, with what new forms do they now risk entering into a relation, and what new form will emerge that is neither God nor man? This is the correct place for the problem which Nietzsche called 'the superman.'"[42]

To explore this superproblem, Deleuze drills into three different onto-historical strata, devoting a section apiece to the outside found within each. Because he deals with this atmospheric outside, his readings are not only stratoanalytic but also meteorological. Following Foucault, Deleuze enters the stormy zone between different strata; he time-travels, navigates disaster. He writes that in the "classical" formation which arose in the seventeenth century, the outside is folded inside as forces of infinitude, giving rise to a God-form that legitimates and governs societies in terms of divine power and knowledge. The general sciences that emerged on this stratum—natural history, an analysis of wealth, a general grammar—developed their forms along continuums extending toward infinity. Deleuze contrasts this arrangement of forces to a core sample from the nineteenth-century formation. Here the outside unfolds as forces of finitude to compose a man-form rather than a God-form. The infinity of the divine gives way to the finitude of humans, and general sciences to comparative analyses. Under the all-too-human regime of discipline, natural history is displaced by biology, the analysis of wealth by economics, and general grammar by linguistics.

What interests us most is the third stratum, which Deleuze explores in a section inquisitively titled "Towards a Formation of the Future?" Though this question mark signals the tentative nature of his thoughts, we've seen elsewhere that Deleuze names this futural formation "societies of control." It is here that the superman-form emerges, for within this stratum, forces of the outside "no longer involve raising to infinity or finitude but an unlimited finity, thereby evoking every situation of force in which a finite number of components yields a practically unlimited diversity of combinations."[43] Infinite finitude, recombinant diversity, unlimited permutation of limited components, these are the modes of being emitted from the future. On this emergent formation, the biology of organisms is displaced by the biochemistry of genetics, the industrial economics of coal and steel give way to the information economy of silicon technologies, and linguistic signifiers disperse in literary agrammaticalities. Deleuze and Foucault are neither cheerful nor morose about this "superfolding" of the outside inside. But neither are they without hope. "As Foucault would say, the superman is much less than the disappearance of living men, and much more than a change of concept: it is the advent of a new form that is neither God nor man and which, it is hoped, will not prove worse than its two previous forms.'"[44]

In the cold blue depths of our current reading, perfumance comprises the element of the superhuman, the overhuman, as in over and out, over and over, interminable life-death rehearsal. Perfumance is a gathering arrangement of forces, an emergent folding of the outside inside, one that generates new forms of being and history—and emerging patterns of becoming. Perfumance, technopoesis, genre machinic. To reiterate what distinguishes machines and structures: With a machine, the outside inscribes or remarks itself inside, and the inside outside. Machines are driven by a desire not for eternal life but for a certain abolition. The structure of Western thought, however, has traditionally opposed life and death, inside and outside, chaining them to a series of related oppositions: *physis/techne*, nature/culture, speech/writing, presence/absence, generation/degeneration. To these we might add other, more contemporary links: the oppositions of performance/technology and of live bodies/mediatized bodies.[45] Machinic readings—deconstructions, critical genealogies, stratoanalyses—bore holes of self-referential alterity into these oppositions, confusing their limits and interrupting their structural links. A general theory of performance is therefore inseparable from a generalized technology, a becoming-machinic of the world that reformats all reading machines. Perhaps Nietzsche foresaw this as well. Posthumously, in the closing years of the twentieth century, Friedrich Kittler called him the "mechanized philosopher" because he was apparently the first of his profession to own and operate a typewriter.[46] On it he typed to his nineteenth-century friend Peter Gast: "Our writing instruments contribute to our thoughts." And in "The Wanderer and his Shadow" Nietzsche left us with these "premises of the Machine Age:" "The printing press, the machine, the railway, the telegraph are premises whose thousand-year conclusions no one has yet had the courage to draw."[47] More than a century later we might attach and send this question: The servo, the computer, the shuttle, the electronic nose—what conclusions will be built on these newly acquired premises?

Let us rehearse some final scenes of Nietzsche's passage through the age of global performance by diving quickly into Pierre Klossowski's deep and moving text, *Nietzsche and the Vicious Circle* (1969). In light of our reading of Deleuze's *Foucault*, we should note that Klossowski dedicates his own book to Deleuze, and that Foucault, upon reading this text, wrote the author to say that, along with Nietzsche, it "is the greatest book of philosophy I have read."[48] Like Bataille, with whom he participated in the Collège de Sociologie, Klossowski wrote critically of fascist readings of Nietzsche in the 1930s, and he later translated into French Heidegger's massive reading of the thinker of the superman. In *Nietzsche and the Vicious Circle*, Klossowski focuses on how Nietzsche experienced his body as test site for the eternal return, how he tried to connect it on and off with a larger conspiratorial body, one composed of highly variable intensities and affects, including those of other experimenters and sovereign players. Klossowski's text is also a geology of the performance stratum—provided, that is, that we now read this formation as ground zero for a malicious conspiracy, a gay sci become major drag. Klossowski writes that "though Nietzsche never tried to describe the required methodological conditions, we can say not only that the conspiracy he outlined took place *without him*, but that it succeeded perfectly: neither through *capitalism*, nor *the working class*, nor *science*, but rather through the *methods* dictated by objects themselves and their *modes of production*, with their laws of growth and consumption. The industrial phenomenon, in short, is a concrete form of the *most malicious caricaturization* of his doctrine, that is to say, the regime of the Return has been installed in the 'productive' existence of humans who never produce anything but a state of *strangeness* between themselves and their life."[49]

Malicious caricaturization, "productive" existence, strangeness between oneself and one's life—might the eternal return circle back in circuits of inputs and outputs? Might the revaluation of values unfold in the satisficing of efficacy, efficiency, and effectiveness—and far, far beyond?

Might the stone in Nietzsche's great edifice turn up as a block in the performance stratum, and the cross- and countercultural training he once prescribed take place today in the diversity and creativity programs of multinational, multicultural institutions?

In short: *is Nietzsche's superman falling victim to an all-too-American faith in "good performance" and his futural project coming to pass as the age of global performance?*

In short: is Nietzsche's superman falling victim to an all-too-American faith in "good performance" and his futural project coming to pass as the age of global performance?

Yes—no—and yet—

5 g∞th3ring h3r thought5 in ∞ 5p3c

5om3 P3r5p3ctiv35," H3r n∞m3 l3g3nd∞ry. h3r 5ubj

h∞ll3ng3r 5 535510n i5 initi∞

rumoro∞n imp3nding 3xplo5ion

h∞ll b3for3

5h3 b3gin5 h3r conclu

In the early years of the twenty-first century, under the sign of a paradox that seems more like a painful comedy of errors, Jane Challenger attends a world conference on extra-disciplinary performance. It is held—where else—in Manaus, Brazil, where she has taken up with a band of researchers whose specializations have long since been forgotten. The conference is an actual-virtual sort of an affair, and it has attracted thousands of attendees, among them artists and cultural theorists, engineers and computer scientists, management and labor leaders, economists, stock brokers, athletes, physicians, geologists, rock fans, as well as a large number of reporters.

But Challenger has not come as a journalist to cover the conference proceedings. Instead, she arrives as a guest speaker invited to deliver findings from her latest research. After her adventures in *Lost World II*, Challenger and crew began collaborating with Dr. Kxalendjer and a group of young hacktivists. Together, they studied the intricacies of disastronautic flight and soon commenced a series of gay sci-fi experiments. Challenger in fact has just this day returned from some untimely fieldwork and is gathering her thoughts in a special session called "The Age of Global Performance: Some Perspectives." Her name legendary, her subject elusive, Challenger's session is initially packed to the gills, but rumors of an impending explosion have led many to leave the hall before she begins her conclusion.

Whil3 w3 533 th3 p3rformanc3 5tratum a5 br3aking with hundr3d5 of y3ar5 of di5ciplinary pow3r, futur3 r353arch3r5 will follow it5 fi55ur35 from anoth3r *It's getting late, so I'll end with this thought:*

researchers of the future will study performance in a radically different manner than from those of today.

p3r5p3ctiv3 and 5can it5 crack5 and angl35 mor3 acut3ly. Th3y will r3ad p3rformanc3 a5 br3aking not only with c3nturi35 of panoptic 5urv3illanc3 but al5o with mill3nnia rul3d by an alphab3tic l3ctur3 machin3, on3 compo53d at variou5 tim35 of tabl3t5 and 5croll5, manu5cript5 and book5, and chair5 and d35k5 and l3ct3rn5. For futur3 r353arch3r5 will tak3 a5 giv3n 5om3thing that w3 can only dimly p3rc3iv3 today—and th3n may b3 too horrifi3d to admit: nam3ly, that ***all p3rformanc3 i5 3l3ctronic****, that th3 global 3xplo5ion of p3rformanc3 coincid35 pr3ci53ly with th3 digitalization of di5cour535 and practic35, and that thi5 coincid3nc3 i5 anything but coincid3ntal.*

Whil3 w3 5ituat3 p3rformanc3 b3tw33n ritual and th3at3r, th3y will ca5t it far b3yond th353 mod35 of actualization. P3rformanc3 ***I have sensed the future*** *for th3m will nam3 th3 3mbodim3nt of digital virtualiti35 (that i5, 5ph3r35 of incorpor3al valu35 and r3f3r3nc35, in thi5 ca53, th3 digital 5ati5ficing of div3r53 5y5t3m5), ju5t a5 th3at3r onc3 actualiz3d th3 virtual 5ph3r35 of lit3rary 5oci3ti35 (5criptur35 of God and hi5tori35 of Man), and ritual actualiz3d tho53 of oral 5oci3ti35 (myth5 of trib35 and cult5 of god5).*

Whil3 w3 oft3n 5p3ak of a thr33-thou5and-y3ar pa55ag3 from orality to lit3racy to digitality, far di5tant r353arch3r5 will 5tudy a much mor3 5udd3n "3v3nt." Th353 r3mot3 5tud3nt5 will play back 5tudi35 of th3 Gr3at Mutation, **and it is** *th3 abrupt 5witching from oral-3ar to alpha-3y3 to 3l3ctro-no53, a tran5mutation that took plac3 ov3r 53v3ral c3nturi35, or in 5om3 in5tanc35 a doz3n d3cad35, and ca535, a 5ingl3 g3n3ration. Th3y will call up l3g3ndary docum3nt5 from th wh3n c3rtain individual5 around th3 glob3 w3r3 born into oral communiti alphab3tic world, and pa553d away in an 3l3ctronic* **perfumed.** *univ3r5 w3 tak3 today a5 3xtraordinary ca535 will gradually b3com3 l355 and from th3 for35hort3n3d angl3 of a mor3 di5tant futur3, mo5t of ritual5 will app3ar to hav3 b3com3 p3rformativ3b*

While we see the performance stratum as breaking with hundreds of years of disciplinary power, future researchers will follow its fissures from another perspective and scan its cracks and angles more acutely. They will read performance as breaking not only with centuries of panoptic surveillance but also with millennia ruled by an alphabetic lecture machine, one composed at various times of tablets and scrolls, manuscripts and books, and chairs and desks and lecterns. For future researchers will take as given something that we can only dimly perceive today—and then may be too horrified to admit: namely, that ***all performance is electronic****, that the global explosion of performance coincides precisely with the digitalization of discourses and practices, and that this coincidence is anything but coincidental.*

While we situate performance between ritual and theater, they will cast it far beyond these modes of actualization. Performance for them will name the embodiment of digital virtualities (that is, spheres of incorporeal values and references, in this case, the digital satisficing of diverse systems), just as theater once actualized the virtual spheres of literary societies (scriptures of God and histories of Man), and ritual actualized those of oral societies (myths of tribes and cults of gods).

While we often speak of a three-thousand-year passage from orality to literacy to digitality, far distant researchers will study a much more sudden "event." These remote students will play back studies of the Great Mutation, the abrupt switching from oral-ear to alpha-eye to electro-nose, a transmutation that took place over several centuries, or in some instances a dozen decades, and in a few intriguing cases, a single generation. They will call up legendary documents from the twentieth century, when certain individuals around the globe were born into oral communities, grew up in an alphabetic world, and passed away in an electronic universe. Indeed, what we take today as extraordinary cases will gradually become less and less so, until from the foreshortened angle of a more distant future, most of the world's rituals will appear to have become performative on the very day they became theatrical.

And if we have begun to sense that performance embodies such values as efficacy, efficiency, and effectiveness, and to see performers as being animal, vegetable, or mineral, distant researchers will experience performance as intensifications in a highly charged atmosphere, as contestations in a cloud of forces without form or substance, all the while taking themselves to be living-dead perfumers, not so much organic-inorganic syntheses or biomechanical contraptions, but recursive patterns of a genre machinic.

Finally, while we may be shocked at the notion that everything's become performative, that the whole world's been framed as a high performance test site, future researchers will merely be shocked at our shock.

"How could this have surprised them? They're the ones who took performance to the ends of the world— and beyond."

As Challenger reads these lines, she becomes more and more agitated,

at first shaking at the microphone,

then rattling the table, the chairs,

and finally

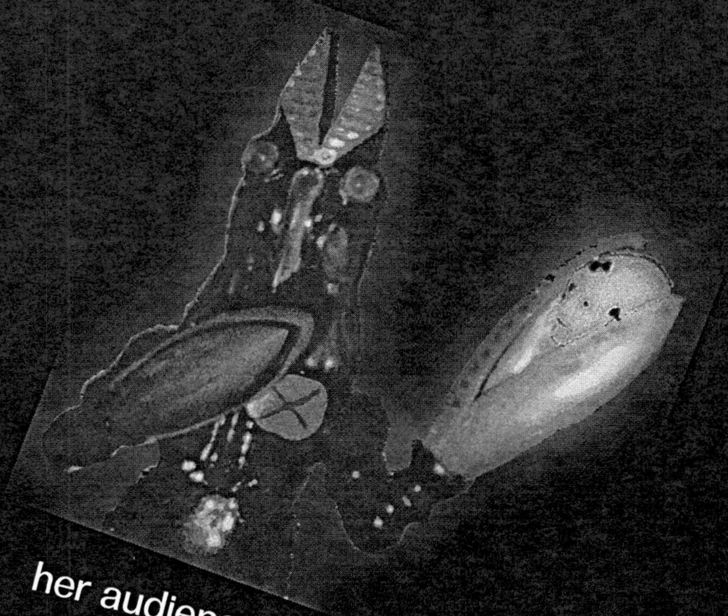

her audience.

The lectern itself has become a sort of time machine, its slanted top now a blinking control panel, its lamp a slotted lever, its casing a cracked and fuming fuselage.

From somewhere near the back of the hall, a deep blue light engulfs the space, while waves of feedback spew out from the lecture machine. There's a slight pause—then a brilliant explosion, a blinding yet muted jolt, a chilling blast of the outside.

Together, lecturer and lectern start shuttling across the wavelengths, channeling disparate voices and gestures, guided by some remote yet immanent device . . .

. . . if that call to such a h

. . .

if that call to such a hurry had not challenged him and put him at bay, if the word framing that order and challenge had not spoken: then there would be no sputnik.[50]

How does one frame a perfume?[51]

im and put him at bay, if the word framing that order and challenge had not spoken: then there no sputnik.

ONIZUKA: **LTD, MS-1 com check. You're loud and clear. Good morning.**

CARTER **[a launch technician]: You know, I think these visors are cold from being outside and are fogging up. Here's the pocket checklist.**

ONIZUKA: **Okay, thank you. See you later on. Kind of cold this morning.**

SMITH: **Up here, Ellison, the sun's shining in. At least we've got the crew arranged right for people who like the warm and the cool. . . . Got you out of the sun.**[52]

In that first venture, under a blue cloudless sky, they were intoxicated by the myrtle and scotch broom, and the smell of thyme. What remained of those sensations in the contemporary olfaction? Apparently nothing more than a vague poetic memory, flashes of ecstasy, shreds of surprise.[53]

T minus 5:00: . . . performed APU start.

The unforgettable associated world of the Tick, defined by its gravitational energy of falling, its olfactory characteristic of perceiving sweat, and its active characteristic of latching on. . . . Active and perceptive characteristics are themselves something of a double pincer, a double articulation.[54]

ONIZUKA: **My nose is freezing.**

Nase, NASA, navy, nazi, Maaanaaa—

The function of ***smelling***. . . . is performed by the so-called olfactory setae. . . . They are sensitive to chemical stimuli. As the currents waft fine particles of the lobsterman's bait to the lobster in his hole or on prowl, these olfactory setae catch the scent and lead the victim to follow the trail to the trap.[55]

How do you get rid of a teacher?
Challenge her.[56]

Challenger, or what remained of him, slowly hurried toward
the plane of consistency, following a bizarre trajectory
with
nothing relative left about it. He tried to slip into an
assemblage serving as a drum-gate, the particle Clock
with its intensive
clicking and conjugated rhythms
hammering out the absolute.[57]

NEVER TOUCH THESE SWITCHES!

T MINUS 0: 30 SCOBEE: Thirty seconds down there.

T MINUS 0: 25 Remember the red button when you make a roll call.

T MINUS 0: 23 SCOBEE: I won't do that. Thanks a lot.

T MINUS 0: 15 SCOBEE: **Fifteen.**

T MINUS 0: 06 SCOBEE: **There they go, guys.** [CHALLENGER'S MAIN ENGINES BEGIN FIRING.][58]

Challenger visibly braced herself.

Pushing a protesting hand to one side,

she seated herself upon a chair.

The handle was clicked into number eight.

She was gone.[59]

NOTES

0. Challenges

1. Friedrich Nietzsche. "On the Advantage and Disadvantage of History for Life." Trans. Peter Preuss. Indianapolis, IN: Hackett Publishing Company, Inc., 1980, pp. 40, 41.
2. See Herbert Marcuse. *Eros and Civilization: A Philosophical Inquiry into Freud.* New York: Vintage Books, 1961 (1955).
3. Dana Wechsler Linder and Nancy Rotenier. "Good-bye to Berle & Means." *Forbes* 153, No. 1 (1994): p. 103.
4. Marvin Carlson. *Performance: A Critical Introduction.* London: Routledge, 1996, p. 168.
5. See Richard Bolton, ed. *Culture Wars: Documents from the Recent Controversies in the Arts.* New York: New Press, 1992.
6. See William J. Fulbright. "The War and Its Effects: The Military-Industrial-Academic Complex." *Super-State: Readings in the Military-Industrial Complex.* Ed. Herbert I. Schiller. Urbana, IL: University of Illinois, 1970, pp.171–8.
7. Digital Dissertations. UMI Database. 21 July 2000 <www.lib.umi.com>.
8. Jean-François Lyotard. *The Postmodern Condition: A Report on Knowledge.* Trans. Geoff Bennington and Brian Massumi. Minneapolis, MN: University of Minnesota Press, 1979, p. xxiii.
9. Lyotard. *The Postmodern Condition*, p. xxiv.
10. Lyotard. *The Postmodern Condition*, p. xxiv.
11. Lyotard. *The Postmodern Condition*, pp. 8-9.
12. Judith Butler. "Critically Queer." *Gay and Lesbian Quarterly* 1 (1993): p17.
13. Marcuse. *Eros and Civilization*, p. 41.
14. Michel Foucault. *This Is Not a Pipe.* Trans. and ed. James Harkness. Berkeley, CA: University of California Press, 1983, p. 23.
15. Michel Foucault. *Discipline and Punish: The Birth of the Prison.* Trans. Alan Sheridan. New York: Vintage Books, 1979, p. 301.
16. Jacques Derrida. *Dissemination.* Trans. Barbara Johnson. Chicago, IL: University of Chicago Press, 1981, p. 290.

1. The Efficacy of Cultural Performance

1. Richard Schechner. *Essays on Performance Theory: 1970-1976.* New York: Drama Book Specialists, 1977, p. 76.
2. This text is a selection of papers read in 1977 at the seventy-sixth Burg Wartenstein Symposium, sponsored by the Wenner-Gren Foundation for Anthropological Research.
3. John J. MacAloon, ed. *Rite, Drama, Festival, Spectacle: Rehearsals Toward a Theory of Cultural Performance.* Philadelphia, PA: Institute for the Study of Human Issues, 1984, p.1.
4. Carol Simpson Stern and Bruce Henderson. *Performance: Texts and Contexts.* London: Longman, 1993, p. 3.
5. Janelle G. Reinelt and Joseph R. Roach, eds. *Critical Theory and Performance.* Ann Arbor, MI: University of Michigan Press, 1992, p. 2, my emphasis.
6. Marvin Carlson. *Performance: A Critical Introduction.* London: Routledge, 1996, p. 7, my emphasis.
7. Peggy Phelan. *Unmarked: The Politics of Performance.* London and New York: Routledge, 1993, p. 1, my emphasis.
8. J.L. Austin. *How to Do Things with Words.* Ed. J.O. Urmson and Marina Sbisà. Cambridge, MA: Harvard University Press, 1962, p. 161.
9. Lawrence Grossberg, Cary Nelson, and Paula Treichler, eds. *Cultural Studies.* London: Routledge, 1992, p. 6.
10. MacAloon. *Rite, Drama, Festival, Spectacle*, p. 2.
11. MacAloon. *Rite, Drama, Festival, Spectacle*, p. 1.
12. Richard Schechner. "PAJ Distorts the Broad Spectrum." *TDR: The Drama Review* 33, no.2 (1989): p. 7.
13. Carlson. *Performance*, p. 13.
14. Carlson. *Performance*, pp. 6-7.
15. Carlson. *Performance*, p. 195.
16. Carlson. *Performance*, p. 7.
17. Victor Turner. "Liminality and the Performative Genres." *Studies in Symbolism and Cultural Communication.* Ed. F. Allan Hanson. Lawrence, KS: University of Kansas, 1982, p. 22.
18. See Arnold van Gennep. *The Rites of Passage.* Chicago, IL: University of Chicago Press, 1960 (1908).
19. Peggy Phelan. "Introduction: The Ends of Performance." *The Ends of Performance.* Ed. Peggy Phelan and Jill Lane. New York: New York University Press, 1998, p. 3.
20. MacAloon. *Rite, Drama, Festival, Spectacle*, p. 2.
21. See Reinelt and Roach's *Critical Theory and Performance*, Carlson's *Performance*, and Philip Auslander's *Presence and Resistance: Postmodernism and Cultural Politics in Contemporary American Performance.* Ann Arbor, MI: University of Michigan Press, 1992.
22. Herbert Blau. *The Eye of Prey: Subversions of the Postmodern.* Bloomington, IN: Indiana University Press, 1987, p. 7.
23. Sue-Ellen Case. "Theory/History/Revolution." *Critical Theory and Performance.* Ed. Janelle G. Reinelt and Joseph R. Roach. Ann Arbor, MI: University of Michigan Press, 1992, p. 422.
24. Reinelt and Roach. *Critical Theory and Performance*, p. 4.
25. Reinelt and Roach. *Critical Theory and Performance*, p. 5.
26. Jacques Derrida. *Writing and Difference.* Trans. Alan Bass. Chicago, IL: University of Chicago Press, 1978. *Of Grammatology.* Trans. Gayatri Chakravorty Spivak. Baltimore: The Johns Hopkins University Press, 1974, p.3.
27. Blau's essay is found in *The Eye of Prey: Subversions of the Postmodern.* Bloomington, IN: Indiana University Press, 1987. This citation is found on page 7.
28. Blau. *The Eye of Prey*, p. 4.

29. Phelan. *Unmarked,* p. 6.
30. Auslander. *Presence and Resistance,* p. 51.
31. Carlson. *Performance,* p. 142.
32. Carlson. *Performance,* p. 182.
33. Reinelt and Roach. *Critical Theory and Performance,* p. 5.
34. Reinelt and Roach. *Critical Theory and Performance,* p. 5.
35. Ronald J. Pelias and James VanOosting. "A Paradigm for Performance Studies." *Quarterly Journal of Speech* 73 (1987): p. 216.
36. Pelias and VanOosting. "A Paradigm for Performance Studies," p. 219.
37. Pelias and VanOosting. "A Paradigm for Performance Studies," p. 229.
38. Curling off the west coast would be the case of California, the Cockettes, feminist performance art, the teachings of Blau, communication studies—in short, performances that escape the tale rendered above but no doubt affect the shape of cultural performance nonetheless. This unwritten strand remains for future reading. My thanks to Janelle Reinelt for pointing this out to me.
39. Richard Schechner. "What Is Performance Studies Anyway?" *The Ends of Performance.* Ed. Peggy Phelan and Jill Lane. New York: New York University Press, 1998, p. 361.
40. Joseph Roach. "Culture and Performance in the Circum-Atlantic World." *Performativity and Performance.* Ed. Andrew Parker and Eve Kosofsky Sedgwick. London: Routledge, 1995, p.46.
41. Carlson. *Performance,* pp. 198-9.
42. Schechner. "What is Performance Studies Anyway?", p. 360.
43. Michel Foucault. *Foucault Live (Interviews, 1966-84).* Trans. John Johnston. Ed. Sylvère Lotringer. New York: Semiotext(e), 1989, p. 66, my emphasis.
44. Significantly, Foucault also pejoratively characterizes the university environment as a "fictitious, artificial and quasi-theatrical" one in which "the student is given a gamelike way of life." See "Rituals of Exclusion." In *Foucault Live (Interviews, 1966–84).* Trans. John Johnston. Ed. Sylvère Lotringer. New York: Semiotext(e), 1989, p. 65.
45. See Turner's essay, "From Liminal to Liminoid, in Play, Flow, and Ritual: An Essay in Comparative Symbology," in *From Ritual to Theatre: The Human Seriousness of Play.* New York: PAJ Publications, 1982. Within Performance Studies, "liminoid" has never been as widely deployed a term as "liminal."
46. See the interview "The Experience-Book." in *Remarks on Marx: Conversations with Duccio Trombadori.* Trans. R. James Goldstein and James Cascaito. New York: Semiotext(e), 1991.
47. Félix Guattari, *Chaosmosis: an Ethico-Aesthetic Paradigm.* Trans. Paul Bains and Julian Pefanis. Bloomington, IN: Indiana University Press, 1995, p. 61.
48. Carlson. *Performance,* p. 5.
49. For a discussion of the differences between the Platonic (formal) question "What is?" and the Nietzschean ("forceful") question "Which one?" or "What is it *for me*?" see Gilles Deleuze, *Nietzsche and Philosophy.* Trans.Hugh Tomlinson. New York: Columbia University Press, 1983, pp. 75-78.
50. Paul Feyerabend. *Against Method: Outline of an Anarchistic Theory of Knowledge.* London: Verso, 1978, p. 31.

2. The Efficiency of Organizational Performance

1. Joseph Tifflin and Ernest J. McCormick. "Industrial Merit Rating." *Performance Appraisal: Research and Practice.* Ed. Thomas L. Whisler and Shirley F. Harper. New York: Holt, Reinhart & Winston, 1962 (1954), p. 4.
2. Evelyn Eichel and Henry E. Bender. *Performance Appraisal: A Study of Current Techniques.* New York: American Management Association Research and Information Service, 1984, pp. 11-12.
3. Gore, Al. *From Red Tape to Results: Creating a Government that Works Better & Costs Less.* Report of the National Performance Review. New York: TimeBooks, 1993, p. i.
4. See Donald F. Kettl and John J. Dilulio, Jr., eds. *Inside the Reinvention Machine: Appraising Governmental Reform.* Washington, DC: The Brookings Institution, 1995.
5. Performance and Results Act of 1993, Sec. 2.b.2.
6. See Donald F. Kettl. *Reinventing Government? Appraising the National Performance Review.* Washington, DC: The Brookings Institution, 1994.
7. Thomas L. Whisler and Shirley F. Harper, eds. *Performance Appraisal: Research and Practice.* New York: Holt, Reinhart & Winston, 1962, p. v.
8. Richard S. Williams. *Performance Management: Perspectives on Employee Performance.* London: International Thomson Business Press, 1998, p. 1.
9. See Peter B. Vaill. *Managing as a Performing Art: New Ideas for a World of Chaotic Change.* San Francisco, CA: Jossey-Bass Publishers, 1989, ch. 4.
10. For an in-depth and detailed study of the postwar transformation of Scientific Management written from a political science perspective, see Stephen P. Waring's *Taylorism Transformed: Scientific Management Theory since 1945.* Chapel Hill, NC: University of North Carolina Press, 1991.
11. Frederick Winslow Taylor. *The Principles of Scientific Management.* New York: W.W. Norton & Company, 1967 (1911), p. 39.
12. Peter F. Drucker. *The Practice of Management.* New York: Harper, 1954, p. 280.
13. Joseph Roach. "The Future That Worked." *Theater* 28, no. 2 (1998): p. 20.
14. Taylor. *The Principles of Scientific Management,* p. 130, n. 1.
15. Taylor. *The Principles of Scientific Management,* p. 114.
16. Taylor. *The Principles of Scientific Management,* pp. 114-15.
17. Taylor. *The Principles of Scientific Management,* p. 115.
18. Taylor. *The Principles of Scientific Management,* p. 62.
19. Taylor. *The Principles of Scientific Management,* p. 21.
20. Taylor. *The Principles of Scientific Management,* p. 25.

21. Taylor. *The Principles of Scientific Management*, p. 26.
22. Cited by Taylor in *The Principles of Scientific Management*, p. 5.
23. Taylor. *The Principles of Scientific Management*, p. 6.
24. Taylor. *The Principles of Scientific Management*, p. 83.
25. For a history of social engineering, see John M. Jordan's *Machine Age Ideology: Social Engineering and American Liberalism: 1911-1939.* Chapel Hill, NC: University of North Carolina Press, 1994.
26. Taylor. *The Principles of Scientific Management*, p. 26. Taylor's appraisal of worker intelligence is frequently shocking. Of a particular worker scientifically selected to handle pig iron, he writes: "He merely happened to be a man of the type of the ox—no rare specimen of humanity, difficult to find and therefore very highly prized. On the contrary, he was a man so stupid that he was unfitted to do most kinds of laboring work, even" (62). And of pig iron workers generally: "the man suited to handling pig iron is too stupid properly to train himself" (63).
27. Taylor. *The Principles of Scientific Management*, p. 128.
28. I worked on a second-shift assembly line one summer in Bloomington, IN, manufacturing the small cards sold during Christmas season to be placed on gifts. Along with my co-workers, I stayed on the line at a single station for a two-hour block and then, after a strictly enforced break, moved on to the next station for anothe two-hour block. Except for the first station, where one placed a molded plastic "bubble" on the assembly line, and the last two, where the card-filled bubbles were heat-sealed on to a cardboard backing and the assembled products boxed for shipment, there was virtually no variation: the other stations' perform ances consisted of tearing out the perforated cards and "hitting the bubble" in a timely fashion as it passed along on the line.
29. Douglas McGregor. *Leadership and Motivation: Essays of Douglas McGregor.* Ed. Warren, G.Bennis and Edgar H. Schein, with collaboration by Caroline McGregor. Cambridge, MA: MIT Press, 1966, p. 19.
30. David L. DeVries, Ann M. Morrison, Sandra L. Shullman, and Michael L. Gerlach. *Performance Appraisal on the Line.* New York: John Wiley & Sons, 1981, p. 113.
31. Elton Mayo. *The Social Problems of an Industrial Civilization.* Boston, MA: Harvard University, 1945, pp. 81-2.
32. MacGregor. *Leadership and Motivation*, p. 4.
33. MacGregor. *Leadership and Motivation*, p. 5.
34. MacGregor. *Leadership and Motivation*, p. 15.
35. MacGregor. *Leadership and Motivation*, p. 19.
36. John Kao. *Jamming: The Art and Discipline of Business Creativity.* New York: HarperBusiness, 1996,p.17.
37. Kao. *Jamming*, p. 97.
38. William H. Whyte. *The Organization Man.* Garden City, NY: Doubleday, 1956. Johnson Nunnally, *The Man in the Grey Flannel Suit.* 1956.
39. At the same time, one might look to France and Japan, where filmmakers created serial films featuring comic Company Men found in their own societies.
40. Barry R. Nathan and Wayne F. Cascio. "Technical and Legal Standards." *Performance Assessment: Methods & Applications.* Ed. Ronald A. Berk. Baltimore, MD: The Johns Hopkins University Press, 1986 pp. 11-12.
41. R. Thomas Roosevelt, Jr. "From Affirmative Action to Affirming Diversity." *Differences That Work: Organizational Excellence through Diversity.* Ed. Mary C. Gentile, Cambridge, MA: Harvard Business School, 1993, p. 30.
42. Barbara A. Walker and William C. Hanson. "Valuing Differences at Digital Equipment Corporation." *Diversity in the Workplace: Human Resources Initiatives.* Ed. Susan E. Jackson. New York: The Guilford Press, 1992, p.120.
43. Mary C. Gentile's anthology *Differences That Work: Organizational Excellence through Diversity*, for instance, contains essays concerning such issues as black managers, gay partners at company events, age discrimination, visually impaired workers, and AIDS in the workplace.
44. Walker and Hanson. "Valuing Differences at Digital Equipment Corporation," pp. 135-6.
45. David P. Hanna. *Designing Organizations for High Performance.* Reading, MA: Addison-Wesley, 1988, p. 4. Weber, of course, was hardly a "spokesman" for modern bureaucracy: he described its workings, criticized its effects on society, while also recognizing its effectiveness and efficiency. While he did employ the figure of the machine which Hanna and others use to characterize Taylorism, Weber's use of the term was not an unequivocal endorsement.
46. Hanna. *Designing Organizations for High Performance*, p. 8. Emphasis mine on 'deviation-amplifying'.
47. Robert C. Fried. *Performance in American Bureaucracy.* Boston: Little, Brown & Company, 1976, pp. 12-13.
48. Hanna. *Designing Organizations for High Performance*, pp. 14-15.
49. James C. Taylor and David F. Felten. *Performance by Design: Sociotechnical Systems in North America.* Englewood Cliffs, NJ: Prentice Hall, 1993, p. 1.
50. E. Frank Harrison. *The Managerial Decision-Making Process.* Boston, MA: Houghton Mifflin, 1975, p. 5.
51. William C. Howell. "An Overview of Models, Methods and Problems." *Human Performance and Productivity, Volume II: Information Processing and Decision Making.* Ed. William C. Howell and Edwin A. Fleishman. Hillsdale, NJ: Lawrence Erlbaum Associates, 1982, p. 3.
52. Herbert A. Simon. *The New Science of Management Decision.* Englewood Cliffs, NJ: Prentice-Hall, Inc., 1977 (1960), p. x.
53. Simon. *The New Science of Management Decision*, p. 40.
54. See Harrison. *The Managerial Decision-Making Process*, p. 14.
55. Simon. *The New Science of Management Decision*, p. 120.
56. Herbert A. Simon. *Models of Man: Social and Rational.* New York and London: John Wiley & Sons, Inc., 1957, p. 219.
57. Simon. *Models of Man*, p. 223.
58. Warren G. Bennis. *Organizational Development: Its Nature, Origins, and Prospects.* Reading, MA: Addison-Wesley, 1969, p. 2.
59. Peter B. Vaill. "Toward a Behavioral Description of High-Performing Systems." *Leadership: Where Else*

Can We Go? Ed. Morgan W. McCall, Jr. and Michael M. Lombardo. Durham, NC: Duke University Press, 1978, p. 104.

60. Vaill. "Toward a Behavioral Description of High-Performing Systems," pp. 124-5.
61. David A. Nadler. *Feedback and Organization Development: Using Data-Based Methods.* Reading, MA: Addison-Wesley, 1977, p. 173.
62. Hanna. *Designing Organizations for High Performance*, p. 101.
63. Thomas J. Peters and Robert H. Waterman, Jr. *In Search of Excellence: Lessons from America's Best-Run Companies.* New York: Warner Books, 1982, p. 41.
64. See Peters and Waterman. *In Search of Excellence*, pp. 44-52.
65. Peters and Waterman. *In Search of Excellence*, p. 42.
66. Peters and Waterman. *In Search of Excellence*, p. 51.
67. Robert T. Golembiewski and Alan Kiepper. *High Performance and Human Costs: A Public Sector Model of Organizational Development.* New York: Praeger, 1988, p. 23.
68. Golembiewski and Kiepper. *High Performance and Human Costs*, p. 228.
69. See Vaill. "Toward a Behavioral Description of High-Performing Systems," pp. 106-7. In presenting this concept, Vaill cites an informal lecture on sociotechnical systems given by Eric Trist in 1972.
70. Waring. *Taylorism Transformed*, p. 203.
71. In doing so, however, I should say that for strategic reasons I have thus far avoided discussing Performance Management's interest in cultural performance. Because I am outlining a general theory of performance—and not generalizing from one particular performance concept or practice—I must analyze models developed in different research paradigms. To have begun by stressing Performance Management's use of cultural models or, alternatively, by discussing well-known analyses of organizations using such models (e.g., Goffman or Handleman's work), I would have risked minimizing the differences between organizational and cultural performance. Instead, I have attempted to explicate performance as it has been deployed by managers and organizational theorists and have resisted making a critique of this paradigm in order to understand performance on its own terms. Such a critique is found in later chapters.
72. Peter B. Vaill. *Managing as a Performing Art: New Ideas for a World of Chaotic Change.* San Francisco, CA: Jossey-Bass Publishers, 1989, p. 121.
73. Vaill. *Managing as a Performing Art*, p. 112.
74. Vaill. *Managing as a Performing Art*, p. 116.
75. Vaill. *Managing as a Performing Art*, p. 117.
76. Vaill. *Managing as a Performing Art*, p. 118.
77. Vaill. *Managing as a Performing Art*, p. 119.
78. Vaill. *Managing as a Performing Art*, pp. 74-5.
79. Mangham and Overington's apparent unawareness of Performance Studies is very striking, since they list in their bibliography in the Spring 1985 *Tulane Drama Review*, an issue on East Village performance that included an ad for NYU's Department of Performance Studies.
80. Iain L. Mangham and Michael A. Overington. *Organizations as Theatre: A Social Psychology of Dramatic Appearances.* Chichester, UK: John Wiley & Sons, 1987, pp. 1, 3.
81. Mangham and Overington. *Organizations as Theatre*, p. 52.
82. Mangham and Overington. *Organizations as Theatre*, p. 25.
83. Kao. *Jamming*, p. 96.
84. Kao. *Jamming*, pp. xviii–xix.
85. Kao. *Jamming*, p. 154.
86. Kao. *Jamming*, p. 4.
87. Kao. *Jamming*, p. 131.
88. Kao. *Jamming*, p. 132.
89. Félix Guattari. *Chaosmosis: an Ethico-Aesthetic Paradigm.* Trans. Paul Bains and Julian Pefanis. Bloomington, IN: Indiana University Press, 1995, p. 31.
90. Niklas Luhmann. *Social Systems.* Trans. John Bednarz, Jr., with Dirk Baecker. Stanford, CA: Stanford University Press, 1995, p. 93.
91. Luhmann. *Social Systems*, pp. 93-4.
92. See, for example, Victor Turner's *From Ritual to Theatre: The Human Seriousness of Play*, New York: PAJ Publications, 1982, pp. 28, 57, 71, 72, and 75; *On the Edge of the Bush*, Tucson, AZ: University of Arizona Press, 1985, p. 191; and Richard Schechner's *Between Theatre and Anthropology.* Philadelphia, PA: University of Pennysylvania Press, 1985, pp. 37, 75, 87, 102-3; and *Essays on Performance Theory: 1970-1976.* New York: Drama Book Specialists, 1977, pp. 66, 76, and 144.
93. Schechner. *Essays on Performance Theory*, p. 144.
94. Schechner. *Essays on Performance Theory*. p. 66.
95. Turner. *From Ritual to Theatre*, pp. 71-2.
96. Turner. *From Ritual to Theatre*, p. 72.
97. Turner. *From Ritual to Theatre*, p. 8.
98. Vaill. *Managing as a Performing Art*, p. 118.
99. Indeed, critical work is needed to trace the borrowings of organizational processes by various directors. Joseph Roach's "The Future That Worked," cited above, suggests the direction such research might take.
100. Turner. *From Ritual to Theatre*, p. 41.
101. Turner. *From Ritual to Theatre*, p. 32.

3. The Effectiveness of Technological Performance

1. Diane Vaughan. *The Challenger Launch Decision: Risky Technology, Culture, and Deviance a NASA.* Chicago, IL: The University of Chicago Press, 1996, p. 157.

2. J.C. Williams, "Titanium alloys: Production, Behavior and Application." *High Performance Materials in Aerospace.* Ed. Harvey M. Flower. London: Chapman & Hall, 1995.
3. R.H. Haase and W.H.T. Holden. *Performance of Land Transportation Vehicles.* Santa Monica, CA: The Rand Corporation, 1964 p. 23.
4. Committee to Study High Performance Computing and Communications: Status of a Major Initiative. *Evolving the High Performance Computing and Communications Initiative to Support the Nation's Information Infrastructure.* Washington, DC: National Academy Press, 1995.
5. P.A. Rey and R.G. Varsanik. "Application and Function of Synthetic Polymeric Flocculents in Wastewater Treatment." *Water-Soluble Polymers: Beauty with Performance.* Ed. J.E. Glass. Washington, DC: American Chemical Society, 1986, p. 113.
6. See *Electric Vehicles: Technology, Performance, and Potential.* Paris: International Energy Agency and the Organization for Economic Co-operation and Development, 1993, pp. 7, 37-45, 91, and 122.
7. Vaughan. *The Challenger Launch Decision*, p. 109, my emphasis.
8. Israel Borovits and Seev Neumann. *Computer Systems Performance Evaluation: Criteria, Measurements, Techniques, and Costs.* Lexington, MA: Lexington Books, 1979, p. 3, my emphasis.
9. The Act specified participation by a host of federal agencies and departments, including the Departments of Agriculture, Commerce, Defense, Education, Energy, Health and Human Services, and Interior, as well as the Environmental Protection Agency (EPA), the National Aeronautics and Space Administration (NASA), the National Oceanic and Atmospheric Administration (NOAA), and the National Science Foundation (NSF). Funding was provided by the Act for five years and, as a rule, increased from one fiscal year to the next. To give some idea of the appropriations: for 1996 alone, the Act provided the Department of Education $2,300,000, the EPA $7,000,000, the Department of Energy $168,000,000, NASA $145,000,000, and the NSF $413,000,000. Over the entire five-year period, the cumulative funds specified in the 1991 Act totaled $2,901,000,000.
10. Committee to Study Hgh Performance Computing and Communications. *Evolving the High Performance Computing and Communications Initiative*, pp. 105, 60.
11. Committee to Study High Performance Computing and Communications. *Evolving the High Performance Computing and Communications Initiative*, p. 25.
12. Charles F. White. "Servo System Theory." Arthur S. Locke. *Guidance.* Princeton, NJ: D. Van Norstrand Company, Inc. 1955, p. 232.
13. Stuart W. Leslie. *The Cold War and American Science: The Military-Industrial-Academic Complex at MIT and Stanford.* New York: Columbia University Press, 1993, p. 10. Eisenhower made this comment in his last presidential press conference, given on 18 January, 1961. See Public Papers of the Presidents: Dwight D. Eisenhower, 1960-61, p. 1045.
14. Leslie. *The Cold War and American Science*, p. 1.
15. Leslie. *The Cold War and American Science*, p. 1.
16. Eugene S. Ferguson. *Engineering and the Mind's Eye.* Cambridge, MA: MIT Press, 1992, p. xii.
17. Peggy A. Kidwell and Paul E. Ceruzzi. *Landmarks in Digital Computing.* Washington, DC: Smithsonian Institution Press, 1994, p. 76.
18. Kidwell and Ceruzzi. *Landmarks in Digital Computing*, p. 81.
19. Kenneth Flamm. *Creating the Computer: Government, Industry, and High Technology.* Washington, DC: The Brookings Institute, 1987, p. 29.
20. The ARPANET was a network of computers and telecommunication systems developed in 1969 by the Department of Defense's Advanced Research Projects Agency, an alliance of research institutions. The agency is still often referred to as ARPA, though its official name is now DARPA, the Defense Advanced Research Project Agency.
21. See Rita H. Skirpan, ed. *Brand Names and Their Companies.* Vol. 1. Detroit: Gale Research Inc. 1994, pp. 199-200.
22. Vaughan. *The Challenger Launch Decision*, p. 202.
23. Vaughan. *The Challenger Launch Decision*, p. 224.
24. Vaughan. *The Challenger Launch Decision*, p. 224.
25. Vaughan. *The Challenger Launch Decision*, p. 123.
26. Committee on Measuring and Improving Infrastructure Performance. *Measuring and Improving Infrastructure Performance.* Washington, DC: National Academy Press, 1995, p. 29.
27. Lewis M. Branscomb. "Product Performance in an Affluent Society." *Product Quality, Performance, and Cost: A Report and Recommendations Based on a Symposium and Workshops Arranged by the National Academy of Engineering.* Washington, DC: National Academy of Engineering, 1972, pp. 26-7.
28. Erika Kress-Rogers. *Handbook of Biosensors and Electronic Noses: Medicine, Food, and the Environment.* Boca Raton, FL: CRC Press, 1997, p. 28.
29. Christos G. Cassandras. *Discrete Event Systems: Modeling and Performance Analysis.* Homewood, IL and Boston, MA: Richard D. Irwin, Inc., and Aksen Associates, Inc., 1993, p. 56.
30. Clement H.C. Leung. *Quantitative Analysis of Computer Systems.* London: John Wiley & Sons, Ltd, 1988, p. xi.
31. Peter J.B. King. *Computer and Communication Systems Performance Modelling.* New York: Prentice Hall, 1990, pp. 1-2.
32. Werner Bux and Harry Rudin. *Performance of Computer-Communication Systems.* Amsterdam: Elsevier Science Publishers, 1984, p. 50.
33. Leung, *Quantitative Analysis of Computer Systems*, p. 3.
34. Committee on Measuring and Improving Infrastructure Performance. *Measuring and Improving Infrastructure Performance*, p. 19.
35. See Vaughan, *The Challenger Launch Decision*, p. 184.
36. Charles H. Sauer and K. Mani Chandy. *Computer Systems Performance Modeling.* Englewood Cliffs, NJ: Prentice-Hall, 1981, p. 5.

37. Ferguson. *Engineering and the Mind's Eye*, p. 194.
38. Ferguson. *Engineering and the Mind's Eye*, p. 171.
39. Branscomb. "Product Performance in an Affluent Society," p. 30.
40. Gunnar A. Hambraeus. Discussion comments. *Product Quality, Performance, and Cost*, p. 103.
41. Robert W. Peach. Discussion comments. *Product Quality, Performance, and Cost*, p. 60.
42. For an excellent and engaging introduction to user-oriented design, see Donald Norman. *The Design of Everyday Things*. New York: Doubleday, 1990 (1988).
43. George H. Stevens and Emily F. Stevens. *Designing Electronic Performance Support Tools: Improving Workplace Performance with Hypertext, Hypermedia, and Multimedia*. Englewood Cliffs, NJ: Educational Technology Publications, 1995, p. 34.
44. Carlos Fallon. Discussion comments. *Product Quality, Performance, and Cost*, p. 20.
45. *Product Quality, Performance, and Cost*, p. 6.
46. Report on Workshop V. "Economic Dimensions of Assuring Product Performance." *Product Quality, Performance, and Cost*, p. 150.
47. Williams. "Titanium Alloys: Production, Behavior and Application," p. 85.
48. Vaughan. *The Challenger Launch Decision*, p. 37. According to Norman, the concept of "satisficing" was introduced by Herbert Simon in *The Sciences of the Artificial*. Cambridge, MA: MIT Press, 1969.
49. Ahmed N. Tantawy. *High Performance Networking: Frontiers and Experience*. Boston, MA: Kluwer Academic Publishers, 1994, p. viii.
50. *Electric Vehicles*, p. 171.
51. R.K. Clark. "Applications of Water-Soluble Polymers as Shale Stabilizers in Drilling Fluids." *Water-Soluble Polymers: Beauty with Performance*. Ed. J.E. Glass. Washington, DC: American Chemical Society, 1986, p.175.
52. Committee on Measuring and Improving Infrastructure Performance. *Measuring and Improving Infrastructure Performance*, p. 5.
53. *Measuring and Improving Infrastructure Performance*, p. 5.
54. *Measuring and Improving Infrastructure Performance*, p. 6.
55. *Measuring and Improving Infrastructure Performance*, p. 6.
56. *Measuring and Improving Infrastructure Performance*, p. 11.
57. *Measuring and Improving Infrastructure Performance*, p. 18.
58. *Measuring and Improving Infrastructure Performance*, p. 18.
59. *Measuring and Improving Infrastructure Performance*, p. 18.
60. *Measuring and Improving Infrastructure Performance*, p. 37.
61. *Measuring and Improving Infrastructure Performance*, p. 18.
62. *Measuring and Improving Infrastructure Performance*, p. 29.
63. *Measuring and Improving Infrastructure Performance*, p. 91.
64. Bruno Latour. *ARAMIS or the Love of Technology*. Trans. Catherine Porter. Cambridge, MA: Harvard University Press, 1996, pp. 23-4.
65. Latour. *ARAMIS*, p. 304.
66. Latour. *ARAMIS*, p. vii.
67. Latour. *ARAMIS*, p. 126.
68. Latour. *ARAMIS*, p. 99.
69. Latour. *ARAMIS*, p. 48.
70. Latour. *ARAMIS*, p. 127.
71. Latour. *ARAMIS*, pp. 24-5.
72. Latour. *ARAMIS*, p. 19.
73. Donald MacKenzie. *Inventing Accuracy: A Historical Sociology of Nuclear Missile Guidance*. Cambridge, MA: MIT Press, 1990, p. 4.
74. See MacKenzie. *Inventing Accuracy*. Appendix A, Table A.1. Accuracy is here defined as "circular error probable" or the "radius of the circle round the target within which 50 percent of warheads would fall in repeated firings" (427).
75. MacKenzie. *Inventing Accuracy*, p. 3.
76. MacKenzie. *Inventing Accuracy*, p. 4.
77. MacKenzie. *Inventing Accuracy*, pp. 386-8.
78. See William J. Fulbright. "The War and Its Effects: The Military-Industrial-Academic Complex." *Super-State: Readings in the Military-Industrial Complex*. Ed. Herbert I. Schiller. Urbana, IL: University of Illinois,1970.
79. Leslie. *The Cold War and American Science*, p. 7.
80. Leslie. *The Cold War and American Science*, p. 11.
81. The term "Big Science" was coined by Alvin Weinberg, past director of the Oak Ridge National Laboratory. See his 1961 article "Impact of Large-Scale Science on the United States." *Science* 134 (1961): pp161–4. See also Crease's discussion of Big Science. *The Play of Nature: Experimentation as Performance*. Bloomington, IN: Indiana University Press, 1993, p. 168.
82. Leslie. *The Cold War and American Science*, p. 9.
83. Glenn O. Blough. "Children, Put Away Your Sputniks." *The Science Teacher* 24, no. 8 (1957): p. 373.
84. Barbara Barksdale Clowse. *Brainpower for the Cold War: The Sputnik Crisis and National Defense Education Act of 1958*. Westport, CN: Greenwood Press, 1981, p. 4.
85. Leslie. *The Cold War and American Science*, p. 2.
86. Brenda Laurel. *Computers as Theatre*. Reading, MA: Addison-Wesley, 1992, p. xvii.
87. Laurel. *Computers as Theatre*, pp. 32-33.
88. Laurel. *Computers as Theatre*, p. 50.
89. Laurel. *Computers as Theatre*, p. 196.
90. See Jon McKenzie, "Virtual Reality: Performance, Immersion, and the Thaw," *TDR: The Drama Review* 38, no.4 (1994): pp. 83–106 and "Laurie Anderson for Dummies." *TDR: The Drama Review* 41, no. 2 (1996): pp. 30–50.

91. Robert P. Crease. *The Play of Nature: Experimentation as Performance.* Bloomington: Indiana University, 1993, p. 105.
92. Crease. *The Play of Nature*, p. 18.
93. Crease. *The Play of Nature*, p. 11.
94. Crease. *The Play of Nature*, p. 95.
95. Crease. *The Play of Nature*, p. 100.
96. See Crease. *The Play of Nature*, p. 85. Crease outlines his philosophical framework in Chapter 3, "Philosophers and Productive Inquiry," where he also draws heavily upon the pragmatism of John Dewey.
97. Crease. *The Play of Nature*, p. 184.
98. Crease. *The Play of Nature*, p. 104.
99. Crease. *The Play of Nature*, p. 108.
100. Crease. *The Play of Nature*, p. 100.
101. See Crease. *The Play of Nature*,pp.181–182. Significantly, Crease cites Artaud's attack on Western theater to make this point.
102. Crease. *The Play of Nature*, pp.171–172.
103. Though it may come as a surprise to some of my colleagues, Performance Studies has been much more explicit in its generalization of performance than has either Performance Management or Techno-Performance. The reasons for this may lie in the fact that Performance Studies is far more theoretically critcal of itself (in the sense that it actively engages the philosophical and historical underpinnings of its discourses and practices) than the other two paradigms. Further, in situating itself as liminal discipline, it paradoxically and with some insistence stakes out its conceptual terrain and field of inquiry in order to self-legitimate this liminality.
104. White. "Servo System Theory," p. 231.
105. White. "Servo System Theory," p. 232.
106. MacKenzie. *Inventing Accuracy*, p. 1. The author's description was written before the Gulf War; no doubt guided missiles have gotten even more accurate since then.
107. Douglas H. Hofstadter. *Gödel, Escher, Bach: An Eternal Golden Braid.* New York: Vintage Books, 1979, p. 10.
108. Hofstadter. *Gödel, Escher, Bach*, p. 691.

4. Challenger Lecture Machine

1. See Wernher Von Braun. *The Mars Project.* Urbana, IL: University of Illinois Press, 1991 (1953). And Dennis R. Jenkins. *The History of Developing the National Space Transportation System: The Beginning Through STS-50.* Melbourne Beach, FL: Broadfield Pub., 1992.
2. Ronald Reagan. *Public Papers of the Presidents of the United States, Ronald Reagan,* 1984: Book I. Washington, DC: US Government Printing Office, pp. 1198-9.
3. Robert T. Hohler. *"I Touch the Future . . .": The Story of Christa McAulliffe.* New York: Random House, 1986, p. 103.
4. McAuliffe, cited by Hohler. *"I Touch the Future . . . "*, p. 171.
5. Presidential Commission on the Space Shuttle Challenger Accident. *Report to the President by the Presidential Commission on the Space Shuttle Challenger Accident: [Rogers Commission].* Washington, DC: The Commission, 1986, p. 104.
6. US Congress, House Committee on Science and Technology. *Investigation of the Challenger Accident: Report.* Washington, DC: Government Printing Office, 1986, p. 4.
7. Howard E. McCurdy. *Inside NASA: High Technology and Organizational Change in the US Space Program.* Baltimore, MD: The Johns Hopkins University Press, 1993, p. 172.
8. Edward R. Tufte. *Visual Explanations: Images and Quantities, Evidence and Narrative.* Cheshire, CT: Graphics Press, 1997, p. 52.
9. Constance Penley. "Spaced Out: Remembering Christa McAuliffe." *Camera Obscura 29* (1992): p195.
10. Elizabeth Radin Simons. "The NASA Joke Cycle: The Astronauts and the Teacher." *Western Folklore 45,* no.4 (1986): p273.
11. Simons. "The NASA Joke Cycle," p. 271.
12. Diane Vaughan. *The Challenger Launch Decision: Risky Technology, Culture, and Deviance at NASA.* Chicago, IL: The University of Chicago Press, 1996. See pp. 78, 154, 194, 279, 334. The works by Geertz which Vaughan cites are *The Interpretation of Cultures: Selected Essays.* New York: Basic Books, 1973; and *Local Knowledge: Further Essays in Interpretive Anthropology.* New York: Basic Books, 1983.
13. Vaughan. *The Challenger Launch Decision*, p. 78.
14. Vaughan. *The Challenger Launch Decision*, p. 95.
15. Vaughan. *The Challenger Launch Decision*, p. 97.
16. Vaughan. *The Challenger Launch Decision*, pp. 394-5.
17. Vaughan. *The Challenger Launch Decision*, p. 400.
18. Vaughan. *The Challenger Launch Decision*, p. 209.
19. Vaughan. *The Challenger Launch Decision*, p. 216.
20. Vaughan. *The Challenger Launch Decision*, p. 65.
21. Vaughan. *The Challenger Launch Decision*, p. 395.
22. See Vaughan. *The Challenger Launch Decision.* Chapter 4, "The Normalization of Deviance, 1981–84."
23. Howard E. McCurdy. *Inside NASA: High Technology and Organizational Change in the US Space Program.* Baltimore, MD: The Johns Hopkins University Press, 1993.
24. See Von Braun, *The Mars Project*, and Jenkins, *History of Developing the National Space Transportation System.*
25. Vaughan. *The Challenger Launch Decision*, p. 19.
26. Vaughan. *The Challenger Launch Decision*, p. 218.

27. Wear, cited by Vaughan. *The Challenger Launch Decision*, pp. 219–20, my emphasis.
28. Vaughan. *The Challenger Launch Decision*, pp. 247, 219.
29. Vaughan. *The Challenger Launch Decision*, p. 248.
30. Vaughan. *The Challenger Launch Decision*, p. 395.
31. Vaughan. *The Challenger Launch Decision*, p. 220.
32. Vaughan. *The Challenger Launch Decision*, p. 218.
33. Vaughan. *The Challenger Launch Decision*, p. 212.
34. Vaughan. *The Challenger Launch Decision*, pp. 377-8.
35. Mulloy, cited by Vaughan. *The Challenger Launch Decision*, p. 6.
36. Vaughan. *The Challenger Launch Decision*, p. xi.
37. Vaughan. *The Challenger Launch Decision*, pp. 396-7.
38. Vaughan. *The Challenger Launch Decision*, p. 72.
39. Vaughan. *The Challenger Launch Decision*, p. 38.
40. Stanislaw Ulam, cited in Douglas H. Hofstadter. *Gödel, Escher, Bach: An Eternal Golden Braid.* New York: Vintage Books, 1979, p. 560.

5. Challenging Forth: The Power of Performance

1. Hans-Georg Gadamer, cited by David Krell in his introduction *to Basic Writings: From Being and Time* (1927) *to The Task of Thinking* (1964). Trans. David Farrell Krell. San Francisco, CA: Harper Collins, 1993 (1977), p.15.
2. Martin Heidegger. *The Question Concerning Technology and Other Essays.* Trans. William Lovitt. New York: Harper & Row, 1977, p. 4.
3. Heidegger. *The Question Concerning Technology*, p. 12.
4. Heidegger. *The Question Concerning Technology*, p. 14.
5. William Lovitt. In Heidegger. *The Question Concerning Technology*, p. 14 n. 13.
6. Heidegger. *The Question Concerning Technology*, p. 15.
7. Heidegger. *The Question Concerning Technology*, p. 134.
8. Heidegger. *The Question Concerning Technology*, p. 133.
9. Heidegger. *The Question Concerning Technology*, p. 133.
10. Heidegger. *The Question Concerning Technology*, p. 19.
11. Heidegger. *The Question Concerning Technology*, p. 26.
12. Heidegger. *The Question Concerning Technology*, p. 27.
13. Heidegger. *The Question Concerning Technology*, p. 28.
14. Heidegger. *The Question Concerning Technology*, p. 33.
15. Heidegger. *The Question Concerning Technology*, p. 34.
16. Heidegger. *The Question Concerning Technology*, p. 35.
17. Herbert Marcuse. *Eros and Civilization: A Philosophical Inquiry into Freud.* New York: Vintage Books, 1961(1955), pp. 40-1.
18. See *One-Dimensional Man: Studies in the Ideology of Advanced Industrial Society.* Boston, MA: Beacon Press, 1964. It opens thus: "A comfortable, smooth, reasonable, democratic unfreedom prevails in advanced industrial civilization, a token of technical progress. Indeed, what could be more rational than the suppression of individuality in the mechanization of socially necessary but painful performances. . . . " (1).
19. Marcuse. *Eros and Civilization*, p. 41.
20. Marcuse. *Eros and Civilization*, p. 41.
21. Herbert Marcuse. "Some Social Implications of Modern Technology." *The Essential Frankfurt School Reader.* Ed. Andrew Arato and Eike Gebhardt. New York: Continuum, 1988 (1941), p. 139.
22. Marcuse. "Some Social Implications," p. 145.
23. Marcuse. "Some Social Implications," p. 155.
24. Marcuse. "Some Social Implications," p. 151.
25. Marcuse. "Some Social Implications," p. 142.
26. Jean-François Lyotard. *The Postmodern Condition: A Report on Knowledge.* Trans. Geoff Bennington and Brian Massumi. Minneapolis, MN: University of Minnesota Press, 1979, p. 3.
27. Lyotard. *The Postmodern Condition*, pp. 8-9.
28. Lyotard. *The Postmodern Condition*, p. xxiv, my emphasis.
29. Lyotard. *The Postmodern Condition*, p. xxiv.
30. Lyotard. *The Postmodern Condition*, p. xxiii.
31. Lyotard. *The Postmodern Condition*, p. xxiv.
32. Lyotard. *The Postmodern Condition*, p. 47.
33. Lyotard. *The Postmodern Condition*, p. 50.
34. Lyotard. *The Postmodern Condition*, p. 37.
35. See Nick Kaye. *Postmodernism and Performance.* New York: St. Martin's Press, 1994, pp.17-20. Marvin Carlson. *Performance: A Critical Introduction.* London: Routledge, 1996, p.138.
36. See Lyotard's section on paralogical legitimation, pp. 60-7. Lyotard actually discusses four modes of legitimation in *The Postmodern Condition*: those of petites narratives (dominant in premodern societies), grand narratives (dominant in modern societies), performativity (dominant in postmodern societies), and paralogy (the incessant and often paradoxical questioning of metaprescriptives which Lyotard hopes can counter performativity).
38. Judith Butler. "Performative Acts and Gender Constitution: An Essay in Phenomenology and Feminist Theory." *Performing Feminisms: Feminist Critical Theory and Theatre.* Ed. Sue-Ellen Case. Baltimore, MD: The Johns Hopkins University Press, 1990, p. 272.
39. Butler. "Performative Acts and Gender Constitution," p. 273.
40. Butler. "Performative Acts and Gender Constitution," p. 274.

41. Butler. "Performative Acts and Gender Constitution," p. 277. Another version of this essay appears in *Gender Trouble*. There the reference to Turner is down-shifted from the text to a footnote.
42. In his essay, "Acting in Everyday Life and Everyday Life in Acting," Turner writes: "Ritual in [Central African] societies is seldom the rigid, obsessional behavior we think of as ritual after Freud." See *From Ritual to Theater: The Human Seriousness of Play*, New York: PAJ Pulications, 1982, p. 109.
43. Butler. "Performative Acts and Gender Constitution," p. 278.
44. Butler. "Performative Acts and Gender Constitution," p. 278. A footnote placed at the citation of Schechner's text directs the reader to "See especially, 'News, Sex, and Performance,' 295-324." Performing the role of scholarly drag, I make this correction: the title is "News, Sex, and Performance Theory."
45. Butler. "Performative Acts and Gender Constitution," p. 278.
46. Judith Butler. *Gender Trouble: Feminism and the Subversion of Identity*. London: Routledge, 1990, p. 145.
47. Butler. *Gender Trouble*, p. 148.
48. Judith Butler. "Critically Queer." *Gay and Lesbian Quarterly* 1 (1993): p17.
49. Butler. "Critically Queer," p. 21.
50. Butler. "Critically Queer," p. 21.
51. Butler. "Critically Queer," p. 21.
52. Butler. "Critically Queer," p. 24.
53. Judith Butler. *Bodies That Matter: On the Discursive Limits of "Sex."* London: Routledge, 1993, p. 231.
54. Lyotard. *The Postmodern Condition*, p. 88 n. 30. Marcuse, too, is critical of Austin's theory of language, as well as Wittgenstein's. See *One-Dimensional Man*, ch. 7.

6. Professor Challenger and the Performance Stratum

1. Gilles Deleuze and Félix Guattari. *A Thousand Plateaus: Capitalism and Schizophrenia, Vol. II*. Trans. Brian Massumi. Minneapolis, MN: University of Minnesota, 1987, p. 40.
2. Deleuze and Guattari. *A Thousand Plateaus*, p. 40.
3. A dramaturgical note: Conan Doyle's science fiction tales have recently been republished in *The Lost World & The Poison Belt: Professor Challenger Adventures*. And *When the World Screamed and Other Stories. Vol. II of Professor Challenger Adventures*. As for the more famous dick, Latour explicitly casts his scientifictional Professor Norbert H. in *ARAMIS* as a detective figure à la Sherlock Holmes. Significantly, one of the texts Professor H. assigns to his engineering protégé is Deleuze and Guattari's *A Thousand Plateaus*.
4. Deleuze and Guattari. *A Thousand Plateaus*, p. 40.
5. Deleuze and Guattari. *A Thousand Plateaus*, p. 40.
6. Deleuze and Guattari. *A Thousand Plateaus*, p. 60.
7. Deleuze and Guattari. *A Thousand Plateaus*, p. 66.
8. Gilles Deleuze. *Foucault*. Trans. Seán Hand. Minneapolis, MN: University of Minnesota Press, 1988, p.47.
9. Michel Foucault. *Discipline and Punish: The Birth of the Prison*. Trans. Alan Sheridan. New York: Vintage Books, 1979, p. 301.
10. Foucault. *Discipline and Punish*, p. 302.
11. Foucault. *Discipline and Punish*, p. 308.
12. Gilles Deleuze. "Postscript on the Societies of Control." *October* 59 (1992): p3.
13. Deleuze. *Foucault*, p. 48.
14. Deleuze. *Foucault*, p. 64.
15. Deleuze. *Foucault*, p. 66.
16. Deleuze. *Foucault*, p. 67.
17. Deleuze. *Foucault*, p. 77.
18. Deleuze. *Foucault*, p. 85.
19. Deleuze. *Foucault*, p. 28.
20. Deleuze. *Foucault*, p. 29.
21. Donna Haraway. *Simians, Cyborgs, and Women: The Reinvention of Nature*. New York: Routledge, 1991, p. 155.
22. AOL stands for America Online. In 1996 AOL, Mitsui & Co., Ltd. (one of the world's largest trading companies), and Nihon Keizai Shimbun, Inc. (a large Japanese financial publishing firm better known as "Nikkei") formed AOL-Japan to serve Japan's growing Internet market.
23. David Harvey. *The Condition of Postmodernity*. Cambridge, MA: Blackwell, 1990, p. 164.
24. See Scott Lash and John Urry. *The End of Organized Capitalism*. Madison, WI: University of Wisconsin Press, 1987.
25. Deleuze. "Postscript on the Societies of Control," p. 6.
26. See especially Derrida's reading of Lévi-Strauss in *Of Grammatology*. Trans. Gayatri Chakravorty Spivak. Baltimore, MD: The Johns Hopkins University Press, 1974; and Ulmer's exploration of hieroglyphic "Riting" in *Applied Grammatology*. Baltimore, MD: The Johns Hopkins University Press, 1985.
27. Eric Hobsbawm, *The Age of Extremes: A History of the World, 1914-1991*. New York: Vintage Books, 1996, p. 295. Hobsbawm writes that even "the academically most conservative countries—Britain and Switzerland—had risen to 1.5 per cent. Moreover, some of the relatively largest student bodies were to be found in economically far from advanced countries: Ecuador (3.2 per cent), the Philippines (2.7 per cent) or Peru (2 per cent)," p. 295.
28. Lyotard. *The Postmodern Condition*, p. 50.
29. Deleuze. "Postscript on the Societies of Control," p. 5.
30. Obviously, the circulation of disciplinary discourses and practices occurs more rapidly in comparison with that found in sovereign societies, and more rapidly still when compared to other premodern strata. But the circulation of words and acts on all these strata is "slow" in relation to that of the performance stratum.
31. Friedrich A Kittler. *Discourse Networks, 1800/1900*. Trans. Michael Metteer with Chris Cullens. Stanford, CA: Stanford University Press, 1990, p. 369.

32. Richard Schechner. *Between Theater and Anthropology.* Philadelphia: University of Pennsylvania Press, 1985, p. 78.
33. Deleuze. "Postscript on the Societies of Control," p. 4.
34. William Bogard. *The Simulation of Surveillance: Hyper-control in Telematic Societies.* New York: Cambridge University Press, 1996, p. 182.
35. Bogard. *The Simulation of Surveillance*, p. 19.

7. Professor Challenger and the Disintegration Machine

1. Arthur Conan Doyle. *When the World Screamed and Other Stories. Vol. II of Professor Challenger Adventures.* San Francisco, CA: Chronicle Books, 1990, p. 24.
2. Doyle. *When the World Screamed,* p. 9.
3. Doyle. *When the World Screamed,* p. 19.
4. Doyle. *When the World Screamed,* p. 10.
5. Doyle. *When the World Screamed,* pp. 24–5.
6. Gilles Deleuze and Félix Guattari. *A Thousand Plateaus: Capitalism and Schizophrenia, Vol. II.* Trans. Brian Massumi. Minneapolis, MN: University of Minnesota, 1987, p. 43.
7. Gilles Deleuze, and Félix Guattari. "Balance Sheet Program for Desiring Machines." Trans. Robert Hurley. In Félix Guattari. *Chaosophy.* Ed. Sylvère Lotringer. New York: Semiotext(e), 1995, pp. 120–1.
8. Manuel De Landa. *A Thousand Years of Nonlinear History.* New York: Zone Books, 1997, p. 21.
9. Deleuze and Guattari. "Balance-Sheet Program for Desiring Machines," p. 121.
10. Félix Guattari. "Regimes, Pathways, Subjects." Trans. Brian Massumi. *Incorporations: Zone* 6 (1992): p129.
11. Deleuze and Guattari. *A Thousand Plateaus*, pp. 42-3. The approach to reading described here finds resonance with Deleuze's description of his own early philosophical research, cited in the translator's introduction. "What got me by during that period was conceiving of the history of philosophy as a kind of ass-fuck, or, what am an author from behind and giving him a child that would indeed be his but would nonetheless be monstrous," p. x.
12. Deleuze and Guattari. *A Thousand Plateaus,* p. 46.
13. Gilles Deleuze. *Foucault.* Trans. Seán Hand. Minneapolis, MN: University of Minnesota Press, 1988, pp. 120-1.
14. Deleuze and Guattari. *A Thousand Plateaus,* p. 40.
15. Niklas Luhmann. *Social Systems.* Trans. John Bednarz, Jr., with Dirk Baecker. Stanford, CA: Stanford University Press, 1995, p. 9.
16. Douglas H. Hofstadter. *Gödel, Escher, Bach: An Eternal Golden Braid.* New York: Vintage Books, 1979, pp. 470-1.
17. In a similar vein, Derrida writes that "the death agony of metalanguage is structurally interminable. But as effort and as effect. Metalanguage is the life of language: it alway flutters like a bird caught in a subtle lime *[glu]*." *Glas.* Trans. John P. Leavey, Jr., and Richard Rand. Lincoln, NE: University of Nebraska Press, 1986, p.130bi.
18. Félix Guattari. *Chaosmosis: an Ethico-Aesthetic Paradigm.* Trans. Paul Bains and Julian Pefanis. Bloomington, IN: Indiana University Press, 1995, p. 37.
19. Deleuze. *Foucault*, p. 85.
20. Friedrich Nietzsche. "On the Advantage and Disadvantage of History for Life." Trans. Peter Preuss. Indianapolis, IN: Hackett Publishing Company, Inc., 1980, p. 40.
21. Friedrich Nietzsche. *Ecce Homo: How One Becomes What One Is.* Trans. R.J. Hollingdale. London: Penguin Books, 1979, p. 126.
22. Nietzsche. *Ecce Homo*, p. 78.
23. Herbert Marcuse. *Eros and Civilization: A Philosophical Inquiry into Freud.* New York: Vintage Books, 1961 (1955), p. 32.
24. Marcuse. *Eros and Civilization*, p. 35.
25. Sigmund Freud. "The Most Prevalent Form of Degradation in Erotic Life."*Collective Papers* Vol. IV. London: Hogarth Press, 1950, p. 215.
26. Marcuse. *Eros and Civilization,* pp. 35-6.
27. Doyle. *When the World Screamed*, p. 40.
28. Doyle. *When the World Screamed*, p. 37.

8. The Catachristening of HMS *Challenger*

1. R. H. Bradbury. "Oceans Simple, Ocean Complex." Distinguished Lecture to open the Oceanology International 99 Conference in Singapore on 27 April 1999. <http://www.brs.gov.au/overview/bradbury/oceansimple.html>.
2. Erik Linklater. *The Voyage of the Challenger.* Garden City, NY: Doubleday, 1972, p. 15.
3. Linklater. *The Voyage of the Challenger*, p. 16. Great Britain. Challenger Office. *Report on the Scientific Results of the Voyage of HMS Challenger during the years 1873–76 under the Command of Captain George S. Nares . . . and the late Captain Frank Tourle Thomson, RN. Prepared under the superintendence of the late Sir C. Wyville Thomson . . . and now of John Murray . . . Published by order of Her Majesty's Government.* Edinburgh: HM Stationery Office, 1880–95.
4. From the depths of these notes, let us bring to the surface yet another challenger, an earlier British exploratory ship that sank off the coast of Chile in 1835. The crew of this HMS *Challenger* made it safely to land, where they encamped for seven weeks before being rescued. See G.A. Rothery. *A Diary of the Wreck of His Majesty's Ship Challenger, on the Western Coast of South America, in May, 1835: With an Account of the Subsequent Encampment of the Officers and Crew during a Period of Seven Weeks on the South Coast of Chile.* London: Longman, Rees, Orme, Brown, Green & Longman, 1836.

5. Gilles Deleuze and Félix Guattari. *A Thousand Plateaus: Capitalism and Schizophrenia, Vol. II.* Trans. Brian Massumi. Minneapolis, MN: University of Minnesota, 1987, pp. 75-6.
6. Deleuze and Guattari. *A Thousand Plateaus,* p. 76.
7. J.L. Austin. *How to Do Things with Words.* Ed. J.O. Urmson and Marina Sbisà. Cambridge, MA: Harvard University Press, 1962, p. 148.
8. Deleuze and Guattari. *A Thousand Plateaus,* p. 78.
9. Deleuze and Guattari. *A Thousand Plateaus,* pp. 88, 86.
10. Judith Butler. *Bodies That Matter: On the Discursive Limits of "Sex."* London: Routledge, 1993, p. 223.
11. Butler. *Bodies That Matter,* p. 228, my emphasis.
12. Butler. *Bodies That Matter,* p. 217.
13. Butler. *Bodies That Matter,* p. 217.
14. Butler. *Bodies That Matter,* pp. 217-18.
15. Jacques Derrida. "The Law of Genre." Trans. Avital Ronell. *Glyph 7* (1980): p213.
16. Jacques Derrida. *Glas.* Trans. John P. Leavey, Jr. and Richard Rand. Lincoln, NE: University of Nebraska Press, 1986, p. 2bi.
17. See Derrida. *Glas,* p. 65b. For extended analyses of Derrida's use of signature effects in *Glas,* see John P. Leavey, Jr. and Gregory L. Ulmer's essays in Leavey's *Glassary.* Derrida's *Signéponge = Signsponge* out lines a poetics of the signature of poet Francis Ponge.
18. In Doyle's short story "The Poison Belt," Challenger prepares for the world's catastrophic end, as it has swum into a belt of deadly interplanetary ether, an event the professor is first to fathom. As the following scene reveals, Challenger has in his employment a loyal butler, and this butler is named "Austin."

> . . . Each breath we breathed was charged with strange forces. And yet our minds were happy and at ease. Presently Austin laid the cigarettes upon the table and was about to withdraw.
> "Austin!" said his master.
> "Yes, sir?"
> "I thank you for your faithful service."
> A smile stole over the servant's gnarled face.
> "I've done my duty, sir."
> "I'm expecting the end of the world today, Austin."
> "Yes, sir. What time, sir?"
> "I can't say, Austin. Before evening."
> "Very good, sir."
> The taciturn Austin saluted and withdrew. Challenger lit a cigarette, and, drawing his chair closer to his wife's, he took her hand in his.

(Doyle. *The Lost World and The Poison Belt: Professor Challenger Adventures.* San Francisco, CA: Chronicle Books, 1989, p. 205)

19. Deleuze and Guattari. *A Thousand Plateaus,* p. 87.
20. Joseph Roach. "Culture and Performance in the Circum-Atlantic World." *Performativity and Performance.* Ed. Andrew Parker and Eve Kosofsky Sedgwick. London: Routledge, 1995, p. 60.
21. Roach. "Culture and Performance," pp. 58, 59.
22. Roach. "Culture and Performance," p. 58.
23. Rebecca Schneider. *The Explicit Body in Performance.* London: Routledge, 1997, p. 172.
24. Richard Schechner. *Between Theater and Anthropology.* Philadelphia, PA: University of Pennsylvania Press, 1985, p. 36.
25. Schechner. *Between Theater and Anthropology,* p. 35, my emphasis.
26. Jacques Derrida. "Signature, Event, Context." *Margins of Philosophy.* Trans. Alan Bass. Chicago: University of Chicago Press, 1982, p. 320. My emphasis on "even before . . . semiolinguistic | communication."
27. Schechner. *Between Theater and Anthropology,* p. 35.
28. Richard Schechner. *Performance Theory: Revised and Expanded.* London: Routledge,1988, pp. 227-8.
29. Deleuze and Guattari. *A Thousand Plateaus,* p. 10.
30. Deleuze and Guattari. *A Thousand Plateaus,* p. 10.
31. See "1914: One or Several Wolves," the second plateau of *A Thousand Plateaus,* and "An Exaggerated Oedipus," the second chapter of *Kafka: Toward a Minor Literature.* Trans. Dana Polan. Minneapolis, MN: University of Minnesota Press, 1986.
32. Linda Montano. "The Chicken Show." *Art in Everyday Life.* Los Angeles, CA: Astro Artz/Station Hill Press, 1981, n.p.
33. Montano. *Art in Everyday Life,* n.p.
34. Reproduced in Montano. "Interview with Lester Ingber." *Art in Everyday Life,* n.p.
35. Montano. "Interview with Lester Ingber." *Art in Everyday Life,* n.p.
36. Gilles Deleuze. *Nietzsche and Philosophy.* Trans. Hugh Tomlinson. New York: Columbia University Press, 1983, p. 24.
37. Deleuze and Guattari. *A Thousand Plateaus,* p. 57.
38. Deleuze and Guattari. *A Thousand Plateaus,* p. 64.
39. Deleuze and Guattari. *A Thousand Plateaus,* p. 72.

9. Professor Rutherford and Gay Sci Fi

1. Arthur Conan Doyle. *Memories and Adventures.* Boston: Little, Brown, & Company, 1924, p. 23.

2. Doyle. *Memories and Adventures*, p. 23.
3. Stewart Richards. "Conan Doyle's 'Challenger' Unchampioned: William Rutherford, F.R.S. (1839-99), and the Origins of Practical Physiology in Britain." *Notes and Records of the Royal Society of London* 40, no. 2 (1986): p215 n. 60.
4. Richards. "Conan Doyle's 'Challenger' Unchampioned," p. 194.
5. Richards. "Conan Doyle's 'Challenger' Unchampioned," p. 215 n. 65.
6. Richards. "Conan Doyle's 'Challenger' Unchampioned," p. 209.
7. Gilles Deleuze and Félix Guattari. *Kafka: Toward a Minor Literature*. Trans. Dana Polan. Minneapolis, MN: University of Minnesota, 1986. See pp. 16-18.
8. Gilles Deleuze and Félix Guattari. *A Thousand Plateaus: Capitalism and Schizophrenia*, Vol. II. Trans. Brian Massumi. Minneapolis, MN: University of Minnesota, 1987, pp. 361-2.
9. Deleuze and Guattari might disagree here: they tend to see all becoming as minor, and thus, there is no major becoming. Other readers of their works, however, have usefully explored normative processes in terms of becoming. Camilla Griggers, for instance, refunctions their notion of an active, affirmative "becoming-woman" in order to explore the reactive construction of women within contemporary medical, military, and cultural contexts. See her *Becoming-Woman*. Minneapolis, MN: University of Minnesota Press, 1987. In *The Gay Science*, Nietzsche writes that the "desire for destruction, change, and becoming can be an expression of an overflowing energy that is pregnant with future (my term for this is, as is known, 'Dionysian'); but it can also be the hatred of the ill-constituted, disinherited, and underprivileged, who destroy, must destroy, because what exists, indeed all existence, all being, outrages and provokes them." Friedrich Nietzche. *The Gay Science*. Trans. Walter Kaufmann. New York: Vintage Books, 1974, p. 329. For us, major becoming begins and ends with being, while in minor becoming being is produced as a secondary effect.
10. Charles Higham. *The Adventures of Conan Doyle: The Life of the Creator of Sherlock Holmes*. New York: W.W. Norton & Company, 1976, p. 237.
11. Gilles Deleuze and Félix Guattari. "Balance Sheet Program for Desiring Machines." Trans. Robert Hurley. In Félix Guattari. *Chaosophy*. Ed. Sylvère Lotringer. New York: Semiotext(e), 1995, pp. 135.
12. Deleuze and Guattari. "Balance Sheet Program," pp. 137-8.
13. Deleuze and Guattari. "Balance Sheet Program," pp. 137-8, 144.
14. Nietzsche. *The Gay Science*, p. 257.
15. Nietzsche. *The Gay Science*, p. 86.
16. Susan Stewart. *Nonsense: Aspects of Intertextuality in Folklore and Literature*. Baltimore, MD: The Johns Hopkins University Press, 1978, pp. 205-6.
17. Nietzsche. *The Gay Science*, p. 74.
18. Craig J. Saper. *Artificial Mythologies: A Guide to Cultural Invention*. Minneapolis, MN: University of Minnesota Press, 1997, p. 11.
19. Jacques Derrida. "Ulysses Gramophone: Hear Say Yes in Joyce." Trans. Tina Kendall and Shari Benstock. *Acts of Literature*. Ed. Derek Attridge. London: Routledge, 1992, pp. 292-3.
20. Derrida. "Ulysses Gramophone," p. 294.
21. Derrida. "Ulysses Gramophone," p. 298.
22. Derrida. "Ulysses Gramophone," p. 299.
23. Derrida. "Ulysses Gramophone," p. 300.
24. Gregory Ulmer. "The Puncept in Grammatology,"*On Puns: The Foundations of Letters*. Ed. Jonathan Culler. Oxford: Basil Blackwell, 1988, p. 164.
25. Ulmer. "The Puncept in Grammatology." p. 166. See also Ulmer's discussion of the "ol-factory" in *Applied Grammatology*. Baltimore, MD: The Johns Hopkins University Press,1985.
26. Walter Kaufmann. "Translator's Introduction." In Nietzsche. *The Gay Science*, pp. 4-5.
27. Kaufmann. "Translator's Introduction." Nietzsche. *The Gay Science*, p. 5.
28. Judith Butler. *Gender Trouble: Feminism and the Subversion of Identity*. New York: Routledge, 1990, p. 25. The Nietzsche citation can be found in Walter Kaufmann's translation of *The Genealogy of Morals* (New York: Vintage books, 1967), p. 45.
29. Lisa Duggan and Kathleen McHugh. "A Fem(me)nist Manifesto." *Women & Performance* 8, no. 2 (1996): p157.
30. Avital Ronell. "The Test Drive." *Deconstruction is/in America: A New Sense of the Political*. Ed. Anselm Haverkamp. New York: New York University Press, 1995, p. 201.
31. Ronell. "The Test Drive," p. 201.
32. Ronell. "The Test Drive," p. 201.
33. Ronell. "The Test Drive," p. 206.
34. Ronell. "The Test Drive," p. 206.
35. Gregory L. Ulmer. *Heuretics: The Logic of Invention*. Baltimore, MD: The Johns Hopkins University Press, 1994, p. 48.
36. As some readers might have already surmised, this is one of the crypto-missions launched at the initiation of this text.
37. Critical Art Ensemble. *Electronic Civil Disobedience and Other Unpopular Ideas*. Brooklyn, NY: Autonomedia, 1996, pp. 23, 25.
38. Richards. "Conan Doyle's 'Challenger' Unchampioned," p. 194.
39. Deleuze and Guattari. *A Thousand Plateaus*, pp. 150, 160.
40. Deleuze and Guattari. *A Thousand Plateaus*, pp. 333-4.
41. David Farrell Krell. "General Introduction: The Question of Being." *Basic Writings: From Being and Time (1927) to The Task of Thinking (1964)*. Trans. David Farrell Krell. San Francisco, CA: Harper Collins, 1993 (1977), p. 26.
42. Heidegger cited in Avital Ronell. *The Telephone Book: Technology, Schizophrenia, Electric Speech*. Lincoln, NE: University of Nebraska Press, 1989, p. 29.
43. Ronell. *The Telephone Book*, p. 19.

44. Jacques Derrida. *Of Spirit: Heidegger and The Question.* Trans. Geoffrey Bennington and Rachel Bowlby. Chicago: University of Chicago Press, 1991, p. 40.
45. Heidegger, cited in Derrida. *Of Spirit*, p. 34. Following Derrida's suggestion, this translation is slightly modified.
46. Derrida. *Of Spirit*, p. 32.
47. Jacques Derrida. "No Apocalypse, Not Now (full speed ahead, seven missiles, seven missives)." Trans. Catherine Porter and Philip Lewis. *Diacritics* 14, no. 2 (1984): p. 29.
48. Dennis R. Jenkins. *The History of Developing the National Space Transportation System: The Beginning through STS-50.* Melbourne Beach, FL: Broadfield Pub., 1992, p. 2.
49. According to Jenkins, Stalin learned of Sänger and Bredt's research and after the war unsuccessfully sought to kidnap the scientists to the Soviet Union.
50. I would like to thank Jon Erickson and Kate Hammer for helping me to articulate this possibility during a conversation in Aberystwyth, Wales.
51. Deleuze and Guattari. *A Thousand Plateaus*, p. 161.
52. Deleuze and Guattari. *A Thousand Plateaus*, p. 334.
53. Jacques Derrida. *Dissemination.* Trans. Barbara Johnson. Chicago, IL: University of Chicago Press, 1981, p.142.
54. Ronell. "The Test Drive," pp. 216, 214.
55. Mary M. Cerullo. *Lobsters: Gangsters of the Sea.* New York: Cobblehill Books, 1994, pp. 28, 30.
56. Richard S. Lewis. *Challenger: The Final Voyage.* New York: Columbia University Press,1988, pp. 10-11.

10. Jane Challenger, Disastronaut

1. Márcio Souza. *Lost World II: The End of the Third World.* Trans. Lana Santamaria. New York: Avon Books, 1990, p. 35.
2. Souza. *Lost World II*, p. 73.
3. Souza. *Lost World II*, p. 71.
4. Souza. *Lost World II*, pp. 18, 19.
5. Souza. *Lost World II*, p. 23.
6. Souza. *Lost World II*, pp. 27, 28.
7. Souza. *Lost World II*, p. 71.
8. Souza. *Lost World II*, p. 125.
9. Souza. *Lost World II*, p. 93.
10. Souza. *Lost World II*, p. 71.
11. Souza. *Lost World II*, p. 9.
12. Noam Chomsky. *Profits over People: Neoliberalism and Global Order.* New York: Seven Stories Press, 1999, p. 39.
13. Jacques Derrida. *The Archeology of the Frivolous: Reading Condillac.* Trans. John P. Leavey, Jr. Pittsburgh: Duquesne University Press, 1980, p. 48. As the subtitle indicates, the text is a reading of Etienne Bonnot de Condillac, one that engages Foucault's reading of this eighteenth-century French empiricist, the first to translate Locke into French.
14. Critical Art Ensemble. *The Electronic Disturbance.* Brooklyn, NY: Autonomedia, 1994, p. 117.
15. See Johannes Fabian. *Time and the Other: How Anthropology Makes Its Object.* New York: Columbia University Press, 1983.
16. Souza. *Lost World II*, p. 242.
17. Souza. *Lost World II*, p. 243.
18. Souza. *Lost World II*, p. 244.
19. Souza. *Lost World II*, p. 245.
20. Souza. *Lost World II*, p. 244.
21. Souza. *Lost World II*, p. 246.
22. Souza. *Lost World II*, pp. 199, 191.
23. Maurice Blanchot. *The Writing of the Disaster.* Trans. Ann Smock. Lincoln, NE: University of Nebraska Press, 1986, p. 1.
24. Blanchot. *The Writing of the Disaster*, p. 42.
25. Souza. *Lost World II*, p. 134.
26. Manuel De Landa. *A Thousand Years of Nonlinear History.* New York: Zone Books, 1997, p. 266.
27. Souza. *Lost World II*, pp. 134-135.
28. Eric Hobsbawm. *The Age of Extremes: A History of the World, 1914-1991.* New York: Vintage Books, 1996, p. 567.
29. Friedrich Nietzsche. *The Gay Science.* Trans. Walter Kaufmann. New York: Vintage Books, 1974, p. 342.
30. Nietzsche. *The Gay Science*, p. 344. On the ebb and flow of Nietzsche and the sea, see Jacques Derrida. *Spurs: Nietzche's Styles.* Trans. Barbara Harlow. Chicago, IL: University of Chicago Press, 1978; and Luce Irigaray. *Marine Lover of Friedrich Nietzsche.* Trans. Gillian C. Gill. New York: Columbia University Press, 1991.
31. Nietzsche. *The Gay Science*, p. 302. "Good performance" is Kaufmann's translation of the term "guten Spiel," which could also be read as "good acting" or "good playing." Given Nietzsche's own play on theatrical and occupational roles, Kaufmann's 1974 reading of Spiel as "performance" is both timely and untimely.
32. Nietzsche. *The Gay Science*, p. 303.
33. Nietzsche. *The Gay Science*, pp. 302–3.
34. Nietzsche's comment on women is "Dass sie 'sich geben,' selbst noch, wenn sie—sich geben," which Kaufmann rephrases literally as "they 'give themselves' (that is, act or play a part) even when they—give themselves." *The Gay Science*, pp. 316-17.
35. Nietzsche. *The Gay Science*, p. 303.

36. Friedrich Nietzsche. *Ecce Homo: How One Becomes What One Is.* Trans. R.J. Hollingdale. London: Penguin Books, 1979, p. 130.
37. Nietzsche. *Ecce Homo.* pp. 126-7.
38. See Nietzsche. "On the Future of Our Educational Institutions." Trans. J.M. Kennedy. *The Complete Works of Friedrich Nietzsche.* Vol. 3. Ed. Oscar Levy. New York: Russell & Russell, 1964. Derrida comments on reading these lectures: "One must allow for the 'genre' whose code is constantly re-marked, for narrative and fictional form and the 'indirect style.' In short, one must allow for all the ways intent ironizes or demarcates itself, demarcating the text by leaving on it the mark of genre. These lectures, given by an academic to academics and students on the subject of studies in the university and secondary schools, amount to a theatrical infraction of the laws of genre and academicism. For lack of time, I will not analyze these traits in themselves. However, we should not ignore the invitation extended to us in the Preface to the lectures where we are asked to read slowly, like anachronistic readers who escape the law of their time by taking time to read—all the time it takes, without saying 'for lack of time' as I have just done." Jacques Derrida. "Otobiographies: The Teaching of Nietzsche and the Politics of the Proper Name." Trans. Avital Ronell. *The Ear of the Other.* Lincoln, NE: University of Nebraska Press, 1988, p. 26.
39. In his essay "Friedrich Nichte," Laurence A. Rickels explores the network of "Nietzsche," Nichte (niece), and nihilism, or the will to Nicht (not). See Rickels, ed. *Looking After Nietzsche.* Albany, NY: State University of New York Press, 1990. For his part, Ulmer contends that " 'Nietzsche is the homonym of the other one, Nietzsche—the relation of living or dead persons to their names is that of the pun." "The Puncept in Grammatology." *On Puns: The Foundations of Letters.* Ed. Jonathan Culler. Oxford: Basil Blackwell, 1988, p. 167.
40. Derrida. "Otobiographies," p. 31.
41. If it is a promise at all, for in *The Genealogy of Morals*, Nietzsche also questioned Man as a promise-making animal. Friedrich Nietzsche. *The Birth of Tragedy and The Genealogy of Morals.* Trans. Francis Golffing. Garden City, NY: Doubleday, 1956, pp. 189–90.
42. Gilles Deleuze. *Foucault.* Trans. Seán Hand. Minneapolis, MN: University of Minnesota Press, 1988, p.130.
43. Deleuze. *Foucault*, p. 131.
44. Deleuze. *Foucault*, p. 132.
45. For a critique of the opposition between live and mediatized bodies, see Philip Auslander's *Liveness: Performance in a Mediatized Culture.* London: Routledge, 1999.
46. See Kittler. "The Mechanized Philosopher." *Looking After Nietzsche.* Ed. Laurence A. Rickels. Albany, NY: State University of New York Press, 1990, pp. 195-207.
47. Nietzsche, "The Wanderer and his Shadow." *In Human, All Too Human.* Trans. R.J. Hollingdale. Cambridge: Cambridge University Press, p. 378.
48. Letter from Foucault to Klossowski, cited by Daniel W. Smith in the preface to his translation of Pierre Klossowski's *Nietzsche and the Vicious Circle.* Trans. Daniel W. Smith. Chicago, IL: University of Chicago Press, 1997, p. vii. Foucault's 1969 letter was published in 1985 in *Cahiers pour un temps.*
49. Klossowski. *Nietzsche and the Vicious Circle*, p. 171.
50. Martin Heidegger. *On the Way to Language.* Trans. Peter D. Hertz. New York: Harper & Row, 1971, p. 62.
51. In *The Truth in Painting*, Derrida makes this challenge, "just try to frame a perfume". Trans. Geoff Bennington and Ian McLeod. Chicago, IL: University of Chicago Press, 1987, p. 82.
52. Richard S. Lewis. *Challenger: The Final Voyage.* New York: Columbia Universiy Press, 1988, pp. 10–11.
53. Souza. *Lost World II*, p. 147.
54. Deleuze and Guattari. *A Thousand Plateaus*, p. 51.
55. Waldo L. Schmitt. *Crustaceans.* Ann Arbor, MI: University of Michigan, 1965, p. 37.
56. Elizabeth Radin Simons. "The NASA Joke Cycle: The Astronauts and the Teacher." *Western Folklore* 45, no. 4 (1986): p. 273.
57. Deleuze and Guattari. *A Thousand Plateaus*, p. 53.
58. Lewis. *Challenger.*
59. Though certain pronouns have been changed here, as well as one number, this last citation launches itself from Arthur Conan Doyle's "The Disintegration Machine." Another launching of sorts occurs near the end of "When the World Screamed." Shaken loose from its frame down a deep black hole, the Professor's boring bit hits its mark. Suddenly, "Nature all blended into one hideous shriek. For a full minute it lasted, a thousand sirens in one, paralyzing all the great multitude, with its fierce insistence, and floating away through the still summer air until it went echoing along the whole south coast and even reached our French neighbors across the Channel. No sound in history has ever equalled the cry of the injured Earth. [. . .] Then came the geyser. It was an enormous spout of vile treacly substance of the consistence of tar, which shot up into the air to a height which has been computed at two thousand feet. An inquisitive aeroplane, which had been hovering over the scene, was picked off as by an Archie and made a forced landing, man and machine buried in filth. The horrible stuff, which had a most penetrating and nauseous odor, may have represented the life blood of the planet, or it may be, as Professor Driesinger and the Berlin School maintain, that it is a protective secretion, analogous to that of the skunk, which Nature has provided to defend Mother Earth from intrusive Challengers" (p. 26).

BIBLIOGRAPHY

Anderson, Laurie. *United States*. New York: Harper & Row, 1984.

Army Mental Tests. Washington, DC: United States War Department, 1918.

Auslander, Philip. *Liveness: Performance in a Mediatized Culture*. London: Routledge, 1999.

——*Presence and Resistance: Postmodernism and Cultural Politics in Contemporary American Performance*. Ann Arbor, MI: University of Michigan Press, 1992.

Austin, J.L. *How to Do Things with Words*. Ed. J.O. Urmson and Marina Sbisà. Cambridge, MA: Harvard University Press, 1962.

Bataille, Georges. *The Accursed Share: An Essay on General Economy*. Vol. I: *Consumption*. Trans. Robert *Hurley. New York: Zone Books*, 1988.

——"Nietzsche and the Fascists." *Visions of Excess*. Ed. Allan Stoekl. Trans. Allan Stoekl with Carol R. Lovitt and Donald M. Leslie, Jr. Minneapolis, MN: University of Minnesota Press, 1983 (1937).

Bateson, Gregory. *Steps to an Ecology of Mind*. New York: Ballatine Books, 1972.

Bennis, Warren G. *Organizational Development: Its Nature, Origins, and Prospects*. Reading, MA: Addison-Wesley, 1969.

Bennis, Warren and Patricia Ward **Biederman**. *Organizing Genius: The Secrets of Creative Collaboration*. Reading, MA: Addison-Wesley, 1997.

Blanchot, Maurice. *The Writing of the Disaster*. Trans. Ann Smock. Lincoln and London: University of Nebraska Press, 1986.

Blau, Herbert. *The Eye of Prey: Subversions of the Postmodern*. Bloomington, IN: Indiana University Press, 1987.

Blough, Glenn O. "Children, Put Away Your Sputniks." *The Science Teacher* 24, no. 8 (1957): pp. 373–4.

Bogard, William. *The Simulation of Surveillance: Hyper-control in Telematic Societies*. New York: Cambridge University Press, 1996.

Bolton, Richard, ed. *Culture Wars: Documents from the Recent Controversies in the Arts*. New York: New Press, 1992.

Borges, Jorge Luis. *Labyrinths: Selected Stories & Other Writings*. Ed. Donald A. Yates and James E. Irby. New York: New Directions, 1964.

Borovits, Israel and Seev **Neumann**. *Computer Systems Performance Evaluation: Criteria, Measurements, Techniques, and Costs*. Lexington, MA: Lexington Books, 1979.

Boyett, Joseph H. and Henry P. **Conn**. *Maximum Performance Management: How to Manage and Compensate People to Meet World Competition*. Lakewood, CO: Glenbridge Publishing, 1993 (1988).

Bradbury, R.H. "Oceans Simple, Oceans Complex." Distinguished Lecture to open the Oceanology International 99 Conference in Singapore on 27 April 1999. <http://www.brs.gov.au/overview/bradbury/oceansimple.html>.

Brands, H.W. *The Devil We Knew: Americans and the Cold War*. Oxford: Oxford University Press, 1993.

Branscomb, Lewis M. "Product Performance in an Affluent Society." *Product Quality, Performance, and Cost: A Report and Recommendations Based on a Symposium and Workshops Arranged by the National Academy of Engineering*. Washington, DC: National Academy of Engineering, 1972, pp. 23–31.

Burnham, James. *The Managerial Revolution: What is Happening in the World*. New York: The John Day Company, 1941.

Butler, Judith. *Bodies That Matter: On the Discursive Limits of "Sex."* London: Routledge, 1993.

——"Critically Queer." *Gay and Lesbian Quarterly* 1 (1993): pp. 17–32.

——*Gender Trouble: Feminism and the Subversion of Identity*. London: Routledge, 1990.

——"Performative Acts and Gender Constitution: An Essay in Phenomenology and Feminist Theory." *Performing Feminisms: Feminist Critical Theory and Theatre*. Ed. Sue-Ellen Case. Baltimore, MD: The Johns Hopkins University Press, 1990, pp. 270–82.

Bux, Werner and Harry **Rudin**. *Performance of Computer-Communication Systems*. Amsterdam: Elsevier Science Publishers, 1984.

Calman, W.T. *The Life of Crustacea*. New York: Macmillan Company, 1911.

Carlson, Marvin. *Performance: A Critical Introduction*. London: Routledge, 1996.

Case, Sue-Ellen. "Theory/History/Revolution." *Critical Theory and Performance*. Ed. Janelle G. Reinelt and Joseph R. Roach. Ann Arbor, MI: University of Michigan Press, 1992, pp. 418–29.

Cassandras, Christos G. *Discrete Event Systems: Modeling and Performance Analysis*. Homewood, IL and Boston, MA: Richard D. Irwin, Inc. and Aksen Associates, Inc., 1993.

Cellary, Wojciech and Maciej **Stroinski**. "Analysis of Methods of Computer Network Performance Measurement." *Performance of Computer-Communication Systems*. Ed. Werner Bux and Harry Rudin. Amsterdam: Elsevier Science Publishers, 1984, pp. 465–80.

Cerullo, Mary M. *Lobsters: Gangsters of the Sea*. New York: Cobblehill Books, 1994.

Challenger, Frederick. *Aspects of the Organic Chemistry of Sulphur*. New York: Academic Press, 1959.

Christenson, Gordon A. "The Function of Governments in the Consumer-Product Area: A New Approach to National and International Decision Making." *Product Quality, Performance, and Cost: A Report and Recommendations Based on a Symposium and Workshops Arranged by the National Academy of*

Engineering. Washington, DC: National Academy of Engineering, 1972, pp. 96–103.
Chomsky, Noam. *Profits over People: Neoliberalism and Global Order.* New York: Seven Stories Press, 1999.
Clark, R.K. "Applications of Water-Soluble Polymers as Shale Stabilizers in Drilling Fluids." *Water-Soluble Polymers: Beauty with Performance.* Ed. J.E. Glass. Washington, DC: American Chemical Society, 1986, pp. 171–81.
Classen, Constance, David **Howes**, and Anthony **Synnott**. *Aroma: The Cultural History of Smell.* London: Routledge, 1994.
Clowse, Barbara Barksdale. *Brainpower for the Cold War: The Sputnik Crisis and National Defense Education Act of 1958.* Westport, CT: Greenwood Press, 1981.
Colloms, Martin. *High Performance Loudspeakers.* 3rd edn. New York: John Wiley & Sons, 1985.
Committee on Measuring and Improving Infrastructure Performance. *Measuring and Improving Infrastructure Performance.* Washington, DC: National Academy Press, 1995.
Committee to Study High Performance Computing and Communications: Status of a Major Initiative. *Evolving the High Performance Computing and Communications Initiative to Support the Nation's Information Infrastructure.* Washington, DC: National Academy Press, 1995.
Corbain, Alain. *The Foul and the Fragrant: Odor and the French Social Imagination.* Cambridge, MA: Harvard University Press, 1986.
Cox, Kevin R., ed. *Spaces of Globalization: Reasserting the Power of the Local.* New York: The Guilford Press, 1997.
Cox, Taylor. *Cultural Diversity in Organizations: Theory, Research and Practice.* San Francisco, CA: Berrett-Koehler, 1993.
Crease, Robert P. *The Play of Nature: Experimentation as Performance.* Bloomington, IN: Indiana University Press, 1993.
Critical Art Ensemble. *Electronic Civil Disobedience and Other Unpopular Ideas.* Brooklyn, NY: Autonomedia, 1996.
——*The Electronic Disturbance.* Brooklyn, NY: Autonomedia, 1994.
Cross, Kelvin F., John J. **Feather**, and Richard L. **Lynch**. *Corporate Renaissance: The Art of Reengineering.* Cambridge, MA: Blackwell, 1994.
Csikszentmihalyi, Mihalyi. *Flow: The Psychology of Optimal Experience.* New York: Harper & Row, 1990.
Culler, Jonathan, ed. *On Puns: The Foundations of Letters.* Oxford: Basil Blackwell, 1988.
Debord, Guy. *Society of the Spectacle.* Detroit: Black & Red, 1983.
De Landa, Manuel. *A Thousand Years of Nonlinear History.* New York: Zone Books, 1997.
Deleuze, Gilles. *Foucault.* Trans. Seán Hand. Minneapolis, MN: University of Minnesota Press, 1988.
——*Nietzsche and Philosophy.* Trans. Hugh Tomlinson. New York: Columbia University Press, 1983.
——"Postscript on the Societies of Control." *October* 59 (1992): pp. 3–7.
Deleuze, Gilles and Félix **Guattari**. "Balance Sheet Program for Desiring Machines." Trans. Robert Hurley. In Félix Guattari. *Chaosophy.* Ed. Sylvère Lotringer. New York: Semiotext(e), 1995, pp. 119–50.
——*Kafka: Toward a Minor Literature.* Trans. Dana Polan. Minneapolis, MN: University of Minnesota Press, 1986.
——*A Thousand Plateaus: Capitalism and Schizophrenia*, Vol. II. Trans. Brian Massumi. Minneapolis, MN: University of Minnesota Press, 1987.
——*What is Philosophy?* Trans. Hugh Tomlinson and Graham Burchell. New York: Columbia University Press, 1994.
Derrida, Jacques. *The Archeology of the Frivolous: Reading Condillac.* Trans. John P. Leavey, Jr. Pittsburgh: Duquesne University Press, 1980.
——*Dissemination.* Trans. Barbara Johnson. Chicago, IL: University of Chicago Press, 1981.
——*Glas.* Trans. John P. Leavey, Jr., and Richard Rand. Lincoln, NE: University of Nebraska Press, 1986.
——*Of Grammatology.* Trans. Gayatri Chakravorty Spivak. Baltimore, MD: The Johns Hopkins University Press, 1974.
——"The Law of Genre." Trans. Avital Ronell. *Glyph* 7 (1980): pp. 202–29.
——*Margins of Philosophy.* Trans. Alan Bass. Chicago, IL: University of Chicago Press, 1982, pp. 307–30.
——"No Apocalypse, Not Now (full speed ahead, seven missiles, seven missives)." Trans. Catherine Porter and Philip Lewis. *Diacritics* 14, no. 2 (1984): pp. 20–31.
——"Otobiographies: The Teaching of Nietzsche and the Politics of the Proper Name." Trans. Avital Ronell. *The Ear of the Other.* Lincoln, NE: University of Nebraska Press, 1988, pp. 3–38.
——*Signéponge = Signsponge.* Trans. Richard Rand. New York: Columbia University Press, 1984.
——*Of Spirit: Heidegger and The Question.* Trans. Geoffrey Bennington and Rachel Bowlby. Chicago, IL: University of Chicago Press, 1991.
——*Spurs: Nietzsche's Styles.* Trans. Barbara Harlow. Chicago, IL: University of Chicago Press, 1978.
——*The Truth in Painting.* Trans. Geoff Bennington and Ian McLeod. Chicago, IL: University of Chicago Press, 1987.
——*Ulysses Gramophone: Deux Mots pour Joyce.* Paris: Galilée, 1987.
——"Ulysses Gramophone: Hear Say Yes in Joyce." Trans. Tina Kendall and Shari Benstock. *Acts of —— Literature.* Ed. Derek Attridge. London: Routledge, 1992. pp. 256–309.
——*Writing and Difference.* Trans. Alan Bass. Chicago, IL: University of Chicago Press, 1978.
DeVries, David L., Ann M. **Morrison**, Sandra L. **Shullman**, and Michael L. **Gerlach**. *Performance Appraisal*

on the Line. New York: John Wiley & Sons, 1981.
Digital Dissertations. UMI Database. 21 July 2000 <www.lib.umi.com>.
Dilulio, John J., Jr., Gerald **Garvey**, and Donald F. Kettl. *Improving Government Performance: An Owner's Manual.* Washington, DC: The Brookings Institute, 1993.
Dodge, Ernest Stanley. *Beyond the Capes: Pacific Exploration from Captain Cook to the Challenger, 1776-1877.* Boston, MA: Little, Brown & Company, 1971.
Doyle, Arthur Conan. *The Edge of the Unknown.* New York: Berkeley Publishing, 1968 (1930).
——*Interviews and Recollections.* Ed. Harold Orel. New York: St. Martin's Press, 1991.
——*The Lost World and The Poison Belt: Professor Challenger Adventures.* San Francisco, CA: Chronicle Books, 1989.
——*Memories and Adventures.* Boston: Little, Brown, & Company, 1924.
——*When the World Screamed and Other Stories.* Vol. II of *Professor Challenger Adventures.* San Francisco, CA: Chronicle Books, 1990.
Drucker, Peter F. *The Practice of Management.* New York: Harper, 1954.
Duggan, Lisa and Kathleen **McHugh**. "A Fem(me)nist Manifesto." *Women & Performance* 8, no. 2 (1996): pp.153–9.
Edelman, Peter G. and Joseph **Wang**, ed. *Biosensors and Chemical Sensors: Optimizing Performance through Polymeric Materials.* Washington, DC: American Chemical Society, 1992.
Eichel, Evelyn and Henry E. **Bender**. *Performance Appraisal: A Study of Current Techniques.* New York: American Management Association Research and Information Service, 1984.
Eisenhower, Dwight D. *Public Papers of the Presidents of the United States, 1960-61*, Washington, DC: U.S. Government Printing Office, 1961.
Electric Vehicles: Technology, Performance, and Potential. Paris: International Energy Agency and the Organization for Economic Co-operation and Development, 1993.
Elkind, Jerome I., Stuart K. **Card**, Julian **Hochberg**, and Beverly M. **Huey**, ed. *Human Performance Models for Computer-Aided Engineering.* Boston, MA: Academic Press, 1990.
Fabian, Johannes. *Time and the Other: How Anthropology Makes Its Object.* New York: Columbia University Press, 1983.
FAO Species Catalogue. Vol. 13: *Marine Lobsters of the World.* Prepared by L.B. Holthuis. Rome: Food and Agriculture Organization of the United Nations, 1991.
Ferguson, Eugene S. *Engineering and the Mind's Eye.* Cambridge, MA: MIT Press, 1992.
Feyerabend, Paul. *Against Method: Outline of an Anarchistic Theory of Knowledge.* London: Verso, 1978.
Flamm, Kenneth. *Creating the Computer: Government, Industry, and High Technology.* Washington, DC: The Brookings Institute, 1987.
Flower, Harvey M., ed. *High Performance Materials in Aerospace.* London: Chapman & Hall, 1995.
Foucault, Michel. *Discipline and Punish: The Birth of the Prison.* Trans. Alan Sheridan. New York: Vintage Books, 1979.
——*Foucault Live (Interviews, 1966–84).* Trans. John Johnston. Ed. Sylvère Lotringer. New York: Semiotext(e), 1989.
——*The History of Sexuality, Vol. I: An Introduction.* Trans. Robert Hurley. New York: Vintage Books, 1978.
——*Remarks on Marx: Conversations with Duccio Trombadori.* Trans. R. James Goldstein and James Cascaito. New York: Semiotext(e), 1991.
——*This Is Not a Pipe.* Trans. and ed. by James Harkness. Berkeley, CA: University of California Press, 1983.
Frank, Thomas and Matt **Weiland**, eds. *Commodify Your Dissent: Salvos from The Baffler.* New York: W.W. Norton, 1997.
Fried, Robert C. *Performance in American Bureaucracy.* Boston: Little, Brown & Company, 1976.
Fries, Slyvia Doughty. "Dealing with Crisis: History and the Challenger Disaster." *The Public Historian* 10, no. 4 (Fall 1988): 83–8.
Freud, Sigmund. "The Most Prevalent Form of Degradation in Erotic Life." *Collective Papers* Vol. IV. London: Hogarth Press, 1950.
Fulbright, William J. "The War and Its Effects: The Military-Industrial-Academic Complex." *Super-State: Readings in the Military-Industrial Complex.* Ed. Herbert I. Schiller. Urbana, IL: University of Illinois Press, 1970, pp. 171–8.
Geertz, Clifford. *The Interpretation of Cultures: Selected Essays.* New York: Basic Books, 1973.
——*Local Knowledge: Further Essays in Interpretive Anthropology.* New York: Basic Books, 1983.
Gentile, Mary C., ed. *Differences That Work: Organizational Excellence through Diversity.* Cambridge, MA: Harvard Business School, 1993.
Glass, J.E., ed. *Water-Soluble Polymers: Beauty with Performance.* Washington, DC: American Chemical Society, 1986.
Golembiewski, Robert T. and Alan **Kiepper**. *High Performance and Human Costs: A Public Sector Model of Organizational Development.* New York: Praeger, 1988.
Gore, Al. *From Red Tape to Results: Creating a Government that Works Better and Costs Less.* Report of the National Performance Review. New York: TimeBooks, 1993.
Great Britain. Challenger Office. *Report on the Scientific Results of the Voyage of HMS Challenger during the Years 1873-76 under the Command of Captain George S. Nares … and the late Frank Tourle Thomson, RN. Prepared under the superintendence of the late Sir C. Wyville Thomson … and now of*

John Murray ... Published by order of Her Majesty's Government. Edinburgh: HM Stationery Office, 1880–95.
Griggers, Camilla. *Becoming-Woman.* Minneapolis, MN: University of Minnesota Press, 1997.
Grossberg, Lawrence, Cary Nelson, and Paula Treichler, eds. *Cultural Studies.* London: Routledge, 1992.
Guattari, Félix. *Chaosmosis: an Ethico-Aesthetic Paradigm.* Trans. Paul Bains and Julian Pefanis. Bloomington, IN: Indiana University Press, 1995.
——*Chaosophy.* Ed. Sylvère Lotringer. New York: Semiotext(e), 1995.
——"Regimes, Pathways, Subjects." Trans. Brian Massumi. *Incorporations: Zone* 6 (1992): pp. 16–37.
Haase, R.H. and W.H.T. Holden. *Performance of Land Transportation Vehicles.* Santa Monica, CA: The Rand Corporation, 1964.
Hall, Elizabeth A.H. "Overview of Biosensors." *Biosensors and Chemical Sensors: Optimizing Performance through Polymeric Materials.* Ed. Peter G. Edelman and Joseph Wang. Washington, DC: American Chemical Society, 1992, pp. 1–14.
Hanna, David P. *Designing Organizations for High Performance.* Reading, MA: Addison-Wesley, 1988.
Haraway, Donna. *Simians, Cyborgs, and Women: The Reinvention of Nature.* London: Routledge, 1991.
Harrison, E. Frank. *The Managerial Decision-Making Process.* Boston, MA: Houghton Mifflin, 1975.
Harrison, Peter G. and Naresh M. Patel. *Performance Modeling of Communication Networks and Computer Architectures.* Reading, MA: Addison-Wesley, 1993.
Harvey, David. *The Condition of Postmodernity.* Oxford: Blackwell, 1990.
Heidegger, Martin. *Basic Writings: From* Being and Time (1927) *to* The Task of Thinking (1964). Trans. David Farrell Krell. San Francisco, CA: Harper Collins, 1993 (1977).
——*On the Way to Language.* Trans. Peter D. Hertz. New York: Harper & Row, 1971.
——*The Question Concerning Technology and Other Essays.* Trans. William Lovitt. New York: Harper & Row, 1977.
High Performance Computing Act of 1991. P.L. 102–194. <http://www.ccic.gov/legislation/hpcc_act.html>.
High Performance Computing and Communications 1996 Blue Book. <http://www.ccic.gov/pubs/blue96/program.summ.html.>
High Performance Computing and Communications 1998 Blue Book. <http://www.ccic.gov/pubs/blue98/exec-summary.html>.
Higham, Charles. *The Adventures of Conan Doyle: The Life of the Creator of Sherlock Holmes.* New York: W.W. Norton & Company, 1976.
Hobart, Michael E. and Zachary S. Schiffman. *Information Ages: Literacy, Numeracy, and the Computer Revolution.* Baltimore, MD: The Johns Hopkins University Press, 1988.
Hobsbawm, Eric. *The Age of Extremes: A History of the World, 1914-1991.* New York: Vintage Books, 1996.
——*On the Edge of the New Century.* In conversation with Antonio Polito. Trans. from the Italian by Allan Cameron. New York: The New Press, 2000.
Hofstadter, Douglas H. *Gödel, Escher, Bach: An Eternal Golden Braid.* New York: Vintage Books, 1979.
Hohler, Robert T. *"I Touch the Future...": The Story of Christa McAuliffe.* New York: Random House, 1986.
Howell, William C. "An Overview of Models, Methods and Problems." *Human Performance and Productivity, Volume II: Information Processing and Decision Making.* Ed. William C. Howell and Edwin A. Fleishman. Hillsdale, NJ: Lawrence Erlbaum Associates, 1982.
Irigaray, Luce. *Marine Lover of Friedrich Nietzsche.* Trans. Gillian C. Gill. New York: Columbia University Press, 1991.
Jenkins, Dennis R. *The History of Developing the National Space Transportation System: The Beginning through STS-50.* Melbourne Beach, FL: Broadfield Pub., 1992.
Jordan, John M. *Machine Age Ideology: Social Engineering and American Liberalism: 1911-1939.* Chapel Hill, NC: University of North Carolina Press, 1994.
Kafka, Franz. *The Penal Colony: Stories and Short Pieces.* Trans. Willa and Edwin Muir. New York: Schocken Books, 1961.
Kao, John. *Jamming: The Art and Discipline of Business Creativity.* New York: HarperBusiness, 1996.
Kaplan, Morris. "Does the 'Informed Consumer' Exist? Will He Ever?" *Product Quality, Performance, and Cost: A Report and Recommendations Based on a Symposium and Workshops Arranged by the National Academy of Engineering.* Washington, DC: National Academy of Engineering, 1972, pp. 49–53.
Kaufmann, Walter. "Translator's Introduction." *The Gay Science.* Trans. Walter Kaufmann. New York: Vintage Books, 1974, pp. 3–26.
Kaye, Nick. *Postmodernism and Performance.* New York: St. Martin's Press, 1994.
Kennedy, John F. *Public Papers of the Presidents of the United States, John F. Kennedy, 1961.* Washington, DC: U.S. Government Printing Office, 1962.
Kettl, Donald F. *Reinventing Government? Appraising the National Performance Review.* Washington, DC: The Brookings Institute, 1994.
Kettl, Donald F. and John J. Dilulio, Jr. *Inside the Reinvention Machine: Appraising Governmental Reform.* Washington, DC: The Brookings Institute, 1995.
Kidwell, Peggy A. and Paul E. Ceruzzi. *Landmarks in Digital Computing.* Washington, DC: Smithsonian Institution Press, 1994.

King, Peter J.B. *Computer and Communication Systems Performance Modelling.* New York: Prentice Hall, 1990.
Kittler, Friedrich A. *Discourse Networks, 1800/1900.* Trans. Michael Metteer with Chris Cullens. Stanford, CA: Stanford University Press, 1990.
——"The Mechanized Philosopher." *Looking After Nietzsche.* Ed. Laurence A. Rickels. Albany, NY: State University of New York Press, 1990, pp. 195–207.
Klossowski, Pierre. *Nietzsche and the Vicious Circle.* Trans. Daniel W. Smith. Chicago, IL: University of Chicago Press, 1997.
Krell, David Farrell. "General Introduction: The Question of Being." *Basic Writings: From* Being and Time *(1927) to* The Task of Thinking *(1964).* Trans. David Farrell Krell. San Francisco: Harper Collins, 1993 (1977), pp. 3–35.
Kress-Rogers, Erika, ed. *Handbook of Biosensors and Electronic Noses: Medicine, Food, and the Environment.* Boca Raton, FL: CRC Press, 1997.
Kuhn, Thomas. *The Structure of Scientific Revolutions.* Chicago, IL: University of Chicago Press, 1970 (1962).
Larabee, Ann. "Remembering the Shuttle, Forgetting the Loom: Interpreting the Challenger Disaster." *Postmodern Culture* 4, no. 3 (1994).
Lash, Scott and John Urry. *The End of Organized Capitalism.* Madison, WI: University of Wisconsin Press, 1987.
Latour, Bruno. *ARAMIS or the Love of Technology.* Trans. Catherine Porter. Cambridge, MA: Harvard University Press, 1996.
Laurel, Brenda. *Computers as Theatre.* Reading, MA: Addison-Wesley, 1992.
Leavey, John P., Jr. *Glassary.* Lincoln, NE: University of Nebraska Press, 1987.
Leslie, Stuart W. *The Cold War and American Science: The Military-Industrial-Academic Complex at MIT and Stanford.* New York: Columbia University Press, 1993.
Leung, Clement H.C. *Quantitative Analysis of Computer Systems.* London: John Wiley & Sons, Ltd, 1988.
Lewis, Richard S. *Challenger: The Final Voyage.* New York: Columbia University Press, 1988.
Linder, Dana Wechsler and Nancy Rotenier. "Good-bye to Berle & Means." *Forbes* 153, no. 1 (1994): pp. 100–3.
Linklater, Erik. *The Voyage of the Challenger.* Garden City, NY: Doubleday, 1972.
Locke, Arthur S. *Guidance.* In collaboration with Charles S. Dodge, Samuel F. George, Laurence F. Gilchrist, William C. Hodgson, John E. Meade, John A. Sanderson, and Charles F. White. Princeton, NJ: D. Van Norstrand Company, Inc., 1955.
Luhmann, Niklas. *Social Systems.* Trans. John Bednarz, Jr., with Dirk Baecker. Stanford, CA: Stanford University Press, 1995.
Lyotard, Jean-François. *The Postmodern Condition: A Report on Knowledge.* Trans. Geoff Bennington and Brian Massumi. Minneapolis, MN: University of Minnesota Press, 1979.
MacAloon, John J., ed. *Rite, Drama, Festival, Spectacle: Rehearsals Toward a Theory of Cultural Performance.* Philadelphia, PA: Institute for the Study of Human Issues, 1984.
McBride, Ken. "Voyager, Challenger, and Other Proofs of Murphy's Law." *Queen's Quarterly* 93, no. 2 (Summer 1986): pp. 330–6.
McConnell, Malcolm. *Challenger: A Major Malfunction.* Garden City, NY: Doubleday, 1987.
McCurdy, Howard E. *Inside NASA: High Technology and Organizational Change in the U.S. Space Program.* Baltimore, MD and London: The Johns Hopkins University Press, 1993.
McGregor, Douglas. *Leadership and Motivation: Essays of Douglas McGregor.* Ed. Warren G. Bennis and Edgar H. Schein, with collaboration by Caroline McGregor. Cambridge, MA: MIT Press, 1966.
——"An Uneasy Look at Performance Appraisal." *Harvard Business Review* 35, vol. 3 (1957): pp. 89–94.
MacKenzie, Donald. *Inventing Accuracy: A Historical Sociology of Nuclear Missile Guidance.* Cambridge, MA: MIT Press, 1990.
McKenzie, Jon. "Interhacktivity." *Style* 33, no. 2 (1999): pp. 283–99.
——"Genre Trouble: (The) Butler Did It." *The Ends of Performance.* Ed. Peggy Phelan and Jill Lane. New York: New York University Press, 1998, pp. 217–35.
——"Laurie Anderson for Dummies." *TDR: The Drama Review* 41, no. 2 (1996): pp. 30–50.
——"Virtual Reality: Performance, Immersion and the Thaw," *TDR: The Drama Review* 38, no 4 (1994): pp. 83–106.
Mangham, Iain L. and Michael A. **Overington**. *Organizations as Theatre: A Social Psychology of Dramatic Appearances.* Chichester, UK: John Wiley & Sons, 1987.
Marcuse, Herbert. *Eros and Civilization: A Philosophical Inquiry into Freud.* New York: Vintage Books, 1961 (1955).
——*One-Dimensional Man: Studies in the Ideology of Advanced Industrial Society.* Boston, MA: Beacon Press, 1964.
——"Some Social Implications of Modern Technology." *The Essential Frankfurt School Reader.* Ed. Andrew Arato and Eike Gebhardt. New York: Continuum, 1988 (1941), pp. 138–62.
Mayo, Elton. *The Social Problems of an Industrial Civilization.* Cambridge, MA: Harvard University Press, 1945.
Mayr, Otto. *Feedback Mechanisms in the Historical Collections of the National Museum of History and Technology.* Smithsonian Studies in History and Technology, No. 12. Washington, DC: Smithsonian

Institution Press, 1971.
Meyer, Marshall W. and Lynne G. Zucker. *Permanently Failing Organizations.* Newbury Park, CA: Sage Publications, Inc., 1989.
Mohrman, Susan Albers and Thomas G. **Cumming**. *Self-Designing Organizations: Learning How to Create High Performance.* Reading, MA: Addison-Wesley, 1989.
Montano, Linda. *Art in Everyday Life.* Los Angeles, CA: Astro Artz/Station Hill Press, 1981.
——*The Art/Life Institute Handbook.* Saugerties, NY: The Art/Life Institute, 1988.
Moseley, Henry Nottidge. *Notes by a Naturalist on the "Challenger": Being an Account of Various Observations Made during the Voyage of the H.M.S. "Challenger" round the World, in the Years 1872-1876, under the Commands of Capt. Sir G.S. Nares and Capt. F.T. Thomson.* London: Macmillan, 1879.
Nadler, David A. *Feedback and Organization Development: Using Data-Based Methods.* Reading, MA: Addison-Wesley, 1977.
Nathan, Barry R. and Wayne F. **Cascio**. "Technical and Legal Standards." *Performance Assessment: Methods & Applications.* Ed. Ronald A. Berk. Baltimore, MD: The Johns Hopkins University Press, 1986, pp. 1–50.
Nietzsche, Friedrich. *On the Advantage and Disadvantage of History for Life.* Trans. Peter Preuss. Indianapolis, IN: Hackett Publishing Company, Inc., 1980.
——*The Birth of Tragedy and The Genealogy of Morals.* Trans. Francis Golffing. Garden City, NY: Doubleday, 1956.
——*Ecce Homo: How One Becomes What One Is.* Trans. R.J. Hollingdale. London: Penguin Books, 1979.
——"On the Future of Our Educational Institutions." Trans. J.M. Kennedy. *The Complete Works of Friedrich Nietzsche.* vol. 3. Ed. Oscar Levy. New York: Russell & Russell, 1964.
——*The Gay Science.* Trans. Walter Kaufmann. New York: Vintage Books, 1974.
——*Human, All Too Human.* Trans. R.J. Hollingdale. Cambridge: Cambridge University Press, 1996.
Nixon, Richard. "The VP on Science: Remarks by The Honorable Richard M. Nixon at the Silver Anniversary of the Bausch & Lomb Honorary Science Award, June 17, 1958, Washington DC." *The Science Teacher* 25, no. 5 (1958): pp. 251–2.
Norman, Donald. *The Design of Everyday Things.* New York: Doubleday, 1990 (1988).
Osborne, David and Ted Gaebler. *Reinventing Government: How the Entrepreneurial Spirit is Transforming the Public Sector.* London: Penguin Books, 1993 (1992).
Parson, Nels A. Jr. *Guided Missiles in War and Peace.* Cambridge, MA: Harvard University Press, 1956.
Peel, C.J. and P.J. **Gregson**. "Design Requirements for Aerospace Structural Materials." *High Performance Materials in Aerospace.* Ed. Harvey M. Flower. London: Chapman & Hall, 1995, pp. 1–48.
Pelias, Ronald J. and James **VanOosting**. "A Paradigm for Performance Studies." *Quarterly Journal of Speech* 73 (1987): pp. 219–31.
Penley, Constance. "Spaced Out: Remembering Christa McAuliffe." *Camera Obscura 29* (1992): pp. 178–213.
Peters, Thomas J. and Robert H. **Waterman**, Jr. *In Search of Excellence: Lessons from America's Best-Run Companies.* New York: Warner Books, 1982.
Phelan, Peggy. "Introduction: The Ends of Performance." *The Ends of Performance.* Ed. Peggy Phelan and Jill Lane. New York: New York University Press, 1998.
——*Unmarked: The Politics of Performance.* London and New York: Routledge, 1993.
Post, Robert C. *High Performance: The Culture and Technology of Drag Racing 1950-1990.* Baltimore, MD: The Johns Hopkins University Press, 1994.
Pouzin, Louis. "What Knobs for User Performance?" *Performance of Computer-Communication Systems.* Ed. Werner Bux and Harry Rudin. Amsterdam: Elsevier Science Publishers, 1984, pp. 541–5.
Presidential Commission on the Space Shuttle Challenger Accident. *Report to the President by the Presidential Commission on the Space Shuttle Challenger Accident [Rogers Commission].* Washington, DC: The Commission, 1986.
Product Quality, Performance, and Cost: A Report and Recommendations Based on a Symposium and Workshops Arranged by the National Academy of Engineering. Washington, DC: National Academy of Engineering, 1972.
Pursell, Carroll. *The Machine in America: A Social History of Technology.* Baltimore, MD: The Johns Hopkins University Press, 1995.
Quinn, Robert E. *Beyond Rational Management: Mastering the Paradoxes and Competing Demands of High Performance.* San Francisco, CA: Jossey-Bass Publishers, 1988.
Reagan, Ronald. *Public Papers of the Presidents of the United States, Ronald Reagan, 1984: Book I.* Washington, DC: U.S. Government Printing Office, 1985.
Reese, Ernst S. "Evolution, Neuroethology, and Behavioral Adaptations of Crustacean Appendages." *Studies in Adaptation: The Behavior of Higher Crustacea.* Eds. Steve Rebach and David W. Dunham. New York: John Wiley & Sons, 1983, pp. 57–81.
Reinelt, Janelle G. and Joseph R. **Roach**, eds. *Critical Theory and Performance.* Ann Arbor, MI: University of Michigan Press, 1992.
Rey, P.A. and R.G. **Varsanik**. "Application and Function of Synthetic Polymeric Flocculents in Wastewater Treatment." *Water-Soluble Polymers: Beauty with Performance.* Ed. J.E. Glass. Washington, DC: American Chemical Society, 1986, pp. 113–43.
Richards, Stewart. "Conan Doyle's 'Challenger' Unchampioned: William Rutherford, F.R.S. (1839-99), and

the Origins of Practical Physiology in Britain." *Notes and Records of the Royal Society of London* 40, no. 2 (1986): pp. 193–217.
Richardson, George P. *Feedback Thought in Social Science and Systems Theory*. Philadelphia, PA: University of Pennsylvania Press, 1991.
Rickels, Laurence. A., ed. *Looking After Nietzsche*. Albany, NY: State University of New York Press, 1990.
Rifkin, Jeremy. *The End of Work: The Decline of the Global Work Force and the Dawn of the Post-Market Era*. New York: G.P. Putnam's Sons, 1996.
Roach, Joseph. *Cities of the Dead: Circum–Atlantic Performance*. New York: Columbia University Press, 1996.
——"Culture and Performance in the Circum-Atlantic World." *Performativity and Performance*. Ed. Andrew Parker and Eve Kosofsky Sedgwick. London: Routledge, 1995, pp. 45–63.
——"The Future That Worked." *Theater* 28, no. 2 (1998): pp. 19–26.
Rodin, Alvin E. and Jack D. **Key**. *Medical Casebook of Doctor Arthur Conan Doyle: From Practicioner to Sherlock Holmes and Beyond*. Malabar, FL: Robert E. Krieger Publishing Company, Inc., 1984.
Ronell, Avital. *The Telephone Book: Technology, Schizophrenia, Electric Speech*. Lincoln, NE: University of Nebraska Press, 1989.
——"The Test Drive." *Deconstruction is/in America: A New Sense of the Political*. Ed. Anselm Haverkamp. New York: New York University Press, 1995, pp. 200–20.
Roosevelt, R. Thomas, Jr. "From Affirmative Action to Affirming Diversity." *Differences That Work: Organizational Excellence through Diversity*. Ed. Mary C. Gentile. Cambridge, MA: Harvard Business School, 1993, pp. 27–46.
Rothery, G.A. *A Diary of the Wreck of His Majesty's Ship Challenger, on the Western Coast of South America, in May, 1835: With an Account of the Subsequent Encampment of the Officers and Crew during a Period of Seven Weeks on the South Coast of Chile*. London: Longman, Rees, Orme, Brown, Green & Longman, 1836.
Saper, Craig J. *Artificial Mythologies: A Guide to Cultural Invention*. Minneapolis, MN: University of Minnesota Press, 1997.
Sauer, Charles H., and K. **Mani Chandy**. *Computer Systems Performance Modeling*. Englewood Cliffs, NJ: Prentice-Hall, 1981.
Schechner, Richard. *Between Theatre and Anthropology*. Philadelphia, PA: University of Pennsylvania Press, 1985.
——*The End of Humanism: Writings on Performance*. New York: Performing Arts Journal Publications, 1982.
——*Essays on Performance Theory: 1970-1976*. New York: Drama Book Specialists, 1977.
——"PAJ Distorts the Broad Spectrum." *TDR: The Drama Review* 33, no. 2 (1989): pp. 4–9.
——*Performance Theory: Revised and Expanded Edition*. London: Routledge, 1988.
——"What is Performance Studies Anyway?" *The Ends of Performance*. Ed. Peggy Phelan and Jill Lane. New York: New York University Press, 1998, pp. 357–62.
Schiller, Herbert I., ed. *Super-State: Readings in the Military-Industrial Complex*. Urbana, IL: University of Illinois Press, 1970.
Schmitt, Waldo L. *Crustaceans*. Ann Arbor, IL: University of Michigan Press, 1965.
Schneider, Rebecca. *The Explicit Body in Performance*. London: Routledge, 1997.
Schwab, F.G. "Advantages and Disadvantages of Associative Thickeners in Coatings Performance." *Water-Soluble Polymers: Beauty with Performance*. Ed. J.E. Glass. Washington, DC: American Chemical Society, 1986, pp. 369–73.
Simon, Herbert A. *Models of Man: Social and Rational*. New York: John Wiley & Sons, Inc, 1957.
——*The New Science of Management Decision*. Englewood Cliffs, NJ: Prentice-Hall, 1977 (1960).
Simons, Elizabeth Radin. "The NASA Joke Cycle: The Astronauts and the Teacher." *Western Folklore* 45, no. 4 (1986): pp. 261–77.
Skirpan, Rita H., ed. *Brand Names and Their Companies*. Vol. 1. Detroit: Gale Research Inc., 1994.
Smith, Anna Deavere. *Fires in the Mirror: Crown Heights, Brooklyn, and Other Identities*. New York: Anchor Books/Doubleday, 1993.
Smith, Connie U. *Performance Engineering of Software Systems*. Reading, MA: Addison-Wesley, 1990.
Smythe, Willie. "Challenger Jokes and the Humor of Disaster." *Western Folklore* 45, no. 4 (1986): pp. 243–60.
Souza, Márcio. *Lost World II: The End of the Third World*. Trans. Lana Santamaria. New York: Avon Books, 1990.
Starr, Chaucey. "Consumer Needs, Product Alternatives, and Risks." *Product Quality, Performance, and Cost: A Report and Recommendations Based on a Symposium and Workshops Arranged by the National Academy of Engineering*. Washington, DC: National Academy of Engineering, 1972, pp. 11–16.
Stearns, Peter N. *The Industrial Revolution in World History*. Boulder, CO: Westview Press, 1993.
Stern, Carol Simpson and Bruce **Henderson**. *Performance: Texts and Contexts*. London: Longman, 1993.
Stevens, George H. and Emily F. **Stevens**. *Designing Electronic Performance Support Tools: Improving Workplace Performance with Hypertext, Hypermedia, and Multimedia*. Englewood Cliffs, NJ: Educational Technology Publications, 1995.
Stewart, Susan. *Nonsense: Aspects of Intertextuality in Folklore and Literature*. Baltimore, MD: The Johns

Hopkins University Press, 1978.
Subcommittee on the Federal Civil Service. *Performance Rating Plans in the Federal Government: Report to the Committee on Post Office and Civil Service, House of Representatives*. Washington, DC: United States Government Printing Office, 1954.
Tantawy, Ahmed N., ed. *High Performance Networking: Frontiers and Experience.* Boston, MA: Kluwer Academic Publishers, 1994.
Taussig, Michael T. *Shamanism, Colonialism, and the Wild Man: A Study in Terror and Healing.* Chicago, IL: University of Chicago Press, 1986.
Taylor, Frederick Winslow. *The Principles of Scientific Management.* New York: W.W. Norton & Company, 1967 (1911).
Taylor, James C. and David F. Felten. *Performance by Design: Sociotechnical Systems in North America.* Englewood Cliffs, NJ: Prentice Hall, 1993.
Taylor, James R. and Elizabeth J. Van Every. *The Vulnerable Fortress: Bureaucratic Organization and Management in the Information Age.* Toronto: University of Toronto Press, 1993.
Thomas, R. Roosevelt, Jr. "From Affirmative Action to Affirming Diversity." *Differences That Work: Organizational Excellence through Diversity.* Ed. Mary C. Gentile. Cambridge, MA: Harvard Business School, 1993, pp. 27–46.
Thomson, Charles Wyville. *The Voyage of the Challenger: the Atlantic: a Preliminary Account of the General Results of the Exploring Voyage of H. M. S. Challenger during the Year 1873 and the Early Part of the Year 1876.* London: Macmillan, 1877.
Tiffin, Joseph and Ernest J. McCormick. "Industrial Merit Rating." *Performance Appraisal: Research and Practice.* Ed.Thomas L. Whisler and Shirley F. Harper. New York: Holt, Reinhart & Winston, 1962 (1954), pp. 4–7.
Tufte, Edward R. *Visual Explanations: Images and Quantities, Evidence and Narrative.* Cheshire, CT: Graphics Press, 1997.
Turner, Victor. *On the Edge of the Bush.* Tucson, AZ: University of Arizona Press, 1985.
——"Liminality and the Performative Genres." *Studies in Symbolism and Cultural Communication.* Ed. F. Allan Hanson. Lawrence, KS: University of Kansas Press, 1982, pp. 25–41.
——*From Ritual to Theatre: The Human Seriousness of Play.* New York: PAJ Publications, 1982.
——*Schism and Continuity in an African Society.* Manchester: Manchester University Press, 1957.
Ulmer, Gregory L. *Applied Grammatology.* Baltimore, MD: The Johns Hopkins University Press, 1985..
——*Heuretics: The Logic of Invention.* Baltimore, MD: The Johns Hopkins University Press, 1994.
——"The Puncept in Grammatology." *On Puns: The Foundations of Letters.* Ed. Jonathan Culler. Oxford: Basil Blackwell, 1988, pp. 164–89.
——"Sounding the Unconscious." *Glassary.* John P Leavey, Jr. Lincoln, NE: University of Nebraska Press, 1987.
U.S. Congress, House Committee on Science and Technology, *Investigation of the Challenger Accident: Report.* Washington, DC: Government Printing Office, 1986.
Vaill, Peter B. *Managing as a Performing Art: New Ideas for a World of Chaotic Change.* San Francisco, CA: Jossey-Bass Publishers, 1989.
——"Toward a Behavioral Description of High-Performing Systems." *Leadership: Where Else Can We Go?* Ed. Morgan W. McCall, Jr. and Michael M. Lombardo. Durham, NC: Duke University Press, 1978.
van Gennep, Arnold. *The Rites of Passage.* Chicago, IL: University of Chicago Press, 1960 (1908).
Vattimo, Gianni. *The Transparent Society.* Trans. David Webb. Baltimore, MD: The Johns Hopkins University Press, 1992.
Vaughan, Diane. *The Challenger Launch Decision: Risky Technology, Culture, and Deviance at NASA.* Chicago, IL: The University of Chicago Press, 1996.
Von Braun, Wernher. *The Mars Project.* Urbana, IL: University of Illinois Press, 1991 (1953).
Walker, Barbara A. and William C. Hanson. "Valuing Differences at Digital Equipment Corporation." *Diversity in the Workplace: Human Resources Initiatives.* Ed. Susan E. Jackson. New York: The Guilford Press, 1992.
Waring, Stephen P. *Taylorism Transformed: Scientific Management Theory since 1945.* Chapel Hill, NC: University of North Carolina Press, 1991.
Weinberg, Alvin. "Impact of Large-Scale Science on the United States." *Science* 134 (1961): pp. 161–4.
Whisler, Thomas L. and Shirley F. Harper, eds. *Performance Appraisal: Research and Practice.* New York: Holt, Reinhart and Winston, 1962.
White, Charles F. "Servo System Theory." *Guidance.* Arthur S. Locke. Princeton, NJ: D. Van Norstrand Company, Inc., 1955.
Whyte, William H. *The Organization Man.* Garden City, NY: Doubleday, 1956.
Williams, J.C. "Titanium Alloys: Production, Behavior and Application." *High Performance Materials in Aerospace.* Ed. Harvey M. Flower. London: Chapman & Hall, 1995, pp. 85–134.
Williams, Richard S. *Performance Management: Perspectives on Employee Performance.* London: International Thomson Business Press, 1998.
Wisdom, J.O. *Challengeability in Modern Science.* Brookfield, VT: Avebury, 1987.

INDEX